0500001017990 6

D1538333

THE ONE BOOK

THE ONE BOOK

Moses D. Powe

FATHERLESS
FATHERS PUBLISHING
A POWEM PUBLISHERS IMPRINT

The One Book

Fatherless Fathers Publishing (A POWEM PUBLISHERS IMPRINT)
1603 Capitol Avenue, Suite 310 A145
Cheyenne, Wyoming 82001
www.mosespowe.com

The illustrations are entirely the product of Fatherless Fathers Publishing.

ISBN (hardcover): 9781735180311
ISBN (paperback): 9781735180328
eISBN: 9781735180304

Library of Congress Control Number: 2020910731

Dedicated to my only begotten son, Sean Moses, and my blessed bride, Blythe.

Thank you to my parents Moses (RIP) and Patricia for giving me life, and to my grandmother Theretha (RIP) for raising me.

A special thank you to my cousin Jonathan Brown. You planted this seed when you said you could see me writing books one day.

This is a book
about the birthday
of a little tot
who loves to play.

Yes, The One Book
will make your head bop
when we sing
at one o'clock.

Tick Tock, Tick Tock.
Oh, what fun!
Soon, Baby will be one.

There's one candle
in the cake.

Hope Baby smiles
for the pic Mom takes.

Tick Tock, Tick Tock.
Oh, what fun!
Soon, Baby will be one.

"Make a wish!"
they will say.

"Eat some cake,

it's your day."

Yummy, yummy,
tastes so sweet.
Baby will squeal,
eating this treat.

Tick Tock, Tick Tock.
Oh, what fun!
Soon, Baby will be one.

Daddy will roll
the birthday ball.

27

And after one step,
Baby will fall.

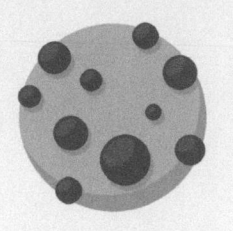

YOU'RE INVITED!

"Uh oh, uh oh,"

YOU'RE INVITED!

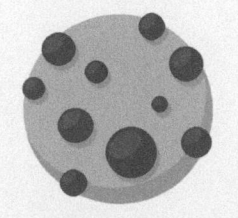

Baby will say,

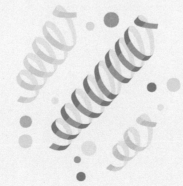

but then grab the ball
and start to play.

Tick Tock, Tick Tock.
Oh, what fun!
Soon, Baby will be one.

Ding! Ding! Ding!
The clock says one.
Let's sing to Baby,
let's have some fun!

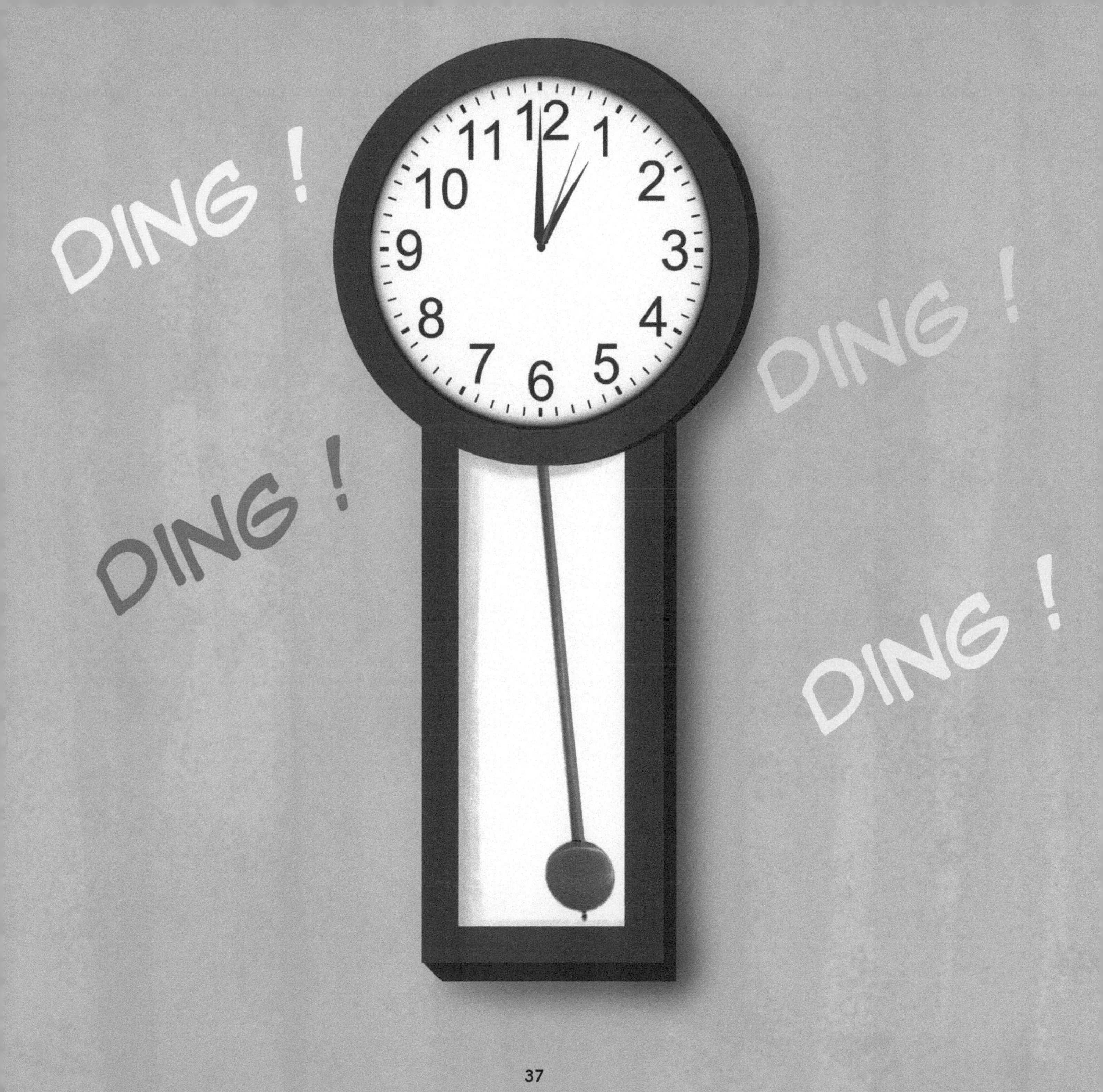
DING!
DING!
DING!
DING!

Happy Birthday!
You're so cute!

YOU'RE INVITED!

Happy Birthday!

PARTY

You're a hoot!

As we sing,
heads do bop.
Baby claps
until we stop.

Baby is tired.

It's time for a nap.

So Baby falls asleep
In Mommy's lap.

Tick Tock,

Tick Tock.

The party is done.
That's the end of the book.
Now Baby is one.

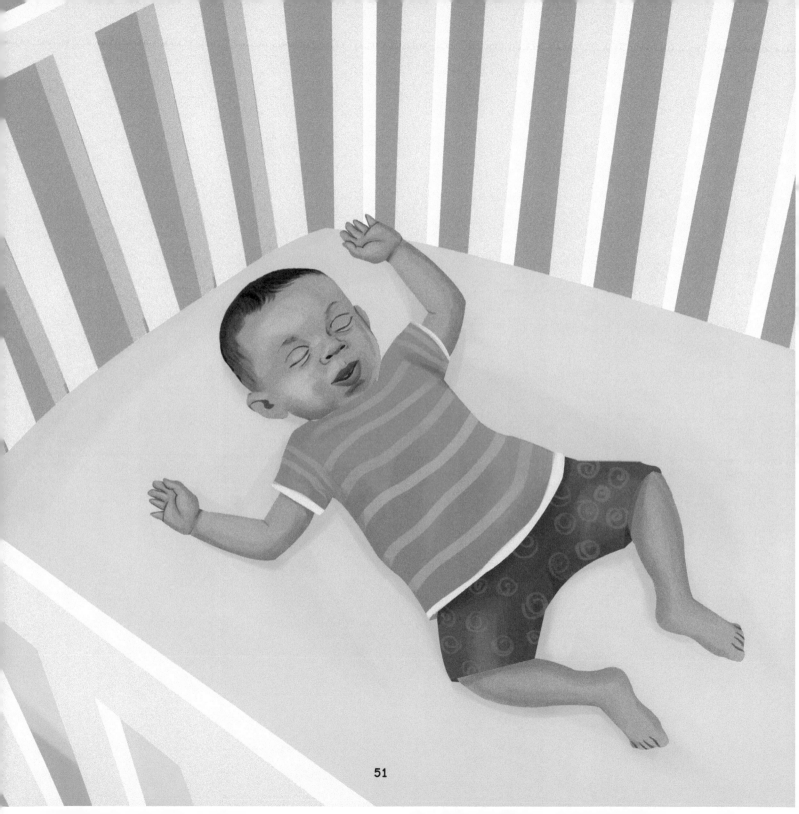

The End

CPSIA information can be obtained
at www.ICGtesting.com
Printed in the USA
LVHW071702291020
670184LV00016B/370

9 781735 180311

TABLE OF CONTENTS

STAR ATTRACTIONS

If you've been a reader of Mobil Travel Guide, you will have heard that this historic brand partnered with another storied media name, Forbes, in 2009 to create a new entity, Forbes Travel Guide. For more than 50 years, Mobil Travel Guide assisted travelers in making smart decisions about where to stay and dine when traveling. With this new partnership, our mission has not changed: We're committed to the same rigorous inspections of hotels, restaurants and spas—the most comprehensive in the industry with more than 500 standards tested at each property we visit—to help you cut through the clutter and make easy and informed decisions on where to spend your time and travel budget. Our team of anonymous inspectors are constantly on the road, sleeping in hotels, eating in restaurants and making spa appointments, evaluating those exacting standards to determine a property's rating.

What kind of standards are we looking for when we visit a proprety? We're looking for more than just high-thread count sheets, pristine spa treatment rooms and white linen-topped tables. We look for service that's attentive, in-dividualized and unforgettable. We note how long it takes to be greeted when you sit down at your table, or to be served when you order room service, or whether the hotel staff can confidently help you when you've forgotten that one essential item that will make or break your trip. Unlike other travel ratings entities, we visit the places we rate, testing hundreds of attributes to compile our ratings, and our ratings cannot be bought or influenced. The Forbes Five Star rating is the most prestigious achievement in hospitality—while we rate more than 8,000 properties in the U.S., Canada, Hong Kong, Macau and Beijing, for 2010, we have awarded Five Star designations to only 53 hotels, 21 restaurants and 18 spas. When you travel with Forbes, you can travel with confidence, knowing that you'll get the very best experience, no matter who you are.

We understand the importance of making the most of your time. That's why the most trusted name in travel is now Forbes Travel Guide.

STAR RATED HOTELS

Whether you're looking for the ultimate in luxury or the best value for your travel budget, we have a hotel recommendation for you. To help you pinpoint properties that meet your needs, Forbes Travel Guide classifies each lodging by type according to the following characteristics:

★★★★★These exceptional properties provide a memorable experience through virtually flawless service and the finest of amenities. Staff are intuitive, engaging and passionate, and eagerly deliver service above and beyond the guests' expectations. The hotel was designed with the guest's comfort in mind, with particular attention paid to craftsmanship and quality of product. A Five Star property is a destination unto itself.

★★★★These properties provide a distinctive setting, and a guest will find many interesting and inviting elements to enjoy throughout the property. Attention to detail is prominent throughout the property, from design concept to quality of products provided. Staff are accommodating and take pride in catering to the guest's specific needs throughout their stay.

★★★These well-appointed establishments have enhanced amenities that provide travelers with a strong sense of location, whether for style or function. They may have a distinguishing style and ambience in both the public spaces and guest rooms; or they may be more focused on functionality, providing guests with easy access to local events, meetings or tourism highlights.

★★The Two Star hotel is considered a clean, comfortable and reliable establishment that has expanded amenities, such as a full-service restaurant.

★The One Star lodging is a limited-service hotel or inn that is considered a clean, comfortable and reliable establishment.

For every property, we also provide pricing information. All prices quoted are accurate at the time of publication; however, prices cannot be guaranteed.

STAR RATED RESTAURANTS

Every restaurant in this book comes highly recommended as an outstanding dining experience.

★★★★★Forbes Five Star restaurants deliver a truly unique and distinctive dining experience. A Five Star restaurant consistently provides exceptional food, superlative service and elegant décor. An emphasis is placed on originality and personalized, attentive and discreet service. Every detail that surrounds the experience is attended to by a warm and gracious dining room team.

★★★★These are exciting restaurants with often well-known chefs that feature creative and complex foods and emphasize various culinary techniques and a focus on seasonality. A highly-trained dining room staff provides refined personal service and attention.

★★★Three Star restaurants offer skillfully-prepared food with a focus on a specific style or cuisine. The dining room staff provides warm and professional service in a comfortable atmosphere. The décor is well-coordinated with quality fixtures and decorative items, and promotes a comfortable ambience.

★★The Two Star restaurant serves fresh food in a clean setting with efficient service. Value is considered in this category, as is family friendliness.

★The One Star restaurant provides a distinctive experience through culinary specialty, local flair or individual atmosphere.

Because menu prices can fluctuate, we list a pricing range rather than specific prices. The pricing ranges are per diner, and assume that you order an appetizer or dessert, an entrée and one drink.

STAR RATED SPAS

Forbes Travel Guide's spa ratings are based on objective evaluations of more than 450 attributes. About half of these criteria assess basic expectations, such as staff courtesy, the technical proficiency and skill of the employees and whether the facility is clean and maintained properly. Several standards address issues that impact a guest's physical comfort and convenience, as well as the staff's ability to impart a sense of personalized service. Additional criteria measure the spa's ability to create a completely calming ambience.

★★★★★Stepping foot in a Five Star spa will result in an exceptional experience with no detail overlooked. These properties wow their guests with extraordinary design and facilities, and uncompromising service. Expert staff cater to your every whim and pamper you with the most advanced treatments and skin care lines available. These spas often offer exclusive treatments and may emphasize local elements.

★★★★Four Star spas provide a wonderful experience in an inviting and serene environment. A sense of personalized service is evident from the moment you check in and receive your robe and slippers. The guest's comfort is always of utmost concern to the well-trained staff.

★★★These spas offer well-appointed facilities with a full complement of staff to ensure that guests' needs are met. The spa facilities include clean and appealing treatment rooms, changing areas and a welcoming reception desk.

MICHIGAN

MICHIGAN HAS A MIGHTY INDUSTRIAL HERITAGE AND IS WELL-KNOWN AS THE BIRTHPLACE of the automobile industry, but rivaling the machines, mines and mills is the nearly $13 billion tourist industry. The two great Michigan peninsulas, surrounded by four of the five Great Lakes, include a vast tapestry of lakeshore beaches, trout-filled streams, more than 11,000 inland lakes, nearly 7 million acres of public hunting grounds, and the cultural attractions of Detroit, Ann Arbor, Grand Rapids, Interlochen and other cities.

Michigan is a four-season vacationland, with tempering winds off the Great Lakes that tame what might otherwise be a climate of extremes. In a land of cherry blossoms, tulips, ski slopes and sugar-sand beaches, you can fish through the ice, snowmobile on hundreds of miles of marked trails, rough it on an uncluttered island or hunt for copper, iron ore, Lake Superior agates or Petoskey stones. One of the country's finest art museums is in Detroit, and Dearborn's The Henry Ford (formerly Henry Ford Museum and Greenfield Village) attracts visitors from all over the world.

A world center for automobile manufacturing, Michigan leads in the production of automobiles and light trucks. More than two-thirds of the nation's tart red cherries are harvested here, and Traverse City hosts the National Cherry Festival each July. This state is also one of the nation's leading producers of blueberries and dry, edible beans. Wheat, hay, corn, oats, turkeys, cattle and hogs are also produced in vast quantities. The Soo Locks at Sault Ste. Marie boast the two longest locks in the world, which can accommodate 1,000-foot-long superfreighters.

French missionaries and explorers, namely Marquette and Joliet, were the first known Europeans to discover the lakes, rivers and streams of Michigan. In their wake came armies of trappers eager to barter with the natives and platoons of soldiers to guard the newly acquired territory. Frenchmen and Native Americans teamed up to fight the British (unsuccessfully) when Ottawa chief Pontiac banded together with other tribes in a bold attempt to overtake Fort Detroit, Fort Michilimackinac and 10 other British forts. The British were forced to retreat into Canada after the American colonies successfully revolted.

Michigan's economic development has come in waves, and following the recession of 2008, the waters have been rough. First, there were trees, the basis for a great lumber industry. These were rapidly depleted. Then copper- and iron-ore mines were discovered. They are now mostly inactive, although the discovery of new copper deposits is leading to renewed activity. The automobile industry, diversified industries and tourism became successful, declined, and now could be poised for a comeback with the development of hybrid and green energy-driven cars. Today, the St. Lawrence Seaway makes Michigan's international port cities and the state's future promising.

ALLEN PARK
See also Dearborn, Detroit
This Detroit suburb is located just 10 miles south of downtown Detroit.

WHERE TO EAT
★★★MORO'S
6535 Allen Road, Allen Park, 313-382-7152; www.morosdining.com
Veal is on the menu at this restaurant, with cuts coming straight from the on-site butcher. Many dishes are prepared tableside, and due to popular demand, the menu never changes. Since opening in 1980, this romantic spot has seen many marriage proposals. It is the perfect setting, after all—dim lighting, a small fireplace, dark wood, brick walls and a singing waiter who performs mid-week from September to May.
International menu. Lunch, dinner. Closed Sunday June-August. Casual attire. $$

ALMA
Home of Alma College and the Michigan Masonic Home, Alma (in Gratiot County) is a pleasant stopping point while driving along Highway 127 north from Lansing.

WHAT TO SEE
ALMA COLLEGE
614 W. Superior St., Alma, 989-463-7111; www.alma.edu
This 87-acre campus offers tours and a 190,000-volume library. The Frank Knox Memorial Room in the Reid-Knox Building has mementos of the former secretary of the navy.

SPECIAL EVENT
HIGHLAND FESTIVAL & GAMES
110 W. Superior St., Alma, 989-463-8979; www.almahighlandfestival.com
Piping, drumming, fiddling, sheaf toss, hammer-throw competitions; art fair and parade.
Memorial Day weekend.

ALPENA
See also Oscoda
The largest city in northeastern Michigan, Alpena has more than 20 miles of shoreline along Thunder Bay, which is notorious for shipwrecks. Once a major commercial fishing and lumber center, Alpena is now a resort community where fishing is one of the main attractions, as is diving among 88 shipwrecks in the bay. The town has retained its late-1800s feel, and restored mansions stand among newer houses.

WHAT TO SEE
DINOSAUR GARDENS PREHISTORIC ZOO
11160 Highway 23 S., Ossineke, 989-471-5477; www.dinosaurgardensllc.com
Authentic reproductions of prehistoric birds and animals.

ISLAND PARK AND ALPENA WILDFOWL SANCTUARY
Highway 23 N. and Long Rapids Road, Alpena
Wildfowl sanctuary, self-guided nature trails, fishing platforms and picnic area.

JESSE BESSER MUSEUM

491 Johnson St., Alpena, 989-356-2202; www.bessermuseum.org

Historical exhibits feature agricultural, lumber and early industrial eras; reconstructed avenue of 1890 shops and businesses; restored cabins, Maltz Exchange Bank (1872), Green School (1895), Jesse Besser exhibit. Science exhibits include geology, natural history and archaeology displays and planetarium shows (Sunday).

Museum: Tuesday-Saturday 10 a.m.-5 p.m., Sunday noon-4 p.m.; closed Monday.

OLD PRESQUE ISLE LIGHTHOUSE AND MUSEUM

5295 Grand Lake Road, Presque Isle, 989-595-9917

Old Presque Isle Lighthouse features a spiral staircase and nautical instruments, marine artifacts and other antiques from the mid-1800s.

May-mid-October, daily.

SPECIAL EVENTS
ART ON THE BAY–THUNDER BAY ART SHOW

Bay View Park, 313 N. Second Ave., Alpena, 989-356-6678;
www.alpenatbarts.org/tbarts/main.html

The original artwork at this show includes quilting, crafts, jewelry, pottery, sculpture, stained glass and painting.

Third weekend in July.

ANN ARBOR

See also Dearborn, Detroit, Jackson, Ypsilanti

Arguably the coolest town in Michigan, Ann Arbor is the home of the University of Michigan, which mingles its campus buildings with city attractions. The university, one of the largest in the United States, brings cultural and artistic flavor to the area. Downtown offers exceptional shops and a variety of eateries. While summer months are usually quiet in Ann Arbor, for four days in July, the city closes off downtown streets and welcomes tens of thousands of visitors for the Street Art Fair, where artisans and craftspeople set up displays and sell their work.

WHAT TO SEE
DELHI

3780 W. Delhi Road, Dexter, 734-426-8211, 800-477-3191; www.metroparks.com

This 53-acre site is home to the Delhi Rapids. Activities include fishing, canoeing (May-September, rentals available), hiking trails, cross-country skiing, picnicking and playground.

DEXTER-HURON METROPARK

6535 Huron River Drive, Ann Arbor, 734-426-8211, 800-477-3191;
www.metroparks.com

This metropark offers fishing, canoeing, hiking trails, cross-country skiing, picnicking and a playground.

EXHIBIT MUSEUM OF NATURAL HISTORY

1109 Geddes Ave., Ann Arbor, 734-764-6085; www.lsa.umich.edu/exhibitmuseum

Anthropology, Michigan wildlife, geology and prehistoric life exhibits can be found at this small natural history museum.

Monday-Saturday 9 a.m.-5 p.m., Sunday noon-5 p.m.

GERALD R. FORD PRESIDENTIAL LIBRARY

1000 Beal Ave., Ann Arbor, 734-741-2218; www.ford.utexas.edu

This research library houses Ford's presidential, vice-presidential and congressional documents.

Monday-Friday 8:45 a.m.-4:45 p.m.

HUDSON MILLS METROPARK

8801 N. Territorial Road, Dexter, 734-426-8211, 800-234-3191; www.metroparks.com

This more than 1,600-acre recreation area offers fishing, boating, canoe rental, hiking, bicycle trails (rentals), an 18-hole golf course, cross-country skiing (winter), picnicking, a playground, camping and an activity center.

KELSEY MUSEUM OF ARCHAEOLOGY

434 S. State St., Ann Arbor, 734-764-9304; www.lsa.umich.edu/kelsey

The museum houses more than 100,000 objects from the civilizations of the Mediterranean.

Tuesday-Friday 9 a.m.-4 p.m., Saturday-Sunday 1-4 p.m.

KEMPF HOUSE CENTER FOR LOCAL HISTORY

312 S. Division, Ann Arbor, 734-994-4898; www.kempfhousemuseum.org

An unusual example of Greek Revival architecture, this restored structure built in 1853 is owned and maintained by the city of Ann Arbor and includes antique Victorian furnishings.

Tours: Sunday 1-4 p.m.; closed January and August.

LAW QUADRANGLE

S. State Street and S. University Avenue, Ann Arbor, 734-764-9322;
www.law.umich.edu/library/info/Pages/default.aspx

This beautiful quadrangle at the University of Michigan includes four beautiful Gothic-style buildings. The law library, with an underground addition, has one of the nation's most extensive collections.

MICHIGAN STADIUM

1 E. Stadium Blvd., Ann Arbor, 734-764-1817; www.umich.edu

Dubbed "The Big House," Michigan Stadium is the largest in the U.S., seating more than 110,000 (and constanly expanding). The two hottest games of the season are with Michigan State (MSU) and Ohio State. MSU is Michigan's biggest intrastate rival, while the Ohio State game (always the last of the season) often determines the Big Ten Championship.

MUSEUM OF ART

1301 S. University, Ann Arbor, 734-764-0395; www.umma.umich.edu
Tuesday-Sunday; closed Monday.

POWER CENTER FOR THE PERFORMING ARTS

121 S. Fletcher, Ann Arbor, 734-763-3333;
www.music.umich.edu/about/facilities/central_campus/power/index.htm
This 1,414-seat theater houses performances of drama, opera, music and dance.

UNIVERSITY OF MICHIGAN

530 S. State St., Ann Arbor, 734-764-1817; www.umich.edu
Established here in 1837 after having moved from Detroit where it was founded, this is one of the largest universities in the country. It makes significant contributions to teaching and research.

SPECIAL EVENTS
ANN ARBOR SUMMER FESTIVAL

522 S. Fourth Ave., Ann Arbor, 734-994-5999; www.annarborsummerfestival.org
This performing arts festival features mime, dance, theater and music, along with lectures, films and exhibits.
Mid-June to early July.

STREET ART FAIR

Ann Arbor, 734-994-5260, 800-888-9487; www.artfair.org
Nearly 1,000 artists and craftspeople display and sell works at this popular fair each summer.
Four days in mid-July.

WHERE TO STAY
★★BELL TOWER HOTEL

300 S. Thayer St., Ann Arbor, 734-769-3010, 800-562-3559; www.belltowerhotel.com
66 rooms. Complimentary continental breakfast. $151-250

★★FOUR POINTS BY SHERATON ANN ARBOR

3200 Boardwalk, Ann Arbor, 734-996-0600, 800-368-7764;
www.fourpointsannarbor.com
197 rooms. Restaurant, bar. $61-150

★RESIDENCE INN BY MARRIOTT

800 Victors Way, Ann Arbor, 734-996-5666, 800-331-3131; www.residenceinn.com
114 rooms, all suites. Complimentary full breakfast. Wireless Internet access. $151-250

★★★WEBER'S INN

3050 Jackson Ave., Ann Arbor, 734-769-2500, 800-443-3050; www.webersinn.com
This full-service hotel offers poolside guest rooms and suites and is located near the University of Michigan (and is often wear the football players stay before a game). Opened in 1937, the rooms have balconies or easy access to

the pool area, large work desks, safes, coffee makers, Gilchrist & Soames bath amenities and Internet access. The pool area features a four-season pool, whirlpool, sundeck, café and teak chaise lounges—a perfect way to relax after a busy day. After spending time at the pool or in the fitness center, guests can enjoy a relaxing dinner of prime rib, steak or seafood at Weber's restaurant.

158 rooms. Complimentary continental breakfast. Restaurant, bar. Fitness center. Pool. $61-150

WHERE TO EAT

★★★BELLA CIAO
118 W. Liberty St., Ann Arbor, 734-995-2107; www.bellaciao.com
This quaint eatery radiates a romantic feeling. The inviting interior includes brick walls and colorful, intriguing art. The menu changes monthly and incorporates seasonal, fresh ingredients into dishes, such as pancetta-wrapped shrimp with lemon-sautéed spinach and grilled polenta or roasted Amish chicken with fresh artichokes and caramelized lemons.
Italian menu. Dinner. Bar. Casual attire. Reservations recommended. Outdoor seating. $36-85

★★THE EARLE
121 W. Washington St., Ann Arbor, 734-994-0211; www.theearle.com
French, Italian menu. Dinner. Closed Sunday in late May-August. Bar. Casual attire. Outdoor seating. $36-85

★★★THE GANDY DANCER
401 Depot St., Ann Arbor, 734-769-0592; www.muer.com
Locals consider this one of the most romantic restaurants in the area. The grand yet intimate atmosphere owes its splendor to the Michigan Central Depot Station, from which it was converted in 1969. The building was originally constructed of granite in 1886 and has two massive stone arches, one of which is in the main entry. Seafood is the main focus, but appealing nonfish options are available, such as the Cajun chicken tortellini and London broil.
American, seafood menu. Lunch, dinner, Sunday brunch. Bar. Children's menu. Business casual attire. Reservations recommended. Valet parking. Outdoor seating. $36-85

★ZINGERMAN'S DELICATESSEN
422 Detroit St., Ann Arbor, 734-663-3354; www.zingermansdeli.com
American, deli menu. Breakfast, lunch, dinner. Children's menu. Casual attire. Outdoor seating. $16-35

AUBURN HILLS
See also Pontiac, Rochester, Troy
Auburn Hills, a 1980s incorporation of the farming communities of Auburn Heights and Avon Township, recently rebuilt its downtown with street lamps and charming shops. Home of the Chrysler Tech Center and dozens of other high-tech companies, the city is best known for Great Lakes Crossing, a mega shopping mall with more than 200 stores. The Detroit Pistons (NBA) and Shock (WNBA) make the Palace of Auburn Hills their home.

WHAT TO SEE
DETROIT PISTONS (NBA)
5 Championship Drive, Auburn Hills, 248-377-0100; www.nba.com/pistons
Professional basketball team.

DETROIT SHOCK (WNBA)
5 Championship Drive, Auburn Hills, 248-377-0100; www.wnba.com/shock
Women's professional basketball team.

GREAT LAKES CROSSING
4000 Baldwin Road, Auburn Hills, 877-746-7452; www.shopgreatlakescrossing.com
With 1.4 million square feet of shops, Great Lakes Crossing is Michigan's top shopping destination. The center also features a high-tech playland, movie theaters, cafés and restaurants.
Daily.

WHERE TO STAY
★★COURTYARD DETROIT AUBURN HILLS
1296 N. Opdyke Road, Auburn Hills, 248-373-4100, 800-321-2211;
www.courtyard.com
148 rooms. High-speed Internet access. Restaurant, bar. $61-150

★★★HILTON SUITES AUBURN HILLS
2300 Featherstone Road, Auburn Hills, 248-334-2222, 800-774-1500;
www.auburnhillssuites.hilton.com
This hotel offers spacious suites with separate sleeping areas, refrigerators and microwaves. The atrium-style lobby is warm and welcoming, and the hotel is situated near several Auburn Hills attractions, including Great Lakes Crossing Shopping Center. The staff even provides guests with complimentary cookies and milk by the lobby fireplace each night.
224 rooms, all suites. Wireless Internet access. Restaurant, bar. Airport transportation available. Pets accepted. $61-150

BATTLE CREEK
See also Kalamazoo, Marshall
Battle Creek was built by two cereal tycoons, W.K. Kellogg and C.W. Post. The Kellogg and Post plants are the largest anywhere, and signs, streets, parks and many public institutions also bear their names. The city, now dubbed the "Cereal Capital of the World," takes its name from a small battle that took place on the banks of the creek in 1825 between a native and a land surveyor. Years later, it was a stop on the Underground Railroad. Abolitionist Sojourner Truth lived here for nearly 30 years.

WHAT TO SEE
BINDER PARK ZOO
7400 Division Drive, Battle Creek, 269-979-1351; www.binderparkzoo.org
Come here to see exotic, endangered and domestic animals in natural exhibits. The 50-acre Wild Africa exhibit includes giraffes, zebras, antelope and African wild dogs and a trading village, ranger station, research camp and

working diamond mine alongside a panoramic African savanna. There is also a children's zoo and special events during Halloween and Christmas.
Mid-April to mid-October, daily.

FORT CUSTER STATE RECREATION AREA
5163 W. Fort Custer Drive, Augusta, 269-731-4200; www.michigan.gov/fortcuster
This recreation area includes a swimming beach, fishing, boating (launch), as well as nature, bridle and bicycle trails and picnic areas. In winter, there is cross-country skiing and snowmobiling.
Daily.

KIMBALL HOUSE MUSEUM
196 Capital Ave. N.E., Battle Creek, 616-965-2613; www.kimballhouse.org
This restored and refurnished Victorian home built in 1886 has an herb garden and country store. Today it displays development of the use of appliances, tools and medical instruments.
Friday 1-4 p.m.; closed January-April.

KINGMAN MUSEUM OF NATURAL HISTORY
175 Limit St., Battle Creek, 269-965-5117; www.kingmanmuseum.org
Exhibits include "Journey Through the Crust of the Earth," "Walk in the Footsteps of the Dinosaurs," "Mammals of the Ice Age," "Window to the Universe," "Planetarium," "Wonder of Life," "Discovery Room" and others.
Tuesday-Friday 9 a.m.-5 p.m., Saturday from 1 p.m.

LEILA ARBORETUM
928 W. Michigan Ave., Battle Creek, 269-969-0270; www.leilaarboretumsociety.org
A 72-acre park containing native trees and shrubs.

SOJOURNER TRUTH GRAVE
Oak Hill Cemetery, South Avenue and Oak Drive, Battle Creek
On the cemetery's Fifth Street is the plain square monument marking the resting place of this remarkable freedom fighter. Born a slave in the 1790s, Truth gained her freedom in the 1820s and crusaded against slavery until her death in 1883. Although uneducated, she had a brilliant mind as well as an unquenchable devotion to her cause.

WILLARD BEACH
Goguac Lake, Battle Creek
Lavishly landscaped with a wide bathing beach, this is a popular spot come summer and includes picnic areas.
Memorial Day-Labor Day, daily.

W.K. KELLOGG BIRD SANCTUARY OF MICHIGAN STATE UNIVERSITY
12685 E. C Ave., Augusta, 269-671-2510; www.kbs.msu.edu/birdsanctuary
Seven kinds of swans and more than 20 species of ducks and geese inhabit the ponds and Wintergreen Lake. You can see one of the finest bird-of-prey collections in the Midwest, along with free-roaming upland game birds.

There is an observation deck and educational displays.
Daily 9 a.m.-7 p.m.

SPECIAL EVENT
CEREAL CITY FESTIVAL
171 W. Michigan Ave., Battle Creek, 800-970-7020; www.kelloggscerealcity.com
This fun festival (who doesn't love cereal?) includes a children's parade, pageant, arts and crafts and, best of all, the world's longest breakfast table to enjoy your morning or all-day treat.
Second Saturday in June.

WHERE TO STAY
★★★MCCAMLY PLAZA HOTEL
50 Capital Ave. S.W., Battle Creek, 269-963-7050, 888-622-2659;
www.mccamlyplazahotel.com
This downtown Battle Creek hotel offers contemporary guest rooms and suites that feature stainless steel accents, granite vanity tops, upholstered headboards and drapes and overstuffed chairs and ottomans. Amenities include a large indoor pool and whirlpool, an exercise room and a business center. Guests can choose Porter's Steakhouse & Cigar Bar for an elegant dinner, or visit J.W. Barleycorn's for casual fare.
239 rooms. Complimentary breakfast. Two restaurants, two bars. $61-150

BAY CITY
See also Midland, Saginaw
Bay City is a historic port community located on Saginaw Bay, which assists Great Lakes freighters as well as seagoing vessels in the handling of millions of tons of products each year. The city is noted for tree-shaded residential areas with new homes and Victorian and Georgian mansions built by 19th-century lumber barons. Retail, specialty dining and entertainment can be found in the Historic Midland Street area on the west side of Bay City.

WHAT TO SEE
BAY CITY STATE RECREATION AREA
3582 State Park Drive, Bay City, 989-667-0717; www.michigan.gov/dnr
This recreation area spans approximately 200 acres and includes beaches, boating docks, hiking trails, picnicking, concessions and camping facilities.

CITY HALL AND BELL TOWER
301 Washington Ave., Bay City, 989-893-1222; www.tourbaycitymi.org
Meticulously restored Romanesque structure from 1895. Council chamber has 31-foot-long woven tapestry depicting the history of Bay City. View of the city and its waterway from bell tower.
Monday-Friday.

SCOTTISH RITE CATHEDRAL
614 Center Ave., Bay City, 989-893-3700; www.supremecouncil.org
The only Scottish Rite Cathedral in the state.
Monday-Friday.

TOBICO MARSH

3582 State Park Drive, Bay City, 989-667-0717; www.michigan.gov/dnr

With 1,700 acres of wetlands, this is the largest remaining wildlife refuge on Saginaw Bay's western shore. Two 32-foot towers allow panoramic viewing of deer, beaver, mink and hundreds of species of waterfowl and song, shore and marsh birds.

Tuesday-Sunday noon-5 p.m.

SPECIAL EVENTS
MUNGER POTATO FESTIVAL

Munger Community Park, 1920 S. Finn Road, Munger, 989-659-2571;
www.mungerpotatofest.com

Celebrate the spud. Potato displays, potato brats and Potato King and Queen contests are featured at this fest, along with live music, a parade and demolition derby.

Four days in late July.

WHERE TO STAY
★★DOUBLETREE HOTEL BAY CITY-RIVERFRONT

1 Wenonah Park Place, Bay City, 989-891-6000; www.doubletree.com

150 rooms. High-speed Internet access. Restaurant, bar. Airport transportation available. $61-150

WHERE TO EAT
★★★FIVE LAKES GRILL

424 N. Main St., Milford, 248-684-7455; www.fivelakesgrill.com

Located about an hour from Detroit in picturesque Milford is this charming restaurant. Chef Brian Polcyn fills his menus with locally grown or raised seasonal ingredients, including several fish from the Great Lakes. There's also a dedicated spot on the menu for slow foods (dishes roasted at low temperatures for hours), such as the veal shank cassoulet and the barbecue-braised short ribs. If you're a fan of charcuterie, there's no place better than here—Polcyn literally wrote the book on it. A sommelier is present nightly to guide guests through the wine list, and the wine cellar boasts more than 500 well-chosen and diverse selections that span the globe.

American menu. Dinner. Closed Sunday. Bar. Children's menu. $36-85

BELLAIRE

See also Boyne City, Gaylord, Glen Arbor, Grayling, Harbor Springs, Peto-skey, Traverse City

As Shanty Creek Resort has grown and expanded, so has the tiny town of Bellaire, which offers several shops and cafés in its charming downtown area. The main attraction of the city remains Shanty Creek, with its two downhill ski resorts, three world-class golf courses, vast network of trails for cross-country skiing, mountain biking and hiking, tennis courts, pools and shopping areas.

WHAT TO SEE
SHANTY CREEK RESORT

1 Shanty Creek Road, Bellaire, 231-533-8621, 800-678-4111; www.shantycreek.com

This popular ski resort includes two separate mountains, five quad, two double chairlifts, four surface lifts; patrol, school, rentals; snowmaking; night skiing; lodge, snowboarding; tubing. All in all, the resort offers thirty trails. The longest run is approximately one mile with a vertical drop of 450 feet. There are also cross-country trails (25 miles).

Thanksgiving-March, daily.

WHERE TO STAY
★★★SHANTY CREEK RESORT

1 Shanty Creek Road, Bellaire, 231-533-8621, 800-678-4111; www.shantycreek.com

Located on more than 4,500 acres of rolling hills, this resort offers three distinct lodges: The Schuss Village features one in a European style at the bottom of Schuss Mountain and offers guest rooms and one- and two-bedroom condos; The Summit Village gives visitors a great view of the snow-covered lakes and forests (considered by many as some of the best views in northern Michigan); and the Cedar River Village, the newest of the three, overlooks the Tom Weiskopf golf course. Onsite activities cover all seasons and include disc golf, hiking, bike trails, skiing, snowboarding and tubing. Guests' pets are welcomed with a package of treats and a map of places to take four-legged friends on walks. The dining options are many, from fine dining to casual post-activity choices.

640 rooms. Restaurant, bar. Beach. Ski in/ski out. Golf. Tennis. $151-250

BIRCH RUN

Buoyed by the more than one million visitors to the Outlets at Birch Run, this town has gone from sleepy to sprawling in just a few years. As a result of all the traffic, attractions outside the outlets have sprung up, including golf courses, museums and a small speedway.

WHAT TO SEE
THE OUTLETS AT BIRCH RUN

12240 S. Beyer Road, Birch Run, 989-624-7467

These outlets are so popular mainly because they are all connected and indoors, so you don't have to go outside in the cold or get in your car to hop from one store to the next. There are more than 200 stores here, including Coach, Nike, J. Crew, Eddie Bauer, Ann Taylor, Laura Ashley, Polo/Ralph Lauren, TJ Maxx, Aldo, Saks Off Fifth, Neiman Marcus Last call, and a lot more. The mall also includes a movie theater and a large food court.

Daily.

BIRMINGHAM

See also Bloomfield Hills, Detroit, Southfield

Chic upscale boutiques and art galleries fill Birmingham's fashionable and charming downtown area. The town is full of upscale boutiques, cozy cafes, popular restaurants and gourmet shops (make a stop in Papa Joe's right on Woodward Avenue, the main street that borders the town). Perhaps the town's biggest appeal is that, unlike many other places in the metro Detroit area, Birmingham is very walker-friendly. Some of the most expensive real estate in the state surrounds this area. Downtown Birmingham is also home to one of the nicest hotels in the area, The Townsend Hotel. You will also find a large movie theater where you can sign up for Dinner and a Movie.

WHERE TO STAY
★★★★THE TOWNSEND HOTEL
100 Townsend St., Birmingham, 248-642-7900, 800-548-4172;
www.townsendhotel.com
Located in the quiet community of Birmingham, where tree-lined streets brim with boutiques and cafés, this hotel is conveniently located less than an hour from Detroit. The guest rooms are handsomely furnished with jewel tones, four-poster beds and full kitchens in the suites and penthouses. The cherry wood paneling and the warm glow of the fireplace make Rugby Grille an inviting space. The Corner bar has appealing interiors that are a perfect match for its Asian-inspired appetizers and creative cocktails.
152 rooms. Pets accepted, some restrictions; fee. High-speed Internet access. Restaurant, bar. Fitness room. Airport transportation available. Business center. $351 and up

WHERE TO EAT
★★★FORTÉ
201 S. Old Woodward Ave., Birmingham, 248-594-7300; www.forterestaurant.com
This see-and-be-seen restaurant is located in the heart of downtown and up-scale Birmingham next to the Downtown Theatre. The tastefully decorated space features lavender ceilings, ocean blue walls, distinctive light fixtures, rich upholstery accents and two giant framed mirrors in the main dining room. The open kitchen allows diners to watch executive chef Ty Gerych create scrumptious dishes such as butternut squash risotto, short ribs and soy-wasabi marinated yellowfin tuna.
International menu. Lunch, dinner. Bar. Business casual attire. Reservations recommended. Valet parking. $36-85

★★★RUGBY GRILLE
100 Townsend St., Birmingham, 248-642-5999; www.townsendhotel.com
Located in the European-style Townsend Hotel, this internationally inspired restaurant's dinner menu features fine steak and chops, fresh seafood and housemade pastas. Breakfast and lunch are also available. The elegant dining room is decorated with an abundance of fresh flowers, cherry wood walls and a cozy fireplace, making it the perfect choice for a special-occasion meal.
International menu. Breakfast, lunch, dinner. Bar. Children's menu. Business casual attire. Reservations recommended. Valet parking. $36-85

BLOOMFIELD HILLS
See also Birmingham, Detroit, Pontiac, Southfield, Troy, Warren
Amasa Bagley followed a Native American trail and cleared land on what is today the business section of this small residential city. It was known as Bagley's Corners, later as Bloomfield Center, and finally as Bloomfield Hills. In 1904, Ellen Scripps Booth and George G. Booth, president of The Detroit

News, bought 300 acres of farmland here, naming it Cranbrook after the English village in which Mr. Booth's father was born. Since then, the estate has turned into a vast cultural and educational complex. Today, Bloomfield Hills ranks as one of the wealthiest cities in the United States. Drive around residential areas to view the city's Tudor and Georgian mansions that date back to the 1920s, as well as modern mansions built by Detroit's professional athletes, entertainers and automotive executives.

WHAT TO SEE
CRANBROOK ACADEMY OF ART MUSEUM
39221 Woodward Ave., Bloomfield Hills, 248-645-3320; www.cranbrookart.edu
This museum is currently closed and under construction until 2011.
Wednesday-Sunday 11 a.m.-5 p.m.

CRANBROOK EDUCATIONAL COMMUNITY
39221 Woodward Ave., Bloomfield Hills, 248-645-3000, 877-462-7262;
www.cranbrook.edu
This well-known campus is the site of the renowned center for the arts, education, science and culture. Located on more than 300 acres, Cranbrook is noted for its exceptional architecture, gardens and sculpture.

CRANBROOK GARDENS
380 Lone Pine Road, Bloomfield Hills, 248-645-3147; www.cranbrook.edu
The lovely gardens here include more than forty acres of formal and informal gardens, trails, fountains and an outdoor Greek theater.
May-August, daily; September, afternoons only; October, Saturday-Sunday afternoons.

CRANBROOK HOUSE
380 Lone Pine Road, Bloomfield Hills, 248-645-3147; www.cranbrook.edu
Tudor-style structure designed by Albert Kahn and built in 1908. Contains exceptional examples of decorative and fine art from the late 19th and early 20th centuries.

CRANBROOK INSTITUTE OF SCIENCE
39221 Woodward Ave., Bloomfield Hills, 248-645-3200; www.cranbrook.edu
This natural history and science museum includes an observatory, nature center, planetarium and laser demonstrations.
Daily 10 a.m.-5 p.m., Friday until 10 p.m.

WHERE TO STAY
★★RADISSON HOTEL DETROIT-BLOOMFIELD HILLS
39475 Woodward Ave., Bloomfield Hills, 248-644-1400, 888-201-1718;
www.radisson.com
151 rooms. High-speed Internet access. Two Restaurants, bar. $151-250

WHERE TO EAT
★★★THE LARK
6430 Farmington Road, West Bloomfield, 248-661-4466; www.thelark.com

Dining at the Lark is like escaping to a quiet European hideaway. The room—a beautiful space with Portuguese-style tile murals and a trellised terrace—is warm and welcoming. The ambitious menu features classics like lobster Thermidor, as well as heartier dishes like rack of lamb Genghis and Chinese oven-roasted duck with figs, dates, almonds and brandy. The world-class wine list fits the seasonal, modern French-influenced menu like a glove. The Lark is also known for its dessert trolley, loaded with every kind of cake, tart, cookie, and pastry imaginable.

French menu. Dinner. Closed Sunday-Monday. Bar. Jacket required. Reservations recommended. Outdoor seating. $36-85

BOYNE CITY
See also Charlevoix, Petosky

Once an industrial center for both logging and leather tanning, Boyne City is now a resort town located at the southern tip of Lake Charlevoix. Fishing, canoeing and kayaking abound in summer, as does golfing on the city's two championship courses. Downhill and cross-country skiing, snowshoeing and snowmobiling keep visitors moving in winter. Nearby Boyne Mountain (six miles southeast) was northern Michigan's first ski resort and is still one of its best.

WHAT TO SEE
BOYNE MOUNTAIN
1 Boyne Mountain Road, Boyne Falls, 231-549-6000, 800-462-6963;
www.boynemountain.com

Triple, six-passenger, three quad, three double chairlifts; rope tow; patrol, school, rentals; snowmaking; lodge, cafeteria, restaurant, bar, nursery. The longest run is one mile with a vertical drop of 500 feet. Cross-country trails (35 miles), rentals (trail ticket; fee).

Late November-mid-April, daily.

BROOKLYN

Like many U.S. cities that offer NASCAR racetracks, Brooklyn has gone from relative obscurity to a popular destination for summer race fans.

WHAT TO SEE
ANTIQUE ALLEY
The 50-mile drive west from Saline to Somerset Center with a side trip up Highway 50 to Brooklyn is known locally as Antique Alley, and it makes for a great day of shopping.

BRICK WALKER TAVERN ANTIQUES
11705 Highway 12, Brooklyn, 517-467-6961

Brick Walker Tavern Antiques, in an 1854 building constructed as a three-story inn along the Detroit-Chicago Pike, features collectible glassware, pottery and china.

CAMBRIDGE JUNCTION HISTORIC STATE PARK/WALKER TAVERN HISTORIC COMPLEX

13220 Highway 50, Cambridge Junction, 517-467-4414; www.michigan.gov/dnr
Walker's farmhouse and tavern, a Federal-style white clapboard house and farm, is a museum interpreting Michigan's frontier history. It was a stopping point for stagecoaches making the arduous trip to Chicago from 1836 to 1855.
May-October.

HIDDEN LAKE GARDENS

6280 Munger Road, Tipton, 517-431-2060; hiddenlakegardens.msu.edu
These "gardens" are spread over nearly 800 acres and feature the Harper collection of dwarf and rare conifers with more than 500 varieties. Hidden Lake also has an 8,000-square-foot tropical plant conservatory and six miles of paved roads through the hilly, oak-hickory woods, meadows and landscaped areas that are good for hiking.
April-October, daily 8 a.m.-dusk; November-March, daily 8 a.m.-4 p.m.

IRISH HILLS ANTIQUES AND OUTDOOR MARKET

10600 Highway 12, Brooklyn, 517-467-4646
Irish Hills Antiques sells antique wood- and coal-burning parlor kitchen stoves, brass cash registers, porcelain signs and gasoline pumps.

IRISH HILLS FUN CENTER

5600 Highway 12, Tipton, 517-431-2217; www.irishhillsgokarts.com
Go-karts and sprint cars for rent, batting cages, miniature golf and paintball arena are enough to keep the kids occupied for an afternoon.
June-August, daily noon-9 p.m.; May and September, Saturday-Sunday 1-7 p.m.; April and October, Saturday-Sunday 1-6 p.m.

22

TURN OF THE CENTURY LIGHTING CO.

116 W. Michigan Ave., Clinton, 517-456-6019
This shop features gas and electric lighting fixtures from the Victorian era as well as period lampshades.

W.J. HAYES STATE PARK

1220 Wamplers Lake Road, Onsted, 517-467-7401
The park features two lakes and wooded sites. Fires are permitted.

SPECIAL EVENT
MICHIGAN INTERNATIONAL SPEEDWAY

12626 Highway 12, Brooklyn, 517-592-6666, 800-354-1010; www.mispeedway.com
NASCAR, ARCA, IROC and Indy Car races on a two-mile oval track.
Mid-June-mid-August.

CADILLAC

See also Traverse City
Named for Antoine de la Mothe Cadillac, founder of Detroit, Cadillac was originally a lumber camp and was once the major lumber center of the area.

Lakes Cadillac and Mitchell offer opportunities for swimming, water skiing and fishing, while nearby Caberfae is known as one of the best ski resorts in the state.

WHAT TO SEE
ADVENTURE ISLAND
6083 E. Highway 155, Cadillac, 231-775-5665;
www.cadillacmichigan.com/adventureisland
This family fun park includes mountain miniature golf, go-karts, batting cages, bumper boats, water slides, concessions, an arcade and a water slide. Memorial Day-Labor Day, daily 10 a.m.-10 p.m.

CABERFAE PEAKS SKI RESORT
Caberfae Road, Cadillac, 231-862-3000; www.caberfaepeaks.com
Quad, triple, three double chairlifts, two T-bars, two rope tows, patrol, school, rentals; snowmaking; bar; snowboard, cross-country and snowmobile trails. Late November-March, daily.

WILLIAM MITCHELL STATE PARK
6093 E. Highway 115, Cadillac, 231-775-7911
This state park occupies approximately 260 acres between Lake Cadillac and Lake Mitchell. It includes a swimming beach, boat docks and rentals, interpretive hiking trails, picnicking, playground and a nature study area.

WHERE TO STAY
★HAMPTON INN
1650 S. Mitchell St., Cadillac, 231-779-2900, 800-426-7866; www.hamptoninn.com
120 rooms. Complimentary continental breakfast. Wireless Internet access. $61-150

WHERE TO EAT
★★HERMANN'S EUROPEAN CAFÉ
214 N. Mitchell St., Cadillac, 231-775-9563; www.chefhermann.com
Continental menu. Lunch, dinner. Closed Sunday. Bar. Children's menu. Casual attire. Outdoor seating. $36-85

★★LAKESIDE CHARLIE'S
301 S. Lake Mitchell, Cadillac, 231-775-5332
American menu. Lunch, dinner, late-night. Bar. Children's menu. Casual attire. Reservations recommended. Outdoor seating. $16-35

CALUMET
See also Copper Harbor, Hancock, Houghton
These days, Calumet is a small town, but it was once a wealthy copper-mining community with a population of 60,000. Thanks to the red sandstone used to build most of the downtown buildings, Calumet looks much like it did 100 years ago, albeit with far fewer residents. Steeped in history and architectural treasures, Calumet has earned national recognition as part of the Keweenaw National Historic Park.

WHAT TO SEE
CALUMET THEATRE
340 Sixth St., Calumet, 906-337-2610; www.calumettheatre.com
Built with boomtown wealth, this ornate theater was host to such stars as Lillian Russell, Sarah Bernhardt, Lon Chaney, Otis Skinner, James O'Neil, Douglas Fairbanks and John Philip Sousa. Guided tours mid-June-September, daily. Live performances throughout the year.

KEWEENAW NATIONAL HISTORICAL PARK
25970 Red Jacket Road, Calumet, 906-337-3168; www.nps.gov/kewe
Established in October 1992 to commemorate the Keweenaw Peninsula's copper mining heritage. Self-guided walking tour; brochures.

UPPER PENINSULA FIREFIGHTERS MEMORIAL MUSEUM
Red Jacket Fire Station, 327 Sixth St., Calumet, 906-337-4579; www.nps.gov
Housed in the historic Red Jacket Fire station, this museum features memorabilia and exhibits spanning almost a century of firefighting history. Monday-Saturday.

CHARLEVOIX
See also Boyne City, Traverse City
This harbor town offers gorgeous sandy beaches on both Lake Michigan and Lake Charlevoix, a 17-mile-long inland lake. Every half hour, the drawbridge stops traffic on Charlevoix's main street to allow sailboats to pass and the Beaver Island Ferry to enter Round Lake Harbor. Visitors walk to the pier to view Lake Michigan and the Charlevoix lighthouse, one of the state's most photographed lighthouses. Tourists can also sample freshly made fudge, caramel apples and ice cream cones while walking a four-block downtown area.

WHAT TO SEE
BEAVER ISLAND BOAT COMPANY
City Dock, 103 Bridge Park Drive, Charlevoix, 231-547-2311, 888-446-4095;
www.bibco.com
A 2¼-hour trip to Beaver Island, the largest island of the Beaver Archipelago. June-September, daily; mid-April-May and October-mid-December, limited schedule. Advance car reservations necessary.

SPECIAL EVENTS
APPLE FESTIVAL
408 Bridge St., Charlevoix, 231-547-2101
Vendors line Charlevoix's main street selling fresh apples, apple pies, cider (with cake-type doughnuts, of course), caramel apples and apple turnovers. Second weekend in October.

VENETIAN FESTIVAL
Charlevoix, 231-547-2101; www.venetianfestival.com
Midway, street and boat parades, fireworks. Fourth week in July.

WATERFRONT ART FAIR

312 Prospect St., Charlevoix, 231-547-2675; www.charlevoixwaterfrontartfair.org

In this juried art show, hundreds of artists display and sell their works in a picturesque setting.

Second Saturday in August.

WHERE TO STAY
★★EDGEWATER INN

100 Michigan Ave., Charlevoix, 231-547-6044, 800-748-0424;
www.edgewater-charlevoix.com

60 rooms, all suites. Wireless Internet access. $151-250

★WEATHERVANE TERRACE INN & SUITES

111 Pine River Lane, Charlevoix, 231-547-9955, 800-552-0025;
www.weathervane-chx.com

68 rooms. Complimentary breakfast. $61-150

WHERE TO EAT
★★★MAHOGANY'S

9600 Clubhouse Drive, Charlevoix, 231-547-3555, 800-618-9796;
www.chxcountryclub.com/mahoganys.phtml

Located at the Charlevoix Country Club, this restaurant offers an elegant dining experience, complete with a fieldstone fireplace and handcrafted mahogany bar. Serving casual lunches on the porch and international cuisine in the dining room, this restaurant is the perfect post-game stopping place. American menu. Dinner, Sunday brunch. Bar. Children's menu. $36-85

★★STAFFORD'S WEATHERVANE

106 Pine River Lane, Charlevoix, 231-547-4311; www.staffords.com

American menu. Lunch, dinner. Bar. Children's menu. Business casual attire. Reservations recommended. Outdoor seating. $16-35

CHEBOYGAN

See also Harbor Springs, Indian River, Mackinaw City

Surrounded by two Great Lakes and large inland lakes, Cheboygan has long been a premier boating and fishing area. You'll also find charming Victorian shops, gorgeous spring blooms and delightful fall color. And because of heavy snowfall, winter activities abound: snowmobiling, cross-country skiing (hundreds of miles of groomed trails), snowshoeing, ice skating, hockey and ice fishing.

WHAT TO SEE
ALOHA STATE PARK

4347 Third St., Cheboygan, 231-625-2522

This park includes roughly 95 acres with swimming, fishing, boating, picnicking, camping. Daily.

CHEBOYGAN OPERA HOUSE

403 N. Huron St., Cheboygan, 231-627-5432; www.theoperahouse.org

This renovated 580-seat auditorium finished in 1877 features events ranging from bluegrass to ballet.

CHEBOYGAN STATE PARK

4490 Beach Road, Cheboygan, 616-627-2811; www.cheboyganstatepark.com

This state park is made up of more than 1,200 acres, and offers swimming, fishing, boating, hiking, cross-country skiing, picnicking and camping. Daily.

THE US COAST GUARD CUTTER MACKINAW

Cheboygan

One of the world's largest icebreakers, with a complement of 80 officers and crew. When in port, the Mackinaw is moored at the turning basin on the east side of the Cheboygan River.

SPECIAL EVENT
CHEBOYGAN COUNTY FAIR

Fairgrounds, 204 E. Lincoln Ave., Cheboygan, 231-627-9611; www.cheboyganfair.com

The attractions at this county fair include horse shows, carnival rides, craft displays and agricultural and animal exhibits.
Early August.

WHERE TO STAY
★BEST WESTERN RIVER TERRACE

847 S. Main St., Cheboygan, 231-627-5688; www.bestwestern.com

53 rooms. High-speed Internet access. Pets accepted. $61-150

★★★INSEL HAUS BED AND BREAKFAST

HCR 1, Bios Blanc Island, 231-634-7393; www.inselhausbandb.com

This pretty 6,200-square-foot home located on the strait of Mackinac is five miles offshore. Guests arrive by ferry, plane or helicopter. Inside, the great room features a beautiful chandelier (the former helm of an old ship), a tiled corner fireplace and a floor-to-ceiling window, which overlooks the grounds. The home can accommodate up to 20 guests at a time and features three kitchens, a private library, antique furniture, Persian rugs and stained-glass accents throughout. The house is surrounded by 1,800 feet of shoreline and a mile of wilderness forests, allowing guests to enjoy various outdoor activities such as cross-country skiing, snow shoeing, bicycling, sailing, hiking, canoeing, swimming, bird-watching and charter fishing. For guests looking for some nightlife, there is a casino 90 minutes away.
9 rooms. Complimentary breakfast. Wireless Internet access. $61-150

WHERE TO EAT
★★HACK-MA-TACK INN

8131 Beebe Road, Cheboygan, 231-625-2919; www.hackmatackinn.com

American menu. Dinner. Closed mid-October-early May. Bar. Children's menu. $36-85

COLDWATER

See also Marshall

Coldwater is renowned for its early 20th-century architecture, which has been carefully preserved. Named for the river that runs through town, Coldwater is best known for the Tibbits Opera House, which features numerous concerts, plays and other events.

WHAT TO SEE
TIBBITS OPERA HOUSE

14 S. Hanchett St., Coldwater, 517-278-6029; www.tibbits.org

This renovated 19th-century Victorian opera house is home to professional summer theater series, art exhibits, a winter concert series, children's programs and community events. Originally owned and operated by businessman Barton S. Tibbits, the house attracted such performers as John Philip Sousa, Ethel Barrymore, P. T. Barnum, John Sullivan and William Gillette. Tours. Monday-Friday.

WING HOUSE MUSEUM

27 S. Jefferson St., Coldwater, 517-278-2871

Originally built in 1875, this historical house museum exhibits Second Empire architectural style. The home includes the original kitchen and dining room in the basement, a collection of Oriental rugs, oil paintings, three generations of glassware, Regina music box and furniture from Empire to Eastlake styles.

Wednesday-Sunday 1-5 p.m., also by appointment.

SPECIAL EVENTS
BRONSON POLISH FESTIVAL DAYS

Bronson, 800-968-9333

Heritage fest, games, vendors, concessions and dancing.
Third week in July.

CAR SHOW SWAP MEET

Coldwater, 517-278-5985; www.carshowswapmeet.com

Antique and classic car show, arts and crafts, vendors; trophies.
Early May.

TIBBITS PROFESSIONAL SUMMER THEATRE SERIES

14 S. Hanchett St., Coldwater, 517-278-6029; www.tibbits.org/summertheatre.htm

Resident professional company produces comedies and musicals.
Late June-August.

COPPER HARBOR

See also Calumet, Houghton

Lumps of pure copper studded the lakeshore and attracted the first explorers to this area, but deposits proved thin and unfruitful. A subsequent lumber boom also ended. Today, this northernmost village is a small but beautiful resort. Streams and inland lakes provide excellent trout, walleye, bass and northern pike fishing. Lake Superior yields trout, salmon and other species.

WHAT TO SEE

ASTOR HOUSE ANTIQUE DOLL & INDIAN ARTIFACT MUSEUM

560 Gratiot St., Copper Harbor, 906-289-4449, 800-833-2470;
www.minnetonkaresort.com

Early items from mining boom days and hundreds of antique dolls.
June-October, daily.

BROCKWAY MOUNTAIN DRIVE

Highways 41 and 26, Copper Harbor

Lookouts. Views of Lake Superior and forests.

COPPER HARBOR LIGHTHOUSE TOUR

Copper Harbor Marina, 326 Shelden Ave., Houghton, 906-289-4966;
www.copperharborlighthouse.com

Twenty-minute boat ride to one of the oldest lighthouses on Lake Superior;
includes guided tour of lighthouse. Trips depart hourly.
Memorial Day-mid-October, daily, weather permitting.

DELAWARE MINE TOUR

7804 Delaware Mine Road, Copper Harbor, 906-289-4688; www.copperharbor.org

Underground guided tour of copper mine dating back to the 1850s.
June-August 10 a.m.-6 p.m., September-October 10 a.m.-5 p.m.

FERRY SERVICE TO ISLE ROYALE NATIONAL PARK

60 Fifth St., Houghton, 906-482-0984; www.nps.gov

Four ferries and a floatplane provide transportation.
June-September, daily; some trips in May.

FORT WILKINS STATE PARK

Highway 41, Copper Harbor, 906-289-4215; www.michigan.gov/dnr

Approximately 200 acres. A historic army post completed in 1844 on Lake
Fanny Hooe. The stockade has been restored and the buildings preserved
to maintain the frontier post atmosphere. Costumed guides demonstrate old
army lifestyle. Fishing, boating, cross-country ski trails, picnicking, playground, concession, camping. Museum with relics of early mining days and
various exhibits depicting army life in the 1870s. Daily.

ISLE ROYALE QUEEN III EVENING CRUISES

Copper Harbor, 906-289-4437; www.isleroyale.com

Narrated 1½-hour cruise on Lake Superior. Reservations recommended.
Early July-Labor Day, evenings.

SNOWMOBILING

326 Shelden Ave., Houghton, 906-482-2388

There is a series of interconnecting trails totaling several hundred miles;
some overlook Lake Superior from high bluffs. Also 17 miles of cross-country trails.
December-March.

SPECIAL EVENTS
ART IN THE PARK
Community Center grounds, Main Street, Copper Harbor, 906-337-4579;
www.keweenaw.info
This juried art show features local and regional artists, food and live entertainment.
Mid-August.

BROCKWAY MOUNTAIN CHALLENGE
Copper Harbor, 906-337-4579; www.keweenaw.info
A 15-kilometer cross-country ski race. February.

FERROUS FROLICS
Iron County Museum, 100 Museum Drive, Caspian, 906-265-2617
Arts, crafts, demonstrations, band concert, flea market.
Third weekend in July.

WHERE TO EAT
★TAMARACK INN
526 Highway 26, Copper Harbor, 906-289-4522
American menu. Breakfast, lunch, dinner. $151-250

DEARBORN
See also Ann Arbor, Detroit, Ypsilanti
Dearborn is the home of the Ford Motor Company's Rouge Assembly Plant, Ford World Headquarters and a complex made up of the Henry Ford Museum, Greenfield Village and other historical attractions. Although Dearborn has a long and colorful history, its real claim to fame is due to Henry Ford, who was born here in 1863.

WHAT TO SEE

GREENFIELD VILLAGE
20900 Oakwood Blvd., Dearborn, 313-271-1620; www.hfmgv.org
This village comprises more than 80 18th- and 19th-century buildings moved here from all over the country to form a community that brings history alive. Homes, shops, schools, mills, stores and laboratories that figured in the lives of such historic figures as Lincoln, McGuffey, Carver, the Wright brothers, Edison and Ford are on display. Among the most interesting are the courthouse where Abraham Lincoln practiced law, the Wright brothers' cycle shop, Henry Ford's birthplace and Edison's Menlo Park laboratory.
Monday-Saturday 9 a.m.-5 p.m., Sunday noon-5 p.m. Interiors also closed January-mid-March.

HENRY FORD ESTATE-FAIR LANE
4901 Evergreen Road, Dearborn, 313-593-5590; www.henryfordestate.com
Built by automotive pioneer Henry Ford in 1915, the mansion cost more than $2 million and stands on 72 acres of property. Designed by William Van Tine, the manse reflects Ford's penchant for simplicity and functionalism. Its systems for heating, water, electricity and refrigeration were entirely self-

sufficient at that time. The powerhouse, boathouse and gardens have been restored, and some original furniture and a children's playhouse have been returned to the premises.

April-December, daily; rest of year, Sunday.

HENRY FORD MUSEUM
20900 Oakwood Blvd., Dearborn, 313-271-1620; www.hfmgv.org
This interesting museum occupies 12 acres and includes major collections in transportation, power and machinery, agriculture, lighting, communications, household furnishings and appliances, ceramics, glass, silver and pewter. Special exhibits, demonstrations and hands-on activities are also part of the fun.

Monday-Saturday 9 a.m.-5 p.m., Sunday noon-5 p.m.

SUWANEE PARK
Dearborn
The park includes an early 20th-century amusement center with antique merry-go-round, steamboat, train ride, restaurant and soda fountain (mid-May-September). In addition, visitors can take narrated rides in a horse-drawn carriage, on a steam train or on a riverboat. 1931 Ford bus rides are also available (mid-May-September). Varied activities are scheduled throughout the year.

SPECIAL EVENTS
FALL HARVEST DAYS
Greenfield Village, 20900 Oakwood Blvd., Dearborn, 313-271-1620; www.hfmgv.org
Fall Harvest Days celebrates turn-of-the-century farm chores, rural home life and entertainment.

Three days in early October.

OLD CAR FESTIVAL
Greenfield Village, 20900 Oakwood Blvd., Dearborn, 313-271-1620; www.hfmgv.org
More than 500 motorized vehicles from 1932 or earlier are on display.
Two days in mid-September.

WHERE TO STAY
★★BEST WESTERN GREENFIELD INN
3000 Enterprise Drive, Allen Park, 313-271-1600, 800-342-5802; www.bestwestern.com
209 rooms. Wireless Internet access. Restaurant, bar. Fitness room. Airport transportation available. $61-150

★★COURTYARD BY MARRIOTT
5200 Mercury Drive, Dearborn, 313-271-1400, 800-321-2211; www.courtyard.com
147 rooms. High-speed Internet access. Airport transportation available. $61-150

★★★MARRIOTT DEARBORN INN
20301 Oakwood Blvd., Dearborn, 313-271-2700, 800-228-9290; www.marriott.com
This property looks more like a bed and breakfast than a hotel. Built in 1931

on the grounds of the Ford Motor Company, this historic spot is located on 23 beautifully landscaped acres with manicured gardens. The grounds consist of a Georgian-style inn built by Henry Ford, two Colonial-style lodges and five Colonial-style houses. Early American décor and furnishings are found throughout this elegant property.

222 rooms. High-speed Internet access. Two restaurants, bar. $151-250

★★★THE RITZ-CARLTON, DEARBORN

300 Town Center Drive, Dearborn, 313-441-2000, 800-241-3333; www.ritzcarlton.com

Located 15 minutes from downtown Detroit, this hotel is part of a nearly seven-acre complex in historic Dearborn. Its distinguished atmosphere and superior service make it a favorite of corporate leaders. The hotel is home to a flurry of charity and business events, and many local weddings. The hotel is also a gourmet destination because of the The Grill. The guest rooms have oversized bathrooms and handsome appointments. Fitness is a priority, and the hotel not only provides a gym and indoor pool, but also extends privileges to the nearby Fairlane Club & Spa.

308 rooms. Wireless Internet access. Restaurant, bar. $251-350

WHERE TO EAT

★★★THE GRILL

300 Town Center Drive, Dearborn, 313-441-2000, 800-241-3333; www.ritzcarlton.com

This mahogany-clad dining room is a civilized retreat. The menu features chef de cuisine Christian Schmidt's American-Continental cuisine, and includes dishes such as an enormous shrimp cocktail; venison soup; Amish chicken with herb spaetzle, spring onions, corn, chantrelles and madeira cream; and morel fettuccine with asparagus, ramps and truffled mushroom broth. Top things off with Bananas Foster made tableside or a slice of the refreshing citrus cheesecake.

American menu. Breakfast, lunch, dinner, Sunday brunch. Bar. Valet parking. $36-85

★★KIERNAN'S STEAK HOUSE

21931 Michigan Ave., Dearborn, 313-565-4260: www.kiernans.com

Seafood, steak menu. Lunch, dinner. Closed holidays. Bar. Valet parking. $36-85

DETROIT

See also Ann Arbor, Birmingham, Bloomfield Hills, Dearborn, Farmington, Mount Clemens, Plymouth, Pontiac, Rochester, Royal Oak, Southfield, St. Clair, Troy, Warren, Ypsilanti

Detroit, a city geared to the tempo of the production line, is the symbol throughout the world of America's automotive industry. Detroit is the birthplace of mass production and the producer of nearly 25 percent of the nation's automobiles, trucks and tractors. This is the city of Ford, Chrysler, Dodge and the U.A.W. Detroit is also a major producer of space propulsion units, automation equipment, plane parts, hardware, rubber tires, office equipment, machine tools, fabricated metal, iron and steel forging and auto stampings and accessories. Being a port and border city, Detroit helps the Michigan Customs District rank among the nation's top five customs districts.

Founded by Antoine de la Mothe Cadillac in the name of Louis XIV of France, this strategic frontier trading post was 75 years old when the American Revolution began. During that time, Detroit was ruled by Henry Hamilton, a British governor hated throughout the colonies as "the hair buyer of Detroit" because he encouraged American Indians to take rebel scalps rather than prisoners. At the end of the war, the British ignored treaty obligations and refused to abandon Detroit. As long as the city remained in British hands, it was both a strategic threat and a barrier to westward expansion. The settlement was finally wrested away by Major General Anthony Wayne at the Battle of Fallen Timbers. On July 11, 1796, the American flag flew over Detroit for the first time.

In 1815, when the city was incorporated, Detroit was still just a trading post. The development of more efficient transportation opened the floodgates of immigration, and the city was on its way to becoming an industrial and shipping hub. Between 1830 and 1860, population doubled with every decade. At the turn of the century, the auto industry took hold.

Detroit was a quiet city before the automobile. The city rocketed out beyond its river-hugging confines, developing dozens of suburbs. Civic planning is now remodeling the face of the community, particularly downtown and along the riverfront.Detroit is one of the few cities in the United States where you can look due south into Canada. The city stretches out along the Detroit River between Lakes Erie and St. Clair, opposite the Canadian city of Windsor, Ontario. The city is 143 square miles in size and almost completely flat. The buildings of the Renaissance Center and Civic Center are grouped about the shoreline, and a network of major highways and expressways radiate from this point like the spokes of a wheel. The original city was laid out on the lines of the L'Enfant plan for Washington, D.C., with a few major streets radiating from a series of circles. As the city grew, a gridiron pattern was superimposed to handle the maze of subdivisions that had developed into Detroit's 200 neighborhoods.

WHAT TO SEE
BELLE ISLE

East Jefferson Avenue and East Grand Boulevard, Detroit, 313-852-4078

Between the U.S. and Canada, in sight of downtown Detroit, this 1,000-acre island park offers nine-hole golf, a nature center, guided nature walks, swimming and fishing (piers, docks). Picnicking, ball fields, tennis and lighted handball courts.

CHARLES H. WRIGHT MUSEUM OF AFRICAN AMERICAN HISTORY

315 E. Warren Ave., Detroit, 313-494-5800; www.maah-detroit.org

Exhibits here trace 400 years of history and achievements of African-Americans. The museum's major exhibit, "The African-American Experience," is an inspiring look at African-American culture.

Sunday 1-5 p.m. Tuesday-Saturday, 9 a.m.-5 p.m.

CHILDREN'S MUSEUM

6134 Second Ave., Detroit, 313-873-8100; www.detroitchildrensmuseum.org

Exhibits at this fun museum include Inuit culture, children's art, folk crafts, birds and mammals of Michigan. Special workshops and programs and plan-

etarium demonstrations are help on Saturdays and during vacations.
Monday-Friday 9 a.m.-4 p.m.

CIVIC CENTER
Woodward and Jefferson avenues, Detroit
Dramatic group of buildings in a 95-acre downtown riverfront setting.

COBO CENTER
1 Washington Blvd., Detroit, 313-877-8111; www.cobocenter.com
Designed to be the world's finest convention-exposition-recreation building, the Cobo Center features an 11,561-seat arena and 720,000 square feet of exhibit area and facilities.
Daily.

COLEMAN A. YOUNG MUNICIPAL CENTER
2 Woodward Ave., Detroit, 313-224-5585
This $27-million, 13-story white marble office building and 19-story tower houses more than 36 government departments and courtrooms. At the front entrance is the massive bronze sculpture, Spirit of Detroit.
Monday-Friday.

DETROIT HISTORICAL MUSEUM
5401 Woodward Ave., Detroit, 313-833-1805; www.detroithistorical.org
Presents a walk-through history along reconstructed streets of Old Detroit, with period alcoves and costumes. Changing exhibits portray city life. The museum rotates exhibits that explore Detroit history, from automotive displays to Motown exhibits.
Tuesday-Friday 9:30 a.m.-5 p.m., Saturday 10 a.m.-5 p.m., Sunday 11 a.m.-5 p.m.

DETROIT INSTITUTE OF ARTS
5200 Woodward Ave., Detroit, 313-833-7900; www.dia.org
This respected art museum tells the history of humankind through artistic creations. Every significant art-producing culture is represented. Exhibits include The Detroit Industry murals by Diego Rivera, Van Eyck's St. Jerome, Bruegel's Wedding Dance and Van Gogh's Self-Portrait. African-American, Indian, Dutch, French, Flemish and Italian collections; Medieval arms and armor; an 18th-century American country house reconstructed with period furnishings.
Frequent special exhibitions, lectures, films. Wednesday-Thursday 10 a.m.-4 p.m., Friday 10 a.m.-9 p.m., Saturday-Sunday 10 a.m.-5 p.m.

DETROIT LIONS (NFL)
Ford Field, 2000 Brush St., Detroit, 313-262-2003; www.detroitlions.com
Professional football team. Located in downtown Detroit, Ford Field was the site of the 2006 Super Bowl.

DETROIT PUBLIC LIBRARY

5201 Woodward Ave., Detroit, 313-833-1000; www.detroit.lib.mi.us

Special collections include National Automotive History, Burton Historical (Old Northwest Territory), Hackley (African-Americans in performing arts), Labor, Maps, Rare Books and U.S. Patents Collection from 1790 to present. There are also murals by Coppin, Sheets, Melchers and Blashfield.
Tuesday-Wednesday noon-8 p.m., Thursday-Saturday 10 a.m.-6 p.m.

DETROIT RED WINGS (NHL)

Joe Louis Arena, 600 Civic Center Drive, Detroit, 313-396-7444;
www.detroitredwings.com

Professional hockey team.

DETROIT SYMPHONY ORCHESTRA HALL

3711 Woodward Ave., Detroit, 313-576-5100; www.detroitsymphony.com

Restored public concert hall, originally made in 1919, features classical programs. The Detroit Symphony Orchestra performs here.

DETROIT TIGERS (MLB)

Comerica Park, 2100 Woodward Ave., Detroit, 313-962-4000; www.tigers.com

Professional baseball team.

DOSSIN GREAT LAKES MUSEUM

100 Strand Drive, Detroit, 313-833-5538; www.glmi.org

See scale models of Great Lakes ships; a restored Gothic salon from Great Lakes liner; marine paintings, reconstructed ship's bridge and full-scale racing boat, Miss Pepsi.
Saturday-Sunday 11 a.m.-5 p.m.

EASTERN MARKET

2934 Russell St., Detroit, 313-833-9300; www.detroiteasternmarket.com

Built originally on the site of an early hay and wood market, this and the Chene-Ferry Market are the two remaining produce/wholesale markets in the city. Today this busy market encompasses produce and meat-packing houses, fish markets and storefronts, offering everything from spices to paper. It is also recognized as the world's largest bedding flower market.
Monday-Saturday.

FISHER BUILDING

3011 W. Grand Blvd., Detroit, 313-874-4444

Designed by architect Albert Kahn, this building was recognized in 1928 as the most beautiful commercial building erected and given a silver medal by the Architectural League of New York. The building consists of a 28-story central tower and two 11-story wings. Housed here are the Fisher Theater, shops, restaurants, art galleries and offices. Underground pedestrian walkways and skywalk bridges connect to a parking deck and 11 separate structures, including General Motors World Headquarters and New Center One.

GREEKTOWN

Monroe Street, Detroit

For more than 100 years, this two-block area of Monroe Street has been known as Greektown. Local restaurants specialize in large portions of Greek specialties, including souvlaki, mousaka, lamb chops, spinach pie and gyros. Greektown bars are especially lively on Fridays and Saturdays, while local shops and groceries celebrate Greek culture every day of the week. To complete your tour of Greektown, visit the Annunciation Greek Orthodox Cathedral that anchors the neighborhood.

GREEKTOWN CASINO

555 E. Lafayette Ave., Detroit, 313-223-2999; www.greektowncasino.com

This buzzing casino is conveniently located in the heart of Greektown and near Comerica Park (Detroit Tigers), Ford Field (Detroit Lions), Max M. Fisher Music Center and the Fox Theater. The casino includes more than 2,400 slot machines, plus a variety of table games, from craps and roulette to blackjack and seven-card stud.

Daily.

HART PLAZA AND DODGE FOUNTAIN

1 Hart Plaza, Detroit, 313-877-8077

A $2 million water display designed by sculptor Isamu Noguchi.

MARINERS' CHURCH

170 E. Jefferson Ave., Detroit, 313-259-2206

Oldest stone church in the city, completed in 1849, this building was moved 800 feet to its present site as part of the Civic Center plan. Since that time it has been extensively restored and a bell tower with carillon has been added. Tours by appointment.

MAX M. FISHER MUSIC CENTER

3711 Woodward Ave., Detroit, 313-576-5111; www.detroitsymphony.com

The home of the Detroit Symphony Orchestra (DSO), the Max M. Fisher Music Center was built around Orchestra Hall, which is reputed to have the best acoustics in the world. In addition, the Max complex includes the Music Box Theater, which is a smaller concert hall, a large rehearsal hall and an educational center.

Monday-Friday 10 a.m.-8 p.m., Saturday on performance days.

MGM GRAND CASINO

1777 Third St., Detroit, 877-888-2121; www.detroit.mgmgrand.com

This large, buzzing casino includes more than 2,000 slot machines, plus games like baccarat, blackjack, poker, roulette and more. It's also a great place for live entertainment and dining, particularly at Bourbon Steak.

Daily.

MICHIGAN CONSOLIDATED GAS COMPANY BUILDING

1 Woodward Ave., Detroit

Glass-walled skyscraper designed by Minoru Yamasaki.

MOTOR CITY CASINO

2901 Grand River Ave., Detroit, 877-777-0711; www.motorcitycasino.com

The Motor City Casino offers more than 2,500 slot machines, plus blackjack, roulette, craps and many other games. A variety of cafés and restaurants can be found here as well. Onsite entertainment takes place all week. Daily.

MOTOWN MUSEUM

2648 W. Grand Blvd., Detroit, 313-875-2264; www.motownmuseum.com

"Hitsville USA," the house where such legends as Diana Ross and the Supremes, Stevie Wonder, Marvin Gaye, the Jackson Five and the Temptations recorded their first songs is located in this historci spot. The museum includes Motown's original Studio A; artifacts, photographs, gold and platinum records, memorabilia. Guided tours are available. Tuesday-Saturday 10 a.m.-6 p.m.

RENAISSANCE CENTER

400 E. Jefferson Ave., Detroit, 313-568-5600

Seven-tower complex on the riverfront; includes a 73-story hotel, offices, restaurants, bars, movie theaters, retail shops and business services.

VETERANS' MEMORIAL BUILDING

151 W. Jefferson Ave., Detroit

Rises on site where Cadillac and the first French settlers landed in 1701. This $5.75-million monument to the Detroit-area war dead was the first unit of the $180-million Civic Center to be completed. The massive sculptured marble eagle on the front of the building is by Marshall Fredericks, who also sculpted Spirit of Detroit at the City-County Building.

WAYNE STATE UNIVERSITY

Cass and Warren avenues, Detroit; www.wayne.edu

This university has 13 professional schools and colleges. The campus also has nearly 100 buildings, some of the most notable being the award-winning McGregor Memorial Conference Center designed by Minoru Yamasaki, the Walter P. Reuther Library of Labor and Urban Affairs and the Yamasaki-designed College of Education. Wayne has a medical campus of 16 acres adjacent in the Detroit Medical Center. Three theaters present performances.

WHITCOMB CONSERVATORY

East Jefferson Avenue and East Grand Boulevard, Detroit, 313-852-4064

Exhibits of ferns, cacti, palms, orchids; special exhibits. Monday-Saturday 10 a.m.-5 p.m.

SPECIAL EVENTS
DETROIT GRAND PRIX

Belle Isle, 1249 Washington Blvd., Detroit; www.detroitgp.com

Indy car race. Friday is Free Prix Day. September.

DETROIT INTERNATIONAL JAZZ FESTIVAL

Hart Plaza and Campus Martius Park, Detroit, 313-447-1248; www.detroitjazzfest.com
Five days of free jazz concerts.
Labor Day weekend.

HAZEL PARK

1650 E. Ten Mile Road, Hazel Park, 248-398-1000; www.hazelparkraceway.com
Harness racing.
April-mid-October, Monday-Tuesday and Thursday-Saturday.

NORTH AMERICAN INTERNATIONAL AUTO SHOW

Cobo Center, 1 Washington Blvd., Detroit, 248-643-0250; www.naias.com
This large auto show attracts executives, media and consumers from all over the world.
January.

NORTHVILLE DOWNS

301 S. Center St., Northville, 248-349-1000; www.northvilledowns.com
Harness racing. Children over 12 years only.
January and October-March, Monday-Tuesday, Thursday, Saturday.

RIVERFRONT FESTIVALS

1 Hart Plaza, Detroit, 313-877-8077
Weekend festivals feature entertainment, costumes, history, artifacts and handicrafts of Detroit's diverse ethnic populations. Different country featured most weekends.
May-September.

THE THEATRE COMPANY-UNIVERSITY OF DETROIT MERCY

8200 W. Outer Drive, Detroit, 313-993-1130
Dramas, comedies in university theater.
September-May.

WOODWARD DREAM CRUISE

Woodward Avenue, Detroit, 800-338-7648; www.woodwarddreamcruise.com
Each year, more than 1.5 million people-watch or ride in 30,000 classic and vintage cars touring Woodward Avenue. The wildly popular event is billed as the world's largest one-day celebration of car culture. A parade-like atmosphere means you'll find plenty to eat and drink, vendors selling T-shirts and other items commemorating the event, and street entertainers providing music and other events.
Third Saturday in August, 9 a.m.-9 p.m., with some events held the preceding Thursday and Friday.

WHERE TO STAY
★★COURTYARD DOWNTOWN DETROIT

333 E. Jefferson St., Detroit, 313-222-7700, 800-321-2211; www.courtyard.com
260 rooms. High-speed Internet access. Restaurant, bar. Airport transportation available. Fitness center. $61-150

★★EMBASSY SUITES HOTEL DETROIT-NOVI/LIVONIA

19525 Victor Parkway, Livonia, 734-462-6000; www.embassysuites.com

239 rooms, all suites. Complimentary full breakfast. Wireless Internet access. Restaurant, bar. Airport transportation available. Fitness center. Pool. $61-150

★★★MARRIOTT DETROIT RENAISSANCE CENTER

Renaissance Center, Detroit, 313-568-8000, 800-352-0831; www.marriott.com

This Marriott hotel is housed in a 73-story building. The world headquarters of General Motors is also located here, along with numerous shops and restaurants. Located along the RiverWalk in the heart of Detroit, the Marriott offers breathtaking views of the Detroit River and Windsor, Ontario. More pluses include large guest rooms and closets, well-appointed facilities and an array of services and amenities for the business or leisure traveler.

1,328 rooms. High-speed Internet access. Restaurant, two bars. Airport transportation available. $151-250

★★★★MGM GRAND DETROIT

1777 Third St., Detroit, 877-888-2121; www.mgmgranddetroit.com

Feel like you're visiting Vegas without leaving Detroit. Located downtown, this mega-resort features non-stop action with a casino, five restaurants and five bars. You can get ready for a big night out at the full-service salon, then refresh and revitalize at the spa the next morning. The rooms and suites are sophisticated and spacious, while unique amenities—such as 42-inch plasma TVs and oversized showers with dual rain showerheads—complete the luxurious experience.

335 rooms, 65 suites. Restaurant, bar. Casino. Fitness center. Pool. Spa. $251-350

★★★OMNI DETROIT RIVER PLACE

1000 River Place Drive, Detroit, 313-259-9500, 800-843-6664; www.omnihotels.com

This elegant hotel (dating to 1902) is located in downtown Detroit on the historic waterfront. It was once the home of the Parke Davis Company, and Stroh's Brewery was also a previous occupant. Guest rooms boast views of the river and the Canadian border. The hotel has a championship croquet court, which is the only U.S.C.A.-sanctioned croquet court in Michigan. Feel free to bring Fido along for the trip—pets under 25 pounds are welcomed, and the hotel offers treats and a walking service.

108 rooms. Wireless Internet access. Restaurant, bar. Airport transportation available. Tennis. Pets accepted. $151-250

WHERE TO EAT
★★★★BOURBON STEAK

MGM Grand Detroit, 1777 S. Third St., Detroit, 313-465-1644;
www.mgmgranddetroit.com

Celebrity chef Michael Mina turns the traditional steakhouse on its head with this super-slick version. The chic space, with sleek furnishings and contemporary design, is equal parts upscale sports club and sultry nightclub. It's a carnivore's delight, as well—offering a variety of cuts of Angus, American kobe and Japanese wagyu beef. But thanks to quirky takes on classics, such

as lobster corn dog appetizers and side dishes including rosemary duck fat fries and truffle mac and cheese, this isn't your typical steakhouse.
American, steakhouse menu. Dinner. Closed Monday. $36-85

★★★CAUCUS CLUB
150 W. Congress St., Detroit, 313-965-4970; www.caucusclubdetroit.com
One of the city's culinary legends, this English-style dining room serves American cuisine with European accents. The jumbo Dover sole in lemon butter is a signature dish and the cozy, dimly lit bar is a popular after-work hangout.
American menu. Lunch, dinner. Closed Sunday. $16-35

★EL ZOCALO
3400 Bagley, Detroit, 313-841-3700; www.elzocalodetroit.com
Mexican menu. Lunch, dinner. Bar. $15 and under

★★FISHBONE'S RHYTHM KITCHEN CAFÉ
400 Monroe St., Detroit, 313-965-4600; www.fishbonesusa.com
Southern, Cajun/Creole menu. Lunch, dinner, Sunday brunch. Bar. Valet parking. $16-35

★★★IRIDESCENCE RESTAURANT
MotorCity Casino Hotel, 2901 Grand River Ave., Detroit, 313-237-6732;
www.motorcitycasino.com
With huge windows that frame drop-dead gorgeous views of the twinkling city lights, you don't have to guess how this restaurant, located atop the MotorCity Casino Hotel, got its name. Everything from the interior design—including hanging lightbulb globes—to the cutting-edge table settings defines urban sophistication. The artfully plated, creative cuisine, much of it organic and seasonal, perfectly complements the swanky atmosphere. Be sure to save room for one of the sugary works of art created by award-winning pastry chef Patricia Nash.
Contemporary American menu. Dinner. Closed Monday. Bar. Reservations recommended. Valet parking. $36-85

★★★OPUS ONE
565 E. Larned St., Detroit, 313-961-7766; www.opus-one.com
Owner Jim Kokas has overseen this dressy dining room for more than 10 years. Executive chef Tim Giznsky creates inventive, American cuisine that can be enjoyed for dinner, weekday power lunches or before heading out to local theater. Try the pan-seared Chilean sea bass with basmati rice, jumbo shrimp in phyllo pastry with potato gratin or rack of New Zealand lamb with potato-fennel gratin.
American menu. Lunch, dinner. Closed Sunday. Bar. Valet parking. $36-85

★★PEGASUS TAVERNA
558 Monroe St., Detroit, 313-964-6800; www.pegasustaverna.com
American, Greek menu. Lunch, dinner. Bar. Children's menu. $16-35

★★★RATTLESNAKE CLUB
300 River Place, Detroit, 313-567-4400; www.rattlesnakeclub.com
This Rivertown destination is where well-known chef Jimmy Schmidt (a James Beard Award winner) offers seasonal, worldly American cuisine. There's also a beautiful riverside dining room and a superior, well-priced wine list. The menu focuses on sustainably harvested and seasonal ingredients, such as wild Alaskan king salmon or tea-cured free-range duck breast. American menu. Lunch, dinner. Closed Sunday. Bar. Outdoor seating. $36-85

★★★SALTWATER
MGM Grand Detroit, 1777 S. Third St., Detroit, 313-465-1646;
www.mgmgranddetroit.com
If Bourbon Steak is Michael Mina's paean to the farm, Saltwater is his love letter to the sea. Entering the elegant dining room feels like stepping aboard a luxury ocean liner, while the seafood-driven menu highlights Mina's talent for turning the standards upside down. Entrées include lobster pot pie, zucchini-wrapped salmon and almond-crusted halibut, but don't miss the signature mussel soufflé or caviar parfait. During the week, the three-course pre-theater menu is a good way to sample the chef's talents.
Contemporary American, seafood menu. Dinner. Closed Sunday-Monday. Bar. No guests under 21. $36-85

★★★THE WHITNEY
4421 Woodward Ave., Detroit, 313-832-5700; www.thewhitney.com
Housed in what was once the home of lumber baron David Whitney Jr., this mansion was built in 1894 out of South Dakota Jasper (a rare pink granite) and was designed in the Romanesque style of architecture. Inside, find Tiffany stained-glass windows and crystal chandeliers. The menu features fish, beef, seafood and lamb and includes dishes like blue cheese soufflé with pecans and apple vinaigrette or Great Lakes whitefish with melted tomato and crispy potato. Enjoy these updated versions of traditional favorites in a variety of rooms including the Music Room, Library or Oriental Room. American menu. Lunch, dinner, Sunday brunch. Closed Monday. Bar. Valet parking. $36-85

★★★WOLFGANG PUCK GRILLE
MGM Grand Detroit, 1777 S. Third St., Detroit, 313-465-1648;
www.mgmgranddetroit.com
Wolfgang Puck's name may be on everything from pans to frozen pizzas, but the quality is always top-notch. His eponymous restaurant in the MGM Grand is no exception. Whether you're enjoying breakfast, lunch or dinner in this casual spot, you'll find upscale comfort food cooked with the freshest ingredients and served by a smiling staff of knowledgeable servers. There's an open kitchen, so even if you can't stand the heat, you'll get a behind-the-scenes look.
American menu. Breakfast, lunch, dinner. Bar. Valet parking. $36-85

SPA
★★★★IMMERSE SPA
MGM Grand Detroit, 1777 S. Third St., Detroit, 313-465-1656;
www.mgmgranddetroit.com

It may be inside the buzzing MGM Grand, but there isn't a better place to unwind than at the serene Immerse Spa. The facility boasts a well-equipped fitness center, indoor pool and full-service salon, but the real beauty of this spa lies in its restorative treatments. From ancient bathing rituals to purifying sea foam facials, this spa uses marine-based products to detoxify and revitalize. Guided relaxation and Japanese tea ceremonies accompany Immerse's signature rituals, which include customized facials and hypnotic massage.

EAST LANSING
See also Jackson

Home to Michigan State University, East Lansing is also known as the cultural and recreational center of mid-Michigan. Street festivals, outdoor concerts and 26 parks make this city a gem.

WHAT TO SEE
JACK BRESLIN STUDENTS EVENTS CENTER
Michigan State University, 1 Birch Road, East Lansing, 517-432-1989, 800-968-2737;
www.breslincenter.com

Home to both Michigan State men's and women's basketball teams, as well as special events and presentations.

PARKS, RECREATION & ARTS
410 Abbott Road, East Lansing, 517-319-6809; www.cityofeastlansing.com

A host of seasonal activities, the East Lansing Hannah Community Center, the Family Aquatic Center, the East Lansing Softball Complex, the Splash Pad and more.
Year-round.

TRILLIUM GALLERY
107 Division St., East Lansing, 517-333-3130; www.michigan.org

Features handcrafted artwork by Michigan artists including glass work, jewelry, pottery and more.

WHARTON CENTER FOR THE PERFORMING ARTS
Michigan State University, East Lansing, 517-353-1982; www.whartoncenter.com

Features various musical, dance, dramatic and arts-oriented performances.

SPECIAL EVENTS
EAST LANSING ART FESTIVAL
410 Abbott Road, East Lansing, 517-319-6804; www.elartfest.com

Artists' work for sale, continuous performances, ethnic foods and children's activities.
Third weekend in May.

SUMMER SOLSTICE JAZZ FESTIVAL

Ann Street Plaza, East Lansing, 517-319-6927; www.eljazzfest.com
Jazz festival featuring a variety of acts.
Mid-June.

WHERE TO STAY
★★★MARRIOTT EAST LANSING AT UNIVERSITY PLACE

300 M.A.C. Ave., East Lansing, 517-337-4440, 800-228-9290; www.marriott.com/lanea
Located in the heart of downtown East Lansing, this hotel is within walking
distance to the campus of Michigan State University as well as shopping and
dining. Guest rooms are spacious and feature plush bed linens and an over-
stuffed chair and ottoman. The glass elevators overlook the hotel's atrium.
180 rooms. Restaurant, bar. $151-250

ELLSWORTH
See also Charlevoix
Tiny Ellsworth, boasting a population of only 483 residents, sits on both
Lake St. Clair and picturesque Ellsworth Lake. Although the town offers few
other amenities, it is home to one of the top restaurants in the state.

WHERE TO EAT
★★★ROWE INN

6303 E. Jordan Road, Ellsworth, 231-588-7351, 866-432-5873; www.roweinn.com
This elegant fine dining restaurant, opened in 1972, is located on the lake in
Ellsworth. The focus here is on cuisine native to Michigan, and the restaurant
boasts an extensive wine list, one of the largest in the state. The signature
dishes include rack of lamb and pecan-stuffed morel mushrooms, but make it
a point to try other offerings or the Rowe's selection of artisanal cheeses.
Country French menu. Dinner, Sunday brunch. Casual attire. Reservations
recommended. Outdoor seating. $36-85

ESCANABA
See also Gladstone, Manistique
The first European settlers in this area were lured by the pine timber, which
they were quick to log. Escanaba is the only ore-shipping port on Lake Michigan. Sports enthusiasts are attracted by the open water and huge tracts of
undeveloped countryside.

WHAT TO SEE
DELTA COUNTY HISTORICAL MUSEUM AND SAND POINT
LIGHTHOUSE

12 Water Plant Road, Escanaba, 906-786-3763; www.deltahistorical.org
See local historical artifacts, including lumber, railroad and maritime indus-
try exhibits at this 1867 restored lighthouse.
June-Labor Day, daily.

HIAWATHA NATIONAL FOREST

2727 N. Lincoln Road, Escanaba, 906-786-4062; www.fs.fed.us/r9/hiawatha
This 893,000-acre forest offers scenic drives, hunting, camping, picnicking,

hiking, horseback riding, cross-country skiing, snowmobiling, winter sports, lake and stream fishing, swimming, sailing, motorboating and canoeing. It has shoreline on three Great Lakes—Huron, Michigan and Superior. The eastern section of the forest is close to Sault Ste. Marie, St. Ignace and the northern foot of the Mackinac Bridge.
Daily.

LUDINGTON PARK
Lakeshore Drive and Luddington Street, Escanaba, 906-786-4141; www.michigan.org
This park offers a plethora of activities, including fishing, boating, swimming, tennis, volleyball, biking, picnicking and more.
April-November, daily.

WHERE TO STAY
★★BEST WESTERN PIONEER INN
2635 Ludington St., Escanaba, 906-786-0602, 877-786-0602; www.bestwestern.com
72 rooms. Restaurant, bar. Pool. High-speed Internet access. $61-150

WHERE TO EAT
★★STONEHOUSE
2223 Ludington St., Escanaba, 906-786-5003
Seafood menu. Lunch, dinner. Closed Sunday. Bar. Children's menu. $36-85

FARMINGTON
See also Birmingham, Detroit, Northville, Southfield
The community feel is evident in the city's downtown, which features the Sundquist Farmington Pavilion and Riley Park, which now host weekly farmers markets and concerts.

WHAT TO SEE
KENSINGTON METROPARK
2240 W. Buno Road, Milford, 248-685-1561;
www.metroparks.com/parks/pk_kensington.php
This park includes more than 4,000 acres on Kent Lake, and features two swimming beaches (Memorial Day-Labor Day, daily), boating, ice fishing, biking/hiking trail, tobogganing, skating, picnicking, concessions and 18-hole golf. You can also take a 45-minute boat cruise on the Island Queen (summer, daily). Also includes nature trails, farm center, nature center.
Daily.

SPECIAL EVENT
FARMINGTON FOUNDERS FESTIVAL
Grand River and Farmington roads, Farmington, 248-477-1199;
www.foundersfestival.com
Ethnic food, arts and crafts, sidewalk sales, carnival, rides, concert, fireworks.
Mid-July.

FARMINGTON HILLS

See also Detroit, Farmington

A pleasant community with more than 600 acres of parkland and public schools that garner national recognition, Farmington Hills is a lovely spot. Its historic district, cultural arts community and location make it a great place to visit.

WHERE TO STAY

★★HOLIDAY INN HOTEL & SUITES FARMINGTON HILLS
37529 Grand River Ave., Farmington Hills, 248-477-7800, 888-465-4329; www.holiday-inn.com
137 rooms. Wireless Internet access. Restaurant, bar. $61-150

WHERE TO EAT

★ANGEL'S CAFE
214 W. Nine Mile Road, Ferndale, 248-541-0888; www.angelscafeofferndale.com
International menu. Lunch, dinner. Closed Monday-Tuesday. $15 and under

★★NAMI SUSHI BAR
201 W. Nine Mile Road, Ferndale, 248-542-6458; www.nami-sushi.com
Japanese menu. Lunch, dinner, late-night. Closed Sunday. Bar. Casual attire. Outdoor seating. $16-35

★THE BLUE NILE
545 W. Nine Mile Road, Ferndale, 248-547-6699; www.bluenilemi.com
Ethiopian menu. Dinner. Closed Monday; holidays. Bar. Casual attire. Outdoor seating. $16-35

★★★TRIBUTE
31425 W. Twelve Mile Road, Farmington Hills, 248-848-9393; www.tributerestaurant.com
This Asian-inspired, contemporary international restaurant attracts a moneyed suburban Detroit crowd. The industrial building and luxuriously whimsical dining room are the property of Lawrence Wisne, a Detroit automotive-industry millionaire whose lavish investment has put this interactive, guest-driven restaurant on the nation's culinary map. Although diners can order à la carte, there are several seven-course menus available and a 21-course menu for those with an adventurous palate. The extensive wine list of more than 2,200 labels gives diners plenty of choices. For a romantic night out, make reservations for the chef's table in the kitchen.
International menu. Dinner. Closed Sunday-Monday. Bar. Business casual attire. Reservations recommended. Valet parking. $36-85

FLINT

See also Holly, Owosso, Saginaw

Once a small, horse-drawn carriage-producing town, Flint is now an automobile manufacturer with the nickname Buick City. One of the largest cities in the state, it is a blue-collar town that led the 20th-century union movement and retains strong union ties.

WHAT TO SEE
CROSSROADS VILLAGE/HUCKLEBERRY RAILROAD

6140 Bray Road, Flint, 810-736-7100, 800-648-7275; www.geneseecountyparks.org

This restored living community of the 1860-1880 period is made up of 28 buildings and sites, including a railroad depot, carousel, Ferris wheel, general store, schoolhouse and several homes. There is also a working sawmill, gristmill, cidermill, blacksmith shop and a eight-mile steam train ride. Paddlewheel riverboat cruises are available and there are special events most weekends.

Memorial Day-Labor Day, Tuesday-Sunday 10 a.m.-5 p.m.; September, weekends; special Halloween programs; December holiday lighting spectacular.

FLINT COLLEGE AND CULTURAL CORPORATION

1198 Longway Blvd., Flint, 810-237-7333; www.flintcultural.org

A complex that includes the University of Michigan-Flint, Mott Community College, Whiting Auditorium, Flint Institute of Music, Bower Theater.

FLINT INSTITUTE OF ARTS

1120 E. Kearsley St., Flint, 810-234-1695; www.flintarts.org

Permanent collections include Renaissance decorative arts, Oriental Gallery, 19th- and 20th-century paintings and sculpture, paperweights; changing exhibits.

Tuesday-Saturday 10 a.m.-5 p.m., Sunday 1-5 p.m.

ROBERT T. LONGWAY PLANETARIUM

1310 E. Kearsley St., Flint, 810-237-3400; www.longwayplanetarium.com

This planetarium includes ultraviolet, fluorescent murals and a Spitz projector. There are also laser light shows and frequent special events, including a laser "spooktakular" for Halloween.

SLOAN MUSEUM

1221 E. Kearsley St., Flint, 810-237-3450; www.sloanmuseum.com

See a collection of antique autos and carriages, most manufactured in Flint. Exhibitions of Michigan history and health and science exhibits.

Monday-Friday 10 a.m.-5 p.m., Saturday-Sunday noon-5 p.m.

SPECIAL EVENT
CRIM FESTIVAL OF RACES

Flint, 810-235-3396; www.crim.org

This annual road event also features a wide range of races, including races for kids. Thousands of people gather to run, including elite athletes from all over the world, while Flint residents line the racecourse to cheer and encourage.

Late August.

WHERE TO STAY
★★HOLIDAY INN

5353 Gateway Centre, Flint, 810-232-5300, 888-570-1770; www.holiday-inn.com

171 rooms. Restaurant, bar. $61-150

★HOLIDAY INN EXPRESS
1150 Longway Blvd., Flint, 810-238-7744, 800-278-1810; www.holiday-inn.com
124 rooms. Complimentary continental breakfast. Airport transportation available. $61-150

FRANKENMUTH
See also Bay City, Flint, Saginaw
This city was settled by 15 immigrants from Franconia, Germany, who came here as Lutheran missionaries to spread the faith to the Chippewas. Frankenmuth has authentic Bavarian architecture, flowerbeds and traditional German hospitality. The charming town is also famous for its all-you-can-eat chicken dinners.

WHAT TO SEE
BRONNER'S CHRISTMAS WONDERLAND
25 Christmas Lane, Frankenmuth, 989-652-9931, 800-255-9327; www.bronners.com
Billing itself as the world's largest Christmas store, Bronner's stocks more than 50,000 trims and gifts from around the world. The store, open since 1945, features a 20-minute multi-image presentation called "World of Bronner's," 260 decorated Christmas trees in varying themes and an outdoor display of 100,000 Christmas lights along Christmas Lane (dusk-midnight). Daily, hours vary by season.

FRANKENMUTH HISTORICAL MUSEUM
613 S. Main St., Frankenmuth, 989-652-9701; www.frankenmuthmuseum.org
Local historical exhibits, hands-on displays, audio recordings and cast-form life figures. Gift shop features folk art.
January-March, Monday-Thursday noon-4 p.m., Friday 10:30 a.m.-5 p.m., Saturday 10 a.m.-5 p.m., Sunday noon-5 p.m.; April-December, Monday-Thursday 10:30 a.m.-5 p.m., Friday 10:30 a.m.-7 p.m., Saturday 10 a.m.-8 p.m., Sunday 11 a.m.-7 p.m.

FRANKENMUTH RIVERBOAT TOURS
445 S. Main St., Frankenmuth, 989-652-8844
Narrated tours along Cass River. May-October, daily (weather permitting).

GLOCKENSPIEL
713 S. Main St., Frankenmuth, 989-652-9941
This 35-bell carillon atop the Frankenmuth Bavarian Inn includes carved wooden figures moving on a track that act out the story of the Pied Piper of Hamelin.

MICHIGAN'S OWN MILITARY & SPACE MUSEUM
1250 S. Weiss St., Frankenmuth, 989-652-8005; www.michigansmilitarymuseum.com
Features uniforms, decorations and photos of men and women from Michigan who served the nation and displays about Medal of Honor recipients, astronauts and former governors.
March-December, Monday-Saturday 10 a.m.-5 p.m., Sunday 11 a.m.-5 p.m.

SPECIAL EVENTS
BAVARIAN FESTIVAL
Heritage Park, 335 S. Main St., Frankenmuth, 989-652-8155, 800-386-3378;
www.bavarianfestival.com
Celebration of German heritage. Music, dancing, parades and other entertainment; food; art demonstrations and agricultural displays. Four days in
early June.

FRANKENMUTH OKTOBERFEST
635 S. Main St., Frankenmuth, 989-652-6106, 800-386-8696; www.frankenmuth.org
Experience an authentic Munich Oktoberfest. Includes German food, music
and entertainment.
Third weekend in September.

WHERE TO STAY
★★FRANKENMUTH BAVARIAN INN LODGE
1 Covered Bridge Lane, Frankenmuth, 989-652-7200, 888-775-6343;
www.bavarianinn.com
354 rooms. Restaurant, two bars. Airport transportation available. $61-150

★ZEHNDER'S BAVARIAN HAUS
730 S. Main St., Frankenmuth, 989-652-0400, 800-863-7999; www.zehnders.com
137 rooms. Children's activity center. Airport transportation available. $151-
250

WHERE TO EAT
★★FRANKENMUTH BAVARIAN INN RESTAURANT
713 S. Main St., Frankenmuth, 989-652-9941, 888-228-2742; www.bavarianinn.com
Continental, German menu. Lunch, dinner. Bar. Children's menu. Casual at-
tire. Reservations recommended. Outdoor seating. $$

GAYLORD
See also Boyne City, Grayling
Known as Michigan's Alpine Village, downtown Gaylord shops give the ap-
pearance of charming, Swiss-inspired chalets. The winter theme is fitting,
given Gaylord's annual snowfall of more than 180 inches. Winter sports
abound in Gaylord, and you'll find more than 300 miles of groomed snow-
mobile trails and numerous cross-country ski trails. With nearly 100 small
lakes, Gaylord is also home to excellent fishing, both in summer and winter.
Gaylord also boasts the best golf experience in Michigan, with two dozen
award-winning courses.

WHAT TO SEE
OTSEGO LAKE STATE PARK
7136 Old Highway 27 S., Gaylord, 989-732-5485; www.michigan.gov/dnr
Approximately 60 acres. Swimming beach, bathhouse, water-skiing, boat-
ing, fishing for pike, bass and perch. Picnicking, playground, concession,
camping.
Mid-April-mid-October.

TREETOPS RESORT

3962 Wilkinson Road, Treetops Village, 989-732-6711, 888-873-3867;
www.treetops.com

Double, two triple chairlifts, four rope tows; patrol, school, rentals; cafeteria, bar. Nineteen runs. The longest run is ½ mile with a vertical drop of 225 feet.

December-mid-March, daily. 10 miles of cross-country trails; 3½ miles of lighted trails.

SPECIAL EVENTS
ALPENFEST

101 W. Main Road, Gaylord, 989-732-6333, 800-345-8621; www.gaylordchamber.com

Participants dress in costumes of Switzerland and there's a carnival, pageant and grand parade.

Third weekend in July.

BRONSON POLISH FESTIVAL DAYS

20 Division St., Coldwater, 800-968-9333, 517-278-0241

Heritage fest, games, vendors, concessions, dancing.

Third week in July.

WINTERFEST

M South Court, Gaylord, 800-345-8621

Ski racing and slalom, cross-country events, snowmobile events, activities for children, snow sculpting, downhill tubing.

Early February.

WHERE TO STAY
★★BEST WESTERN ALPINE LODGE

833 W. Main St., Gaylord, 989-732-2431, 800-684-2233; www.bestwestern.com

130 rooms. Complimentary continental breakfast. Wireless Internet access. Restaurant, bar. Pool. Pets accepted. $61-150

★★★GARLAND RESORT & GOLF COURSE

4700 N. Red Oak Road, Lewiton, 989-786-2211, 877-442-7526; www.garlandusa.com

This family-run resort caters to golfers with four championship courses surrounded by 3,500 acres of pristine wilderness. Lessons, practice facilities and a well-stocked pro shop enhance the experience. During the winter months, miles of cross-country ski trails attract skiers. You can also rent mountain bikes, fish in the Garland ponds, or take a guided nature trail hike. From the main lodge to the golf cottages, villas and condos, the accommodations are comfortable, and the interiors reflect the rugged setting.

60 rooms. Closed mid-March-April. Restaurant, bar. $61-150

WHERE TO EAT
★★SUGAR BOWL

216 W. Main St., Gaylord, 989-732-5524, 866-230-0272

American menu. Breakfast, lunch, dinner. Closed last week in March and first two weeks in April. Bar. Children's menu. Casual attire. Reservations recommended. $16-35

GLADSTONE

With year-round outdoor activities, Gladstone offers something for everyone. The town is located on Little Bay de Noc, a deep harbor that accommodates boats of all sizes. Fishing in summer and winter is popular, and the Sports Park offers winter activities including skiing and tubing. Take a picnic lunch to the bay in summer or fall for beautiful sunsets and a stunning show of color.
See also Escanaba.

WHERE TO EAT
★★LOG CABIN SUPPER CLUB
7531 Highway Two, Gladstone, 906-786-5621
American menu. Lunch, dinner. Closed holidays. Bar. Children's menu. $16-35

GLEN ARBOR
See also Leland, Traverse City
This community, situated on Lake Michigan, lies just north of Sleeping Bear Dunes National Lakeshore. Because of its unique location next to one of Michigan's top attractions, Glen Arbor caters to tourists with boutiques, art galleries and shops selling local crafts. A popular stop is Cherry Republic on Lake Street, which sells only cherry products from the region, including jam, pie and barbecue sauce.

WHERE TO STAY
★★★THE HOMESTEAD
Wood Ridge Road, Glen Arbor, 231-334-5000; www.thehomesteadresort.com

Located in Leelanau County and on the shore of Lake Michigan, this resort sits on many acres of wooded land—the setting is private and breathtaking. Visitors can choose to stay in a small hotel, an inn, a lodge or privately owned guest homes when they stay at this resort. The quaint resort town of Glen Arbor is within a two-mile drive, as are the popular Sleeping Bear Sand Dunes National Park and Lakeshore.
130 rooms. Closed mid-March-April, November-late December. Restaurant. Children's activity center. Beach. $151-250

WHERE TO EAT
★★LA BÉCASSE
9001 S. Dunn's Farm Road, Maple City, 231-334-3944; www.restaurantlabecasse.com
French menu. Dinner. Closed Monday; Tuesday (May-mid-June); also mid-October-late December, mid-February-early May. Reservations recommended. Outdoor seating. $16-35

★WESTERN AVENUE GRILL
6410 Western Ave., Glen Arbor, 231-334-3362; www.westernavegrill.com
American menu. Dinner. Bar. Children's menu. Casual attire. $16-35

GRAND HAVEN

See also Grand Rapids, Holland, Muskegon

A stream of produce for all the Midwest flows through this port city at the mouth of the Grand River. The port has the largest charter fishing fleet on Lake Michigan and is also used for sport fishing, recreational boating and as a Coast Guard base. Connecting the pier to downtown shops is a boardwalk and park.

WHAT TO SEE
GRAND HAVEN STATE PARK
1001 Harbor Ave., Grand Haven, 616-798-3711; www.michigan.gov/dnr
This park encompasses almost 50 acres on Lake Michigan beachfront. Spend the day swimming, fishing or picnicking.
Daily.

HARBOR STEAMER
301 N. Harbor Drive, Grand Haven, 616-842-8950; www.harborsteamer.com
This stern-wheel paddleboat cruises to Spring Lake.
Mid-May-September, daily.

HARBOR TROLLEYS
440 N. Ferry St., Grand Haven, 616-842-3200; www.grandhaven.org
These trolleys take two different routes: Grand Haven trolley operates between downtown and state park; second trolley goes to Spring Lake.
Monday-Friday 6 a.m.-5:30 p.m., Saturday 9 a.m.-3:30 p.m.

MUNICIPAL MARINA
101 N. Harbor Drive, Grand Haven, 616-847-3478; www.grandhaven.org
Contains 57 transient slips; stores and restaurants; trolley stop.

MUSICAL FOUNTAIN
Dewey Hill, 1 N. Harbor Drive, Grand Haven, 616-842-2550; www.grandhaven.org
Said to be the world's largest electronically controlled musical fountain; water, lights and music are synchronized.
Special Christmas nativity scene in December covering all of Dewey Hill.
Programs Memorial Day-Labor Day, evenings; May and rest of September, Friday-Saturday only.

SPECIAL EVENTS
COAST GUARD FESTIVAL
113 N. Second St., Grand Haven, 888-207-2434; www.coastguardfest.org
Includes a parade, carnival, craft exhibit, ship tours, pageant, variety shows and fireworks.
Late July-early August.

GREAT LAKES KITE FESTIVAL
Grand Haven State Park, 106 Washington Ave., Grand Haven, 616-846-7501;
www.mackite.com
Giant kites fly in the air throughout the day, weather permitting. Various kite

demonstrations are held on the main field.
May.

ON THE WATERFRONT BIG BAND CONCERT SERIES
421 Columbus St., Grand Haven, 616-842-2550; www.grandhaven.org
Wednesday evenings. July-August.

POLAR ICE CAP GOLF TOURNAMENT
Spring Lake, 1 S. Harbor Drive, Grand Haven, 800-303-4097; www.visitgrandhaven.com
18-hole, par-three golf game on ice.
Late January.

WINTERFEST
120 Washington Ave., Grand Haven, 616-842-4499; www.winterfestonline.org
Music, dance, parade, children's activities.
Late January.

WHERE TO STAY
★BEST WESTERN BEACON INN
1525 S. Beacon Blvd., Grand Haven, 616-842-4720; www.bestwestern.com
101 rooms. Airport transportation available. Pool. High-speed Internet. $61-150

GRAND MARAIS
See also Munising
On the shore of Lake Superior, Grand Marais has a harbor with a marina and is surrounded by cool, clear lakes, trout streams and agate beaches. In winter, there is snowmobiling and cross-country skiing.

SPECIAL EVENTS

500-MILER SNOWMOBILE RUN
Downtown Grand Marais, 906-494-2447; www.sno-trails.net
While this run is not a race per se, participants must accumulate 500 miles in no less than 14 hours and no more than 24 hours.
Mid-January.

MUSIC AND ARTS FESTIVAL
Downtown Grand Marais, Grand Marais, 906-494-2447
Second weekend in August.

GRAND RAPIDS
See also Grand Haven, Holland, Muskegon
Grand Rapids, a widely known furniture center and convention city, is located on the site where Louis Campau established a Native American trading post in 1826. The city derives its name from the rapids in the Grand River, which flows through the heart of the city. There are 50 parks here, covering 1,270 acres. Calvin College and Calvin Seminary are located here, and sev-

eral other colleges are in the area.

Former president Gerald R. Ford was raised in Grand Rapids and represented the Fifth Congressional District in Michigan from 1948 to 1973, when he became the nation's vice president.

WHAT TO SEE
BERLIN RACEWAY
2060 Berlin Fair Drive, Marne, 616-726-7373; www.berlinraceway.com
Late-model stock car, sportsman stock car and super stock car racing.
May-September, Friday-Sunday.

BLANDFORD NATURE CENTER
1715 Hillburn Ave. N.W., Grand Rapids, 616-735-6240; www.blandfordnaturecenter.org
More than 140 acres of woods, fields and ponds with self-guiding trails; guided tours; interpretive center has exhibits, live animals, furnished pioneer garden, one-room schoolhouse.
Monday-Friday, also Saturday-Sunday afternoons.

CANNONSBURG SKI AREA
6800 Cannonsburg Road, Cannonsburg, 616-874-6711, 800-253-8748;
www.cannonsburg.com
Quad, triple, double chairlift; two T-bars, eight rope tows.
Late November-mid-March, Saturday-Sunday 9 a.m.-10 p.m.; holidays 9 a.m.-4 p.m.

FREDERIK MEIJER GARDENS AND SCULPTURE PARK
1000 E. Beltline Ave. N.E., Grand Rapids, 616-957-1580, 888-957-1580;
www.meijergardens.org
This botanic garden and sculpture park includes a 15,000-square-foot glass conservatory, a desert garden, exotic indoor and outdoor gardens and more than 60 bronze works.
Monday-Saturday 9 a.m.-5 p.m., Sunday noon-5 p.m.

GERALD R. FORD MUSEUM
303 Pearl St. N.W., Grand Rapids, 616-254-0400; www.fordlibrarymuseum.gov
Exhibits trace the life and public service of the 38th president of the United States. The museum includes a 28-minute introductory film on Ford; reproduction of the White House Oval Office; educational exhibits on the U.S. House of Representatives and the presidency; and even the original burglar tools used in the Watergate break-in.
Daily 9 a.m.-5 p.m.

GRAND RAPIDS ART MUSEUM
101 Monroe Center N., Grand Rapids, 616-831-1000; www.gramonline.org
Collections include Renaissance, German Expressionist, French and American paintings, graphics and a children's gallery augmented by special traveling exhibitions.
Tuesday-Sunday.

JOHN BALL ZOO

1300 W. Fulton St., Grand Rapids, 616-336-4301; www.johnballzoosociety.org
Located in 100-acre park, the zoo features more than 700 animals, the Living Shores Aquarium, an African Forest exhibit and children's zoo.
Mid-May-Labor Day, daily 10 a.m.-6 p.m.; rest of the year, daily 10 a.m.-4 p.m.

LA GRANDE VITESSE

County Building, Grand Rapids
This 42-ton stabile was created by Alexander Calder.

MEYER MAY HOUSE

450 Madison Ave. S.E., Grand Rapids, 616-246-4821; www.meyermayhouse.com
This Frank Lloyd Wright house from the late Prairie period was finished in 1908 has been authentically restored with architect-designed furniture, leaded-glass windows, lighting fixtures, rugs and textiles.
Tours begin at visitor center (442 Madison Ave. S.E.). Tuesday, Thursday, Sunday; schedule varies.

PANDO

8076 Belding Road N.E., Rockford, 616-874-8343; www.pandopark.com
Six rope tows, seven lighted runs; patrol, school, rentals, grooming equipment, snowmaking; cafeteria. Vertical drop of 125 feet. Seven miles of cross-country trails; three miles of lighted trails, rentals. Night skiing.
December-March, daily.

THE PUBLIC MUSEUM OF GRAND RAPIDS

272 Pearl St. N.W., Grand Rapids, 616-456-3997; www.grmuseum.org
Located in the Van Andel Museum Center, this museum features exhibits of interactive history and natural science, including mammals, birds, furniture, Native American artifacts, re-creation of 1890s Grand Rapids street scene and a 1928 carousel. The Chaffee Planetarium offers sky shows and laser light shows.
Tuesday-Saturday 9 a.m.-5 p.m.

SPECIAL EVENTS
COMMUNITY CIRCLE THEATER

John Ball Park Pavilion, 1300 W. Fulton St., Grand Rapids, 616-456-6656;
www.circletheatre.org
Mid-May-September.

NORTHERN MINNESOTA VINTAGE CAR SHOW AND SWAP MEET

Itasca County Fairgrounds, Grand Rapids, 218-326-0234;www.exploreminnesota.com
This large car show features classic antique cars and roaring street rods, along with a giant swap meet for some outdoor shopping.
Late July.

TALL TIMBER DAYS FESTIVAL

1 N.W. Third St., Grand Rapids, 218-326-6619, 800-472-6366; www.grandmn.com
This downtown celebration features chainsaw carving, an arts-and-crafts fair, canoe races, a parade and lumberjacks climbing 40-foot logs.
First weekend in August.

WHERE TO STAY
★★★AMWAY GRAND PLAZA

187 Monroe Ave. N.W., Grand Rapids, 616-774-2000, 800-253-3590;
www.amwaygrand.com
Opened in 1913 as the Pantlind Hotel, this Michigan landmark quickly earned a reputation for providing a distinguished residence for out-of-town-ers. Fronting the Grand River, the hotel is conveniently located in Grand Rapids's business and entertainment district. The lobby is topped by a magnificent gold-leaf ceiling. The guest rooms are appointed in either classically elegant or modern décor, with the Tower Rooms featuring views of the river and city. The 1913 Room, with its fine continental cuisine, is the jewel in the crown, featuring a Louis XVI style and classic, French-inspired cuisine.
682 rooms. Restaurants, bar. Pool. Tennis. $151-250

★★★CROWNE PLAZA

5700 28th St. S.E., Grand Rapids, 616-957-1770, 800-957-9575;
www.crowneplaza.com/grr-airport
Located one mile from the Grand Rapids Airport and minutes from the largest shopping center in western Michigan, the Crowne Plaza is a convenient choice. Spacious rooms include overstuffed chairs, comfortable beds and CDs of relaxing, serene music. In nice weather, drinks and light fare are served under a gazebo or on the outdoor patio.
320 rooms. Restaurant, bar. Pets accepted. $61-150

★★RAMADA PLAZA GRAND RAPIDS EAST

3333 28th St. S.E., Grand Rapids, 616-949-9222, 800-333-3333; www.ramada.com
187 rooms. Complimentary continental breakfast. Wireless Internet access.
Restaurant, bar. Airport transportation available. $61-150

WHERE TO EAT
★★★★1913 ROOM

Amway Grand Plaza, 187 Monroe Ave. N.W., Grand Rapids, 616-774-2000,
800-253-3590; www.amwaygrand.com
This fine-dining restaurant is ideal for special occasions. The Louis XVI-style room is filled with white-linen topped tables and overseen by a polished, confident staff. The menu, which features classic dishes with French influences, includes standouts like grilled beef filet and lobster terrine, or seared Atlantic salmon with horseradish crust. A chef's tasting menu with accompanying wines is available for those who want to savor the talents of the creative kitchen staff.
Continental menu. Lunch, dinner. Reservations recommended. $36-85

★★ARNIE'S

3561 28th St. S.E., Grand Rapids, 616-956-7901; www.arniesrestaurants.com

American menu. Breakfast, lunch, dinner. Children's menu. Casual attire. $16-35

★★CHARLEY'S CRAB

63 Market St. S.W., Grand Rapids, 616-459-2500, 800-989-9949; www.muer.com

American, seafood menu. Lunch, dinner, Sunday brunch. Bar. Children's menu. Business casual attire. Reservations recommended. Valet parking. Outdoor seating. $36-85

★★★THE CHOP HOUSE

190 Monroe Ave. N.W., Grand Rapids, 616-451-6184, 888-456-3463;
www.thechophouserestaurant.com

The Chop House is located in downtown Grand Rapids across from the Convention Center and Amway Grand Plaza hotel. The centerpiece of the room is its beautiful black granite bar, accented with colorful floor-to-ceiling pillars and oil prints. The menu zeros in on the best in Midwestern, grain-fed meats and USDA Prime beef—look for Australian rib lamb chops, caviar and fresh lobster. A dessert and cigar lounge called La Dolce Vita, located on the lower level of the restaurant, is an intimate spot, and the wine cellar displays a variety of reds. All in all, a place perfect for any special occasion.
Steak menu. Dinner. Closed Sunday. Bar. Casual attire. Reservations recommended. $36-85

★★PIETRO'S BACK DOOR PIZZERIA

2780 Birchcrest St. S.E., Grand Rapids, 616-452-7488; www.pietros-rcfc.com

Italian menu. Lunch, dinner. Bar. Children's menu. Casual attire. Outdoor seating. $16-35

★★SAN CHEZ BISTRO

38 W. Fulton St., Grand Rapids, 616-774-8272; www.sanchezbistro.com

Spanish, tapas menu. Lunch, dinner, late-night. Bar. Children's menu. Casual attire. Outdoor seating. $16-35

★★SAYFEE'S

3555 Lake Eastbrook Blvd. S.E., Grand Rapids, 616-949-5750; www.sayfees.com

American menu. Lunch, dinner, late-night. Closed Sunday. Bar. Business casual attire. Outdoor seating. $36-85

GRAYLING

See also Gaylord, Houghton Lake

Named for a fish related to both trout and salmon, Grayling has long ties to fishing in its two major rivers, the Au Sable and the Manistee. In fact, fishing was so popular in the area during the late 1800s that the grayling became extinct by 1930. Today, while its most popular fish lives on in name only, Grayling still offers world-class trout fishing. Because Grayling's annual snowfall reaches nearly 200 inches, snow sports, including cross-country skiing and snowmobiling are also popular in the area.

WHAT TO SEE
HARTWICK PINES STATE PARK
4216 Ranger Road, Grayling, 989-348-7068; www.michigan.gov/dnr
This park is approximately 9,700 acres. Marked cross-country ski trails, picnicking, playground, concession, camping can all be found here. Also includes a lumberman's museum and one of the few remaining stands of virgin white pine in the world.
Daily.

SPECIAL EVENTS
AU SABLE RIVER FESTIVAL
213 N. James St., Grayling, 989-348-2921, 800-937-8837;
www.graylingchamber.com/id19.html
Arts and crafts, parade, car show.
Last full weekend in July.

WINTER WOLF FESTIVAL
213 N. James St., Grayling, 800-937-8837
Early February.

WHERE TO STAY
★★HOLIDAY INN
2650 Interstate 75 Business Loop, Grayling, 989-348-7611, 800-292-9055;
www.holiday-inn.com
151 rooms. Wireless Internet access. Restaurant, bar. $61-150

HANCOCK
See also Calumet, Copper Harbor, Houghton
Located across the Portage Waterway from Houghton, Hancock is the home of Finlandia University, the only Finnish college in the United States, established in 1896. Hancock's homes are built on 500-foot bluffs that offer a delightful view of the Keeweenau Peninsula and Lake Superior, but the nearly vertical streets can make for treacherous driving.

WHAT TO SEE
FINNISH-AMERICAN HERITAGE CENTER
601 Quincy St., Hancock, 906-487-7347; www.finlandia.edu
This center, located on the campus of Suomi College, houses the Finnish-American Historical Archives, a museum, theater, art gallery and the Finnish-American Family History Center.
Tuesday-Saturday 8 a.m.-4:30 p.m. Special events evenings and weekends.

QUINCY MINE STEAM HOIST, SHAFTHOUSE, TRAM RIDES AND MINE TOURS
49750 US Highway 41, Hancock, 906-482-3101; www.quincymine.com
This 790-ton hoist was used at the Quincy Copper Mine between 1920 and 1931. It could raise 10 tons of ore at a speed of 3,200 feet per minute from an inclined depth of more than 9,000 feet. Tour of mine shafts available.
Mid-May-mid-October, daily.

SPECIAL EVENT
HOUGHTON COUNTY FAIR
Fairgrounds, 1500 Birch St., Hancock, 906-482-6200; www.houghtoncountyfair.com
A demolition derby, monster truck show and horse show tournament are among the events at this fair.
Late August.

WHERE TO STAY
★BEST WESTERN COPPER CROWN MOTEL
235 Hancock Ave., Hancock, 906-482-6111, 800-780-7234; www.bestwestern.com
47 rooms. Pets accepted. Indoor pool. $61-150

HARBOR SPRINGS
See also Petoskey
Known as a year-round vacation spot, Harbor Springs is a picturesque town on Little Traverse Bay that boasts sandy beaches and two of Michigan's most popular ski resorts. Downtown Harbor Springs overflows with pricey but quaint shops and eateries. Drive through Wequetonsing, a summer-only community of mansion-size cottages nestled in the heart of Harbor Springs. Cycle, walk or in-line skate to Petoskey on a paved bike trail that links the two cities.

WHAT TO SEE
ANDREW J. BLACKBIRD MUSEUM
368 E. Main St., Harbor Springs, 231-526-7731
Museum of the Ottawa; artifacts.
Memorial Day-Labor Day, daily; September-October, weekends.

BOYNE HIGHLANDS
600 Highlands Drive, Harbor Springs, 231-526-3000, 800-462-6963;
www.boynehighlands.com
Four triple, four quad chairlifts, rope tow; patrol, school, rentals, snowmaking. Cross-country trails (four miles); rentals.
Thanksgiving weekend-mid-April, daily.

NUB'S NOB
500 Nub's Nob Road, Harbor Springs, 231-526-2131, 800-754-6827;
www.nubsnob.com
Two double, three quad, three triple chairlifts; patrol, school, rentals, snowmaking. The longest run is one mile with a vertical drop of 427 feet.
Thanksgiving-Easter, daily. Half-day rates. Cross-country trails (same seasons, hours as downhill skiing); night skiing (five nights/week).

WHERE TO STAY
★BEST WESTERN OF HARBOR SPRINGS
8514 Highway 119, Harbor Springs, 231-347-9050, 800-937-8376;
www.bestwestern.com
50 rooms. Complimentary breakfast. Fitness center. Pool. Spa. $61-150

★★BOYNE HIGHLANDS RESORT

600 Highlands Pike, Harbor Springs, 231-526-3000, 800-462-6963;
www.boynehighlands.com

164 rooms. Closed mid-October-Thanksgiving, most of April. Restaurants.
Bars. $61-150

★★★KIMBERLY COUNTRY ESTATE

2287 Bester Road, Harbor Springs, 231-526-7646; www.kimberlycountryestate.com

Just four minutes outside town, this colonial plantation estate on 25 acres
is wrapped in pillared balconies overlooking its swimming pool and Wequetonsing Golf Course. Rooms have English country décor and four-poster
beds and fresh flowers. The hotel will put together a picnic lunch for a trip to
the beach. In the evening, guests are treated to wine as well as bedtime sherry
and chocolate truffles.

Eight rooms. Closed April. Complimentary breakfast. $151-250

WHERE TO EAT

★LEGS INN

6425 S. Lake Shore Drive, Cross Village, 231-526-2281; www.legsinn.com

Eastern European menu. Lunch, dinner. Closed late October-late May. Bar.
Children's menu. Outdoor seating. $16-35

★★★THE NEW YORK

101 State St., Harbor Springs, 231-526-1904; www.thenewyork.com

Established in 1904, this American bistro is housed in a Victorian-style former hotel building. Interesting artwork lines the walls, and the dining room
looks out onto a popular downtown street, making this a great place to people-watch. Diners can also request a table overlooking Little Traverse Bay's
waterfront area for a more romantic view. Locals come for the delicious seafood dishes and other delicacies made with fresh ingredients and homegrown
herbs, and to partake in the award-winning wine list, which features more
than 350 vintages.

American menu. Dinner. Closed April. Bar. Children's menu. Casual attire.
Reservations recommended. $16-35

★★PIER RESTAURANT

102 E. Bay St., Harbor Springs, 231-526-6201; www.staffords.com

American menu. Lunch, dinner, late-night, brunch. Bar. Children's menu.
Casual attire. Reservations recommended. Outdoor seating. $16-35

HOLLAND

See also Grand Haven, Grand Rapids, Saugatuck

In 1847, a group of Dutch settlers seeking religious freedom left the Netherlands and settled in this area because its sand dunes and fertile land reminded
them of their homeland. Today, much of the population is of Dutch descent, as
evidenced by the mid-May Tulip Time Festival, which features millions of tulips, wooden shoemaking, dancing and Dutch delicacies. The town prides itself
on being the center of Dutch culture in the United States. The city is located at
the mouth of the Black River, on the shores of Lake Macatawa, and has developed a resort colony along the shores of Lakes Macatawa and Michigan.

WHAT TO SEE
CAPPON HOUSE

228 W. Ninth St., Holland, 616-392-6740, 888-200-9123; www.hollandmuseum.org

This Italianate house from 1874 was the home of the first mayor of Holland and has original furnishings and millwork.

June-October, Wednesday-Saturday 1-4p.m.; November-May, Friday-Saturday 1-4 p.m.

DUTCH VILLAGE

12350 James St., Holland, 616-396-1475, 800-285-7177; www.dutchvillage.com

The village include buildings of Dutch architecture, canals, windmills and tulips everywhere. You can also see Dutch dancing and listen to street organs. Have a pair of wooden shoes carved just for you.

Mid-April-late October, daily.

HOLLAND MUSEUM

31 W. 10th St., Holland, 616-392-1362, 888-200-9123; www.hollandmuseum.org

Features decorative arts from the Netherlands Collection and the Volendam Room. Permanent and changing exhibits pertaining to local history.

Monday, Wednesday, Friday-Saturday, 10a.m.-5p.m.; Thursday, 10a.m.-8p.m., Sunday, 2-5 p.m.

HOLLAND STATE PARK

2215 Ottawa Beach Road, Holland, 616-399-9390

This 143-acre park includes a ¼-mile beach on Lake Michigan and offers swimming, boating, fishing, picnicking, playground and more.

HOPE COLLEGE

141 E. 12th St., Holland, 616-395-7000; www.hope.edu

Tours of campus. Theater series July-August.

LITTLE NETHERLANDS

1 Lincoln Ave., Holland, 616-355-1030; www.windmillisland.org

A miniature reproduction of old Holland; 20-minute film on Dutch windmills in the posthouse; klompen dancing in summer; exhibits, tulips.

VELDHEER'S TULIP GARDENS AND DE KLOMP WOODEN SHOE & DELFTWARE FACTORY

12755 Quincy St., Holland, 616-399-1900; www.veldheer.com

Visit the only delftware factory in the United States; factory tours. Visitors can try on wooden shoes and talk to the artisans who made them.

WINDMILL ISLAND

Seventh Street and Lincoln Avenue, Holland, 616-355-1030; www.cityofholland.com

The 225-year-old windmill De Zwaan ("the swan") is the only operating imported Dutch windmill in the United States. It was relocated here by special permission of the Dutch government, as the remaining windmills in the Netherlands are all considered historic monuments. It is still used today to grind flour.

April-May, July-August, Monday-Saturday 9 a.m.-6 p.m., Sunday 11:30 a.m.-6 p.m.; June, September-October, Monday-Saturday 10 a.m.-5 p.m., Sunday 11:30 a.m.-5 p.m.

SPECIAL EVENT
TULIP TIME FESTIVAL
238 S. River Avenue, Holland, 616-396-4221, 800-822-2770; www.tuliptime.org
A celebration of Dutch heritage featuring 1,800 klompen dancers, three parades, street scrubbing, Dutch markets, musical and professional entertainment and millions of tulips.
Eight days in mid-May.

WHERE TO STAY
★COUNTRY INN BY CARLSON HOLLAND
12260 James St., Holland, 616-396-6677, 800-456-4000; www.countryinns.com
116 rooms. Complimentary continental breakfast. Business center. $61-150

★★HOLIDAY INN
650 E. 24th St., Holland, 616-394-0111, 800-279-5286; www.innhotwlsgroup.com
168 rooms. Restaurant. Bar. $61-150

WHERE TO EAT
★84 EAST FOOD & SPIRITS
84 E. Eighth St., Holland, 616-396-8484; www.84eastpasta.com
Italian menu. Lunch, dinner. Closed Sunday. Bar. Children's menu. Casual attire. $16-35

★★★ALPENROSE
4 E. Eighth St., Holland, 616-393-2111; www.alpenroserestaurant.com
The space that houses this charming restaurant used to be the home of a run-of-the-mill discount store. Located in downtown Holland, it is now filled with hand-carved woodwork, stained-glass windows and chairs and tables from Austria and Germany—all contributing to the Alpine aesthetic the restaurant embraces. Locals come for the famous chicken shortcake, a mainstay on the changing menu. Dinner isn't the only popular meal here—the Sunday brunch and lunch buffet also draw crowds.
International menu. Lunch, dinner, Sunday brunch. Children's menu. Casual attire. Reservations recommended. Outdoor seating. $36-85

★PEREDDIES
447 Washington Square, Holland, 616-394-3061; www.pereddiesrestaurant.com
Italian menu. Lunch, dinner. Closed Sunday. Bar. Casual attire. $16-35

★★★PIPER
2225 S. Shore Drive, Macatawa, 616-335-5866; www.piperrestaurant.com
With its location overlooking Lake Macatawa, this casually elegant restaurant serves cuisine with professional, friendly service. Try the shrimp nachos, artichoke ravioli or the chicken paella.
American menu. Dinner. Closed Sunday-Monday in winter. Bar. Children's menu. $36-85

HOLLY
See also Detroit, Flint, Pontiac

Entering the city of Holly is like stepping back in time. At the summer Renaissance Festival, the 16th century comes alive with armor-clad knights on horseback, sword swallowers and other entertainers, jousting contests and feasts. The 19th-century storefronts beckon at Historic Battle Alley and Dickens's Victorian novels are celebrated during the winter Dickens Festival.

WHAT TO SEE
DAVISBURG CANDLE FACTORY
634 Broadway, Davisburg, 248-634-4214, 800-748-9440; www.candlefactorymi.com

Located in a 125-year-old building, this factory produces unique and beautiful handcrafted candles.

Demonstrations by appointment (weekdays). Monday-Saturday 10 a.m.-5 p.m., Sunday noon-4 p.m.

DTE ENERGY MUSIC CENTER
7774 Sashabaw Road, Clarkston, 248-377-0100; www.palacenet.com

This outdoor ampitheater features summer concerts by top performers. Seats are available close to the stage, but many concertgoers choose to bring blankets for the much cheaper and more charming, lawn area.

HISTORIC BATTLE ALLEY
110 Battle Alley, Holly, 248-634-5208; www.hollyhotel.com

Once known for its taverns and brawls, Battle Alley is now a restored 19th-century street featuring antiques, boutiques, specialty shops, crafter and dining at the Historic Holly Hotel. On the Alley is a mosaic of the bicentennial logo made from 1,000 red, white and blue bricks.

Daily.

MOUNT HOLLY SKI AREA
13536 S. Dixie Highway, Holly, 248-634-8269, 800-582-7256; www.skimtholly.com

Three quad, three triple, double chairlift, six rope tows; patrol, school, rentals, snowmaking. Vertical drop 350 feet. Night skiing.

December-March, daily.

SPECIAL EVENTS
CARRYNATION FESTIVAL
103 N. Saginaw, Holly, 248-634-1900; www.carrynation.org

Recreation of Carry Nation's 1908 visit to Holly. The "temperance crusader" charged down Battle Alley with her famed umbrella, smashing bottles and a few heads along the way. Pageant, parade, antique car show and crafts show. Weekend after Labor Day.

DICKENS FESTIVAL
Holly, 248-634-1900; www.mainstreetholly.com/dickens

Recreates the Dickensian period with carolers, town crier, strolling characters, skits, bell choirs, street hawkers, carriage rides.

Weekends in December.

MICHIGAN RENAISSANCE FESTIVAL

12500 Dixie Highway, Holly, 248-634-5552, 800-601-4848; www.michrenfest.com
Festivities include jousting tournaments, entertainment, food and crafts in Renaissance-style village.
Eight weekends in August-September.

WHERE TO EAT
★★HISTORIC HOLLY HOTEL

110 Battle Alley, Holly, 248-634-5208; www.hollyhotel.com
Seafood, steak menu. Lunch, dinner, Sunday brunch. Bar. $36-85

HOUGHTON

See also Calumet, Hancock
Houghton and its sister city, Hancock, face each other across the narrowest part of Portage Lake. This is the area of America's first mining capital, the scene of the first great mineral strike in the Western Hemisphere. The copper-bearing geological formations are believed to be the oldest rock formations in the world. The great mining rush of 1843 and the years following brought people from all over Europe. Two main ethnic groups are identifiable today: Cornishmen, who came from England and made popular the pasties available throughout the Upper Peninsula, and Finns, who have made this their cultural center in the United States.

WHAT TO SEE
A.E. SEAMAN MINERALOGICAL MUSEUM

Electrical Energy Resources Center, 1400 Townsend Drive, Houghton, 906-487-2572;
www.museum.mtu.edu
Exhibits one of the nation's best mineral collections.
Monday-Friday 9 a.m.-4:30 p.m., Saturday noon-4 p.m.

FERRY SERVICE TO ISLE ROYALE NATIONAL PARK

800 E. Lakeshore Drive, Houghton, 906-482-0984; www.nps.gov
Four ferries and a float plane provide transportation.
June-September, daily; some trips in May.

MICHIGAN TECHNOLOGICAL UNIVERSITY

1400 Townsend Drive, Houghton, 906-487-1885; www.mtu.edu
One of the finest engineering and mining schools in the United States, Michigan Tech also features one of the country's premier hockey teams. Campus tours leave from University Career Center in the Administration Building.

MONT RIPLEY SKI AREA

1400 Townsend Drive, Houghton, 906-487-2340; www.aux.mtu.edu/ski
Double chairlift, T-bar; patrol, school, rentals, snowmaking.
Early December-late March, daily.

SPECIAL EVENTS
BRIDGEFEST
326 Shelden Ave., Houghton, 906-482-2388; www.bridgefestfun.com
Parade, arts and crafts show, entertainment, powerboat races, fireworks.
Father's Day weekend. Mid-June.

WINTER CARNIVAL
Michigan Technological University, 1400 Townsend Drive, Houghton, 906-487-2818; www.mtu.edu
Snow sculptures and statues; dogsled and snowshoe racing, broomball, ski-
ing, skating; skit contests; Queen Coronation and Snowball Dance.
Late January-early February.

WHERE TO STAY
★★BEST WESTERN FRANKLIN SQUARE INN
820 Shelden Ave., Houghton, 906-487-1700, 888-487-1700; www.bestwestern.com
104 rooms. Restaurant. Bar. Fitness Center. Pets accepted. $61-150

HOUGHTON LAKE
See also Grayling
The Houghton Lake area is the gateway to a popular north country resort area,
including three of the largest inland lakes in the state and 200,000 acres of
state forests. It's best known for fishing, including ice fishing in winter. Houghton Lake has also become popular among snowmobilers because of the heavy
snowfall that accumulates in the middle portion of the Lower Peninsula.

WHAT TO SEE
HIGGINS LAKE
Houghton Lake
One of the most beautiful in America, Higgins Lake covers 10,317 acres and
has 25 miles of sandy shoreline.

HOUGHTON LAKE
Houghton Lake
This is the largest inland lake in Michigan and the source of the Muskegon
River. This lake has a 32-mile shoreline and 22,000 acres of water, as well
as 200 miles of groomed and marked snowmobile trails. A variety of resorts
are in the area.

ST. HELEN LAKE
Houghton Lake
This pine-bordered lake has 12 miles of shoreline.

SPECIAL EVENT
TIP-UP TOWN USA ICE FESTIVAL
1625 W. Houghton Lake Drive, Houghton Lake, 989-366-5644; www.houghtonlakechamber.org
Tip-up is an ice-fishing term for the way anglers set up their gear to signal
that a fish is on the line. The Tip-Up Town USA Ice Festival features ice fish-

ing contests, games, food, parade, fireworks and carnival.
Third and fourth weekend in January.

WHERE TO STAY
★BEST WESTERN BEACHFRONT
4990 W. Houghton Lake Drive, Houghton Lake, 989-366-9126, 800-780-7234;
www.bestwestern.com
60 rooms. Complimentary continental breakfast. High-speed Internet access.
$61-150

INDIAN RIVER
Located on beautiful Burt Lake and the Sturgeon and Pigeon rivers, Indian
River is a sport-lover's paradise. Visitors and locals enjoy hunting, fishing,
canoeing, kayaking, snowmobiling, snowshoeing and cross-country skiing.

WHAT TO SEE
BURT LAKE STATE PARK
6635 State Park Drive, Indian River, 231-238-9392; www.michigan.gov/dnr
Set on approximately 400 acres, this park offers a beach, water-skiing, fishing for walleyed pike and perch, boating, picnicking, playground, concession
and camping.
May-October, daily.

STURGEON & PIGEON RIVER OUTFITTERS
4271 S. Straits Highway, Indian River, 231-238-8181; www.bigbearadventures.com
Go canoeing, tubing or kayaking with this company.
May-mid-September.

WHERE TO STAY
★HOLIDAY INN EXPRESS
4375 Brudy Road, Indian River, 231-238-3000, 888-255-3365; www.holiday-inn.com
50 rooms. Complimentary continental breakfast. High-speed Internet access.
$61-150

INTERLOCHEN
See also Beulah, Frankfort, Traverse City
This picturesque farming community is the cultural and artistic center of
northern Michigan. Throughout the year, but especially in summer, the city
hosts performances by big-name entertainers that rival those found in the
largest cities in the U.S. The nearby state park offers one of the only virgin
white pine forests left in the world.

WHAT TO SEE
INTERLOCHEN CENTER FOR THE ARTS
4000 Highway 137, Interlochen, 231-276-7200; www.interlochen.org
The Interlochen Arts Academy, a fine arts boarding high school, is located
here. Concerts by students, faculty and internationally known guests; art
exhibits, drama and dance productions. Approximately 2,500 students as-
semble here every summer to study music, art, drama and dance.

INTERLOCHEN STATE PARK

South Highway 137, Interlochen, 231-276-9511
A 187-acre park with sand beach on Green and Duck lakes.
Swimming, bathhouse, fishing, boating.

SPECIAL EVENT
INTERLOCHEN ARTS CAMP

Interlochen Center for the Arts, 4000 Highway 137, Interlochen, 231-276-7200;
www.interlochen.org
A variety of performing arts events by students and visiting professionals.
Mid-June-early September.

IRON MOUNTAIN

See also Iron River, Ishpeming
After more than a half-century of production, the underground shaft mines
of high-grade ore deposits here have closed. Abandoned mines, cave-ins and
a huge Cornish mine pump, preserved as tourist attractions, are reminders
of mining days.

WHAT TO SEE
CORNISH PUMPING ENGINE & MINING MUSEUM

300 Kent St., Iron Mountain, 906-774-1086
Features largest steam-driven pumping engine built in the United States,
weighing 160 tons with 40-foot-diameter flywheel in engine; also includes
display of underground mining equipment used in Michigan; World War II
glider display.
Mid-May-September, daily; rest of year, by appointment.

IRON MOUNTAIN IRON MINE

Highway 2, Vulcan, 906-563-8077; www.ironmountainironmine.com
Mine train tours 2,600 feet of underground drifts and tunnels 400 feet below
surface. Working machinery, museum.
Tours June-mid-October, daily.

LAKE ANTOINE PARK

Lake Antoine, Iron Mountain, 906-774-8875
Swimming, boating, water-skiing; nature trail, picnicking, concession, im-
proved county campgrounds; band concerts.
Memorial Day-Labor Day, daily.

MENOMINEE RANGE HISTORICAL MUSEUM

300 E. Ludington St., Iron Mountain, 906-774-4276; www.menomineemuseum.com
More than 100 exhibits depict life on the Menominee Iron Range in the
1880s and early 1900s; one-room school, Victorian parlor, trapper's cabin,
country store.
Mid-May-September, daily; rest of year, by appointment.

PINE MOUNTAIN LODGE

Pine Mountain Road, Iron Mountain, 906-774-2747, 800-553-7463;
www.pinemountainresort.com

Triple, two double chairlifts, rope tow; snowmaking, patrol, school, rentals; nine-hole golf; two tennis courts; indoor/outdoor pools. The longest run is ¾ of a mile with a vertical drop of 500 feet. Also includes cross-country trails. Late November-early April, daily.

SPECIAL EVENTS
FESTIVAL OF THE ARTS

600 S. Stevens Ave., Iron Mountain, 906-774-2945

Crafts demonstrations, antique car show, concerts, square and folk dancing, community theater, international foods.
Mid-June-mid-August.

PINE MOUNTAIN SKI JUMPING TOURNAMENT

Pine Mountain Lodge, Pine Mountain Road, Iron Mountain, 906-774-2747
January.

WOOD-BEE CARVERS SHOW

600 S.Stevens Ave., Iron Mountain, 906-774-2945
Wood carvers' competition and show.
October.

WHERE TO STAY
★COMFORT INN

1555 N. Stephenson Ave., Iron Mountain, 906-774-5505, 866-774-5505;
www.comfortinn.com

60 rooms. Complimentary continental breakfast. Fitness center. $61-150

IRON RIVER

See also Iron Mountain

Just north of the Wisconsin-Michigan state line, Iron River was one of the last of the large mining towns to spring up on the Menominee Range. Lumbering has also played a prominent part in the town's past. Ottawa National Forest lies a few miles to the west, and a Ranger District office is located here.

WHAT TO SEE
IRON COUNTY MUSEUM

100 Museum Drive, Caspian, 906-265-2617; www.ironcountymuseum.com

This indoor/outdoor museum has 22 buildings, which include a miniature logging exhibit with more than 2,000 pieces. Iron mining dioramas; more than 100 major exhibits; log homestead; 1896 one-room schoolhouse; logging camp, home of composer Carrie Jacobs-Bond; Lee-LeBlanc Willife Art Gallery. Annual ethnic festivals (Scandinavian, Polish, Italian, Yugoslavian).
Mid-May-October, Monday-Saturday 9 a.m.-5 p.m., Sunday 1-5 p.m.; rest of year, by appointment.

SKI BRULE

397 Brule Mountain Road, Iron River, 906-265-4957, 800-362-7853; www.skibrule.com

Four chairlifts, two T-bars, pony lift, rope tow; patrol, school, rentals, snowmaking. 17 runs. The longest run is one mile with a vertical drop of 500 feet.

November-April, daily. Cross-country trails.

SPECIAL EVENTS
BASS FESTIVAL

Crystal Falls, 906-265-3822; www.iron.org

Canoe races on the Paint River, softball game, barbecue, music and events at Runkle Park and Runkle Lake.

First weekend in July.

FERROUS FROLICS

Iron County Museum, 100 Museum Drive, Caspian, 906-265-2617; www.iron.org

Arts, crafts, demonstrations, band concert, flea market.

Third weekend in July.

IRON COUNTY FAIR

Fairgrounds, North Seventh Avenue and West Franklin Street, Iron River, 888-879-4766; www.ironcountyfair.org

This down-home county fair features a carnival, rodeo, horse races, and arts and crafts.

Four days in late August.

UPPER PENINSULA CHAMPIONSHIP RODEO

Fairgrounds, 50 E. Genesee St., Iron River, 906-265-3822; www.upprorodeo.com

The first rodeo here was held in 1968 and has been going strong ever since.

Late July.

★★★★★ **MICHIGAN**

67

IRONWOOD

See also Houghton, Iron Mountain, Ishpeming

Ironwood is a center for summer and winter recreation. The first part of Gogebic County to be settled, the town was linked at first with fur trading. It quickly blossomed into a mining town when a deposit of iron was found in what is now the eastern section of the city. John R. Wood, one of the first mining captains, was known as "Iron" because of his interest in ore—thus, the name Ironwood.

WHAT TO SEE
BIG POWDERHORN MOUNTAIN

Powderhorn Road, Bessemer, 906-932-4838, 800-501-7669; www.bigpowderhorn.net

Nine double chairlifts; patrol, school, rentals; three restaurants, cafeteria, three bars, nursery. 25 runs. The longest run is one mile with a vertical drop of 600 feet.

Thanksgiving-early April, daily 9 a.m.-4 p.m.

BLACKJACK

Blackjack Road, Bessemer, 906-229-5115, 800-848-1125; www.skiblackjack.com

Four double chairlifts, two ropes tow; patrol, school, rentals. The longest run is one mile with a vertical drop of 465 feet.

November-March, daily.

COPPER PEAK SKI FLYING

Copper Peak Road, Ironwood, 906-932-3500; www.copperpeak.org

The only ski flying facility in North America and one of six in the world. Athletes test their skills in an event that requires more athletic ability than ski jumping. Skiers reach speeds of more than 60 miles per hour and fly farther than 500 feet. International tournament is held every winter. In summer, chairlift and elevator rides take visitors 240 feet above the crest of Copper Peak for a view of three states, Lake Superior and Canada.

Mid-June-Labor Day, daily; September-October, weekends.

HIAWATHA: WORLD'S TALLEST INDIAN

Houk Street, Ironwood

This statue of the famous Iroquois stands 52 feet high and looks north to the legendary "shining big-sea-water"—Gitchee Gumee, otherwise known as Lake Superior.

LITTLE GIRL'S POINT PARK

104 S. Lowell St., Ironwood, 906-932-1420; www.gogebic.org/lgp.htm

Notable for the agate pebbles on the beaches. Picnic tables, campsites; Native American burial grounds.

May-September.

MOUNT ZION

4946 Jackson Road, Ironwood, 906-932-3718

This is one of the highest points on the Gogebic Range, located 1,150 feet above Lake Superior. Double chairlift, two rope tow; patrol, school, rentals. The longest run is ¾ mile with a vertical drop of 300 feet.

Mid-December-March, Tuesday-Sunday. Two miles of cross-country ski trails, equipment rentals.

OTTAWA NATIONAL FOREST

2100 E. Cloverland Drive, Ironwood, 906-932-1330; www.fs.fed.us

This national forest includes wooded hills, picturesque lakes and streams, waterfalls, a nursery, harbor, scenic trails and more.

Daily.

SPECIAL EVENT
GOGEBIC COUNTY FAIR

Fairgrounds, 104 S. Lowell St., Ironwood, 906-932-2700;
www.gogebiccountyfair.homestead.com

Carnival rides, harness racing, horse shows and live music are among the activities at this county fair.

Second weekend in August.

WHERE TO STAY
★COMFORT INN

210 E. Cloverland Drive, Ironwood, 906-932-2224, 800-572-9412; www.comfortinn.com
61 rooms. Complimentary continental breakfast. Wireless Internet access.
$61-150

ISHPEMING
See also Iron Mountain, Marquette
Iron mines gave birth to this city and still sustain it. Skiing is the basis of its
recreation and tourism business. The national ski jumping championships
are held here annually. In 1887, three Norwegians formed a ski club in Ishpeming, which is a Native American word for "high grounds." That ski club
eventually became the U.S. Ski Association, which hosts the National Ski
Hall of Fame and Ski Museum, located here.

WHAT TO SEE
NATIONAL SKI HALL OF FAME AND SKI MUSEUM

610 Palms Ave., Ishpeming, 906-485-6323; www.skihall.com
Affiliated with the U.S. Ski Association, this museum houses national tro-
phies and displays of old skis and ski equipment, and includes a replica of the
oldest-known ski and ski pole in the world. The Roland Palmedo National
Ski Library includes a collection of ski publications.
Monday-Saturday 10 a.m.-5 p.m.

SUICIDE BOWL

Ishpeming, 906-485-4242
Includes five ski-jumping hills from mini-hill to 70-meter hill. There are also
four cross-country trails; one is lighted for evening use.

VAN RIPER STATE PARK

851 County Road AKE, Champion, 906-339-4461; www.michigan.gov/dnr
Approximately 1,000 acres on Lake Michigamme. Swimming, water-skiing,
bathhouse, fishing, boating, hunting, hiking, picnic grounds, camping.
Daily.

SPECIAL EVENT
ANNUAL SKI JUMPING CHAMPIONSHIPS

National Ski Hall of Fame, 610 Palms Ave., Ishpeming, 906-485-6323; www.skihall.com
Paul Bietila Memorial. Also cross-country ski race. February.

WHERE TO STAY
★★BEST WESTERN COUNTRY INN

850 Highway 41 W., Ishpeming, 906-485-6345, 800-780-7234; www.bestwestern.com
60 rooms. Complimentary breakfast. Pets accepted; fee. $61-150

JACKSON
See also Ann Arbor, Battle Creek, Lansing
In Jackson on July 6, 1854, the Republican Party was officially born at a
convention held outdoors, as there was no hall large enough to accommodate

the delegates. Each year, the city attracts thousands of tourists, who use it as a base to explore more than 200 natural lakes in Jackson County.

WHAT TO SEE
CASCADES FALLS PARK
1992 Warren Ave., Jackson, 517-788-4320; www.co.jackson.mi.us/parks
Approximately 465 acres. Fishing ponds and pier, paddle-boating (rentals); picnicking, playground; 18-hole miniature golf, driving range; fitness and running trail; basketball, tennis and horseshoe courts; restaurant.

CASCADES-SPARKS MUSEUM
Brown Street and Denton Road, Jackson, 517-788-4320
Depicts early history of falls and its builder, Captain William Sparks; original drawings, models, audiovisual displays.
Memorial Day-Labor Day.

DAHLEM ENVIRONMENTAL EDUCATION CENTER
7117 S. Jackson Road, Jackson, 517-782-3453; www.dahlemcenter.org
This pretty nature center includes five miles of easy trails through forests, fields, marshes.
Tuesday-Sunday.

ELLA SHARP MUSEUM
3225 Fourth St., Jackson, 517-787-2320; www.ellasharp.org
Complex includes Victorian farmhouse, historic farm lane, one-room schoolhouse, log cabin, galleries with rotating art and historic exhibits; studios; planetarium; visitor center.
Tuesday-Friday 10 a.m.-4 p.m., Saturday 11 a.m.-4 p.m.

ELLA SHARP PARK
3225 Fourth St., Jackson, 517-788-4040; www.ellasharppark.com
This park is made up of approximately 530 acres and includes an 18-hole golf course, tennis courts, ballfields, swimming pool, miniature golf, picnic facilities and formal gardens.
Daily.

REPUBLICAN PARTY FOUNDING SITE
West Franklin and Second streets, Jackson
You can't miss this landmark—it's marked with a tablet dedicated by President William Howard Taft.

SPARKS ILLUMINATED CASCADES WATERFALLS
1992 Warren Ave., Jackson, 517-788-4320
Approximately 500 feet of water cascading over 16 waterfalls and six fountains in continually changing patterns of light, color and music.
Memorial Day-Labor Day, nightly.

WATERLOO FARM MUSEUM
9998 Waterloo-Munith Road, Waterloo Township, 517-596-2254;
www.waterloofarmmuseum.org
Tours of furnished pioneer farmhouse (1855-1885), bakehouse, windmill, farm workshop, barn, milk cellar, log house, granary.
June-August, Tuesday-Sunday afternoons; September, Saturday-Sunday. Pioneer Festival second Sunday in October.

SPECIAL EVENTS
CIVIL WAR MUSTER & BATTLE REENACTMENT
Cascade Falls Park, 1992 Warren Ave., Jackson, 517-788-4320
Thousands of participants recreate a different Civil War battle each year; living history demonstrations, parades, food, entertainment.
Third weekend in August.

HOT AIR BALLOON JUBILEE
Jackson County Airport, 3606 Wildwood Ave., Jackson, 517-782-1515;
www.hotairjubilee.com
Competitive balloon events; skydivers; arts and crafts.
Mid-July.

JACKSON COUNTY FAIR
Jackson County Fairgrounds, 200 W. Ganson St., Jackson, 517-788-4405
The Jackson County Fair includes stage shows, displays of produce, handicrafts, farm animals, midway shows and rides.
Second week in August.

ROSE FESTIVAL
Ella Sharp Park, 212 W. Michigan Ave., Jackson, 517-787-2065;
www.jacksonrosefestival.org
Parade, pageant, garden tours, entertainment.
Mid-May-mid-June.

WHERE TO EAT
★★KNIGHT'S STEAKHOUSE & GRILL
2125 Horton Road, Jackson, 517-783-2777; www.knightsrestaurants.com
Steak menu. Dinner. Closed Sunday. Bar. Children's menu. Casual attire. $16-35

KALAMAZOO
See also Battle Creek, Paw Paw, Three Rivers
The name is derived from the American Indian name for the Kalamazoo River, which means "where the water boils in the pot." The concept is noted not only in the community's name but also in its cultural, industrial and recreational makeup.

WHAT TO SEE
BITTERSWEET SKI AREA

600 River Road, Otsego, 269-694-2820; www.skibittersweet.com

Quad, four triple chairlifts, double chairlift, five rope tows; school, rentals. 16 trails. The longest run is 2,300 feet with a vertical drop of 300 feet. There is also night skiing.

December-March, Monday-Thursday noon-10 p.m., Friday 10 a.m.-10:30 p.m., Saturday 9 a.m.-10:30 p.m., Sunday 9 a.m.-10 p.m.

BRONSON PARK

200 W. South St., Kalamazoo

A bronze tablet marks the spot where Abraham Lincoln made an antislavery speech in 1856.

ECHO VALLEY

8495 E. H Ave., Kalamazoo, 269-349-3291; www.echovalleyfun.com

Tobogganing and ice skating (rentals).

December-March, Friday-Sunday.

GILMORE-CCCA MUSEUM

6865 Hickory Road, Hickory Corners, 269-671-5089; www.gilmorecarmuseum.org

More than 120 antique autos tracing the significant technical developments in automotive transportation on 90 acres of landscaped grounds can be found at this interesting museum.

May-October; Monday-Friday 9 a.m.-5 p.m., Saturday-Sunday 9 a.m.-6 p.m.

KALAMAZOO AIR ZOO

6151 Portage Road, Portage, 269-382-6555; www.airzoo.org

This is home to more than 70 beautiful historic and restored aircraft of the World War II period, many of which are still in flying condition. Also includes exhibits, video theater, flight simulator and observation deck.

Tours of Restoration Center: May-September. Flight of the Day: May-September, afternoons. Daily.

KALAMAZOO COLLEGE

1200 Academy St., Kalamazoo, 269-337-7300; www.kzoo.edu

This private, liberal arts college has red-brick streets and Georgian architecture that characterize this school, one of the 100 oldest colleges in the nation. A 3,023-pipe organ is in Stetson Chapel; Bach Festival (March); Festival Playhouse (June-July).

KALAMAZOO INSTITUTE OF ARTS

314 S. Park St., Kalamazoo, 269-349-7775; www.kiarts.org

The Kalamazoo Institute of Arts includes galleries, a school, shop, library and auditorium. Stop here to see a collection of 20th-century American art and circulating exhibits.

Tuesday-Wednesday, Friday-Saturday 10 a.m.-5 p.m., Thursday 10 a.m.-8 p.m., Sunday noon-5 p.m.

KALAMAZOO NATURE CENTER

7000 N. Westnedge Ave., Kalamazoo, 269-381-1574; www.naturecenter.org

This nature center includes a restored 1860s pioneer homestead tours by appointment); barnyard (May-Labor Day); and nature trails.
Monday-Saturday 9 a.m.-5 p.m., Sunday 1-5 p.m.

TIMBER RIDGE SKI AREA

7500 23½ St., Gobles, 269-694-9449, 800-253-2928; www.timberridgeski.com

Four chairlifts, Pomalift, three rope tows; patrol, school, snowmaking. Store, repairs, rentals. Total of 15 trails.
Late November-mid-March, Monday-Friday 11 a.m.-10 p.m., Saturday 9 a.m.-10 p.m., Sunday 9 a.m.-8 p.m.

WESTERN MICHIGAN UNIVERSITY

1903 W. Michigan Ave., Kalamazoo, 269-387-1000; www.wmich.edu

Contemporary plays, musical comedies, operas and melodramas are offered in the Shaw and York theaters. Touring professional shows, dance programs and entertainers can be found in Miller Auditorium, while dance and music performances are featured in the Irving S. Gilmore University Theatre Complex. Art exhibits are in Sangren Hall and East Hall.

SPECIAL EVENTS
WINE AND HARVEST FESTIVAL

Downtown Paw Paw, 269-655-1111; www.wineandharvestfestival.com

First weekend in September.

WHERE TO STAY
★★★BAY POINTE INN AND RESTAURANT

11456 Marsh Road, Shelbyville, 269-672-8111, 888-486-5253; www.baypointeinn.com

Overlooking Gun Lake, this modern inn is located in a charming resort area 30 minutes from Grand Rapids and Kalamazoo. A lobby features a fireplace and a flat-screen TV. A marina, beach and small shops are all nearby. The Terrace Grille Restaurant is a nice spot for dinner.
38 rooms. Complimentary breakfast. Restaurant, bar. Beach. $151-250

★BEST WESTERN HOSPITALITY INN

3640 E. Cork St., Kalamazoo, 269-381-1900, 800-780-7234; www.bestwestern.com

124 rooms. Complimentary breakfast. Pets accepted; fee. Fitness center. $61-150

★FAIRFIELD INN BY MARRIOTT KALAMAZOO EAST

3800 E. Cork St., Kalamazoo, 269-344-8300, 800-228-2800; www.fairfieldinn.com

119 rooms. Complimentary breakfast. Pets not accepted. $61-150

★★RADISSON PLAZA HOTEL AT KALAMAZOO CENTER

100 W. Michigan Ave., Kalamazoo, 269-343-3333, 800-333-3333; www.radisson.com

281 rooms. Restaurant, bar. Fitness center. $151-250

WHERE TO EAT
★★★BRAVO
5402 Portage Road, Kalamazoo, 269-344-7700; www.bravokalamazoo.com

The contemporary décor, fresh dishes and welcoming atmosphere make this Italian restaurant an excellent choice for lunch or dinner. Bravo is located about one block from the airport and is easily accessible from Interstate 94. Its interior features a large wine display, open wood ovens, candlelit tables, natural wood and a fireplace in the main dining room. Expect dishes such as grilled stuffed pork chops filled with proscuitto ham and mozzarella with blue cheese mashed potatoes, or chicken gnocchi in mushrooms and cream served on crispy potato and spinach gnocchi.

American, Italian menu. Lunch, dinner, Sunday brunch. Closed holidays. Bar. Children's menu. $16-35

★★★WEBSTER'S
100 W. Michigan Ave., Kalamazoo, 269-343-4444; www.webstersrestaurant.com

Located in the heart of downtown on the second floor of the Radisson Hotel, this contemporary, club-like restaurant features an elegant copper and brass display kitchen that turns out fresh seafood and grilled steaks as well as tableside caesar salads and freshly prepared desserts. Live music entertains diners on Friday and Saturday nights.

American menu. Dinner. Closed Sunday; holidays. Bar. $36-85

LANSING
See also Jackson

When Lansing became the capital of Michigan in 1847, it consisted of one log house and a sawmill. Today, in addition to state government, Lansing is the headquarters for many trade and professional associations and has much heavy industry. R.E. Olds, who built and marketed one of America's earliest automobiles, started the city's industrial growth. Lansing is the home of the Lansing Automotive Division of General Motors and many allied industries. East Lansing, a neighboring community, is the location of the Michigan State University Spartans and is part of the capital city in all respects except government.

WHAT TO SEE
BOARSHEAD THEATER
Center for the Arts, 425 S. Grand Ave., Lansing, 517-484-7800; www.boarshead.org

A regional center with a professional resident theater company.

BRENKE RIVER SCULPTURE AND FISH LADDER
300 N. Grand Ave., Lansing

Located at North Lansing Dam on the Riverfront Park scenic walk, this sculpture encompasses the ladder designed by artist/sculptor Joseph E. Kinnebrew and landscape architect Robert O'Boyle.

FENNER NATURE CENTER
2020 E. Mount Hope Ave., Lansing, 517-483-4224; www.lansingmi.gov/parks/fenner

Park features a bald eagle, two waterfowl ponds, replica of a pioneer cabin and garden, and five miles of nature trails through a variety of habitats. Nature center with small animal exhibits open Tuesday-Sunday. Trails daily 8 a.m.-dusk.

IMPRESSION 5 SCIENCE CENTER

200 Museum Drive, Lansing, 517-485-8116; www.impression5.org

The center has more than 200 interactive, hands-on exhibits, including a computer lab, chemistry experiments; restaurant.
Monday-Saturday 10 a.m.-5 p.m., closed holidays.

LEDGES

133 Fitzgerald Park Drive, Grand Ledge, 517-627-7351;
www.grandledgemi.com/parks.htm

Edging the Grand River, the Ledges are 300-million-year-old quartz sandstone. They are considered a good area for the experienced rock climbers.
Daily.

MICHIGAN HISTORICAL MUSEUM

702 W. Kalamazoo St., Lansing, 517-373-3559; www.michigan.gov

Exhibits at this small historical museum include a copper mine, sawmill and 54-foot-high relief map of Michigan. There are also audiovisual programs and hands-on exhibits.
Daily; closed holidays.

MICHIGAN STATE UNIVERSITY

1200 E. Michigan Ave., Lansing, 517-353-1855; www.msu.edu

Founded as the country's first agricultural college and forerunner of the nationwide land-grant university system, MSU, located on a 5,300-acre landscaped campus with 7,800 different species and varieties of trees, shrubs and vines, is known for its research, Honors College and many innovations in education. Among the interesting features of the campus are Abrams Planetarium; Horticultural Gardens; W. J. Beal Botanical Garden; Breslin Student Events Center; Wharton Center for Performing Arts; Michigan State University Museum; and Kresge Art Museum.

POTTER PARK ZOO

1301 S. Pennsylvania Ave., Lansing, 517-483-4222; www.potterparkzoo.org

This zoo on the Red Cedar River has more than 400 animals. You will also find educational programs, camel and pony rides, playground, concession and picnic facilities.
Daily.

R.E. OLDS TRANSPORTATION MUSEUM

240 Museum Drive, Lansing, 517-372-0529; www.reoldsmuseum.org

Named after Ransom Eli Olds, the museum houses Lansing-built vehicles including Oldsmobile, REO, Star and Durant autos. Aside from older models, there is also a collection of newer "concept" cars from some of today's top manufacturers and car designers.
Tuesday-Saturday 10 a.m.-5 p.m., Sunday noon-5 p.m.

STATE CAPITOL BUILDING

North Capital and West Michigan avenues, Lansing, 517-373-2353

Dedicated in 1879, this was one of the first state capitol buildings to emulate the dome and wings of the U.S. Capitol in Washington, D.C. Interior walls and ceilings reflect the work of many skilled artisans, muralists and portrait painters.

Tours daily.

WOLDUMAR NATURE CENTER

5739 Old Lansing Road, Lansing, 517-322-0030; www.woldumar.org

This 188-acre wildlife preserve has nature walks and trails open for hiking and skiing.

Daily, dawn-dusk.

SPECIAL EVENT
EAST LANSING ART FESTIVAL

410 Abbott Road, East Lansing, 517-319-6884; www.elartfest.com

Artists' work for sale, continuous performances, ethnic foods, children's activities. Third weekend in May.

WHERE TO STAY
★★CLARION HOTEL & CONFERENCE CENTER

3600 Dunckel Drive, Lansing, 517-351-7600, 877-424-6423; www.lansingclarion.com

141 rooms. Complimentary continental breakfast. Wireless Internet access. Restaurant, bar. $61-150

★★COURTYARD BY MARRIOTT

2710 Lake Lansing Road, Lansing, 517-482-0500, 800-321-2211; www.courtyard.com

129 rooms. High-speed Internet access. $61-150

★FAIRFIELD INN BY MARRIOTT EAST LANSING

2335 Woodlake Drive, Okemos, 517-347-1000, 800-568-4421; www.fairfieldinn.com

78 rooms. Complimentary continental breakfast. Wireless Internet access. $61-150

★HAMPTON INN LANSING

525 N. Canal Road, Lansing, 517-627-8381, 800-426-7866; www.hamptoninn.com

105 rooms. Complimentary continental breakfast. High-speed Internet access. Airport transportation available. Pets accepted. Business center. Fitness center. $61-150

★★HOLIDAY INN LANSING/SOUTH CONVENTION CENTER

6820 S. Cedar St., Lansing, 517-694-8123, 800-465-4329; www.holiday-inn.com

300 rooms. Wireless Internet access. Restaurant, bar. $61-150

★★★MARRIOTT EAST LANSING AT UNIVERSITY PLACE

300 M.A.C. Ave., East Lansing, 517-337-4440, 800-228-9290; www.marriott.com/lanea

Located in the heart of downtown East Lansing, this hotel is within walking distance of the campus of Michigan State University as well as shopping and dining. Guest rooms are spacious and feature luxury bed linens and over-stuffed chairs and ottomans.

180 rooms. High-speed Internet access. Restaurant, bar. $151-250

★★RADISSON HOTEL LANSING
111 N. Grand Ave., Lansing, 517-482-0188, 800-333-3333;
www.radisson.com/lansingmi
257 rooms. Wireless Internet access. Restaurant, bar. $151-250

★★★SHERATON LANSING HOTEL
925 S. Creyts Road, Lansing, 517-323-7100, 800-325-3535; www.sheratonlansing.com
Located on the west side of Lansing, this full-service hotel is only a five-minute drive from the Capitol and Lansing Mall. The hotel offers a complimentary shuttle service for attractions within a five-mile radius. Christie's Bistro offers a popular Sunday brunch. Dogs accompanying their owners are given a special pet bed, food, water dishes and treats.

212 rooms. High-speed Internet access. Restaurant, bar. Airport transportation available. $151-250

LELAND
See also Glen Arbor, Traverse City
Leland, located on the western side of the Leelanau Peninsula, is a fishing town through and through. It was built on a bustling commercial fishing trade, and today, the major attraction is Fishtown, former fishing shacks, now weathered and gray, that are now gift shops, galleries and a fresh fish store.

WHAT TO SEE
BOAT TRIPS TO MANITOU ISLANDS
Leland Harbor, 207 W. River St., Leland, 231-256-9061
The Mishe-Mokwa makes daily trips in summer, including overnight camping excursions, to North and South Manitou islands. There are also evening cocktail cruise.
June-August, daily; May, September-October, Monday, Wednesday, Friday-Sunday.

WHERE TO STAY
★★LELAND LODGE
565 E. Pearl St., Leland, 231-256-9848; www.lelandlodge.com
18 rooms. Complimentary continental breakfast. Restaurant, bar. $61-150

WHERE TO EAT
★★BLUEBIRD
102 River St., Leland, 231-256-9081; www.leelanau.com/bluebird
Seafood menu. Lunch, dinner, Sunday brunch. Closed first three weeks in November; also Monday in April-mid-June, after Labor Day-October. Bar. Children's menu. $16-35

★★COVE
111 River St., Leland, 231-256-9834; www.thecoveleland.com

Seafood menu. Lunch, dinner. Closed Mid-October-mid-May. Bar. Children's menu. Outdoor seating. $16-35\

LUDINGTON
See also Manistee

A large passenger car ferry and freighters keep this important Lake Michigan port busy. First named after Father Jacques Marquette, in honor of the missionary explorer who died here in 1675, the community later adopted the name of its more recent founder, James Ludington, a lumber baron. Ludington draws vacationers because of its long stretch of beach on Lake Michigan and miles of forests, lakes, streams and dunes surrounding the town. The Pere Marquette River offers Chinook salmon.

WHAT TO SEE
AUTO FERRY/S.S. BADGER
701 Maritime Drive, Ludington, 231-843-1509, 800-841-4243; www.ssbadger.com

Instead of driving all the way around Lake Michigan, you can drive right onto the S.S. Badger and ride across. This car ferry takes passengers and vehicles on a four-hour trip to Manitowoc, Wisconsin. Amenities aboard the ferry include include a game room, movie screenings, staterooms and food service. May-October, daily.

LUDINGTON PUMPED STORAGE HYDROELECTRIC PLANT
3225 S. Lakeshore Drive, Ludington, 800-477-5050

Scenic overlooks beside Lake Michigan and the plant's 840-acre reservoir. One of the world's largest facilities of this type.

April-November, daily.

LUDINGTON STATE PARK
Highway 116 N., Ludington, 231-843-8671; www.ludingtonfriends.com

Approximately 4,500 acres on lakes Michigan and Hamlin and the Sable River make up this state park. Plenty of recreational activities are on hand, including swimming, water-skiing, fishing, boating, hunting, cross-country skiing and more. Visitor center.

May-September.

MASON COUNTY CAMPGROUND AND PICNIC AREA
5906 W. Chauvez Road, Ludington, 231-845-7609

Picnicking, playground, camping.

Memorial Day-Labor Day, daily.

WHITE PINE VILLAGE
1687 S. Lakeshore Drive, Ludington, 231-843-4808; www.historicwhitepinevillage.org

Historical buildings recreate small-town Michigan life in the late 1800s. Village includes a general store, trapper's cabin, courthouse/jail, town hall, one-room school and more.

June-early September, Tuesday-Sunday.

WHERE TO STAY
★★RAMADA INN

4079 W. Highway 10, Ludington, 231-845-7311, 800-707-7475; www.ramada.com
116 rooms. Restaurant, bar. Complimentary breakfast. Pets accepted. Fitness center. Business center. $61-150

WHERE TO EAT
★★SCOTTY'S

5910 E. Ludington Ave., Ludington, 231-843-4033; www.scottysrestaurant.com
American menu. Dinner. Bar. Children's menu. Casual attire. $16-35

MACKINAC ISLAND
See also Mackinaw City, St. Ignace

Because cars aren't allowed on the island—leaving horse-drawn carriages and bicycles as the chief modes of transportation—Mackinac Island retains the atmosphere of the 19th century. In view of the five-mile-long Mackinac Bridge, the largest expansion bridge in the world, it has been a famous resort for the last century. The island was called "great turtle" by Native Americans, who believed that its towering heights and rock formations were shaped by supernatural forces. Later, because of its strategic position, the island became the key to the struggle between England and France for control of the rich fur trade of the Great Northwest. Held by the French until 1760, it became British after Wolfe's victory at Quebec, was turned over to the United States at the close of the American Revolution, reverted to the British during the War of 1812 and finally was restored to the United States.

With the decline of the fur trade in the 1830s, Mackinac Island began to develop its potential as a resort area. Southern planters and their families summered here prior to the Civil War; wealthy Chicagoans took their place in the years following. Today, the island remains the home of the governor's summer mansion, where a long line of Michigan governors have spent at least a portion of their vacations. Carriages and bicycles can be rented. Passenger ferries make regularly scheduled trips to the island from Mackinaw City and St. Ignace, or visitors can reach the island by air from St. Ignace, Pellston or Detroit.

WHAT TO SEE
ARNOLD MACKINAC ISLAND FERRY

Mackinac Island, 906-847-3351, 800-542-8528; www.arnoldline.com
Large fast ferries traveling to Mackinac Island.
May-December, daily.

BEAUMONT MEMORIAL
Mackinac Island
Monument to Dr. William Beaumont, who charted observations of the human digestive system by viewing this action through an opening in the abdomen of a wounded French-Canadian.
Mid-June-Labor Day, daily.

BENJAMIN BLACKSMITH SHOP

Market Street, Mackinac Island
A working forge in replica of blacksmith shop dating from 1880s.
Mid-June-Labor Day, daily.

FORT MACKINAC

7127 Huron Road, Mackinac Island, 906-847-3328;
www.mackinacparks.com
High on a bluff overlooking the Straits of Mackinac, this 18th- and 19th-century British and American military outpost has massive limestone ramparts, cannon, a guardhouse, blockhouses, barracks, costumed interpreters and reenactments.
Mid-May-mid-October, daily.

INDIAN DORMITORY

Mackinac Island
Built in 1838 as a place for Native Americans to live during annual visits to the Mackinac Island office of the U.S. Indian Agency, this dormitory includes interpretive displays, craft demonstrations and murals depicting scenes from Longfellow's Hiawatha.
Mid-June-Labor Day, daily.

MACKINAC ISLAND STATE PARK

300 S. Washington Square, Mackinac Island, 906-847-3328; www.mackinacparks.com
This park comprises approximately 80 percent of the island. Michigan's first state park has views of the straits of Mackinac, prehistoric geological formations such as Arch Rock and shoreline and inland trails. Visitor center at Huron Street has informative exhibitsand guidebooks (mid-May-mid-October, daily). British Landing Nature Center (May-Labor Day).

80

MARQUETTE PARK

401 E. Fair Ave., Mackinac Island
More than 60 varieties of lilacs dominate this park.

SHEPLER'S MACKINAC ISLAND FERRY

556 E. Central Ave., Mackinaw City, 231-436-5023; www.sheplersferry.com
This ferry departs from 556 E. Central Ave., Mackinaw City or from downtown St. Ignace.
Early May-early November.

STAR LINE FERRY

587 N. State St., St. Ignace, 906-643-7635, 800-638-9892; www.mackinacferry.com
Hydro Jet service from Mackinaw City and St. Ignace.
May-October.

SPECIAL EVENTS
LILAC FESTIVAL

Main Street, Mackinac Island, 800-454-5227; www.mackinacislandlilacfestival.com
Second week in June.

SAILING RACES

7274 N. Main St., Mackinac Island, 906-847-3783; www.mackinacisland.org

Port Huron to Mackinac and Chicago to Mackinac. Mid-late July.

WHERE TO STAY
★★★GRAND HOTEL

1 Grand Ave., Mackinac Island, 906-847-3331, 800-334-7263; www.grandhotel.com

The hotel, an island landmark built in 1887, sits regally on a bluff overlooking the Straits of Mackinac. Sit in one of the giant rocking chairs on the longest front porch in America and watch the Great Lake freighters glide by. The interior is traditionally decorated. The hotel offers a variety of accommodations, shops, afternoon tea and carriage rentals.

385 rooms. Closed December-mid-May. Restaurant, bar. Golf. Tennis. $351 and up

★★★HOTEL IROQUOIS ON THE BEACH

298 Main St., Mackinac Island, 906-847-3321; www.iroquoishotel.com

This Victorian hotel was originally built in 1902 as a private residence. Run by the McIntire family since 1954, the hotel offers guest rooms and suites (garden side rooms, suites or deluxe rooms) at a lakefront location on the Straits of Mackinac at the confluence of Lake Michigan and Lake Huron. Enjoy fine dining at the Carriage House or a drink at the Piano Bar.

46 rooms. Closed November-April. Restaurant, bar. Beach. $251-350

★★★ISLAND HOUSE

6966 Main St., Mackinac Island, 906-847-3347, 800-626-6304;
www.theislandhouse.com

The Island House, built in 1852, is Mackinac Island's oldest operating hotel. After a short ferry ride to the island, guests are welcomed to the hotel with the aroma of fresh-baked cookies. The 1852 Grill Room offers delicious dining. The lovely front porch offers a quiet spot to take in the view.

93 rooms. Closed mid-October-mid-May. Complimentary breakfast. Restaurant, bar. $151-250

★★★MISSION POINT RESORT

1 Lakeshore Drive, Mackinac Island, 906-847-3312, 800-833-7711;
www.missionpoint.com

This luxurious getaway looks and feels like a country inn, yet it operates with the amenities and services of a top-notch resort. Guests are greeted at the ferry dock and taken via horse-drawn carriage to the resort. The guest rooms are decorated with nautical, lodge and northern Michigan themes and have garden, forest or Lake Huron views. Activities abound, from an 18-hole putting green to bicycle rentals to hayrides and lawn bowling. In summer, the turn-of-the-20th-century movie theater shows first-run and classic films on Monday evenings. The seven-story-high Tower Museum offers historical information on the resort, the island and the straits and Great Lakes ships. The resort's four restaurants attract diners with casual fare and friendly service.

242 rooms. Closed November-late December. Four restaurants, bar. $251-350

WHERE TO EAT
★★CARRIAGE HOUSE
298 Main St., Mackinac Island, 906-847-3321; www.iroquoishotel.com
American menu. Breakfast, lunch, dinner. Closed mid-October-Memorial Day. Bar. Children's menu. Outdoor seating. $36-85

MACKINAW CITY
See also Cheboygan, Mackinac Island, St. Ignace
The only place in America where one can see the sun rise on one Great Lake (Huron) and set on another (Michigan), Mackinaw City sits in the shadow of the five-mile-long Mackinac Bridge. The French trading post built here became Fort Michilimackinac in about 1715. It was taken over by the British in 1761 and was captured by American Indians two years later. The British reoccupied the fort in 1764. The fort was rebuilt on Mackinac Island between 1780-1781. Today, the area is not only the gateway to the island, but a shopping destination.

WHAT TO SEE
ARNOLD MACKINAC ISLAND FERRY
Arnold Line Docks, Mackinac Island, 906-847-3351, 800-542-8528;
www.arnoldline.com
Large, fast ferries traveling to Mackinac Island.

COLONIAL MICHILIMACKINAC
102 E. Straits Ave., Mackinaw City, 231-436-5563; www.mackinacparks.com
Reconstructed French and British outpost and fur-trading village. Costumed interpreters provide music and military demonstrations, pioneer cooking and crafts, children's programs and reenactments.

MACKINAC BRIDGE
Mackinaw City
This imposing structure has reduced crossing time to the Upper Peninsula over the Straits of Mackinac to 10 minutes. Connecting Michigan's upper and lower peninsulas between St. Ignace and Mackinaw City, the 8,344-foot distance between cable anchorages makes it one of the world's longest suspension bridges. Total length of the steel superstructure is 19,243 feet. Height above water at midspan is 199 feet and clearance for ships is 155 feet.

MACKINAC BRIDGE MUSEUM
231 E. Central Ave., Mackinaw City, 231-436-5534; www.mackinacparks.com
See displays on the construction and maintenance of the bridge. Features original pieces of equipment.
Daily.

MILL CREEK
9001 S. Highway 23, Mackinaw City, 231-436-7301; www.mackinacparks.com
This scenic 625-acre park features working water-powered sawmill from 1790, nature trails, forest demonstration areas, maple sugar shack, active beaver colony and more. Sawmill demonstrations take place beteen mid-

June-Labor Day, Monday-Friday. Stop by the visitor center for information..
Mid-May-mid-October, daily.

SHEPLER'S MACKINAC ISLAND FERRYS
556 E. Central Ave., Mackinaw City, 231-436-5023; www.sheplersferry.com
Early May-early November.

WILDERNESS STATE PARK
903 E. Wilderness Park Drive, Carp Lake, 231-436-5381, 800-447-2757;
www.wildernessstatepark.net
Approximately 8,200 acres. Beaches, water-skiing, fishing, boating, hunting
in season, snowmobiling, cross-country skiing, picnic areas, playgrounds.
Trailside cabins, camping.

SPECIAL EVENTS
COLONIAL MICHILIMACKINAC PAGEANT
Mackinaw City, 231-436-5574; www.mackinawchamber.com
Pageant and reenactment of Chief Pontiac's capture of the frontier fort in
1763. Parade, muzzle-loading contests. Three days during Memorial Day
weekend.

MACKINAC BRIDGE WALK
Mackinaw City, 517-347-7891, 800-434-8642; www.mackinacbridge.org
Michigan's governor leads the walk, which begins in St. Ignace at 7 a.m., on
the north side of the bridge, and ends in Mackinaw City, on the south side.
Buses return you to your starting point.
Labor Day.

MACKINAW MUSH SLED DOG RACE
Mackinaw City, 231-436-5574; www.mackinawchamber.com
The biggest dog sled race in the contiguous United States. First week in
February.

SPRING/FALL BIKE TOURS
Mackinaw City, 231-436-5574
Biannual bicycle rides, ranging from 25 to 100 miles. Mid-June-mid-Sep-
tember.

VESPER CRUISES
Mackinaw City, 906-847-3351, 800-542-8528; www.arnoldline.com/Vesper.htm
Cruises depart on Sunday evenings from the Old State Dock. July-Septem-
ber.

WINTERFEST
Mackinaw City, 231-436-5574; www.mackinawchamber.com
The winter activities at this three-day festival include professional snow
sculpting, ice fishing, sleigh rides and buffalo chip hockey.
Mid-January.

WHERE TO STAY
★CLARION HOTEL BEACHFRONT
905 S. Huron, Mackinaw City, 231-436-5539, 800-413-8826; www.choicehotels.com
115 rooms. Closed November-mid-April. Complimentary full breakfast. Wireless Internet access. Beach. Airport transportation available. $61-150

★COMFORT INN LAKESIDE
611 S. Huron St., Mackinaw City, 231-436-5057, 800-903-2564;
www.comfortinnmackinaw.com
60 rooms. Closed November-April. Complimentary full breakfast. Wireless Internet access. Beach. $61-150

LIDAY INN EXPRESS
364 Louvingny St., Mackinaw City, 231-436-7100, 800-465-4329;
www.expressmackinaw.com
102 rooms. Complimentary continental breakfast. Wireless Internet access. $61-150

★QUALITY INN & SUITES BEACHFRONT
917 S. Huron Ave., Mackinaw City, 231-436-5051, 877-436-5051; www.qualityinn.com
74 rooms. Closed mid-November-mid-April. Complimentary full breakfast. Wireless Internet access. Beach. $61-150

★RAMADA LIMITED WATERFRONT
723 S. Huron Ave., Mackinaw City, 231-436-5055, 888-852-4165; www.ramada.com
42 rooms. Closed November-April. Complimentary continental breakfast. Wireless Internet access. Beach. $61-150

WHERE TO EAT
★★'NEATH THE BIRCHES
14277 Mackinaw Terrace, Mackinaw City, 231-436-5401;
Steak, seafood menu. Dinner. Closed late October-mid-May. Bar. Children's menu. $16-35

★PANCAKE CHEF
327 E. Central Ave., Mackinaw City, 231-436-5578, 888-436-5578;
www.pancakechef.com
American menu. Breakfast, lunch, dinner. $15 and under

MANISTEE
See also Ludington
With Lake Michigan on the west and the Manistee National Forest on the east, this site was once the home of 1,000 Native Americans who called it Manistee, or "spirit of the woods." In the mid-1800s, this community was a thriving lumber town, serving as headquarters for more than 100 companies. When the timber supply was exhausted, the early settlers found other sources of revenue. Manistee is rich in natural resources including salt, oil and natural gas.

WHAT TO SEE
HURON-MANISTEE NATIONAL FOREST
1755 S. Mitchell St., Cadillac, 800-821-6263; www.fs.fed.us
This 520,968-acre forest is the Manistee section of the Huron-Manistee National Forest. The forest includes the Lake Michigan Recreation Area, which contains trails and panoramic views of the sand dunes and offers beaches; fishing in the Pine, Manistee, Little Manistee, White, Little Muskegon and Pere Marquette rivers; boating; hiking, bicycle and vehicle trails; hunting for deer and small game, camping and picnicking. Winter sports include downhill and cross-country skiing, snowmobiling, ice fishing and ice sailing. Daily.

MANISTEE COUNTY HISTORICAL MUSEUM
Russell Memorial Building, 425 River St., Manistee, 231-723-5531
If you enjoy looking at old items, pay a visit to this museum, which includes fixtures and fittings of an 1880 drugstore and early general store. Also includes Victorian period rooms, historical photographs, Civil War and marine collections, plus antique dolls, costumes and housewares.
Tuesday-Saturday 10 a.m.-5 p.m.

OLD WATERWORKS BUILDING
West First Street, Manistee, 231-723-5531
Logging wheels, early lumbering, shipping and railroad exhibits; Victorian parlor, barbershop, shoe shop, kitchen.
Late June-August, Tuesday-Saturday.

RAMSDELL THEATRE AND HALL
101 Maple St., Manistee, 231-723-9948; www.ramsdell-theater.org
Constructed by T.J. Ramsdell, pioneer attorney, this opulent building built in 1903 is home to the Manistee Civic Players, who present professional and community productions throughout the year; also art and museum exhibits.
Tours June-August, Wednesday and Saturday; rest of year, by appointment.

★★★★★ MICHIGAN

85

SPECIAL EVENTS
NATIONAL FOREST FESTIVAL
50 Filer St., Manistee, 231-723-2575; www.manisteecountychamber.com
Boat show; car show; U.S. Forestry Service forest tours; parades, athletic events, raft and canoe races, Venetian boat parade, fireworks. Sponsored by the Chamber of Commerce.
Week of July Fourth.

SHOOT TIME IN MANISTEE
Manistee, 231-723-9006; www.manisteecountychamber.com
Traditional shooting events, costumed participants.
Late June.

VICTORIAN PORT CITY FESTIVAL
Manistee, 231-723-2575; www.manisteecountychamber.com
Includes musical entertainment, street art fair, antique auto exhibit, food,

schooner rides and more.
Early September.

MANISTIQUE
See also Grand Marais, Munising, Newberry, Paradise
Manistique, the county seat of Schoolcraft County, has a bridge in town named "the Siphon Bridge" that is partially supported by the water that flows underneath it. The roadway is approximately four feet below the water level. Fishing for salmon is good in the area.

WHAT TO SEE
FAYETTE HISTORIC STATE PARK
13700 13.25 Lane, Garden, 906-644-2603
Fayette, formerly an industrial town producing charcoal iron (1867-1891), is now a ghost town. Self-guided tour of restored remains; interpretive center (May-October).

INDIAN LAKE
Highway 2, Manistique, 906-341-2355
Approximately 550 acres. Swimming, sand beach, bathhouse, water-skiing, boating; fishing for pike, perch, walleye, bass and bluegill; hiking, picnicking, camping.
Daily.

PALMS BOOK STATE PARK
Highway 455 and Highway 149, Manistique, 906-341-2355; www.michigan.gov/dnr
Approximately 300 acres. Here is Kitch-iti-kipi, the state's largest spring, 200 feet wide, 40 feet deep; 16,000 gallons of water per minute form a stream to Indian Lake. Observation raft for viewing the spring. No camping allowed. Closed in winter.

SPECIAL EVENT
SCHOOLCRAFT COUNTY SNOWMOBILE POKER RUN
Manistique, 906-341-5010; www.schoolcraftcountychamber.com
Late January.

WHERE TO STAY
★BEST WESTERN BREAKERS MOTEL
6770 W. Highway 2, Manistique, 906-341-2410, 888-335-3674; www.bestwestern.com
40 rooms. Private beach opposite. $61-150

MARQUETTE
See also Ishpeming
The largest city in the Upper Peninsula, Marquette is the regional center for retailing, government, medicine and iron ore shipping. Miles of public beaches and picnic areas flank the dock areas on Lake Superior. Rocks rise by the water and bedrock runs just a few feet below the surface. The city is named for the missionary explorer Father Jacques Marquette, who made

canoe trips along the shore here between 1669 and 1671. At the rear flank of the city is sand-plain blueberry country, as well as forests and mountains of granite and iron.

WHAT TO SEE
MARQUETTE COUNTY HISTORICAL MUSEUM
213 N. Front St., Marquette, 906-226-3571; www.marquettecohistory.org
Exhibits of regional historical interest; J.M. Longyear Research Library. Monday-Friday.

MARQUETTE MOUNTAIN SKI AREA
4501 County Road, Marquette, 906-225-1155, 800-944-7669;
www.marquettemountain.com
Three double chairlifts, rope tow; patrol, school, rentals, snowmaking, night skiing, weekly NASTAR; cafeteria, bar, nursery. The longest run is 1¼ miles with a vertical drop of 600 feet.
Late November-April, daily 9:30 a.m.-5 p.m. Cross-country trails (three miles) nearby.

MOUNT MARQUETTE SCENIC OUTLOOK AREA
Highway 41, Marquette
Provides a lovely view.
May-mid-October, daily.

NORTHERN MICHIGAN UNIVERSITY
140 Presque Isle Ave., Marquette, 906-227-1700, 800-682-9797; www.nmu.edu
The 300-acre campus includes the Superior Dome, the world's largest wooden dome, which spans 5.1 acres, Lee Hall Gallery and a five-acre technology and applied sciences center. Olson Library has Tyler Collection on Early American literature. The school has been designated an Olympic Education Center.

PRESQUE ISLE PARK
Lakeshore Boulevard, Marquette, 906-228-0460
Picnic facilities (four picnic sites for the disabled), swimming. A bog walk in Presque Isle Park features 4,000-foot trail with plank walkways and observation decks; self-guided with interpretive sign boards at 10 conservation points.
May-October, daily; rest of year, open only for winter sports.

SUGAR LOAF MOUNTAIN
County 550, Marquette
A 3,200-foot trail leads to the summit for a panoramic view of the Lake Superior coastline and forestland.

UPPER HARBOR ORE DOCK
Marquette
Several million tons of ore are shipped annually from this site. The loading of ore freighters is a fascinating sight to watch.

UPPER PENINSULA CHILDREN'S MUSEUM

123 W. Baraga Ave., Marquette, 906-226-3911, 888-590-8726; www.upcmkids.org

All exhibits are products of kids' imaginations; regional youth planned their conceptual development.

Admission: adults $5, children $5, Infants free, family rate $25.00.

Monday-Wednesday 10 a.m.-6 p.m., Thursday 10 a.m.-7:30 p.m., Friday 10 a.m.-8 p.m., Saturday 10 a.m.-6 p.m., Sunday noon-5 p.m.

SPECIAL EVENTS
ART ON THE ROCKS

Presque Isle Park, Lakeshore Boulevard, Marquette, 906-225-1952;
www.artontherocks.org

Nationwide art display and sale.

Last full weekend in July.

HIAWATHA MUSIC FESTIVAL

Tourist Park, Marquette, 906-226-8575; www.hiawathamusic.org

Bluegrass, traditional music festival.

Third weekend in July.

INTERNATIONAL FOOD FESTIVAL

Ellwood Mattson Lower Harbor Park, Marquette, 906-249-1595

Ethnic foods, crafts, music.

July Fourth weekend.

SEAFOOD FESTIVAL

Ellwood Mattson Lower Harbor Park, Marquette, 906-226-6591; www.marquette.org

Seafood is served at the many booths of this festival.

Weekend before labor day.

UP 200 DOG SLED RACE

Marquette, 800-544-4321

Dog sled race; features food, games, entertainment, dog-sledding exhibitions.

Mid-late February.

MARSHALL

See also Battle Creek, Coldwater

Marshall was at one time slated to be Michigan's capital—a grand governor's mansion was built, land was set aside for the capitol and wealthy and influential people swarmed into the town. In 1847, Marshall lost its capital bid to Lansing. Today, many of the elaborate houses and buildings of the period remain, and more than 30 historical markers dot the city's streets.

WHAT TO SEE
AMERICAN MUSEUM OF MAGIC

107 E. Michigan Ave., Marshall, 269-781-7570; www.americanmuseumofmagic.org

Display of vintage magical equipment, rare posters, photographs and personal effects of well-known magicians.

By appointment.

HONOLULU HOUSE MUSEUM

107 N. Kalamazoo Ave., Marshall, 269-781-8544, 800-877-5163;
www.marshallhistoricalsociety.org

This exotic structure, which blends traditional Italianate architecture with tropical motifs of island plantation houses, was built by the first U.S. Consul to the Sandwich Islands (now Hawaii) in 1860. The museum includes period furnishings and artifacts. It also serves as the headquarters of the Marshall Historical Society, which provides free self-guided walking tour.

May-September, daily noon-5 p.m.; rest of year, weekends

SPECIAL EVENTS
HISTORIC HOME TOUR

Marshall, 800-877-5163; www.marshallmich.com

Informal tours of nine 19th-century homes, including Honolulu House, Governor's Mansion and Capitol Hill School.

First weekend after Labor Day.

WELCOME TO MY GARDEN TOUR

Marshall, 269-781-5434; www.marshallmich.com

Tour of Marshall's most distinctive gardens.

Second weekend in July.

WHERE TO EAT
★CORNWELL'S TURKEYVILLE

18935 15 1/2 Mile Road, Marshall, 269-781-4293, 800-228-4315; www.turkeyville.com

American menu. Lunch, dinner. Children's menu. Casual attire. Outdoor seating. $16-35

★★SCHULER'S RESTAURANT & PUB

115 S. Eagle St., Marshall, 269-781-0600, 877-724-8537; www.schulersrestaurant.com

American menu. Lunch, dinner, Sunday brunch. Bar. Children's menu. Reservations recommended. Outdoor seating. $36-85

MENOMINEE

See also Marinette

Because of water transportation and water power, many manufacturing industries are located in Menominee. Green Bay and the Menominee River form two sides of the triangular city. Across the river is the sister city of Marinette, Wisconsin. Established as a fur-trading post, and later a lumbering center, Menominee County is the largest dairy producer in the state of Michigan. Menominee is an American Indian word for "wild rice," which once grew profusely on the riverbanks.

WHAT TO SEE
FIRST STREET HISTORIC DISTRICT

10th Ave., Menominee

Variety of specialty shops located in a setting of restored 19th-century buildings. Marina, parks, restaurants, galleries.

HENES PARK
Henes Park Drive and Third Street, Menominee, 906-863-2656;
www.cityofmenominee.org
Small zoo with deer yards, nature trails, bathing beach and picnic area.
Memorial Day-mid October, daily.

J.W. WELLS STATE PARK
N7670 Highway 35, Cedar River, 906-863-9747; www.michigan.gov/dnr
Approximately 700 acres, including two miles along Green Bay and 1,400
feet along Big Cedar River. Swimming, bathhouse, water-skiing, fishing,
boating (ramp); hunting, snowmobiling, cross-country skiing, picnicking,
playground, camping, cabins and shelters.

MENOMINEE MARINA
Doyle Drive, Menominee, 906-863-8498; www.menomineemarina.com
One of the best small-craft anchorages on the Great Lakes. Swimming beach,
lifeguard.
May-October, daily.

STEPHENSON ISLAND
Menominee
Reached by bridge that also carries traffic between the sister cities on High-
way 41. On island are picnic areas and a historical museum.

MIDLAND
See also Bay City, Mount Pleasant, Saginaw
Midland owed its prosperity to the lumber industry until Herbert Henry Dow
founded the Dow Chemical Company in 1897. Today, Dow still dominates
Midland's attractions, from the Dow Museum to Dow Gardens. The city also
boasts beautiful parks and trails.

WHAT TO SEE
ARCHITECTURAL TOUR
315 Post St., Midland, 989-839-2744; www.abdow.org
Self-guided driving tour of buildings designed by Alden B. Dow, son of Herbert H. Dow. The younger Dow studied under Frank Lloyd Wright at Taliesin.
He designed more than 45 buildings in Midland, including the architect's
house and studio, churches, Stein House (his Taliesin apprentice project) and
the Whitman House, for which he won the 1937 Grand Prix for residential architecture. Many buildings are privately owned and not open to the public.

CHIPPEWA NATURE CENTER
400 S. Badour Road, Midland, 989-631-0830; www.chippewanaturecenter.com
On more than 1,000 acres; 14 miles of marked and mowed trails; wildflower
walkway and pond boardwalk; Homestead Farm; reconstructed 1870s log
cabin, barn, sugarhouse, one-room schoolhouse; visitor center; museum depicting evolutionary natural history of the Saginaw Valley; auditorium, library; seasonal programs.
Daily.

DOW GARDENS

1809 Eastman Ave., Midland, 989-631-2677, 800-362-4874; www.dowgardens.org

These gardens, originally the grounds of the residence of Herbert H. Dow, founder of the Dow Chemical Company (which is based in Midland), include 110 acres of trees, flowers, streams and waterfalls, as well as a greenhouse and conservatory.

Tours by appointment. Daily 9 a.m.-dusk.

MIDLAND CENTER FOR THE ARTS

1801 W. St. Andrews, Midland, 989-631-5930; www.mcfta.org

This center houses the Alden B. Dow Museum of Science and Art, which features temporary exhibits and includes the Hall of Ideas, a permanent interactive exhibit. It also hosts concerts and plays. The Dow architectural tour begins here.

Tuesday-Saturday 10 a.m.-6 p.m., Sunday noon-6 p.m.

SPECIAL EVENTS

FALL FESTIVAL

Chippewa Nature Center, 400 S. Badour Road, Midland, 989-631-0830; www.chippewanaturecenter.org

Second weekend in October.

MAPLE SYRUP FESTIVAL

Chippewa Nature Center, 400 S. Badour Road, Midland, 989-631-0830; www.chippewanaturecenter.org

Third Saturday in March.

MATRIX: MIDLAND FESTIVAL

Midland Center for the Arts, 1801 West St. Andrews Road, Midland, 989-631-7980; www.mcfta.org

Celebration of the arts, sciences, humanities; classical and popular music, theater, dance; lectures by noted professionals.

Late June-September.

MICHIGAN ANTIQUE FESTIVALS

Midland Michigan Fairgrounds, 2156 N. Rudy Court, Midland, 989-687-9001; www.miantiquefestival.com

Over 1,000 vendors inside and outside.

Early June, late July, late September.

WHERE TO STAY

★★BEST WESTERN VALLEY PLAZA RESORT

5221 Bay City Road, Midland, 989-496-2700, 800-825-2700; www.valleyplazaresort.com

236 rooms. Complimentary breakfast. Restaurant, bar. Pets accepted. $61-150

★★HOLIDAY INN

1500 W. Wackerly St., Midland, 989-631-4220, 800-465-4329; www.holiday-inn.com

235 rooms. Complimentary breakfast. Restaurant, bar. Pets accepted. $61-150

MONROE

See also Detroit

Originally called Frenchtown because of the many French families that settled here, this city on Lake Erie was renamed in 1817 in honor of President James Monroe. The river that flows through the center of the city was named the River Aux Raisin because of the many grapes growing in the area. At one time, Monroe was briefly the home of General George Armstrong Custer of Little Big Horn fame.

WHAT TO SEE

CABELA'S

110 Cabela Blvd. E., Dundee, 734-529-4700, 800-581-4420; www.cabelas.com

Cabela's offers the world's largest hunting, fishing and outdoor store, attracting more than six million visitors per year. Cabela's is more than just a store; the 225,000-square-foot center offers museum-quality mounted animals, aquarium and gun collections; a shooting range; two hotels; three restaurants, including a café that features wild game; a beef jerky outlet.

Monday-Saturday 8 a.m.-9 p.m., Sunday 10 a.m.-7 p.m.

MONROE COUNTY HISTORICAL MUSEUM

126 S. Monroe St., Monroe, 734-243-7137; www.co.monroe.mi.us

Exhibits of General George Custer, Woodland Native Americans pioneers, War of 1812; trading post, country store museum.

Summer, daily; rest of year, Wednesday-Sunday.

RIVER RAISIN BATTLEFIELD VISITOR CENTER

1402 Elm Ave., Monroe, 734-243-7136

Interprets fierce War of 1812 battle of River Raisin. Nearly 1,000 U.S. soldiers from Kentucky clashed with British, Native American and Canadian forces on this site in January of 1813. Only 33 Americans escaped death or capture. Exhibits of weapons and uniforms, dioramas; fiber optic audiovisual map program.

Memorial Day-Labor Day, daily; rest of year, weekends.

STERLING STATE PARK

2800 State Park Road, Monroe, 734-289-2715; www.michigan.gov/dnr

On 1,001 acres, this park offers swimming, water-skiing, fishing, boating (ramp); hiking, picnicking, a playground, concessions and camping.

YELLOWSTONE LAKE STATE PARK

8495 Lake Road, Blanchardville, 608-523-4427, 800-947-8757;
www.dnr.wi.gov/org/land/parks

This 968-acre park on Yellowstone Lake offers swimming, water-skiing, fishing, boating, hiking, cross-country skiing, snowmobiling, picnicking, playground, concessions and camping.

Daily.

MONROE COUNTY FAIR

Monroe County Fairgrounds, 3775 S. Custer Road, Monroe, 734-241-5775
Rides, concessions, merchant buildings.
Late July-early August.

MOUNT CLEMENS
See also Detroit, Troy, Pontiac
On the banks of the Clinton River, Mount Clemens has a central shopping district marked by restaurants, shops and a large fountain.

WHAT TO SEE
ART CENTER
125 Macomb Place, Mount Clemens, 586-469-8666; www.theartcenter.org
Exhibits and classes, sponsors tours. Holiday Fair (December). Tuesday-Thursday 10 a.m.-5 p.m., Friday 10 a.m.-6 p.m., Saturday 10 a.m.-5 p.m., Sunday noon-4 p.m. Closed Monday.

CROCKER HOUSE
15 Union St., Mount Clemens, 586-465-2488; www.crockerhousemuseum.com
This Italianate building built in 1869, home of the Macomb County Historical Society, was originally owned by the first two mayors of Mount Clemens. Period rooms. March-December, Tuesday-Thursday; also first Sunday of the month.

METRO BEACH METROPARK
31300 Metropolitan Parkway, Mount Clemens, 586-463-4581, 800-234-6534;
www.metroparks.com
Park features ¾-mile beach (late May-September, daily), pool (Memorial Day-Labor Day, daily; fee), bathhouse, boating, marinas, ramps, launch, dock (fee); 18-hole par-three golf course, miniature golf, shuffleboard, tennis, group rental activity center, playgrounds. Picnicking, concessions. Nature center.
Free admission Tuesday. Daily.

MOUNT PLEASANT
See also Alma, Clare, Midland
Home of the aptly named Central Michigan University, Mount Pleasant sits smack in the middle of the state. The city's Soaring Eagle Casino is a major tourist attraction, and Mount Pleasant is also rich in championship golf courses, including the Pohl Cat and Riverwood Golf Club.

WHAT TO SEE
CENTER FOR CULTURAL & NATURAL HISTORY
Mount Pleasant, Rowe Hall
Includes 45 exhibits and dioramas on anthropology, history and natural science. Daily.

CENTRAL MICHIGAN UNIVERSITY

204 W. Hall, Mount Pleasant, 989-774-4000; www.cmich.edu
Established 1892, the university is home to 16,300 students.

CLARKE HISTORICAL LIBRARY

409 Park Library, Mount Pleasant, 989-774-3352; www.clarke.cmich.edu
Rare books, manuscripts, historical documents of the Northwest Territory
and more are housed at this library. There is also a children's library and
changing exhibits.
School year, Monday-Friday.

SOARING EAGLE CASINO

6800 Soaring Eagle Blvd., Mount Pleasant, 989-775-7777, 888-732-4537;
www.soaringeaglecasino.com
This popular casino includes a 2,500-seat Bingo Hall, slot machines, blackjack, craps and roulette. There is also a spa onsite.
Daily.

SPECIAL EVENTS
MAPLE SYRUP FESTIVAL

Shepherd, 989-828-6486; www.shepherdmaplesyrupfestival.org
Pancake and sausage meals, maple syrup and candy sales, arts and crafts, and
a parade are among the features of this festival.
Last weekend in April.

ZONTA APPLE FEST

McIntosh Orchards, Mount Pleasant, 989-772-0114
Find fresh apple cider, home-baked apple desserts, arts and crafts, live music
and children's games at this festival.
First weekend in October.

WHERE TO STAY
★★★SOARING EAGLE CASINO & RESORT

6800 Soaring Eagle Blvd., Mount Pleasant, 989-775-7777, 877-232-4532;
www.soaringeaglecasino.com
This popular resort and casino has a Native American theme. Guest rooms
have king-sized beds and patios or balconies. Some deluxe rooms offer in-
room Jacuzzi tubs. The property has multiple dining and entertainment options onsite.
512 rooms. Three restaurants, bar. Spa. Casino. $61-150

WHERE TO EAT
★★★THE EMBERS

1217 S. Mission St., Mount Pleasant, 989-773-5007; www.theembersdine.com
The signature one-pound pork chop is the main attraction at this restaurant
in Mount Pleasant. Locals and visitors alike enjoy filling up at the delicious
smorgasbord held here the first and third Thursday of each month. Tease, a
more casual dining option, is also available within the building.
American menu. Dinner. Bar. Children's menu. Casual attire. $36-85

★★★WATER LILY

6800 Soaring Eagle Blvd., Mount Pleasant, 989-775-5496, 888-232-4532;
www.soaringeaglecasino.com

Located inside of the Soaring Eagle Casino & Resort, Water Lily is an elegant dining destination that offers a menu of regional American cuisine for both breakfast and dinner. A number of egg dishes are featured at breakfast, including the market fresh omelet, with ham, sausage, mushrooms, bacon, spinach, cheddar cheese, tomatoes and onions. Seafood dominates the menu at dinner, with choices such as seafood pasta, yellowfin tuna niçoise and crab Randolph, but a few beef and chicken entrées are also available.
American menu. Dinner. Bar. Casual attire. Valet parking. $36-85

MUNISING

See also Gladstone, Manistique, Marquette, Newberry
Colorful sandstone formations, waterfalls, sand dunes, agate beaches, hiking trails and outdoor recreational facilities are part of the Hiawatha National Forest and the Pictured Rocks National Lakeshore, which stretches eastward from Munising along 42 miles of the south shore of Lake Superior. Camping areas are plentiful in the Hiawatha National Forest and on Lake Superior.

WHAT TO SEE
PICTURED ROCKS BOAT CRUISE

City Pier, 355 Elm Ave., Munising, 906-387-2379; www.picturedrocks.com
A 37-mile cruise on the Miners Castle, Pictured Rocks, Grand Island or Miss Superior. June-early October, daily.

SPECIAL EVENT
PICTURED ROCKS ROAD RACE

Alger Centennial Arena, Varnum Street, Munising, 906-387-2379;
www.algercounty.com/roadrace
Course runs over wooded, hilly trails, roads passing waterfalls, streams and Lake Superior.
Late June.

WHERE TO EAT
★SYDNEY'S

Highway 28 E., Munising, 906-387-4067; www.sydneysrestaurant.com
American menu. Breakfast, lunch, dinner, Sunday brunch. Bar. $15 and under

MUSKEGON

Muskegon County is located in the western part of the lower peninsula, along 26 miles of Lake Michigan shoreline. Muskegon Channel, which runs from Lake Michigan through the sand dunes to Muskegon Lake, opens the harbor to world trade. It has 80 miles of waterfront, including 10 miles of public waterfront and 3,000 acres of public parks—an acre for every 50 people in the county. The downtown area has been enclosed as a climate-controlled shopping and business mall.

Muskegon Lake, largest of 40 lakes in Muskegon County, is the focal point of the area comprised of Muskegon, Muskegon Heights, North Muskegon,

Norton Shores, Roosevelt Park and surrounding townships. Fishing for coho, Chinook salmon and other fish is good here. Ice fishing is popular in the winter months. The first freshwater reef in North America, a natural fish attractant, is located in Lake Michigan, off Pere Marquette Park.

WHAT TO SEE
GILLETTE VISITOR CENTER
6585 Lake Harbor Road, Muskegon, 231-798-3573; www.michigan.gov/dnr
This visitors center includes a dune interpretive center. See multi-image slide presentations on the Great Lakes and dune habitats; also includes a dune ecology exhibit, hands-on classroom, seasonal animal exhibits and more. Daily.

HACKLEY AND HUME HISTORIC SITE
West Webster and Sixth streets, Muskegon, 231-722-7578;
www.muskegonmuseum.org
These two restored Queen Anne/Victorian mansions were built by two wealthy lumbermen between 1888 and 1889.
Tours mid-May-September, Wednesday, Saturday-Sunday; also some weekends in December.

MICHIGAN'S ADVENTURE AMUSEMENT PARK
4750 Whitehall Road, Muskegon, 231-766-3377; www.miadventure.com
More than 24 amusement rides, including the Wolverine Wildcat, the largest wooden roller coaster in the state. Corkscrew roller coaster, Mammoth River water slide, log flume; games, arcade. There is also a water park with wave pool, lazy river, body flumes, tube slides and family play areas.
Mid-May-early September, daily.

MUSKEGON MUSEUM OF ART
296 W. Webster Ave., Muskegon, 231-720-2570; www.muskegonartmuseum.org
Permanent collection includes American and European paintings, an extensive print collection, Tiffany and contemporary glass, paintings by Hopper, Inness, Whistler, Homer, Wyeth and others.
Tuesday-Wednesday, Friday-Saturday 10 a.m.-4:30 p.m., Thursday 10 a.m.-8 p.m., Sunday noon-4:30 p.m.

MUSKEGON STATE PARK
3560 Memorial Drive, Muskegon, 231-744-3480, 800-447-2757;
www.muskegonstatepark.com
A 1,165-acre area with a replica of a frontier blockhouse on one of the park's highest sand dunes. The park features swimming, beaches, bathhouse, water skiing, fishing, boating (ramp, launch), as well as 12 miles of hiking trails, cross-country skiing, skating rink, a luge run, picnicking, concession, playground and camping.

MUSKEGON TROLLEY COMPANY
Muskegon, 231-724-6420; www.matsbus.com
Two routes cover the north side, south side and downtown; each trolley stops

at 11 locations, including Hackley and Hume Historic Site, USS Silversides, Muskegon State Park.

Memorial Day-Labor Day, daily; no trips during special events.

P.J. HOFFMASTER STATE PARK

6585 Lake Harbor Road, Muskegon, 231-798-3711, 800-447-2757;

www.michigan.gov/dnr

The more than 1,000 acres here include forest-covered dunes along 2½ miles of Lake Michigan shoreline. You will find a sandy beach and 10 miles of trails. Climb to the top of the dunes. There is also cross-country skiing (3 miles of trails) in winter. The park has picnicking, concession and camping facilities. Visitor center has displays and exhibits on dune formation.

Daily.

USS SILVERSIDES AND MARITIME MUSEUM

1346 Bluff St., Muskegon, 231-755-1230; www.silversides.org

Famous World War II submarine that served with Pacific Fleet along Japan's coasts. The Silversides's outstanding aggressive war record includes sinking 23 enemy ships, embarking on special mine laying and reconnaissance missions, and rescuing two American aviators downed in air strikes over Japan. Guided tours. June-August: daily; April-May and September-October: Saturday-Sunday.

SPECIAL EVENTS

BLUEBERRY FESTIVAL

Fruitland Township Park, 4545 Nestrom Road, Muskegon, 231-766-3208;

www.fruitlandtwp.org

Late July.

MUSKEGON AIR FAIR

99 Sinclair Drive, Muskegon, 231-798-4596; www.muskegonairport.com

More than 100 military and civilian aircraft; displays.

Mid-July.

MUSKEGON SHORELINE SPECTACULAR

Pere Marquette Park, 1601 Beach St., Muskegon, 231-737-5791

Concerts, sporting events, arts and crafts, hot air balloon rides.

Labor Day weekend.

MUSKEGON SUMMER CELEBRATION

587 W. Western Ave., Muskegon, 231-722-6520; www.summercelebration.com

Family music and entertainment parade, midway, food and beer tents, Venetian boat parade.

Late June to early July.

WHERE TO STAY

★★HOLIDAY INN

939 Third St., Muskegon, 231-722-0100, 800-846-5253; www.holiday-inn.com

200 rooms. Wireless Internet access. Restaurant, bar. $61-150

WHERE TO EAT
★RAFFERTY'S DOCKSIDE
601 Terrace Point Blvd., Muskegon, 231-722-4461; www.shorelineinn.com
American menu. Lunch, dinner, Sunday brunch. Bar. Children's menu. Casual attire. Reservations recommended. Outdoor seating. $16-35

★★TONY'S BISTRO
211 S. Seaway Drive, Muskegon, 231-739-7196; www.tonysbistro.net
Steak menu. Lunch, dinner. Closed Sunday. Bar. Children's menu. $16-35

NEW BUFFALO
See also Niles, St. Joseph
Because of its proximity to large Midwestern cities, New Buffalo and the Harbor County area is a popular resort community for year-round vacationers. Sandy Lake Michigan beaches beckon, and numerous shops, galleries and antiques stores make this area a vacationer's paradise.

WHAT TO SEE
RED ARROW HIGHWAY
Interstate 94 and Union Pier, New Buffalo
Many antiques stores, inns, galleries, shops and restaurants can be found along this road that travels from Union Pier to Sawyer, between Lake Michigan and the Interstate.

WARREN DUNES STATE PARK
12032 Red Arrow Highway, Sawyer, 269-426-4013; www.michigan.gov/dnr
Occupying 1,499 acres of land on the shores of Lake Michigan, this park offers swimming, hiking, picnicking, playground, concession, camping and cabins. There are 200 acres of virgin forest in Warren Woods.
Daily.

NEWBERRY
See also Paradise, Soo Junction
Located in the middle of the eastern Upper Peninsula, Newberry is centrally located to all of the U.P.'s attractions: Lake Superior, Tahquamenon Falls, Paradise and Whitefish Bay, Pictured Rocks and the Hiawatha National Forest. Enjoy hunting in the fall, a range of sports in winter and fishing and blueberry picking in summer.

WHAT TO SEE
LUCE COUNTY HISTORICAL MUSEUM
411 W. Harrie St., Newberry, 906-293-5946; www.exploringthenorth.com
This restored Queen Anne structure, completed in 1894, has stone on the lower portion that is Marquette or Jacobsville sandstone, some of the oldest rock in the country. Originally a sheriff's residence and jail, it was saved from razing and is now a museum. The stateroom fireplace is original; many of the rooms have been refurbished to hold records, books and other artifacts; jail cells are still intact.
Tuesday-Thursday 2-4 p.m.

SENEY NATIONAL WILDLIFE REFUGE

Highway 77, Seney, 906-586-9851; www.fws.gov/midwest/seney

On 95,455 acres, this wildlife refuge is home to Canada geese, bald eagles, sandhill cranes, loons, deer, beaver, otter and several species of ducks. Visitor center has exhibits, films and information on wildlife observation. Fishing; picnicking, limited hunting. Pets on leash only.
Mid-May-September, daily.

SPECIAL EVENTS
LUMBERJACK DAYS

Tahquamenon Logging Museum, Highway 123, Newberry, 800-831-7292

Wood carvings, traditional music, logging contests, lumberjack breakfast.
Weekend in late August.

MICHIGAN FIDDLERS' JAMBOREE

7964 M-123, Newberry, 906-293-8711; www.michiganfiddlers.com

Music, dancing and concessions are featured at this jamboree presented by the original Michigan Fiddler's Association.
Weekend in late September.

WHERE TO STAY
★BEST WESTERN NEWBERRY

12956 Highway 28, Newberry, 906-293-4000, 800-293-3297; www.bestwestern.com

66 rooms. Complimentary continental breakfast. $61-150

★COMFORT INN

13954 Highway 28, Newberry, 906-293-3218, 800-228-5150; www.comfortinn.com

54 rooms. Complimentary continental breakfast. $61-150

NILES

See also New Buffalo, St. Joseph

Niles calls itself the "city of four flags" because the banners of France, England, Spain and the United States each have flown over the area. Montgomery Ward and the Dodge brothers are native sons of the town.

WHAT TO SEE
FERNWOOD BOTANIC GARDENS

13988 Range Line Road, Niles, 269-695-6491; www.fernwoodbotanical.org

The scenic grounds at this botanical garden comprise more than 100 acres of woodland trails, spring-fed ponds, a tall grass prairie and nearly 20 gardens, including rock and fern gardens and a lovely Japanese garden. A nature center features interesting hands-on educational exhibits and panoramic bird observation windows.
Tuesday-Sunday.

FORT ST. JOSEPH MUSEUM

508 E. Main St., Niles, 269-683-4702; www.ci.niles.mi.us

This museum contains one of the top five Sioux art collections in the nation,

including autobiographical pictographs by Sitting Bull and Rain-In-The-Face. Other collections are Fort St. Joseph and Potawatomi artifacts, local history memorabilia.
Wednesday-Friday 10 a.m.-4 p.m., Saturday 10 a.m.-3 p.m.

SPECIAL EVENTS
FOUR FLAGS AREA APPLE FESTIVAL
1740 Lake St., Niles, 269-683-8870; www.fourflagsapplefestival.org
This four-day festival offers carnival rides, a parade, arts and crafts and food vendors.
Fourth week in September.

RIVERFEST
Riverfront Park, Niles, 269-684-5766; www.nilesriverfest.net
Crafts, games, food, entertainment, raft race.
Early August.

NORTHVILLE
See also Farmington, Plymouth
Northville is located on the western outskirts of the Detroit metro area. Incorporated as a village in 1867 and as a city in 1955, the surrounding area is known for undulating hills and its lovely rural surroundings. Victorian architecture is the hallmark of the town, and many of the homes in its historic district were built before the 1930s. A thriving arts community and a quaint downtown are big draws.

WHAT TO SEE
ART HOUSE
215 W. Cady, Northville, 248-344-0497; www.ci.northville.mi.us
Local artists' work on display, plus various other arts events.

SPECIAL EVENT
NORTHVILLE DOWNS
301 S. Center St., Northville, 248-349-1000; www.northvilledowns.com
Harness racing. Children over 12 years only.
January and October-March, Monday-Tuesday, Thursday, Saturday.

WHERE TO EAT
★★LITTLE ITALY RISTORANTE
227 Hutton St., Northville, 248-348-0575; www.littleitalynorthville.com
Italian menu. Lunch, dinner. Bar. Children's menu. Business casual attire. Reservations recommended. Valet parking. Outdoor seating. $36-85

★★ROCKY'S OF NORTHVILLE
41122 W. Seven Mile Road, Northville, 248-349-4434; www.rockysnorthville.com
American menu. Lunch, dinner. Closed holidays. Bar. Children's menu. $16-35

ONTONAGON

See also Houghton, Ironwood

Ontonagon is a beautiful, sleepy town on the shores of Lake Superior that is unspoiled by tourists. Its quaint drawbridge stops traffic every now and then, but the pace of this town is so slow, you'll hardly notice. Nearby Porcupine Mountains and Lake of the Clouds offer rugged hiking trails that reward you with breathtaking mountaintop views.

WHAT TO SEE

PORCUPINE MOUNTAINS WILDERNESS STATE PARK

412 S. Boundry Road, Ontonagon, 906-885-5275; www.michigan.gov/dnr

This 63,000-acre forested, mountainous semiwilderness area harbors otters, bears, coyotes, bald eagles and many other species. There are many streams and lakes with fishing for bass, perch and trout; boating (launch); hunting in season for grouse, deer and bear; downhill and cross-country skiing, snowmobiling; hiking trails with overnight rustic cabins (reservations available) and shelters; scenic overlooks, waterfalls, abandoned mine sites. Visitor center. Picnicking, playground, camping. Daily.

OSCODA

See also Tawas City

This is a resort community where the Au Sable River empties into Lake Huron. Formerly a heavily populated logging town, Oscoda is now an outdoor lover's paradise, with trout and salmon fishing, canoeing and hunting.

WHAT TO SEE

HURON-MANISTEE NATIONAL FOREST

1755 S. Mitchell St., Cadillac, 231-775-2421; www.fs.fed.us

This 427,000-acre forest is the Huron section of the Huron-Manistee National Forest. A major attraction of the forest is the Lumberman's Monument overlooking the Au Sable River. A three-figure bronze memorial depicting a timber cruiser, sawyer and river driver commemorates the loggers who cut the timber in Michigan The visitor center at the monument offers interpretations of this colorful era (Memorial Day-Labor Day).

Scenic drives; beaches, swimming, streams, lakes, ishing, canoe trips; hunting for deer and small game, camping, picnicking, winter sports areas.

PADDLE-WHEELER BOAT TRIPS

Au Sable River Queen, Foote Dam, 1775 W. River Road, Oscoda, 989-739-7351;
www.ausableriverqueen.net/main.html

This paddle-wheeler makes 19-mile (two-hour) round-trips on Au Sable River. Memorial Day-mid-October, daily; schedule may vary. Advanced reservations are recommended.

SPECIAL EVENTS

AU SABLE RIVER INTERNATIONAL CANOE MARATHON

4440 Highway 23 N., Oscoda, 989-739-7322; www.oscodachamber.com

This 120-mile marathon begins in Grayling and ends in Oscoda. Last weekend in July.

PAUL BUNYAN DAYS
Oscoda, 989-739-7322
Lumberjack show, chainsaw carving competition, children's events.
Third weekend in September.

OWOSSO
See also Flint, Lansing
Owosso's most famous sons were James Oliver Curwood, author of many wildlife novels about the Canadian wilderness, and Thomas E. Dewey, governor of New York and twice the Republican presidential nominee. The city, rising on the banks of the Shiawassee River, is home to five parks and many industries.

WHAT TO SEE
CURWOOD CASTLE
224 Curwood Castle Drive, Owosso, 517-723-8844;
www.dupontcastle.com/castles/curwood.htm
This replica of a Norman castle, thought to be architecturally unique in the state, was used as a studio by James Oliver Curwood, author and conservationist. It is maintained as a museum with Curwood memorabilia and local artifacts displayed.
Tuesday-Sunday 1-5 p.m.

SPECIAL EVENTS
CURWOOD FESTIVAL
308 W. Main St., Owosso, 989-723-2161; www.curwoodfestival.com
River raft, bed and canoe races, juried art show, pioneer displays and demonstrations, fun run, parade, entertainment.
First full weekend in June.

SHIAWASSEE COUNTY FAIR
County Fairgrounds, 2900 E. Hibbard Road, Corunna, 989-743-3611;
www.shiawasseecountyfair.com
Agricultural and home economics exhibits, rides. First week in August.

PARADISE
See also Sault Ste. Marie
Although residents number only a few hundred, Paradise offers plenty of delights for travelers. With sandy beaches, fishing, blueberries, gorgeous fall colors and a variety of winter sporting opportunities, Paradise has something for everyone. It is probably best known for its two natural assets: Tahquamenon Falls and Whitefish Bay, the bay legendary freighter the Edmund Fitzgerald was attempting to reach before disappearing just 15 miles away.

WHAT TO SEE
GREAT LAKES SHIPWRECK MUSEUM AND WHITEFISH POINT LIGHT STATION
18335 N. Whitefish Point Road, Paradise, 888-492-3747; www.shipwreckmuseum.com
Near Whitefish Bay, where the Edmund Fitzgerald and more than 300 other

ships sank in the unforgiving waters of Lake Superior, the Great Lakes Shipwreck Museum pays tribute to these fallen ships. To get the most out of your experience, stay overnight at the light station, where you're asked to take on a few simple tasks to keep the lighthouse in operation.

TAHQUAMENON FALLS STATE PARK
41382 W. Highway 123, Paradise, 906-492-3415; www.michigan.gov/dnr
Approximately 35,000 acres of scenic wilderness includes Upper and Lower Falls. Swimming, fishing, boating (rentals, launch); snowmobiling, cross-country skiing, hunting in season, playground, picnicking, concession; camping near rapids and near shore of Whitefish Bay, Lake Superior.

PAW PAW
See also Kalamazoo
The center of an important grape-growing area, this town takes its name from the Paw Paw River, so designated by Native Americans for the papaw trees that grew along its banks.

WHAT TO SEE
MAPLE LAKE
Paw Paw
Created in 1908 when river waters were dammed for electric power. Boating and swimming on Maple Island; picnicking.

ST. JULIAN WINE COMPANY
716 S. Kalamazoo St., Paw Paw, 269-657-5568; www.stjulian.com
The oldest and largest winery in the state offers wine tasting and tours, which begin every half hour.
Monday-Saturday 9 a.m.-6 p.m., Sunday noon-5 p.m.

WARNER VINEYARDS
706 S. Kalamazoo St., Paw Paw, 269-657-3165, 800-756-5357; www.warnerwines.com
Produces wine and juices. Tours and tasting.
Daily.

PELLSTON
See also Mackinaw City, Petoskey
As you enter and leave Pellston, a sign advertises this city as the coldest spot in North America. But its real claim to fame is a small international airport that links northern Michigan to Canada and the rest of the United States. With Mackinaw City just 15 miles north, flying into Pellston is the fastest way to get to the Straits of Mackinac and Mackinac Island.

WHERE TO STAY
★THE CROOKED RIVER LODGE
6845 Highway 31 N., Alanson, 231-548-5000, 866-548-0700;
www.crookedriverlodge.com
40 rooms. Indoor spa. $61-150

PENTWATER

See also Mackinaw City, Petoskey

Located on Lake Michigan, Pentwater is a quiet town that retains much of its Victorian charm. Look for unique shops in downtown Pentwater; among the most popular are stores that specialize in antiques from the town's logging heyday around 1900.

WHERE TO EAT
★HISTORIC NICKERSON INN
262 W. Lowell St., Pentwater, 231-869-6731; www.nickersoninn.com
International menu. Dinner. Closed Sunday-Thursday in April-May; also January-March. Children's menu. Casual attire. Outdoor seating. $16-35

PETOSKEY

See also Boyne City, Charlevoix, Harbor Springs, Indian River

A popular resort nestled in a hillside overlooking Little Traverse Bay, Petoskey is known for its historic Gaslight Shopping District. These downtown shops connect to Waterfront Park, which features a walking path, playground, recreation area and marina. A bike path connects Petoskey northward to Harbor Springs and southward to Charlevoix, offering opportunities to bike, in-line skate and walk among these charming cities. Petoskey State Park and numerous local parks offer hiking trails and beaches.

WHAT TO SEE
LITTLE TRAVERSE HISTORICAL MUSEUM
Waterfront Park, 100 Depot Court, Petoskey, 231-347-2620; www.petoskeymuseum.org
Housed in a former railroad depot, visitors can see historical exhibits from the area's Native American, pioneer and Victorian past.
May-November, daily.

PETOSKEY STATE PARK
2475 Highway 119, Petoskey, 231-347-2311
A 305-acre park with swimming beach, beach house, fishing; hiking, cross-country skiing, picnicking, playground, camping.
Daily.

ST. FRANCIS SOLANUS INDIAN MISSION
West Lake Street, Petoskey
Built of square hand-cut timbers and held together by dovetailed corners, this 1859 church is the oldest structure in Petoskey. Native American burial grounds (not open to the public) are adjacent to the church. Mass is still held at the church once a year on the feast of St. Francis Solatonus, July 14.

SPECIAL EVENT
ART IN THE PARK
Pennsylvania Park, 401 E. Mitchell St., Petoskey, 231-347-4150; www.petoskey.com
Approximately 125 exhibitors display their artwork at this downtown park location.
Third Saturday in July.

WHERE TO STAY
★★★STAFFORD'S BAY VIEW INN

2011 Woodland Ave., Petoskey, 231-347-2771, 800-258-1886;
www.thebayviewinn.com

Built in 1866, this historic Victorian-style inn features a green mansard roof, sun room, library and an outdoor porch. The inn overlooks Little Traverse Bay. Guest rooms are quaint (period furnishings and antiques) and relaxing—no televisions or telephones. Breakfast, Sunday brunch and dinner menus are offered at the Roselawn Dining Room, the inn's in-house restaurant.

31 rooms. Closed April, late October-late November; also Sunday-Thursday in March and early-late December. Complimentary breakfast. Restaurant, bar. $151-250

★★★RENAISSANCE INN AT BAY HARBOR

3600 Village Harbor Drive, Bay Harbor, 231-439-4000, 800-362-6963;
www.innatbayharbor.com

This resort is nestled on five acres alongside Lake Michigan. Golf is a major attraction, with 162 holes just outside the hotel, 27 of them part of the property itself. The spa soothes with a wide variety of pampering treatments, including massages, facials, hydrotherapy and wellness packages. The inn's suites have a classic appeal, while three-bedroom cottages offer spacious accommodations with views of the Crooked Tree Golf Club. From the photographs of Victorian cruise ships lining the walls at Sagamore's to the dark wood and leather interior at the South American lounge, this resort celebrates its history in its restaurants as well.

218 rooms. Closed two-three weeks in April and November. High-speed Internet access. Restaurant, bar. Airport transportation available. $251-350

WHERE TO EAT
★★ANDANTE

321 Bay St., Petoskey, 231-348-3321

American menu. Dinner. Closed Monday; also November-April. Bar. Business casual attire. Reservations recommended. $36-85

★★STAFFORD'S BAY VIEW INN

2011 Woodland Ave., Petoskey, 231-347-2771; www.thebayviewinn.com

American menu. Breakfast, lunch, dinner, Sunday brunch. Closed a few weeks in March-April and November. Bar. Casual attire. Reservations recommended. $36-85

PLYMOUTH

See also Farmington

Spend a day shopping and eating in downtown Plymouth, which offers two dozen restaurants and cafés, plus plenty of chic boutiques for retail therapy.

SPECIAL EVENTS
FALL FESTIVAL

Plymouth, 734-453-3331; www.plymouthfallfestival.com

Antiques mart, music and ethnic food.
First weekend after Labor Day.

ICE SCULPTURE SPECTACULAR

Kellogg Park, Plymouth, 734-453-1540; www.ci.plymouth.mi.us

Hundreds of ice sculptures line the streets and fill Kellogg Park, as professional and student chefs compete with each other carving huge blocks of ice; the sculptures are lighted at night.

January.

WHERE TO STAY
★FAIRFIELD INN

5700 Haggerty Road, Canton, 734-981-2440, 800-228-2800; www.fairfieldinn.com

188 rooms. Complimentary continental breakfast. High-speed Internet access. $61-150

WHERE TO EAT
★★AH-WOK

41563 W. Ten Mile Road, Novi, 248-349-9260

Chinese menu. Lunch, dinner. Bar. Children's menu. Casual attire. $15 and under

★★ERNESTO'S

41661 Plymouth Road, Plymouth, 734-453-2002; www.ernestos1.com

Italian menu. Lunch, dinner. Closed Monday. Bar. Outdoor seating. $16-35

PONTIAC

See also Auburn Hills, Bloomfield Hills, Detroit, Holly, Southfield

What was once the summer home of Chief Pontiac of the Ottawas is now the home of the Pontiac division of General Motors. A group of Detroit businessmen established a village here that became a way station on the wagon trail to the West. The Pontiac Spring Wagon Works, in production by the middle 1880s, is the lineal ancestor of the present industry. Pontiac is easily accessible by train. The Wolverine train travels daily between Pontiac and Chicago. Pontiac is surrounded by 11 state parks, and 400 lakes are within a short distance nearby.

WHAT TO SEE
ALPINE VALLEY SKI RESORT

6775 E. Highland, White Lake, 248-887-4183; www.skialpinevalley.com

10 chairlifts, 10 rope tows; patrol, school, rentals, snowmaking. The longest run is ½ mile with a vertical drop of 320 feet.

November-March, daily.

HIGHLAND

3500 Wixon Road, Pontiac, 248-685-2433

On 5,524 wooded acres. Swimming, bathhouse, fishing, boating (launch); hiking, horseback riding, hunting in season, cross-country skiing, picnicking, playground, concession, camping.

PONTIAC LAKE

7800 Gale Road, Waterford

Pontiac Lake spans approximately 3,700 acres and offers swimming, water-skiing, fishing, boating (launch); horseback riding, riding stable, hunting in season, archery and rifle ranges, winter sports, picnicking, playground, concession, camping.

WHERE TO STAY

★★★MARRIOTT PONTIAC AT CENTERPOINT

3600 Centerpoint Parkway, Pontiac, 248-253-9800, 800-228-9290; www.marriott.com

A peaceful place to stay that is located virtually in the middle of everything the Detroit area has to offer, including Somerset Mall, Ford Field and Palace of Auburn Hills. Guest rooms are standard but spacious, with queen- or king-sized beds and ergonomic work areas. The outdoor pool is a nice touch during warmer months.

295 rooms. Restaurant. High-speed Internet access. Pool. $151-250

PORT AUSTIN

See also Bay City

Port Austin sits at the tip of Michigan's thumb, an area known for farming sugar beets, melons, blueberries and potatoes. The city boasts beautiful sunrises and sunsets over Lake Huron, as well as a charming downtown. Sandy beaches and dunes are perfect for strolling or shell hunting. Nearby Pointe aux Barques, a small bit of land that extends into Lake Huron, beckons you to drive among its luxurious summer mansions, which were built over the last 125 years.

WHAT TO SEE

ALBERT E. SLEEPER STATE PARK

6573 State Park Road, Caseville, 989-856-4411; www.michigan.gov/dnr

Spanning 723 acres, this park includes sandy beaches and offers plenty of recreational activities, including fishing, hunting, hiking, cross-country skiing, picnicking, a playground and camping.

Daily.

HURON CITY MUSEUM

7930 Huron City Road, Port Austin, 989-428-4123; www.huroncitymuseums.com

Nine preserved buildings from the 1850-1890 Victorian era, including the LaGasse Log Cabin, Phelps Memorial Church, Point aux Barques U.S. Life Saving Station, Hubbard's General Store, Community House/Inn, Brick Museum. Buildings house period furnishing and memorabilia.

Tours. July-Labor Day, Thursday-Monday.

PORT HURON

See also St. Clair

Port Huron is famous for its sandy beaches and Fort Gratiot Lighthouse. The famous International Blue Water Bridge (toll), south of the lighthouse, crosses to Sarnia, Ontario. Port Huron's historic downtown shopping district also offers interesting shops and boutiques.

WHAT TO SEE
HURON LIGHTSHIP MUSEUM
1115 Sixth St., Port Huron, 810-982-0891; www.phmuseum.org

Lightships were constructed as floating lighthouses, anchored in areas where lighthouse construction was not possible, using their powerful lights and fog horns to guide ships safely past points of danger. Built in 1920, the Huron was stationed at various shoals in Lake Michigan and Lake Huron until her retirement in 1971.

June-September, Wednesday-Sunday afternoons or by appointment.

LAKEPORT STATE PARK
7605 Lakeshore Road, Lakeport, 810-327-6765; www.michigan.gov/dnr

This mark is made up of more than 600 acres on Lake Huron and includes a beach. There is water-skiing, fishing for perch, boating, hiking, picnicking, concession, playground and camping.

Daily.

MUSEUM OF ARTS AND HISTORY
1115 Sixth St., Port Huron, 810-982-0891; www.phmuseum.org

Historical and fine arts exhibits; pioneer log home, Native American collections, Thomas Edison's boyhood home archaeological exhibit, marine lore, natural history exhibits, period furniture and lectures.

Wednesday-Sunday.

SPECIAL EVENTS
FEAST OF THE STE. CLAIRE
Pine Grove Park, Port Huron, 810-985-7101

See a reenactment of 18th-century crafts, lifestyles and battles at this popular and quirky festival. There is also a variety foo and entertainment as well.

Memorial Day weekend.

MACKINAC RACE
Port Huron, 810-985-7101

Mid-July.

WHERE TO STAY
★COMFORT INN
1700 Yeager St., Port Huron, 810-982-5500, 800-228-5150; www.comfortinn.com

80 rooms. Complimentary continental breakfast. Indoor pool. $61-150

★★THOMAS EDISON INN
500 Thomas Edison Parkway, Port Huron, 810-984-8000, 800-451-7991;
www.thomasedisoninn.com

149 rooms. Complimentary continental breakfast. Restaurant, bar. $61-150

WHERE TO EAT
★★FOGCUTTER
511 Fort St., Port Huron, 810-987-3300; www.fogcutterrestaurant.com

Seafood, steak menu. Lunch, dinner. Bar. Children's menu. $151-250

ROCHESTER

See also Auburn Hills, Pontiac, Troy

As you drive into Rochester, you coast down gentle hills that offer a spectacular view of this charming city, located in the heart of the hills of Oakland County. Sandwiched between much-larger cities like Rochester Hills, Auburn Hills and Troy, Rochester still retains its small-town feel. Stroll along the downtown sidewalks and window shop at the extensive array of clothing and shoe stores, home-furnishing shops and other boutiques. When you're ready to rest, stop in any of the city's cafés or coffeehouses.

WHAT TO SEE
OAKLAND UNIVERSITY

2200 N. Squirrel Road, Rochester, 248-370-2100; www.oakland.edu

This university is on the grounds of the former Meadow Brook Farms estate of Mr. and Mrs. Alfred G. Wilson. The Eye Research Institute is internationally recognized; the Center for Robotics and Advanced Automation promotes education, research and development in high technology and manufacturing methods.

MEADOW BROOK HALL

2200 N. Squirrel Road, Rochester, 248-370-3140; www.oakland.edu

This English Tudor mansion was built by lumber baron Alfred Wilson and his wife, Matilda Dodge The spectacular structure has nearly all of its original furnishings and art. The library and Wilson's personal office have hand-carved paneling; the dining room has a sculptured ceiling and table that can seat several dozen guests; a two-story ballroom has elaborate stone and woodwork. Outside the mansion is Knole Cottage, Francis Wilson's playhouse featuring pint-sized luxury accommodations. The hall serves as a cultural and conference center for the university.
Daily.

MEADOW BROOK THEATRE

Oakland University, 207 Wilson Hall, Rochester, 248-377-3300; www.mbtheatre.com

Professional company.
Early October-mid-May, Tuesday-Sunday; matinees Wednesday, Saturday-Sunday.

OAKLAND UNIVERSITY ART GALLERY

2200 N. Squirrel Road, Rochester, 248-370-3005; www.oakland.edu/ouag

Series of contemporary, primitive and Asian art exhibitions, including permanent collection of African art; outdoor sculpture garden adjacent to music festival grounds. October-May, Tuesday-Sunday.

SPECIAL EVENT
MEADOW BROOK MUSIC FESTIVAL

3554 Walton Blvd., Rochester, 248-377-0100; www.palacenet.com

Concerts at Meadow Brook are a local treat and feature popular and classical artists. Dining and picnicking facilities are on hand.
Mid-June-August.

WHERE TO STAY
★★★ROYAL PARK HOTEL
600 E. University Drive, Rochester, 248-652-2600; www.royalparkhotel.net
This luxurious boutique hotel, just 30 minutes from Detroit, is a modern homage to the English manor style. Attention to detail is found throughout, from the glass conservatory to the four-poster beds in some rooms and suites. Brookshire Restaurant offers dishes like pappardelle with baby spinach, wild mushrooms and puttanesca, or cedar plank Arctic char with roma tomato gratin and asparagus.
143 rooms. Wireless Internet access. Two restaurants, bar. $251-350

ROYAL OAK
See also Birmingham, Bloomfield Hills, Detroit
Just 30 years ago, Royal Oak was a Detroit bedroom community, with a fading downtown and no personality. Today, a revitalized Royal Oak is one of Michigan's trendiest cities, a place where stylish shops and chic restaurants line the downtown area. The Detroit Zoo, ranked among the best zoos in the nation, is located in the city.

WHAT TO SEE
DETROIT ZOO
8450 W. 10 Mile Road, Royal Oak, 248-541-5717; www.detroitzoo.org
The Detroit Zoo is one of the world's outstanding zoos, with 40 exhibits featuring more than 1,300 animals in natural habitats. It includes chimpanzee, reptile, bear, butterfly, hummingbird and Arctic animal exhibits.
Daily.

WHERE TO EAT
★ATHENS CONEY ISLAND
32657 Woodward Ave., Royal Oak, 248-549-1488; www.AthensConeyIsland.com
American menu. Breakfast, lunch, dinner. Closed holidays. Children's menu. $15 and under

SAGINAW
See also Bay City, Flint, Frankenmuth, Midland
When this was the land of the Sauk, the trees grew so thick that it was always night in the swamps on both sides of the Saginaw River. When the loggers "brought daylight to the swamp," the city became the timber capital of the world. When the trees were depleted, Saginaw turned its attention to industry and agriculture. Today, it is the home of numerous General Motors plants and offers a variety of museums, art galleries, performing art venues and cultural centers. Saginaw is also home to two sports teams, the Saginaw Spirit minor league hockey team and the Great Lake Storm, which is a part of the Continental Basketball Association.

WHAT TO SEE
CASTLE MUSEUM OF SAGINAW COUNTY HISTORY
500 Federal, Saginaw, 989-759-2861; www.castlemuseum.org
Housed in a replica of a French chateau, this museum includes collections

pertaining to the history of the Saginaw Valley and central Michigan. Daily.

CHILDREN'S ZOO
1730 S. Washington Ave., Saginaw, 989-759-1408; www.saginawzoo.com
Small animals, including llamas, macaws, swans, snakes and porcupines. Contact yard featuring goats; train and pony rides; lectures; educational programs.
Mid-May-Labor Day, daily.

JAPANESE CULTURAL CENTER & TEA HOUSE
527 Ezra Rust Drive, Saginaw, 989-759-1648
Unique showplace on Lake Linton, designed by Yataro Suzue; gift from sister city of Tokushima, Japan.
Tuesday-Sunday.

MARSHALL M. FREDERICKS SCULPTURE GALLERY
Saginaw Valley State University, 7400 Bay Road, University Center, 989-964-7125; www.svsu.edu/mfsm
Houses an extraordinary collection of more than 200 works by the world-renowned sculptor.
Tuesday-Sunday.

SAGINAW ART MUSEUM
1126 N. Michigan Ave., Saginaw, 989-754-2491; www.saginawartmuseum.org
Permanent and changing exhibits of paintings, sculpture, fine art; children's gallery; historic formal garden. Tuesday-Sunday.

SPECIAL EVENTS
GREAT LAKES RENDEZVOUS
Saginaw, 989-754-2928
Third weekend in August.

SAGINAW COUNTY FAIR
515 N. Washington Ave., Saginaw, 989-752-7164; www.visitsaginawvalley.com
Late July.

WHERE TO STAY
★HAMPTON INN
2222 Tittabawassee Road, Saginaw, 989-792-7666, 800-426-7866; www.hamptoninn.com
120 rooms. Complimentary continental breakfast. Fitness center. Pool. $61-150

SAUGATUCK
See also Holland, South Haven
Long one of the major art colonies in the Midwest, Saugatuck is now a year-round resort area. It offers swimming off the beautiful beaches, hiking and cross-country skiing in the dunes, canoeing and boating on the Kalamazoo

River, yachting from marinas and a charming shopping area. The northern end of the village covers an ancient Native American burial ground. During the summer months, arts and crafts shows are abundant.

WHAT TO SEE
FENN VALLEY VINEYARDS AND WINE CELLAR
6130 122nd Ave., Fennville, 269-561-2396; www.fennvalley.com
Self-guided tour overlooking wine cellar; audiovisual program, wine tasting. Daily.

KEEWATIN MARITIME MUSEUM
Harbour Village, 219 Union St., Douglas, 269-857-2464;
www.keewatinmaritimemuseum.com
Tours of a restored, turn-of-the-century, passenger steamship of the Canadian Pacific Railroad, the S.S. Keewatin, maintained as an "in-service" ship; features original, elegant furnishings, carved paneling and brass fixtures. The quadruple-expansion engine room also is open to tours.
Memorial Day-Labor Day, daily 10 a.m.-4:30 p.m.

MASON STREET WAREHOUSE
Saugatuck Center for the Arts, 400 Culver St., Saugatuck, 269-857-4898;
www.masonstreetwarehouse.org
This theater company stages summertime theater performances in downtown Saugatuck, from comedies to musicals and other lighthearted fare.
June-September, Tuesday-Sunday.

SAUGATUCK DUNE RIDES
6495 Washington Road, Saugatuck, 269-857-2253; www.saugatuckduneride.com
Buggy rides over the sand dunes near Lake Michigan.
Cash and travelers checks only. Late April-September, Monday-Saturday 10 a.m.-5:30 p.m., Sunday noon-5:30 p.m.; October, Saturday 10 a.m.-5:30 p.m., Sunday noon-5:30 p.m.

SPECIAL EVENTS
HALLOWEEN HARVEST FESTIVAL
Saugatuck, 269-857-1701; www.saugatuck.com
Events at this festival include country music, storytelling, arts and crafts and a parade.
Late October.

HARBOR DAYS
132 Mason St., Saugatuck, 269-857-1701
Venetian boat parade, family activities.
Last weekend in July.

TASTE OF SAUGATUCK
Saugatuck, 269-857-1701
Enjoy the variety of foods from area restaurants at this street festival.
Late August.

WHERE TO STAY
★★THE BELVEDERE INN
3656 63rd St., Saugatuck, 269-857-5777; www.thebelvedereinn.com
10 rooms. Wireless Internet access. Complimentary full breakfast. Restaurant. $151-250

WHERE TO EAT
★★THE BELVEDERE INN RESTAURANT
3656 63rd St., Saugatuck, 269-857-5777; www.thebelvedereinn.com
French menu. Dinner. Closed Monday-Tuesday. Casual attire. $16-35

★CHEQUERS
220 Culver St., Saugatuck, 269-857-1868; www.chequersofsaugatuck.com
Continental, English pub menu. Lunch, dinner. Bar. Children's menu. $36-85

★★RESTAURANT TOULOUSE
248 Culver St., Saugatuck, 269-857-1561; www.restauranttoulouse.com
French menu. Dinner. Bar. Children's menu. Casual attire. Outdoor seating. $16-35

SAULT STE. MARIE
See also Mackinac Island, Mackinaw City, Newberry, Paradise
Sault Ste. Marie is the home of one of the nation's great engineering marvels—the locks of St. Mary's River. Along the river, the locks lower or raise lake and ocean vessels 21 feet between Lake Superior and Lake Huron in 6 to15 minutes. From April to December, about 100 vessels a day pass through with no toll charge. The cascades of the river, which made the locks necessary, give the city its name: the French word for a cascade is sault and the name of the patron saint was Mary. Combined, the two made Sault de Sainte Marie or "Leap of the Saint Mary."

The only entrance into Canada for almost 300 miles, the Sault Ste. Marie community began in 1668 when Father Jacques Marquette built the first mission church here. An international bridge spans the St. Mary's River to Sault Ste. Marie, Ontario.

WHAT TO SEE
FEDERAL BUILDING
East Portage Avenue, Sault Ste. Marie
Grounds occupy what was the site of Jesuit Fathers' mission and later the original site of Fort Brady, first built in 1822, before it was moved. Ground floor houses River of History Museum, an interpretive center depicting the history of the St. Mary's River.

THE HAUNTED DEPOT
317 W. Portage Ave., Sault Ste. Marie, 906-635-0093
Guided tours through depot's many unusual chambers; visitors can "fall uphill" in the mystery bedroom, walk through a "storm" in the cemetery or "lose their heads" at the guillotine.
June-October, daily.

LAKE SUPERIOR STATE UNIVERSITY

650 W. Easterday Ave., Sault Ste. Marie, 906-635-6841; www.lssu.edu

This hillside campus was the second site of historic Fort Brady after it was moved from its original location. Many old buildings, including some that were part of the fort, still stand. Library's Marine Collection on Great Lakes Shipping open on request. Carillon concerts (June-September, twice daily; free). Headquarters of the famous Unicorn Hunters, official keepers of the Queen's English.

MUSEUM SHIP VALLEY CAMP AND GREAT LAKES MARITIME MUSEUM

Great Lakes Marine Hall of Fame, 501 E. Water St., Sault Ste. Marie, 906-632-3658

Ship's store, picnic area and park.

Mid-May-mid-October, daily.

SOO LOCKS

119 Park Place, Sault Ste. Marie, 906-632-3311

The famous locks can be seen from both the upper and lower parks paralleling the locks. The upper park has three observation towers. There is a scale model of the locks at the east end of the MacArthur Lock and a working lock model, photos and a movie in the visitor building in the upper park.

March-February, daily.

SOO LOCKS BOAT TOURS

515 and 1157 E. Portage Ave., Sault Ste. Marie, 906-632-6301; www.soolocks.com

Two-hour narrated excursions travel through the Soo Locks, focusing on their history. Sunset dinner cruises (approximately 2¾ hours; reservations suggested).

Mid-May-mid-October, daily.

TOWER OF HISTORY

326 E. Portage Ave., Sault Ste. Marie, 906-632-3658, 888-744-7867;
www.thevalleycamp.com

A 21-story observation tower with a 20-mile view of Canadian and American cities; show in lobby, displays.

Mid-May-mid-October, daily 10 a.m.-6 p.m.

TWIN SOO TOUR

315-317 W. Portage Ave., Sault Ste. Marie, 906-635-5241

Guided tour (two to four hours) of both Canadian and American cities of Sault Ste. Marie; provides view of Soo Locks; passengers may disembark in Canada.

June-October, daily.

WHERE TO STAY

★BEST WESTERN SAULT STE. MARIE

4333 Interstate 75 Business Spur, Sault Ste. Marie, 906-632-2170, 800-297-2858;
www.bwsault.com

110 rooms. Complimentary continental breakfast. $61-150

★QUALITY INN & SUITES CONFERENCE CENTER

3290 Interstate 95 Business Spur, Sault Ste. Marie, 906-635-6918, 877-424-6423;
www.choicehotels.com
130 rooms. Complimentary continental breakfast. Pets accepted. Pool.
$61-150

★★RAMADA PLAZA HOTEL OJIBWAY

240 W. Portage Ave., Sault Ste. Marie, 906-632-4100, 800-654-2929;
www.ramada.com
71 rooms. Wireless Internet access. Two restaurants, two bars. Pool.
$61-150

WHERE TO EAT
★ANTLER'S

804 E. Portage Ave., Sault Ste. Marie, 906-632-3571
Steak menu. Lunch, dinner. Bar. Children's menu. $16-35

★★FREIGHTERS' DINING ROOM

240 W. Portage St., Sault Ste. Marie, 906-632-4100, 800-654-2929;
www.waterviewhotels.com
Seafood menu. Breakfast, lunch, dinner, Sunday brunch. Bar. Children's
menu. $36-85

SLEEPING BEAR DUNES NATIONAL LAKESHORE

See also Frankfort, Glen Arbor, Leland, Traverse City

In 1970, Congress designated the Manitou Islands and 35 miles of mainland
Lake Michigan shoreline in the vicinity of Empire as Sleeping Bear Dunes
National Lakeshore. Today, the park welcomes more than one million visi-
tors per year. A lighthouse built in 1871 stands guard over the waterways.

An Ojibwa legend tells of a mother bear who, with her two cubs, tried to
swim across Lake Michigan from Wisconsin to escape from a forest fire.
Nearing the Michigan shore, the exhausted cubs fell behind. The mother bear
climbed to the top of a bluff to watch and wait for her offspring. They never
reached her. Today she can still be seen as the Sleeping Bear, a solitary dune
higher than its surroundings. Her cubs are the Manitou Islands, which lie a
few miles offshore.

The lakeshore's variety of landforms supports a diversity of interrelated
plant habitats. Sand dune deserts contrast sharply with hardwood forests. The
71,000-acre lakeshore contains stands of pine, dense cedar swamps and a few
secluded bogs of sphagnum moss. Against this green background are stands
of white birch. In addition, the park supports many kinds of animal life, including porcupine, deer, rabbit, squirrel, coyote and raccoon. More than 200
species of birds may be seen. Bass, bluegill, perch and pike are plentiful, and
salmon are numerous in the fall.

Dune Climb takes visitors up 150 feet on foot through the dunes for a panoramic view of Glen Lake and the surrounding countryside. Pierce Stocking
Scenic Drive, a seven-mile loop, a road with a self-guiding brochure available, offers visitors an opportunity to view the high dunes and overlooks

from their cars (May-October; park pass required).

Sleeping Bear Point Maritime Museum, one mile west of Glen Haven on Highway 209, located in the restored U.S. Coast Guard Station, contains exhibits on the activities of the U.S. Life-Saving Service and the U.S. Coast Guard, and the general maritime activities these organizations have aided on the Great Lakes. A restored boathouse contains original and replica surf boats and other related rescue equipment (Memorial Day-Labor Day, daily).

South Manitou Island, an eight-square-mile, 5,260-acre island with 12 miles of shoreline, has a fascinating history. Formed from glacial moraines more than 10,000 years ago, the island slowly grew a forest covering. European settlers and the U.S. Lighthouse Service, attracted by the forest and the natural harbor, established permanent sites here as early as the 1830s. On the southwest corner is the Valley of the Giants, a grove of white cedar trees more than 500 years old. There are three developed campgrounds on the island and ranger-guided tours of the 1873 lighthouse.

Nearby North Manitou Island is a 28-square-mile wilderness with 20 miles of shoreline. All travel is by foot and is dependent on weather. Camping is allowed under wilderness regulations; no ground fires are permitted. There is no safe harbor or anchorage on either of the Manitou islands, however, from May-October, the islands are accessible by commercial ferry service from Leland.

Camping is available at D. H. Day Campground (May-November) and Platte River Campground (year-round); camping is limited to 14 days. Pets on leash only. Information may be obtained from the headquarters in Empire (daily). The visitor center has information on park passes, self-guided trails, hiking, cross-country skiing, evening campfire programs, maritime and natural history exhibits, and other park activities.

SOO JUNCTION
See also Newberry, Paradise

Once just an Upper Peninsula railroad stop, Soo Junction grew into a town in its own right in the early 20th century. Tourists visit today because of the city's wide range of outdoor activities, from hiking to snowmobiling. Fall colors are exquisite, and Soo Junction is in close proximity to Hiawatha National Forest, Lake Superior, Whitefish Bay, the city of Paradise and Tahquamenon Falls.

WHAT TO SEE
TOONERVILLE TROLLEY AND RIVERBOAT TRIP TO TAHQUAMENON FALLS
Soo Junction Road, Soo Junction, 906-876-2311, 888-778-7246; www.superiorsights.com/toonerville/index.html

Narrated 6½-hour, 53-mile round-trip through Tahquamenon region via narrow-gauge railroad and riverboat, with 1¼-hour stop at Upper Tahquamenon Falls. Trolley leaves Soo Junction (mid-June-early October, daily). Also 1¾-hour train tour.

July-August, Tuesday-Saturday.

SOUTH HAVEN
See also Saugatuck
A five-mile beach on Lake Michigan and surrounding lakes make sport fishing a popular summer activity in South Haven. Numerous marinas and charter boat services are available in the area. Views are stunning as the sun sets on Lake Michigan, and South Haven's charming boutiques make shopping an attractive pastime.

WHAT TO SEE
LIBERTY HYDE BAILEY MUSEUM
903 S. Bailey Ave., South Haven, 269-637-3251
See the 19th-century house of the famous botanist and horticulturist; includes family memorabilia, period furnishings and Native American artifacts.
Tuesday and Friday afternoons.

MICHIGAN MARITIME MUSEUM
260 Dyckman Ave., South Haven, 269-637-8078, 800-747-3810;
www.michiganmaritimemuseum.org
Exhibits of Great Lakes maps, photographs, maritime artifacts, historic boats; public boardwalk and park.
Monday, Wednesday-Saturday 10 a.m.-5 p.m., Sunday noon-5 p.m.

VAN BUREN STATE PARK
23960 Ruggles Road, South Haven, 269-637-2788, 800-447-2757;
www.michigan.org/dnr
326 acres include scenic wooded sand dunes. Swimming, bathhouse; hunting, picnicking, playground, concession, camping.

SPECIAL EVENTS
BLUEBERRY FESTIVAL
300 Broadway St., South Haven, 269-637-0800
Arts and crafts, entertainment, children's parade, 5K run.
Second weekend in August.

HARBORFEST
546 Phoenix St., South Haven, 269-637-5252; www.southhaven.org
Harborfest features dragon boat races, arts and crafts, musical entertainment and children's activities.
Third weekend in June.

WHERE TO EAT
★CREOLE TAVERN
515 Williams St., South Haven, 269-637-8435
Cajun/Creole menu. Lunch, dinner, late-night. Closed early September-late May. Bar. Children's menu. Casual attire. Reservations recommended. Outdoor seating. $16-35

★★
★★ MICHIGAN
★★
★

SOUTHFIELD

See also Birmingham, Bloomfield Hills, Detroit, Farmington, Northville, Plymouth, Pontiac

Southfield, a northwestern suburb of Detroit, is the largest office center in the Detroit metro area. It is also home to the Lawrence Institute of Technology and has branch campuses of Wayne State University, Central Michigan University and the University of Phoenix.

WHERE TO EAT

★★★MORTON'S, THE STEAKHOUSE

1 Towne Square, Southfield, 248-354-6006; www.mortons.com

The Southfield location of this Chicago-based, upscale steakhouse chain offers the signature tableside presentation of menu favorites, such as steaks and lobster, along with fresh vegetables, which are presented on a cart by the animated staff. The masculine setting, featuring a wine cellar, cherry wood furniture and tray ceilings, is perfect for business dinners.

American, Steak menu. Dinner. Bar. Business casual attire. Reservations recommended. Valet parking. $36-85

★★SWEET LORRAINE'S CAFÉ

29101 Greenfield Drive, Southfield, 248-559-5985; www.sweetlorraines.com

International menu. Lunch, dinner, brunch. Closed holidays. Children's menu. Business casual attire. $16-35

ST. CLAIR

See also Detroit, Mount Clemens, Port Huron, Warren

Home to the world's largest freshwater boardwalk situated along Lake St. Clair, this city is meant for water lovers. Whether you go to sail, water ski, snorkel or just park your boat at the city's 200-slip marina and stroll through downtown, St. Clair is a charming getaway.

WHERE TO EAT

★★RIVER CRAB

1337 N. River Road, St. Clair, 810-329-2261; www.muer.com

Seafood menu. Lunch, dinner, Sunday brunch. Bar. Children's menu. Outdoor seating. $36-85

★★ST. CLAIR INN

500 N. Riverside, St. Clair, 810-329-2222; www.stclairinn.com

American menu. Breakfast, lunch, dinner. Bar. Children's menu. Outdoor seating. $36-85

ST. IGNACE

See also Mackinac Island, Mackinaw City

Located at the north end of the Mackinac Bridge, across the Straits of Mackinac from Mackinaw City, St. Ignace was founded more than 300 years ago by the famous missionary/explorer Jacques Marquette. St. Ignace is the gateway to Michigan's Upper Peninsula, which offers beautiful scenery and vast opportunities for outdoor recreation.

WHAT TO SEE
ARNOLD MACKINAC ISLAND FERRY
Mackinac Island, Arnold Line Docks, 906-847-3351, 800-542-8528;
www.arnoldline.com
The largest, fastest ferries traveling to Mackinac Island.

CASTLE ROCK
Castle Rock Road, St. Ignace, Mackinac Bridge, 906-643-8268; www.stignace.com
Climb the 170 steps to the top of this 200-foot-high rock to see excellent views of Mackinac Island and Lake Huron. Also features statues of Paul Bunyan and Babe, the blue ox.
Daily.

FATHER MARQUETTE NATIONAL MEMORIAL
St. Ignace, adjacent to Mackinac Bridge Authority Plaza
This 52-acre memorial pays tribute to the life and work of the famed Jesuit explorer who came to area in the 1600s.

MARQUETTE MISSION PARK AND MUSEUM OF OJIBWA CULTURE
500 N. State St., St. Ignace, 906-643-9161
Gravesite of Father Marquette. Museum interprets 17th-century Native American life and the coming of the French.
Memorial Day-Labor Day, daily; after Labor Day-September, Tuesday-Saturday.

STATUE OF FATHER MARQUETTE
Marquette Mission Park, St. Ignace, 906-228-0460; www.mqtcty.org
On top of a bluff overlooking the site of the first settlement.

SPECIAL EVENTS
ARTS AND CRAFTS DOCKSIDE AND ST. IGNACE POWWOW
560 N. State St., St. Ignace, 906-643-8717; www.saintignace.org
Juried show held in conjunction with the Bridge Walk; traditional Native American powwow.
Labor Day weekend.

MACKINAC BRIDGE WALK
1213 Center St., St. Ignace, 517-347-7891, 800-434-8642; www.michiganfitness.org
The only day each year when walking across the bridge is permitted (some lanes open to motor vehicles). Michigan's governor leads the walk, which begins in St. Ignace at 7 a.m., on the north side of the bridge, and ends in Mackinaw City, on the south side. Buses return you to your starting point.
Labor Day.

WHERE TO STAY
★BEST WESTERN HARBOUR POINTE LAKEFRONT
797 N. State St., Saint Ignace, 906-643-6000, 800-642-3318; www.bestwestern.com
150 rooms. Closed November-April. Complimentary breakfast. $61-150

★DAYS INN SUITES MACKINAC COUNTY
1067 N. State St., Saint Ignace, 906-643-8008, 800-732-9746; www.daysinn.com
105 rooms. Closed one week late December. Complimentary breakfast. Beach. $61-150

★QUALITY INN
561 Boulevard Drive, Saint Ignace, 906-643-9700, 800-906-4656; www.qualityinn.com
54 rooms. Complimentary breakfast. $61-150

ST. JOSEPH
See also New Buffalo, Niles
St. Joseph, or St. Joe, as it's known to locals, was built around the shipping and lumber industries, and many of its 19th-century mansions remain. The downtown features fashionable boutiques, art galleries and cafés. Take a picnic dinner to sandy, beautiful Silver Beach and stay for one of St. Joe's renowned sunsets—prime viewing is at either of the town's two lighthouses.

WHAT TO SEE
CURIOUS KIDS' MUSEUM
415 Lake Blvd., St. Joseph, 269-983-2543; www.curiouskidsmuseum.org
Interactive museum for children with such exhibits as balloon flying and apple picking. Kids can even run their own TV station.
Wednesday-Saturday 10 a.m.-5 p.m., Sunday noon-5 p.m.

DEER FOREST CHILDREN'S AMUSEMENT PARK
6800 Marquette Drive, Coloma, 269-468-4961, 800-752-3337;
www.deerforest.com/directn.htm
Spanning approximately 30 acres, this park houses more than 500 animals and birds. There frequent events and picnicking.
Memorial Day-Labor Day, daily.

KRASL ART CENTER
707 Lake Blvd., St. Joseph, 269-983-0271; www.krasl.org
Three galleries house contemporary and traditional works, fine and folk arts, local and major museum collections; art reference library; lectures, tours, films; gift shop.
Monday-Thursday, Saturday 10 a.m.-4 p.m., Friday 10 a.m.-1 p.m., Sunday 1-4 p.m.

SARETT NATURE CENTER
2300 Benton Center Road, St. Joseph, 269-927-4832; www.sarett.com
This bird sanctuary is run by the Michigan Audubon Society and features 350 acres of habitat, including beaches, meadows, wooded trails, swamp forests and marshes.
Tuesday-Friday 9 a.m.-5 p.m., Saturday 10 a.m.-5 p.m., Sunday 1-5 p.m.

WARREN DUNES STATE PARK
12032 Red Arrow Highway, Sawyer, 269-426-4013; www.michigan.gov/dnr
On 1,499 acres on Lake Michigan. Swimming, beach house; hiking, pic-

nicking, playground, concession, camping, cabins. Warren Woods offers 200 acres of virgin forest. Daily.

SPECIAL EVENTS
BLOSSOMTIME FESTIVAL
151 E. Napier Ave., St. Joseph, 269-926-7397; www.blossomtimefestival.org
A spring salute to agriculture, industry and recreation in southwest Michigan; Blessing of the Blossoms; Blossomtime Ball, Grand Floral Parade. Early May.

KRASL ART FAIR
707 Lake Boulevard, Lake Bluff Park, St. Joseph, 269-983-0271; www.krasl.org
One of the major art shows in the state. Second weekend in July.

SAILING FESTIVAL
120 State St., St. Joseph, 269-985-1111; www.sjtoday.org
This family festival features music, horse-drawn trolley rides, food booths, arts and crafts and more.
Labor Day weekend.

VENETIAN FESTIVAL
401 Lake Blvd., St. Joseph, 269-983-7917; www.venetian.org
Boat parades, fireworks, concerts, land and water contests, races, sandcastle sculptures, food booths, photography competition. Mid-July.

WHERE TO STAY
★BEST WESTERN TWIN CITY INN & SUITES
1598 Mall Drive, Benton Harbor, 269-925-1880, 866-668-3548
50 rooms. Complimentary continental breakfast. Wireless Internet access. $61-150

TAWAS CITY
See also Oscoda
In Tawas City and its sister city East Tawas, summer days along Lake Huron are slow and comfortable. Take in quaint shops, grab a bite at a café or ice cream shop and walk barefoot on the sandy beach. Anglers celebrate their sport with both a winter and a summer festival, while bird watchers gather in spring and fall to watch the migratory stops of warblers and other songbirds.

SPECIAL EVENT
TAWAS BAY WATERFRONT ART SHOW
Tawas City Park, 402 Lake St., Tawas City, 989-362-8643; www.tawas.com
More than 200 professional and amateur artists display art and craftwork; juried show.
First weekend in August.

THREE RIVERS

See also Battle Creek, Kalamazoo

The historic, tastefully restored downtown area of Three Rivers is listed on the National Register of Historic Places and features exceptional Victorian architecture. In addition to viewing the buildings themselves, stop in the quaint shops, galleries and studios located throughout the Three Rivers streetscape.

WHAT TO SEE

SWISS VALLEY SKI AREA

Patterson Hill Road, Jones, 269-244-5635; www.skiswissvalley.com

Two quad, triple chairlift, four rope tows; patrol, school, rentals, ski shop, snowmaking. Vertical drop 225 feet. Night skiing.

December-March, daily.

TRAVERSE CITY

See also Beulah, Glen Arbor

A one-acre cherry orchard, planted here in the 1880s, has multiplied to such an extent that today the entire region produces more than 75 million pounds of cherries a year. The city's beaches are legendary, and the views of Lake Michigan's Grand Traverse Bay are gorgeous. There are six ski areas within 35 miles of town. More than 30 public and private golf courses are also found in the area.

WHAT TO SEE

CLINCH PARK

181 E. Grandview Parkway, Traverse City, 231-922-4904

Zoo and aquarium featuring animals native to Michigan (mid-April-November, daily). Con Foster Museum has exhibits on local history, Native American and pioneer life, and folklore (Memorial Day-Labor Day, daily).

DENNOS ART CENTER

1701 E. Front St., Traverse City, 231-995-1055; www.dennosmuseum.org

Three galleries; including one of the largest collections of Inuit art in the Midwest.

Daily.

SCHOONER MADELINE

322 Sixth St., Traverse City, 231-946-2647; www.maritimeheritagealliance.org

Full-scale replica of 1850s Great Lakes sailing ship. Original Madeline served as first schoolhouse in the Grand Traverse region.

Tours early May-late September, Wednesday-Sunday afternoons.

TALL SHIP MALABAR

13390 S. West-Bay Shore Drive, Traverse City, 231-941-2000

Tours of the classic topsail schooner (late May-early October, four times daily).

SPECIAL EVENTS
DOWNTOWN TRAVERSE CITY ART FAIR
100 E. Front St., Traverse City, 231-264-8202

More than 100 artists participate in this juried art fair featuring painting, jewelry, photography, weaving, pottery, glassworks and sculpture.
Late August.

MESICK MUSHROOM FESTIVAL
10798 Maple Road, Traverse City, 231-885-2679; www.mesick-mushroomfest.org

Carnival, rodeo, baseball tournament, flea market, music, parade, mushroom contest, food wagons.
Second weekend in May.

NATIONAL CHERRY FESTIVAL
108 W. Grandview Parkway, Traverse City, 231-947-4230; www.cherryfestival.org

This very popular festival features more than 150 activities, including pageants, parades, concerts and, of course, lots of cherries.
Early July.

WHERE TO STAY
★BAYSHORE RESORT
833 E. Front St., Traverse City, 231-935-4400, 800-634-4401;
www.bayshore-resort.com

120 rooms. Complimentary full breakfast. Wireless Internet access. Pool. Beach. $$

★★CRYSTAL MOUNTAIN RESORT
12500 Crystal Mountain Drive, Thompsonville, 231-378-2000, 800-968-9686;
www.crystalmountain.com

250 rooms. Restaurant, bar. Children's activity center. $

★★★GRAND TRAVERSE RESORT AND SPA
100 Grand Traverse Village Blvd., Acme, 231-534-6000, 800-748-0303;
www.grandtraverseresort.com

Approximately eight miles north of Traverse City, this resort sits on several acres of rolling hills, with a spectacular view of East Grand Traverse Bay. The hotel features a lobby with marble floors and fresh flowers throughout. Numerous activities abound—summer activities include golf, tennis, jet skiing and boat rentals at their beach, while in winter there's cross-country skiing, sleigh rides, ice skating and snowmobiling. Shops and numerous food and beverage options are available onsite. The beauty of the area will leave guests relaxed and invigorated.

660 rooms. Restaurant, bar. Children's activity center. Spa. Airport transportation available. $151-250

★★★GREAT WOLF LODGE
3575 N. Highway 31 S., Traverse City, 231-941-3600, 866-478-9653;
www.greatwolflodge.com

This family-friendly property is located within one mile of the Horizon Outlet Mall, within two miles of the Grand Traverse mall and within five miles of downtown Traverse City. Each room is decorated with pine log furniture. The theme is carried throughout the interior and exterior of the hotel, and the lobby features a huge stone fireplace. The main draw is the 51,000-square-foot indoor water park, complete with slides, pools for all ages and a floating river. Outside, there is a pool area, with basketball hoops and dunking pails that fill with water and splash guests.

300 rooms, all suites. Restaurant, bar. $$

★★PARK PLACE HOTEL
300 E. State St., Traverse City, 231-946-5000, 800-748-0133;
www.park-place-hotel.com
140 rooms. Wireless Internet access. Restaurant, bar. Airport transportation available. Pets accepted. Pool. $

WHERE TO EAT
★AUNTIE PASTA'S
2030 S. Airport Road, Traverse City, 231-941-8147
Italian menu. Lunch, dinner. Bar. Children's menu. Casual attire. Outdoor seating. $16-35

★★★BOWERS HARBOR INN
13512 Peninsula Drive, Traverse City, 231-223-4222; www.bowersharborinn.net
This historic converted family mansion was built in the 1800s and overlooks West Grand Traverse Bay. It is located approximately nine miles out on Old Mission Peninsula, a scenic and curvy drive along the bay. The interior features beautiful dark wood floors and wood trim. Favorites, such as fish in a bag, rack of lamb, lobster tails, steaks and seafood, are served in a fine-dining atmosphere and accompanied by an extensive wine list. An acoustic guitarist performs Wednesday through Saturday from May to October.
American menu. Dinner. Closed January-April, Sunday-Thursday. Bar. Children's menu. Reservations recommended. $36-85

★SCHELDE'S
714 Munson Ave., Traverse City, 231-946-0981
American menu. Lunch, dinner, brunch. Bar. Children's menu. Casual attire. Reservations recommended. $16-35

TROY
See also Bloomfield Hills, Detroit, Pontiac, Warren
The year 1819 saw the first land grants for an area that was eventually to become Troy. By 1837, the city was becoming a center for trade between Detroit and Pontiac. Today, Troy is the home of many large corporations.

WHAT TO SEE
STONY CREEK METROPARK
1460 Mead Road, Rochester, 586-781-4242, 800-477-7756
Stoney Creek is a popular place with locals for early morning runs (many organizations meet here to train for marathons). It is also a popular spot for biking, thanks to a six-mile loop that goes around a lake and down pretty

tree-shaded paths. The area spans more than 4,000 acres and includes beaches with lifeguards (Memorial Day-Labor Day, daily), fishing, boating (ramp, rentals), bicycling (rentals, trails), winter sports, picnicking, playground, and golf. Pets on leash only.
Daily.

TROY MUSEUM AND HISTORICAL VILLAGE
60 W. Wattles Road, Troy, 248-524-3570; www.ci.troy.mi.us/Museum
This village museum includes an 1820 log cabin, the 1832 Caswell House, the 1877 Poppleton School, an 1880 general store, an 1890 blacksmith shop and a 1900 print shop.
Tuesday-Sunday.

WHERE TO STAY
★FAIRFIELD INN BY MARRIOTT
DETROIT-TROY/MADISON HEIGHTS
32800 Stephenson Highway, Madison Heights, 248-588-3388, 800-228-2800; www.fairfieldinn.com
121 rooms. Complimentary continental breakfast. Wireless Internet access.
$61-150

WHERE TO EAT
★★MON JIN LAU
1515 E. Maple Road, Troy, 248-689-2332; www.monjinlau.com
Pacific-Rim/Pan-Asian menu. Lunch, dinner. Bar. Business casual attire. Reservations recommended. Outdoor seating. $36-85

★★PICANO'S
3775 Rochester Road, Troy, 248-689-8050; www.picanos.com
Italian menu. Lunch, dinner. Bar. Children's menu. Casual attire. Valet parking. $16-35

WAKEFIELD
See also Ironwood
Located at the far western tip of the Upper Peninsula, Wakefield is a quintessential Upper Peninsula town, with plenty of winter sports to enjoy, including downhill and cross-country skiing, snowmobiling, snowshoeing, ice fishing, skating and pick-up hockey. Sunday Lake provides summer fun as well.

WHAT TO SEE
INDIANHEAD MOUNTAIN-BEAR CREEK SKI RESORT
500 Indianhead Road, Wakefield, 906-229-5181, 800-346-3426; www.indianheadmtn.com
Quad, triple, three double chairlifts; Pomalift, two T-bars; beginner's lift; patrol, school, rentals; snowmaking. The longest run is one mile with a vertical drop of 638 feet.
November-mid-April, daily.

WARREN

See also Bloomfield Hills, Detroit, St. Clair, Troy

Warren, a northern suburb of Detroit, is the third-largest city in Michigan. It is home of the General Motors Technical Center, designed by Eero Saarinen, as well as other offices of many large automotive manufacturers. A small farmland community until the 1930s, Warren erupted almost overnight when General Electric's Carboloy Division established a factory in the area. Soon other major manufacturers set up plants in Warren and the city boomed.

WHERE TO STAY

★★BEST WESTERN GEORGIAN INN

31327 Gratiot Ave., Roseville, 586-294-0400, 800-477-1466; www.bestwestern.com

111 rooms. Restaurant, bar. Pets accepted. Outdoor heated pool. $61-150

★★COURTYARD BY MARRIOTT

30190 Van Dyke Ave., Warren, 586-751-5777, 800-321-2211; www.courtyard.com

147 rooms. Restaurant, bar. Wireless Internet access. $61-150

★HOLIDAY INN EXPRESS

11500 Eleven Mile Road, Warren, 586-754-9700, 800-465-4329; www.holiday-inn.com

124 rooms. Complimentary continental breakfast. High-speed Internet access. $61-150

WHERE TO EAT

★★★ANDIAMO ITALIA

7096 E. 14 Mile Road, Warren, 586-268-3200; www.andiamoitalia.com

This family-owned, authentic Italian restaurant is very popular among locals (there are several other locations around the Detroit area) and it is usually a busy, lively place every night of the week. The main dining room's ceiling mural at this location creates an open, airy feeling, which makes for an ideal setting to enjoy the made-from-scratch fare that includes several good pasta dishes and fresh vegetables for sides. Diners can also choose a complementary wine from the extensive list. For regular guests, there are personal cellars with engraved nameplates.

Italian menu. Lunch, dinner. Bar. Reservations recommended. $16-35

WHITEHALL

See also Muskegon

Whitehall and its sister city, Montague, sit about five miles off Lake Michigan on White Lake. Both are unpretentious, slow-paced towns with soda fountains and delightful shops, and both offer excellent opportunities for canoeing and bird watching on the White River.

WHAT TO SEE

MONTAGUE CITY MUSEUM

Church and Meade streets, Montague, 231-894-6813

History of lumbering era, artifacts; displays on Montague resident Nancy Ann Fleming, who was Miss America 1961.

June-August, Saturday-Sunday.

WHITE RIVER LIGHT STATION MUSEUM

6199 Murray Road, Whitehall, 231-894-8265

This museum is located in an 1875 lighthouse made of Michigan limestone and brick; ship relics and artifacts include binnacle, ship's helm, chronograph, compasses, sextant, charts, models, photographs, paintings.
Memorial Day-Labor Day, Tuesday-Sunday; September, weekends.

WORLD'S LARGEST WEATHER VANE

Highway 31, Montague

This 48-foot-tall structure weighs 4,300 pounds and is topped with a model of the lumber schooner Ella Ellenwood that once traveled the Great Lakes.

SPECIAL EVENTS
SUMMER CONCERT SERIES

124 W. Hanson St., Whitehall, or White Lake Music Shell, Launch Ramp Road,
Montague, 231-893-4585

Grab a blanket or lawn chair and enjoy the sounds of jazz, folk, country and swing music.
Every Tuesday in mid-June-late August.

WHITE LAKE ARTS & CRAFTS FESTIVAL

Funnel Field, Whitehall, 231-893-4585; www.whitelake.org

150 exhibitors.
Father's Day weekend.

YPSILANTI

See also Ann Arbor, Dearborn, Detroit

Home to Eastern Michigan University, Ypsilanti was established as an American Indian trading post and later named for a young Greek patriot, Demetrius Ypsilanti. The city had stations on the Underground Railroad before the Civil War. A two-block area, known as Depot Town, has renovated 150-year-old houses and storefronts, as well as antique shops and restaurants and many fine examples of Greek Revival architecture. In late July, Depot Town hosts the Summer Beer Festival.

WHAT TO SEE
EASTERN MICHIGAN UNIVERSITY

202 Welch Hall, Ypsilanti, 734-487-1849; www.emich.edu

The university is home to Quirk/Sponberg Dramatic Arts Theaters, Pease Auditorium, Bowen Field House, Rynearson Stadium, Olds Student Recreation Center; Ford Art Gallery with changing exhibits (Monday-Saturday; 734-487-1268); Intermedia Art Gallery. Tours, by appointment, depart from historic Starkweather Hall. Daily.

FORD LAKE PARK

9075 S. Huron River Drive, Ypsilanti, 734-485-6880; www.twp.ypsilanti.mi.us

This park offers fishing, boating (launch; fee); volleyball, tennis and handball courts; horseshoes, softball field, four picnic shelters.
Daily; some fees May-September.

YPSILANTI HISTORICAL MUSEUM

220 N. Huron St., Ypsilanti, 734-484-0080; www.ypsilantihistoricalmuseum.org

Victorian house with 11 rooms, including a special children's room and craft room; exhibits. Ypsilanti Historical Archives are located here and are open for research pertaining to local history and genealogy.
Thursday, Saturday-Sunday 2-4 p.m.

YPSILANTI MONUMENT AND WATER TOWER

Cross and Washtenaw streets, Ypsilanti

Marble column with a bust of Demetrius Ypsilanti, Greek patriot. Century-old water tower.

SPECIAL EVENTS
SUMMER BEER FESTIVAL

Depot Town, Ypsilanti, 734-483-4444; www.michiganbrewersguild.org

At this festival, eat, dance and sample 100 different beers from more than 35 breweries. Local brewers dish the dirt on beer-making techniques.
Late July.

YPSILANTI HERITAGE FESTIVAL

Riverside Park, Ypsilanti, 734-483-4444; www.ypsilantiheritagefestival.com

Classic cars, arts and crafts, 18th-century encampment, jazz competition and continuous entertainment. Third weekend in August.

WHERE TO EAT
★★HAAB'S

18 W. Michigan Ave., Ypsilanti, 734-483-8200, 888-431-4222;
www.haabsrestaurant.com

American menu. Lunch, dinner. Bar. Children's menu. Casual attire. $16-35

MINNESOTA

ALTHOUGH KNOWN AS THE MOTHER OF THE MISSISSIPPI, AND DOTTED BY MORE THAN 4,000 square miles of water surface, Minnesota is not the "Land of 10,000 Lakes" as it so widely advertises—a recount indicates that the figure is closer to 12,000. Natives of the state may tell you that the lakes were stamped out by the hooves of folk hero Paul Bunyan's giant blue ox, Babe; geologists maintain that retreating glaciers during the Ice Age are responsible. The lakes are certainly one of Minnesota's main draws.

Although Minnesota borders Canada and is 1,000 miles from either ocean, it is nevertheless a seaboard state. The St. Lawrence Seaway makes Duluth, which is located on Lake Superior, an international harbor and the world's largest inland freshwater port.

Taking full advantage of all that water is easy: Fish in a lake, canoe in the Boundary Waters along the Canadian border, or search out the Northwest Angle (near Baudette), which is so isolated that until recently it could be reached only by boat or plane. In winter, ice fish, snowmobile or ski the hundreds of miles of downhill and cross-country areas. The outdoors not your thing? Minneapolis and St. Paul—the Twin Cities—offer spectator sports, nightlife, shopping, music, theater and sightseeing.

Explored by American-Indians, fur traders and missionaries since the dawn of its known history, Minnesota surged ahead on the economic tides of lumber, grain and ore. Today, the state has 79,000 farms covering 28 million acres. Agricultural production ranks high in sugar beets, butter, turkeys, sweet corn, soybeans, sunflowers, spring wheat, hogs and peas. Manufacturing is important as well, and the state is a wholesale transportation hub and the financial and retailing center of the Upper Midwest. The Mall of America in Bloomington is the country's largest mall.

Minnesota passed through Spanish, French and British rule before becoming part of the United States in segments in 1784, 1803 and 1818. Determined a territory in 1849, Minnesota was admitted as a state less than a decade later. The Dakota (Sioux) War was a turning point in the state's history, claiming the lives of 400 settlers and an unknown number of Native American in 1862, and marking the end of Sioux control in the domain they called "the land of the sky-tinted waters." The vast forests poured out seemingly unending streams of lumber and with the first shipment of iron ore in 1884, Minnesota was on its way to a mining, farming and factory future.

Now, dense forests, vast grain fields, rich pastures, wilderness parks, outstanding hospitals and universities, high-tech corporations and a thriving arts community make the state a well-rounded destination.

AFTON
See also Bloomington, Faribault, Lakeville, Minneapolis, Northfield, St. Paul
About 15 miles east of downtown Saint Paul, Afton is home to Afton Alps, the biggest ski and snowboard resort in the Twin Cities area.

WHERE TO EAT
★★AFTON HOUSE
3291 S. St. Croix Trail, Afton, 651-436-8883, 877-436-8883; www.aftonhouseinn.com
American menu. Lunch, dinner, Sunday brunch. Closed Monday (January-April). Bar. Children's menu. Casual attire. Reservation recommended. $36-85

AITKIN
See also Brainerd, Onamia
Once the bed of Lake Aitkin and since drained by the deep channel of the Mississippi, the city now produces wild rice and other crops. Fishing enthusiasts, bound for one of the hundreds of lakes in Aitkin County, often stop here.

WHAT TO SEE
RICE LAKE NATIONAL WILDLIFE REFUGE
36289 Highway 65, McGregor, 218-768-2402, 800-877-8339; www.planetware.com
An 18,127-acre refuge that includes 4,500-acre Rice Lake, the refuge includes migration and nesting area for ducks and Canada geese along the Mississippi Flyway, walking and auto trails and fishing.
Daily.

SAVANNA PORTAGE STATE PARK
55626 Lake Place, McGregor, 218-426-3271; www.dnr.state.mn.us
A 15,818-acre wilderness area built around an historic portage linking the Mississippi River and Lake Superior, the state park has swimming, fishing, boating, canoeing, hiking, cross-country skiing, snowmobiling, picnicking and camping.

SPECIAL EVENTS
FISH HOUSE PARADE
24 Third St., Aitkin Downtown, 218-927-2316; www.aitkin.com/fhp.htm
This parade features unusual floats, decorated ice-fishing houses and appearances by celebrity guests.
Friday after Thanksgiving.

RIVERBOAT HERITAGE DAYS
Aitkin, 218-927-2316; www.aitkin.com/rbd.htm
Celebrating its ties with the riverboat era, this town's summer festival includes a parade, music, food, children's activities and historical displays.
Mid-July.

WHERE TO STAY
★COUNTRY INN BY CARLSON DEERWOOD
23884 Front St., Deerwood, 218-534-3101, 800-456-4000; www.countryinns.com
38 rooms. Complimentary breakfast. Pool. Pets accepted. $61-150

★★RUTTGER'S BAY LAKE LODGE
25039 Tame Fish Lake Road, Deerwood, 218-678-2885, 800-450-4545;
www.ruttgers.com
30 rooms. Restaurant, bar. Pool. Golf. $

ALBERT LEA
See also Austin, Blue Earth
An important agriculture, manufacturing and distribution center, Albert Lea bears the name of the officer who surveyed the area. Known as the Crossroads of the Upper Midwest because both Interstate 35 and Interstate 90 cross the city, the town has two excellent museums.

WHAT TO SEE
FREEBORN COUNTY HISTORICAL MUSEUM, LIBRARY AND VILLAGE
1031 N. Bridge St., Albert Lea, 507-373-8003; www.smig.net/fchm
Restored buildings include a schoolhouse, general store, sheriff's office and jail, blacksmith and wagon shops, post office, train depot, church and log cabin. The museum has displays of tools, household items, firefighting equipment, toys and musical instruments. The library specializes in Freeborn County history and genealogy.
May-September, Tuesday-Saturday.

MYRE-BIG ISLAND STATE PARK
Route 3, Albert Lea, 507-379-3403; www.dnr.state.mn.us
The state park features 1,600 acres of prairie pothole landscape including rare white pelicans and hundreds of wildflowers, plus hiking, cross-country skiing and camping.

WHERE TO STAY
★HOLIDAY INN EXPRESS
821 Plaza St., Albert Lea, 507-373-4000, 800-465-4329; www.holiday-inn.com
52 rooms. Complimentary continental breakfast. Pool. High-speed Internet access. $61-150

ALEXANDRIA
See also Glenwood, Sauk Centre
Easy access to hundreds of fish-filled lakes attracts a steady stream of tourists to this city, which has a manufacturing base. Red River fur traders first explored this area, followed by settlers, one of whom gave the city his name.

WHAT TO SEE
LAKE CARLOS STATE PARK
2601 County Road 38 N.E., Alexandria, 320-852-7200; www.dnr.state.mn.us
With 1,236-acres, this park offers swimming, fishing and a boat ramp, plus hiking, bridle trails, ski trails, snowmobiling, picnicking and camping.

RUNESTONE MUSEUM

206 Broadway, Alexandria, 320-763-3160; www.runestonemuseum.org

Runic inscriptions on graywacke stone carry a 1362 date, which supports the belief of North American exploration long before Columbus discovered the New World. Found at the roots of a tree in 1898, the stone and its authenticity has been the subject of great controversy. The museum also includes restored log cabins, farm artifacts, horse-drawn machinery and a schoolhouse.

Winter, Monday-Friday 9 a.m.-5 p.m., Saturday 10 a.m.-3:30 p.m.; mid-May-mid-October, Monday-Friday 9 a.m.-5 p.m., Saturday 9 a.m.-3:30 p.m., Sunday 11 a.m.-3:30 p.m.

VIKINGLAND BAND FESTIVAL

Runestone Museum, 206 Broadway, Alexandria, 320-763-3161, 800-235-9441;
www.vkinglandbandfestival.com

Twenty select high school marching bands compete in the state's largest summer marching band competition.

Last Sunday in June.

WHERE TO STAY
★★HOLIDAY INN

5637 Highway 29 S., Alexandria, 320-763-6577, 800-465-4329; www.holiday-inn.com

149 rooms. High-speed Internet access. Restaurant, bar. Fitness center. Indoor pool. $61-150

ANOKA

See also Minneapolis, St. Paul

Once rivaling Minneapolis as the metropolitan center of the state, Anoka continues as a thriving industrial city at the confluence of the Mississippi and Rum rivers. A city of parks and playgrounds, Anoka is minutes away from 10 well-stocked lakes.

WHAT TO SEE
ANOKA COUNTY HISTORY CENTER

2135 Third Ave. N., Anoka, 763-421-0600; www.ac-hs.org

Built in 1904 as a home and medical office for two doctors, the history center holds photographs and artifacts.

Tuesday 10 a.m.-8 p.m., Wednesday-Friday 10 a.m.-5 p.m., Saturday 10 a.m.-4 p.m.

WHERE TO EAT
★★THE VINEYARD

Highways 10 and 169, Anoka, 763-427-0959; www.thevineyardmn.com

American menu. Bar. Children's menu. Casual attire. Dinner, Sunday brunch. $16-35

AUSTIN

See also Albert Lea, Owatonna

Named for a pioneer settler, Austin became the county seat after two citizens stole the county records from another contender. The Hormel Institute, a unit of the graduate school of the University of Minnesota, does research on fats and oils and their effects on heart disease.

SPECIAL EVENTS
MOWER COUNTY FAIR
Mower County Fairgrounds, 700 12th St. S.W., Austin, 507-433-1868;
www.mowercountyfair.com
A Midwest steer show, tractor pull, 4-H fair, carnival and old-time fiddlers contest are among the events at this county fair.
Mid-August.

SPAMTOWN USA FESTIVAL/SPAM JAM
1937 SPAM Blvd., Austin, 507-437-5100; www.spam.com
Activities, which are held in various locations throughout the city, include a parade, concerts, a street dance, a canoe sprint and fireworks.
Mid-June.

WHERE TO STAY
★★HOLIDAY INN
1701 Fourth St. N.W., Austin, 507-433-1000, 800-985-8850; www.hiaustin.com
121 rooms. Complimentary breakfast. Restaurant, bar. Fitness center. $61-150

BAUDETTE
See also International Falls, Roseau
On the Rainy River, Baudette is the gateway to the waters and thousands of islands of the Lake of the Woods area. Across the border from Ontario, it is an important trade and commerce center for a farm area producing seed potatoes, flax, alfalfa, clover and small grain crops. It is also a 24-hour port of entry, with a toll-free bridge to Canada.

WHAT TO SEE
LAKE OF THE WOODS
Highway 172, Baudette, 218-634-1174, 800-382-3474; www.lakeofthewoods.com
This lake is partly in the United States, partly in Canada. More than 2,000 square miles in area, with 14,000 charted islands and 65,000 miles of shore-line, it's known for its fishing (especially walleyed pike), sandy beaches and scenic beauty.

WHERE TO STAY
★AMERICINN
Highway 11 W., Baudette, 218-634-3200, 866-370-8008; www.americinn.com
53 rooms. Pool. Pets accepted. Complimentary breakfast. $61-150

BAYPORT
See also Minneapolis, St. Paul
Bayport is a small town on the St. Croix River, surrounded by river bluffs and beautiful views.

WHERE TO EAT
★★★BAYPORT COOKERY
328 Fifth Ave. N., Bayport, 651-430-1066; www.bayportcookery.com

With only one nightly seating, diners can expect an adventure of innovative cuisine at this St. Croix River Valley destination. Even city dwellers travel to experience the food, which features artistic presentations of local ingredients such as New York strip steak with cauliflower, sunchokes and Guinness sauce, or Alaskan halibut with miso, corn coulis and pioppini mushrooms. American menu. Dinner. Casual attire. Reservations recommended. Outdoor seating. Closed Monday. $36-85

BEMIDJI
See also Bigfork, Grand Rapids, Park Rapids, Thief River Falls

Logging and Native American trails, wooded shorelines and scenic rivers are just a few minutes away from this town on Lake Bemidji. Bemidji started as a trading post, and then became a lumber boomtown and dairy and farming center. Once strictly a summer vacation area, Bemidji is host to winter sports enthusiasts, spring anglers, fall hunters and nature lovers.

WHAT TO SEE
BEMIDJI STATE UNIVERSITY
1500 Birchmont Drive N.E., Bemidji, 218-755-2001; www.bemidjistate.edu

This university is renowned for peat research, its music programs, environmental studies, accounting and industrial technology. Guided tours are available.

BEMIDJI TOURIST INFORMATION CENTER
300 Bemidji Ave., Bemidji, 800-458-2223; www.visitbemidji.com

The center houses a collection of Paul Bunyan tools and artifacts with amusing descriptions. Fireplace of the States has stones from every state (except Alaska and Hawaii) and most Canadian provinces. Memorial Day-Labor Day, daily; October-April, Monday-Saturday.

LAKE BEMIDJI STATE PARK
3401 State Park Road N.E., Bemidji, 218-308-2300; www.dnr.state.mn.us

This 1,688-acre park offers swimming, picnicking, fishing and hiking in a virgin pine forest. Boating, cross-country skiing, camping and biking are also available as well as naturalist programs and a visitor center.

WHERE TO STAY
★BEST WESTERN BEMIDJI INN
2420 Paul Bunyan Drive N.W., Bemidji, 218-751-0390, 877-857-8599;
www.bestwestern.com

59 rooms. Complimentary breakfast. Pool. Pets accepted. Fitness center. $61-150

★★RUTTGER'S BIRCHMONT LODGE
7598 Bemidji Road N.E., Bemidji, 218-444-3463, 888-788-8437; www.ruttger.com

31 rooms. Restaurant, bar. Pets accepted. Tennis. $61-150

BIGFORK

See also Bemidji, International Falls

This is a tiny town (population about 470) in Minnesota's beautiful lake country.

WHAT TO SEE
SCENIC STATE PARK

56956 Scenic Highway 7, Bigfork, 218-743-3362; www.dnr.state.mn.us

This primitive area of 3,000 acres has seven lakes, swimming, fishing, boating, hiking, cross-country skiing, snowmobiling, picnicking, camping, lodging and interpretive programs.

WHERE TO EAT
★★THE TIMBERWOLF INN

Highway 38 and Jack the Horse Road, Marcell, 218-832-3990; www.timberwolfinn.com

American menu. Lunch, dinner. $15 and under

BLOOMINGTON

See also Minneapolis, St. Paul

Bloomington, located south of Minneapolis, is the state's fifth-largest city. The Mall of America, the largest shopping mall in the United States, draws an astounding 2.5 million visitors each year, more than Walt Disney World, the Grand Canyon and Graceland combined. But Bloomington has more than stores. A 10,000-acre wildlife refuge offers opportunities to view bald eagles and other wildlife, hike, cycle and horseback ride, while the city's zoo is considered one of the finest in the nation.

WHAT TO SEE
MALL OF AMERICA

60 E. Broadway, Bloomington, 952-883-8800; www.mallofamerica.com

This complex houses more than 600 stores and restaurants. The mall also features plenty of non-shopping activities for kids, such as Knott's Camp Snoopy, the LEGO Imagination Center; Golf Mountain miniature golf course; a movie complex; and Underwater World, a walk-through aquarium. Monday-Saturday 10 a.m.-9:30 p.m., Sunday 11 a.m.-7 p.m.

MINNESOTA VALLEY NATIONAL WILDLIFE REFUGE

3815 American Blvd., Bloomington, 952-854-5900;
www.fws.gov/Midwest/MinnesotaValley

One of the only urban wildlife refuges in the nation, this 34-mile corridor of marsh and forest is home to coyotes, badgers and bald eagles and offers miles of trails for hiking, biking, horseback riding and skiing.
Daily; visitor center: Tuesday-Sunday 9 a.m.-5 p.m.

MINNESOTA ZOO

13000 Zoo Blvd., Apple Valley, 952-431-9200, 877-660-4629; www.mnzoo.com

Simulated natural habitats here house 450 species of animals and 2,000 varieties of plants.
Daily.

VALLEYFAIR

1 Valleyfair Drive, Shakopee, 952-445-6500; www.valleyfair.com

A 68-acre family amusement park bordering the Minnesota River has more than 75 rides and attractions, including four roller coasters, three water rides, an antique carousel and special rides for children. Entertainment includes an IMAX theater and musical shows.

Memorial Day-Labor Day, daily; May and September, some weekends.

SPECIAL EVENT
RENAISSANCE FESTIVAL

Highways 169 S. and 41, Shakopee, 952-445-7361

Expect entertainment, ethnic foods, 250 arts and crafts shops, games and equestrian events at this re-creation of a 16th-century Renaissance village celebrating a harvest holiday.

Seven weekends beginning mid-August.

WHERE TO STAY
★★EMBASSY SUITES

7901 34th Ave. S., Bloomington, 952-854-1000, 800-362-2779;

www.embassysuites.com

219 rooms, all suites. Restaurant, bar. Pool. Fitness center. $151-250

★★★MARRIOTT MINNEAPOLIS AIRPORT BLOOMINGTON

2020 E. American Blvd., Bloomington, 952-854-7441, 800-228-9290;

www.marriott.com

Located just five minutes from the airport, this hotel is adjacent to the famous Mall of America, the largest shopping mall in the country. Guests can also visit nearby restaurants and more.

472 rooms. Restaurant, bar. Airport transportation available. Pool. Business center. High-speed Internet access. Fitness center. $151-250

WHERE TO EAT
★★CIAO BELLA

3501 Minnesota Drive, Bloomington, 952-841-1000; www.ciaobellamn.com

Italian menu. Lunch, dinner. Bar. Casual attire. Outdoor seating. $36-85

★DA AFGHAN

929 W. 80th St., Bloomington, 952-888-5824; www.daafghan.com

Afghani menu. Lunch (Thursday-Friday), dinner. Closed Monday. Children's menu. Casual attire. $15 and under

★DAVID FONG'S

9329 Lyndale Ave. S., Bloomington, 952-888-9294; www.davidfongs.com

Chinese menu. Lunch, dinner. Closed Sunday. Bar. Children's menu. Casual attire. $16-35

★★★KINCAID'S

8400 Normandale Lake Blvd., Bloomington, 952-921-2255; www.kincaids.com

Touted as a fish, chop and steak house, this restaurant delivers with a menu of well-portioned dishes, such as rock salt-roasted prime rib. The décor is reminiscent of a turn-of-the-century saloon, and the service continues this relaxed social-center style. $36-85

★★LA FOUGASSE
5601 W. 78th St., Bloomington, 952-835-1900; www.lafougasseminneapolis.com
French, Mediterranean menu. Lunch, dinner, Sunday brunch. Bar. Casual attire. Valet parking. Outdoor seating. $16-35

BLUE EARTH
See also Albert Lea, Fairmont
Blue Earth gets its name from the Blue Earth River, which circles the town. The river was given the American Indian name "Mahkota" (meaning "blue earth") for blue-black clay found in the high river banks. The town is the birthplace of the ice cream sandwich, and a 55½-foot statue of the Jolly Green Giant stands in Green Giant Park.

WHAT TO SEE
FARIBAULT COUNTY HISTORICAL SOCIETY
405 E. Sixth St., Blue Earth, 507-526-5421; www.rootsweb.ancestry.com
The Wakefield House is maintained as a pioneer home with furnishings depicting life between 1875 and 1900. Also look for an 1870 rural school, an original log house, an Episcopal Church from 1872, the Etta C. Ross Museum and an antique museum.
Tuesday-Saturday 2-5 p.m., or by appointment.

WOODLAND SCHOOL AND KROSCH LOG HOUSE
405 E. Sixth St., Blue Earth, 507-526-5421
The Woodland School is furnished as one-room schools were in the early 20th century. The Krosch Log House was once home to a family of 11 children.

SPECIAL EVENT
UPPER MIDWEST WOODCARVERS AND QUILTERS EXPO
405 E. Sixth St., Blue Earth, 507-526-2916; www.blueearthchamber.com
Creative quilters and skilled carvers display their crafts.
Mid-August.

BRAINERD
See also Aitkin, Little Falls, Onamia
Brainerd calls itself the hometown of Paul Bunyan and is the center of lore and legend about the giant folk hero lumberjack and his blue ox, Babe. On the Mississippi River at the geographical center of the state, the city was once part of a dense forest used by the Chippewa as a hunting ground and blueberry field. Created by the Northern Pacific Railroad, Brainerd was named for the wife of a railroad official. There are 465 pine-studded, sandy-bottomed lakes within a 25-mile radius and more than 180 lodging choices.

WHAT TO SEE
CROW WING COUNTY HISTORICAL SOCIETY MUSEUM
320 Laurel St., Brainerd, 218-829-3268
This restored sheriff's residence and remodeled jail features exhibits on domestic life, logging, mining and the railroad.
Memorial Day-Labor Day, Monday-Friday 10 a.m.-4 p.m.; rest of the year, Tuesday-Friday 1-5 p.m., Saturday 10 a.m.-3 p.m., closed first week in August.

PAUL BUNYAN STATE TRAIL
Highway 371 and Excelsior Road, Brainerd; www.paulbunyantrail.com
This 100-mile recreational trail is for joggers, walkers, bikers, hikers and snowmobilers (rentals available). The trail passes by six communities, nine rivers and 21 lakes.

WHERE TO STAY
★★CRAGUN'S RESORT AND HOTEL ON GULL LAKE
11000 Cragun's Road, Brainerd, 218-825-2700, 800-272-4867; www.craguns.com
285 rooms. Restaurant, bar. Airport transportation available. Tennis. $61-150

★★GRAND VIEW LODGE
23521 Nokomis Ave., Nisswa, 218-963-2234, 800-432-3788; www.grandviewlodge.com
77 rooms. Restaurant, bar. Airport transportation available. Tennis. $151-250

★★MADDEN'S ON GULL LAKE
11266 Pine Beach Peninsula, Brainerd, 218-829-2811; www.maddens.com
279 rooms. Restaurant, bar. Closed mid-October-mid-April. Tennis. $61-150

WHERE TO EAT
★BAR HARBOR SUPPER CLUB
8164 Interlachen Road, Lake Shore, 218-963-2568; www.barharborsupperclub.com
American menu. Lunch, dinner. Bar. Children's menu. Casual attire. Outdoor seating. $16-35

★★IVEN'S ON THE BAY
19090 Highway 371, Brainerd, 218-829-9872; www.ivensonthebay.com
International menu. Lunch, dinner. Bar. Children's menu. Casual attire. Reservations recommended. Outdoor seating. $36-85

BURNSVILLE
See also Farmington, Lakeville, Minneapolis, St. Paul
This farming community is home to a ski resort and more than 3,300 acres of parks and wildlife refuge.

WHERE TO EAT
★LEEANN CHIN
14023 Aldrich Ave. S., Burnsville, 952-898-3303; www.leeannchin.com
Chinese menu. Lunch, dinner. Casual attire. Outdoor seating. $15 and under

CROOKSTON
See also Thief River Falls
Crookston is the major city of the broad and level Red River Valley, carved by glacial Lake Agassiz. The area is known for the huge catfish that live by the dam on Red Lake River, which is also an excellent canoeing route. For a taste of old-fashioned, homemade candy and drinks from a soda fountain, visit Widman's Candy Store on South Broadway.

SPECIAL EVENT
OX CART DAYS
Central Park, Ash and Robert streets, Crookston, 800-809-5997;
www.visitcrookston.com
Held in the city's Central Park, this festival includes ox-cart races, battle of the bands, pageants, parades and fireworks.
Third weekend in August.

DETROIT LAKES
See also Moorhead, Park Rapids
A French missionary visiting this spot more than 200 years ago commented on the beautiful Detroit (strait), and this came to be the name of the town. Lakes were added to promote the 412 lakes found within 25 miles of the town. Tourism and agriculture are major sources of income.

WHAT TO SEE
TAMARAC NATIONAL WILDLIFE REFUGE
35704 County Highway 26, Rochert, 218-847-2641
On 43,000 acres, this refuge has 21 lakes, abundant wild rice, picnicking and fishing, plus trumpeter swans, grouse, beaver, deer and a flyway sanctuary for thousands of songbirds, ducks and geese.
Visitor center: Memorial Day-Labor Day, daily; rest of year, Monday-Friday.

SPECIAL EVENTS
BECKER COUNTY FAIR
Becker County Fairgrounds, West Lake Drive and Rossman Avenue, Detroit Lakes,
218-847-8407; www.beckercountyfair.tripod.com
This county fair has been held for more than 100 years and features musical entertainment, a 4-H show, pony rides, a demolition derby and arts and crafts.
Late July.

POLAR FEST
101 City Park Road, Detroit Lakes, 218-817-9202; www.visitdetroitlakes.com
This fest includes sports, entertainment and a polar plunge.
Mid-February.

WHERE TO STAY
★★CLUB HOUSE HOTEL
1155 Highway 10 E., Detroit Lakes, 218-847-2121, 800-465-4329; www.dlinn.com
102 rooms. Restaurant. Pool, whirlpool. Beach. Fitness center. Business center. $61-150

WHERE TO EAT
★★FIRESIDE
1463 E. Shore Drive, Detroit Lakes, 218-847-8192; www.firesidedl.com
American menu. Lunch, dinner, Sunday brunch. Bar. Children's menu. Casual attire. Outdoor seating.
Closed Monday-Friday (late November-March). $36-85

★LAKESIDE 1891
200 W. Lake Drive, Detroit Lakes, 218-847-1891
American menu. Lunch, dinner, late-night. Bar. Children's menu. Casual attire. Outdoor seating. $16-35

DULUTH
See also Two Harbors, Virginia
Located at the western tip of Lake Superior, Duluth is a world port thanks to the St. Lawrence Seaway. This gives the products of Minnesota and the Northwestern states better access to markets around the world.

High bluffs rise from the lakeshore, protecting the harbor from the elements. Minnesota Point, a sandbar extending seven miles from Minnesota to the Wisconsin shore, protects the inner harbor. There are two ways for ships to enter the Duluth-Superior Harbor: by way of the Superior side, called the Superior Entry, and the Duluth Ship Canal, with an aerial lift bridge located a few blocks south of downtown Duluth. The distance between the two is about eight miles.

The great Minnesota northwoods begin almost at the city's boundaries, and from here the North Shore Drive follows Lake Superior into Canada. Other highways fan out to the lake country, the great forests and south to the Twin Cities.

WHAT TO SEE
AERIAL LIFT BRIDGE
525 Lake Ave. S., Foot of Lake Avenue, Duluth, 218-722-3119;
www.duluthshippingnews.com
At 138 feet high, 336 feet long and 900 tons, this bridge connects the mainland with Minnesota Point, lifting 138 feet in less than a minute to let ships through.

DEPOT, ST. LOUIS COUNTY HERITAGE AND ARTS CENTER
506 W. Michigan St., Duluth, 218-727-8025; www.duluthdepot.org
This building was originally Union Depot, but now houses three museums, a visual arts institute and four performing arts organizations.
Daily.

DULUTH CHILDREN'S MUSEUM

506 W. Michigan St., Duluth, 218-733-7543; www.duluthchildrensmuseum.org.
This museum covers natural, world and cultural history and features a giant walk-through tree in the habitat exhibit.

DULUTH LAKEWALK

600 E. Superior St., Duluth, 800-438-5884; www.visitduluth.com
Walk along Lake Superior to the Aerial Lift Bridge and see statues, kiosks and horse and buggy rides along the way.

DULUTH-SUPERIOR EXCURSIONS

323 Harbor Drive, Duluth, 218-722-6218; www.vistafleet.com
This two-hour tour of Duluth-Superior Harbor and Lake Superior takes place on the Vista King and Star.
Mid-May-mid-October, daily.

FITGER'S BREWERY COMPLEX

600 E. Superior St., Duluth, 218-722-8826, 888-348-4377; www.fitgers.com
This historic renovated brewery was transformed into more than 25 specialty shops and restaurants on the shore of Lake Superior.
Monday-Saturday 10 a.m.-9 p.m., Sunday 11 a.m.-5 p.m.

GLENSHEEN

3300 London Road, Duluth, 218-726-8910, 888-454-4536; www.d.umn.edu/glen
This historic 22-acre Great Lake estate on the west shore of Lake Superior is owned by the University of Minnesota.
May-October, daily 9:30 a.m.-4 p.m.; November-April, Saturday-Sunday 11 a.m.-2 p.m.

JAY COOKE STATE PARK

780 Highway 210 E., 218-384-4610; www.dnr.state.mn.us
Located on 8,813 acres of rugged country, this park includes fishing, cross-country skiing, snowmobiling, picnicking, camping and a visitors' center.

LAKE SUPERIOR MARITIME VISITORS CENTER

600 Lake Ave. S., Duluth, 218-727-2497; www.lsmma.com
Look for ship models, relics of shipwrecks, reconstructed ship cabins and exhibits related to the maritime history of Lake Superior and Duluth Harbor and the Corps of Engineers. Vessel schedules and close-up views of passing ship traffic are also offered.
March 25-late December, daily.

LAKE SUPERIOR ZOOLOGICAL GARDENS

72nd Avenue West and Grand Avenue, Duluth, 218-730-4900; www.lszoo.org
This 12-acre zoo has more than 80 exhibits and picnicking.
Summer, daily 10 a.m.-5 p.m.; winter, daily 10 a.m.-4 p.m.

S.S. WILLIAM A. IRVIN

301 Harbor Drive, Duluth, 218-722-5573; www.williamairvin.com

Enjoy guided tours of the former flagship of the United States Steel's Great Lakes fleet that sailed inland waters from 1938 to 1978. Explore the decks and compartments of the restored 610-foot ore carrier, including the engine room, elaborate guest staterooms, galley, pilothouse, observation lounge and elegant dining room.

Daily.

SPIRIT MOUNTAIN SKI AREA

9500 Spirit Mountain Place, Duluth, 218-628-2891, 800-642-6377; www.spiritmt.com

Ski area includes double chairlifts, ski patrol, a school, rentals and snowmaking, plus a bar, cafeteria and children's center.

November-March, daily.

ST. LOUIS COUNTY HISTORICAL SOCIETY

506 W. Michigan St., Duluth, 218-733-7586

This depicts the settlement of northern Minnesota, including logging, mining, railroading and pioneer life exhibits.

UNIVERSITY OF MINNESOTA, DULUTH

1049 University Drive, Duluth, 218-726-8000; www.d.umn.edu

Established in 1902, the university has 7,800 students.

SPECIAL EVENTS
BAYFRONT BLUES FESTIVAL

Bayfront Park, Commerce Street and Canal Park Drive, Duluth, 218-394-6831; www.bayfrontblues.com

This music festival features a variety of blues artists performing on three stages.

Mid-August.

GRANDMA'S MARATHON

Duluth, 218-727-0947; www.grandmasmarathon.com

Held each year in mid-June, Grandma's Marathon is one of the largest marathons in the United States, with 9,000 participants. The beautiful course runs along Lake Superior, beginning in Two Harbors and ending in Duluth. Registration usually begins early in the year and closes by March.

Mid-June.

WHERE TO STAY
★BEST WESTERN EDGEWATER

2400 London Road, Duluth, 218-728-3601, 800-777-7925; www.bestwestern.com

235 rooms. Complimentary breakfast. Pets accepted. $61-150

★COMFORT INN

408 Canal Park Drive, Duluth, 218-727-1378, 877-424-6423; www.comfortinn.com

82 rooms. Complimentary continental breakfast. Pool. $61-150

★DAYS INN
909 Cottonwood Ave., Duluth, 218-727-3110, 800-329-7466;
www.daysinnduluthmn.com
86 rooms. Complimentary continental breakfast. Pets accepted. $61-150

★FITGER'S INN
600 E. Superior St., Duluth, 218-722-8826, 888-348-4377; www.fitgers.com
62 rooms. Complimentary continental breakfast. High-speed Internet access.
Bar. $61-150

★★RADISSON HOTEL DULUTH
505 W. Superior St., Duluth, 218-727-8981, 800-333-3333;
www.radisson.com/duluthmn
268 rooms. Wireless Internet access. Restaurant, bar. Pets accepted. $61-150

WHERE TO EAT
★★★BELLISIO'S
405 Lake Ave. S., Duluth, 218-727-4921; www.grandmasrestaurants.com
This restaurant features floor-to-ceiling wine racks and white tablecloths
with full table settings to help guests enjoy a true Italian experience.
Italian menu. Lunch, dinner. Bar. Casual attire. Reservations recommended.
Outdoor seating. $16-35

★★BENNETT'S ON THE LAKE
600 E. Superior St., Duluth, 218-722-2829; www.bennettsonthelake.com
American menu. Breakfast, lunch, dinner. Sunday brunch. $16-35

★FITGER'S BREWHOUSE
600 E. Superior St., Duluth, 218-279-2739; www.brewhouse.net
American menu. Lunch, dinner. $15 and under

★GRANDMA'S SALOON & GRILL/CANAL PARK
522 Lake Ave. S., Duluth, 218-727-4192, 800-706-7672;
www.grandmasrestaurants.com
American menu. Lunch, dinner. $16-35

★★PICKWICK
508 E. Superior St., Duluth, 218-727-8901; www.pickwickrestaurant.com
American menu. Lunch, dinner. Closed Sunday. Bar. Children's menu. Reservations recommended. $16-35

★SCENIC CAFE
5461 N. Shore Drive, Duluth, 218-525-6274; www.sceniccafe.com
International menu. Lunch, dinner. $15 and under

★★TOP OF THE HARBOR
505 W. Superior St., Duluth, 218-727-8981; www.radisson.com/duluthmn
American menu. Breakfast, lunch, dinner. Children's menu. Reservations
recommended. Outdoor seating. $16-35

ELK RIVER
See also Anoka, Minneapolis, St. Cloud, St. Paul

Although it's just 35 miles from Minneapolis and St. Paul, Elk River is a peaceful, simple community located on the banks of the Mississippi River. Elk River native Oliver Kelley started the Grange, an almost union-like organization of farmers that quickly spread across the country and boasted more than 1 million members at its peak.

WHAT TO SEE
OLIVER H. KELLEY FARM
15788 Kelley Farm Road, Elk River, 763-441-6896; www.mnhs.org

This farm is the birthplace of National Grange and organized agriculture. Now, it's a living history farm of the mid-19th century.
Memorial Day-Labor Day, Monday, Thursday-Saturday 10 a.m.-5 p.m., Sunday noon-5 p.m.; September, Saturday 10 a.m.-5 p.m., Sunday noon-5 p.m.

WHERE TO EAT
★LINDEY'S PRIME STEAKHOUSE
3600 Snelling Ave. N., Arden Hills, 866-491-0538; www.theplaceforsteak.com

Steak menu. Lunch, dinner. Bar. Children's menu. Casual attire. Closed Sunday. $16-35

ELY
See also Grand Marais, Superior National Forest, Tower

A vacation and resort community, Ely is also the gateway to one of the finest canoeing areas—the Boundary Waters Canoe Area Wilderness—and is in the heart of the Superior National Forest. From the Laurentian Divide, south of here, all waters flow north to the Arctic.

WHAT TO SEE
DOROTHY MOLTER MUSEUM
2002 E. Sheridan, Ely, 218-365-4451; www.canoecountry.com/dorothy

Dorothy Molter was the last living resident of the Boundary Waters Canoe Area Wilderness—she died in December 1986. The museum features two of her furnished cabins as they were in the wilderness.
Memorial Day-Labor Day, Monday-Saturday 10 a.m.-5:30 p.m., Sunday noon-5:30 p.m.; May, September, Saturday-Sunday.

INTERNATIONAL WOLF CENTER
1396 Highway 169, Ely, 800-359-9653; www.wolf.org

This center houses a wolf pack and exhibits. Look for animal tracking, hikes and tours of abandoned wolf dens and wolf communication mini-classes.
May-mid-October, daily; November-April, Saturday-Sunday.

TOM AND WOODS' MOOSE LAKE WILDERNESS CANOE TRIPS
5855 Moose Lake Road, Ely, 800-322-5837

This outfit specializes in ultra-lightweight canoe trips.
May-September.

SPECIAL EVENT
VOYAGEUR WINTER FESTIVAL
528 E. Sheridan St., Ely, 218-365-3398; www.elywinterfestival.com
Snow sculptures by local, state and international artists are the highlight at
this festival, which celebrates the area's culture, history and art.
Early February.

EVELETH
See also Hibbing, Tower, Virginia
The site of a large taconite operation, Eveleth sees mines within a 50-mile
radius that produce a large amount of the nation's requirements of iron ore.
Located about one mile west of town on County Highway 101, Leonidas
Overlook provides a panoramic view of the taconite mining and Minntac
Mine.

WHAT TO SEE
U.S. HOCKEY HALL OF FAME
801 Hat Trick Ave., Eveleth, 218-744-5167, 800-443-7825; www.ushockeyhall.com
This museum honors American hockey players and the sport.
Monday-Saturday 9 a.m.-5 p.m., Sunday 10 a.m.-3 p.m.

WHERE TO STAY
★★DAYS INN
701 Hat Trick Ave., Eveleth, 218-744-2703, 800-329-7466; www.daysinneveleth.com
142 rooms. Restaurant, bar. Pets accepted. Pool. $61-150

FAIRMONT
See also Blue Earth, Jackson
Fairmont, the seat of Martin County, is 10 miles north of Iowa. Situated on a
north-south chain of lakes, fishing and water sports are popular here. A group
of English farmers who arrived in the 1870s and were known as the "Fairmont sportsmen" introduced fox hunting into southern Minnesota.

WHAT TO SEE
FAIRMONT OPERA HOUSE
45 Downtown Plaza, Fairmont, 507-238-4900, 800-657-3280;
www.fairmontoperahouse.com
Built in 1901, this historic theater has been completely restored.
Guided tours: Monday-Friday 8 a.m.-5 p.m., also by appointment.

MARTIN COUNTY HISTORICAL SOCIETY AND PIONEER MUSEUM
304 E. Blue Earth Ave., Fairmont, 507-235-5178; www.co.martin.mn.us/mchs
Operated by the Martin County Historical Society, this museum features pioneer memorabilia and Native American artifacts.
Monday-Friday 8:30 a.m.-4:30 p.m., Saturday-Sunday by appointment.

WHERE TO STAY
★★HOLIDAY INN
1200 Torgerson Drive, Fairmont, 507-238-4771, 800-465-4329; www.holiday-inn.com
105 rooms. Restaurant, bar. Pets accepted. Pool. $61-150

WHERE TO EAT
★THE RANCH FAMILY RESTAURANT
1330 N. State St., Fairmont, 507-235-3044; www.theranchrestaurant.com
American menu. Breakfast, lunch, dinner. Bar. Children's menu. Casual attire. $16-36

FARIBAULT
See also Lakeville, Le Sueur, Mankato, Northfield, Owatonna, St. Peter
In 1826, Alexander Faribault, a French-Canadian fur trader, built the largest of his six trading posts here. Faribault now is known for Faribo wool blankets and Tilt-A-Whirl amusement rides. The town, seat of Rice County, is surrounded by 20 area lakes and 3,000 acres of parkland. Faribault is also home to several historic landmarks, including the Cathedral of Our Merciful Saviour, built in 1869, and the limestone buildings of Shattuck-St. Mary's Schools, founded in 1858.

WHAT TO SEE
ALEXANDER FARIBAULT HOUSE
12 N.E. First Ave., Faribault, 507-334-7913; www.rchistory.org/afarbhouse.html
A house of the fur trader for whom the town was named, this building features period furnishings, a museum of Native American artifacts and historical items.
May-September, Monday-Friday 1-4 p.m., October-April, by appointment.

FARIBAULT WOOLEN MILL COMPANY
1819 Second Ave. N.W., Faribault, 507-334-1644, 800-448-9665; www.faribowool.com
Look for wool blankets and other items made in a century-old mill on the Cannon River.
Mill tours: Monday-Friday, 10 a.m. and 2 p.m., closed first two weeks in July.

FERGUS FALLS
See also Alexandria, Detroit Lakes, Moorhead
Fergus Falls was named in honor of James Fergus, who financed Joseph Whitford, a frontiersman who led an expedition here in 1857. The town is the seat of Otter Tail County, which has 1,029 lakes. The city has a remarkable park and recreation system.

WHAT TO SEE
GLENDALOUGH STATE PARK
25287 Whitetail Lane, Battle Lake, 218-864-0110
This largely undeveloped, 1,900-acre state park includes six lakes and more than nine miles of shoreline. The largest at 335 acres, Annie Battle Lake is a designated Heritage Fishery, which means that it offers plenty of bass,

panfish and walleye but also imposes restrictions that ensure fishing levels remain stable. Also look for bird-watching, hiking, picnicking, observation areas and camping sites.
Daily, 9 a.m.-4 p.m.

WHERE TO STAY
★DAYS INN
610 Western Ave., Fergus Falls, 218-739-3311, 800-329-7466; www.daysinn.com
57 rooms. Complimentary continental breakfast. Pool. $61-150

WHERE TO EAT
★★MABEL MURPHY'S EATING LTD
Highway 210 W., Fergus Falls, 218-739-4406; www.mabelmurphysmn.com
American menu. Lunch, dinner. Bar. Children's menu. $16-35

GLENWOOD
See also Alexandria, Morris, Sauk Centre
Located on the banks of Lake Minnewaska, the 13th largest lake in Minnesota, Glenwood's identity is intertwined with fishing.

WHAT TO SEE
POPE COUNTY HISTORICAL MUSEUM
809 S. Lakeshore Drive, Glenwood, 320-634-3293
Visit the Helbing Gallery of American Indian arts and crafts, the country store and the school and church for exhibits of local history, farm machinery and artifacts and a furnished log cabin circa 1880.
Tuesday-Saturday 10 a.m.-5 p.m.

WHERE TO EAT
★★MINNEWASKA HOUSE SUPPER CLUB
24895 Highway 28, Glenwood, 320 634-4566, 800-828-0882; www.merchantcircle.com

American menu. Lunch, dinner. Bar. Children's menu. Business casual attire. $16-35

GRAND MARAIS
See also Grand Portage, Lusten
This municipality on the rocky north shore of Lake Superior is the major community in the northeast point of Minnesota. The area resembles the tip of an arrow and is known as "arrowhead country." The cool climate and pollen-free air, as well as lake and stream fishing, abundant wildlife, water sports, camping and stretches of wilderness, make this a leading resort area.

WHAT TO SEE
GUNFLINT TRAIL
Grand Marais, 800-338-6932; www.gunflint-trail.com
The trail penetrates an area of hundreds of lakes where camping, picnicking, fishing and canoeing are available.

SPECIAL EVENT
FISHERMAN'S PICNIC
13 N. Broadway Ave., Grand Marais, 218-387-2524, 888-922-5000;
www.grandmarais.com/fishermans.html
Expect a parade, rides, dancing and food.
First week in August.

WHERE TO STAY
★★BEARSKIN LODGE
124 E. Bearskin Road, Grand Marais, 218-388-2292, 800-338-4170; www.bearskin.com
15 rooms. Restaurant. $61-150

★BEST WESTERN SUPERIOR INN AND SUITES
Highway 61 E., Grand Marais, 218-387-2240, 800-842-8439; www.bestwestern.com
66 rooms. Complimentary breakfast. Pets accepted. Business Center. $61-150

WHERE TO EAT
★BIRCH TERRACE
601 W. Highway 61, Grand Marais, 218-387-2215
American menu. Dinner. Closed Monday-Friday November-April. Bar. Children's menu. Casual attire. Reservations recommended. Outdoor seating. $16-35

GRAND PORTAGE
See also Grand Marais
The Ojibwas named this area "gitche onigaming," meaning "great carrying place" because canoers took a trail through the area to avoid the steep and dangerous falls on the Pigeon River. With so much traffic carrying canoes around the falls, the savvy North West Company established a post, making Grand Portage a vibrant commercial center for more than 30 years.

WHAT TO SEE
FERRY SERVICE TO ISLE ROYALE NATIONAL PARK
White Bear Lake, Grand Portage, 715-392-2100, 888-746-2305;
www.grand-isle-royale.com
From Grand Portage, there is passenger ferry service to Isle Royale National Park within Michigan state waters.

GRAND PORTAGE NATIONAL MONUMENT
315 S. Broadway, Grand Portage, 218-387-2788; www.nps.gov
This area was once a rendezvous point and central supply depot for fur traders operating between Montreal and Lake Athabasca. The partially reconstructed summer headquarters of the North West Company includes a stockade, great hall, kitchen and warehouse. The Grand Portage begins at the stockade and runs 8½ miles northwest from Lake Superior to the Pigeon River. Primitive camping is available at Fort Charlotte (accessible only by hiking the Grand Portage or by canoe).
Mid-May-mid-October, Daily.

GRAND RAPIDS
See also Hibbing
At the head of navigation on the Mississippi River, Grand Rapids was named for nearby waters. For years it served as a center for logging. Paper production and tourism are the principal industries today. Seat of Itasca County, Grand Rapids serves as a diverse regional center at the western end of the Mesabi Iron Range. A number of open pit mines nearby have observation stands for the public. The forested area surrounding the town includes more than a thousand lakes. Four of them—Crystal, Hale, Forest and McKinney—are within the city limits.

WHAT TO SEE
CHIPPEWA NATIONAL FOREST
200 Ash Ave. N.w., Cass Lake, 218-335-8600; www.fs.fed.us
The forest has 661,400 acres of timbered land; 1,321 lakes, with 699 larger than 10 acres; swimming, boating, canoeing, hiking, hunting, fishing, picnicking, camping and winter sports.

FOREST HISTORY CENTER
2609 County Road 76, Grand Rapids, 218-327-4482; www.mnhs.org/places/sites/fhc
The center includes a museum building, recreated 1900 logging camp and log drive wanigan maintained by Minnesota Historical Society.
June-Labor Day, Monday-Saturday 10 a.m.-5 p.m., Sunday noon-5 p.m., October-May, Monday-Friday 8 a.m.-4:30 p.m.

JUDY GARLAND BIRTHPLACE AND MUSEUM
2727 Highway 169 S., Grand Rapids, 218-327-9276, 800-664-5839;
www.judygarlandmuseum.com
The childhood home of Judy Garland features a one-acre memorial garden with 50 Judy Garland rose bushes.
Daily 10 a.m.-5 p.m.

SPECIAL EVENTS
ITASCA COUNTY FAIR
Fairgrounds, 1336 N.E. Third Ave., Grand Rapids, 218-326-6619; www.grandmn.com
This county fair features cattle barns, 4-H competitions, food and fun.
Mid-August.

NORTHERN MINNESOTA VINTAGE CAR SHOW AND SWAP MEET
Itasca County Fairgrounds, Grand Rapids, 218-326-0234; www.exploreminnesota.com
This large car show features classic antique cars and roaring street rods, along with a giant swap meet for some outdoor shopping.
Late July.

TALL TIMBER DAYS FESTIVAL
1 N.W. Third St., Grand Rapids, 218-326-6619, 800-472-6366; www.grandmn.com
This downtown celebration features chainsaw carving, an arts-and-crafts fair, canoe races, a parade and lumberjacks climbing 40-foot logs.
First weekend in August.

WHERE TO EAT
★★SAWMILL INN
2301 Pokegama Ave., Grand Rapids, 218-326-8501, 800-667-7508;
www.sawmillinn.com
American menu. Breakfast, lunch, dinner. $$

GRANITE FALLS
See also Marshall, Redwood Falls, Willmar
The falls for which this city is named still power the town's energy needs through its hydroelectric plant. Founded by mill workers, the town today is known for its outdoor adventure areas; two state parks are nearby.

WHAT TO SEE
LAC QUI PARLE STATE PARK
County Road 33 and Highway 7, Montevideo, 320-752-4736; www.dnr.state.mn.us
Approximately 529 acres on the Lac qui Parle and Minnesota rivers, this park has dense timber, swimming, fishing, boating, hiking, riding, cross-country skiing, picnicking and camping.
Daily.

OLOF SWENSSON FARM MUSEUM
151 Pioneer Drive, Montevideo, 320-269-7636
This 22-room, brick, family-built farmhouse, barn and family burial plot on a 17-acre plot was the home of Olof Swensson, who ran unsuccessfully for governor of Minnesota, but won the title of mayor from the community out of its respect and admiration for him.
Memorial Day-Labor Day, Sunday.

HASTINGS
See also Minneapolis, Northfield, Red Wing, St. Paul
Diversified farming and industry are the mainstays of this community, which was founded by a trader who felt the area was a good town site.

WHAT TO SEE
AFTON ALPS
6600 Peller Ave. S., Hastings, 651-436-5245, 800-328-1328; www.aftonalps.com
Find 15 double chairlifts, two rope tows, patrol, a school and rentals here. The longest run is 3,000 feet with a vertical drop of 330 feet.
November-March, Daily.

ALEXIS BAILLY VINEYARD
18200 Kirby Ave., Hastings, 651-437-1413; www.abvwines.com
This is the first vineyard to make wine with hundred percent Minnesota-grown grapes. Wine tastings: May-Thanksgiving, Friday-Sunday 11 a.m.-5:30 p.m. Group tours by appointment.

CARPENTER ST. CROIX VALLEY NATURE CENTER
12805 St. Croix Trail, Hastings, 651-437-4359; www.carpenternaturecenter.org
This environmental education center has more than 15 miles of hiking trails

and one mile of shoreline on the St. Croix River. There are various seasonal programs and activities as well.
Daily 8 a.m.-4:30 p.m.

TREASURE ISLAND RESORT AND CASINO
5734 Sturgeon Lake Road, Welch, 800-222-7077; www.treasureislandcasino.com
This 24-hour casino offers blackjack, slots, bingo, pull-tabs and national and local entertainment. Daily.

WHERE TO EAT
★★MISSISSIPPI BELLE
101 E. Second St., Hastings, 651-437-4814; www.mississippibelle.net
Italian menu. Lunch, dinner. Closed Monday. Bar. Children's menu. Casual attire. $16-35

HIBBING
See also Eveleth, Grand Rapids, Virginia
Hibbing is home the world's largest open-pit iron mine, which produced one-quarter of the ore mined in the country during World War II. Located on the Mesabi (Native American for "sleeping giant") Iron Range, Hibbing mines and processes taconite, yielding a rich iron concentrate. Frank Hibbing, the town's founder, built the first hotel, sawmill and bank. In 1918, when the Hull-Rust pit encroached on the heart of town, the community was moved on wheels two miles south. The move was not completed until 1957. A local bus line, begun here in 1914 with an open touring car, is now the nationwide Greyhound Bus system. Hibbing was also the boyhood home of singer-guitarist Bob Dylan. Each year the town celebrates the legend with Dylan Days (www.dylandays.com), a series of musical events and tours.

WHAT TO SEE
HULL-RUST MAHONING MINE

401 Penobscot Road, Hibbing, 218-262-4166
Individual mines have merged through the years into a single pit producing hundreds of millions of tons. The deepest part of pit, on the east side, dips 535 feet into earth. Also look for an observation building and self-guided walking tours.
Mid-May-September, Monday-Saturday 9 a.m.-5 p.m., Sunday 1-5 p.m.

MCCARTHY BEACH STATE PARK
7622 McCarthy Beach Road, Side Lake, 218-254-7979
Approximately 2,566 acres, this virgin pine forest also has two lakes with swimming, fishing and boating, plus cross-country skiing, hiking, snowmobiling, camping and naturalist activities.

MINNESOTA MUSEUM OF MINING
Memorial Park Complex, 900 W. Lake St., Chisholm, 218-254-5543;
www.fnbchisholm.com/mining
The museum records the past 70 years of iron mining with equipment, exhibits and models. Also on display are jet and rotary drills, a steam engine, ore

cars, a railroad caboose, 120-ton Euclid and fire trucks, the first Greyhound bus and a steam railroad diorama.

Memorial Day-Labor Day, Monday-Saturday 9 a.m.-5 p.m., Sunday 1-5 p.m.

HINCKLEY
See also Mora

Located at a convenient stop between the Twin Cities and Duluth, Hinckley's major attraction is the Fire Museum, which describes the Hinckley Fire of September 1, 1894—the worst single-day disaster in Minnesota.

WHAT TO SEE
HINCKLEY FIRE MUSEUM
106 Highway 61, Hinckley, 320-384-7338; www.sunsetweb.com/hinckley

This old Northern Pacific Railroad Depot houses a museum that depicts the disastrous forest fire that swept across Hinckley in 1894.

May-mid-October, Tuesday-Saturday 10 a.m.-5 p.m., Sunday noon-5 p.m.

ST. CROIX STATE PARK
30065 St. Croix Road, Hinckley, 320-384-6591; www.dnr.state.mn.us

A 34,037-acre space, this park features lake swimming, fishing and canoeing plus hiking, riding trails, cross-country skiing, snowmobiling, picnicking, a six-mile blacktop wooded bike trail and camping.

WHERE TO STAY
★DAYS INN
104 Grindstone Court, Hinckley, 320-384-7751, 800-559-8951; www.daysinn.com

69 rooms. Complimentary continental breakfast. Pets accepted. Pool. $61-150

WHERE TO EAT
★CASSIDY'S
Interstate 35 and Highway 48, Hinckley, 320-384-6129

American menu. Breakfast, lunch, dinner. Children's menu. $15 and under

★TOBIE'S
404 Fire Monument Road, Hinckley, 320-384-6174; www.tobies.com

American menu. Breakfast, lunch, dinner. Bar. Casual attire. $16-35

INTERNATIONAL FALLS
See also Baudette, Kabetogama, Superior National Forest

In addition to tourism, converting trees and wood chips into paper is big business here. The town takes its name from a 35-foot drop of the Rainy River, now concealed by a reservoir above a dam that harnesses the water power. International Falls is a port of entry to Canada by way of Fort Frances, Ontario.

WHAT TO SEE
BRONKO NAGURSKI MUSEUM
214 Sixth Ave., International Falls, 218-283-4316; www.bronkonagurski.com
This museum highlights the life and career of football hero Bronko Nagurski with exhibits, a diorama, audiovisual programs, photographs and archives.

SMOKEY THE BEAR STATUE
Smokey Bear Park, Third Street and Sixth Avenue
Look for the giant symbol of the campaign against forest fires, plus a 22-foot-high thermometer in the park, which electronically records the temperature.

WHERE TO STAY
★★HOLIDAY INN
1500 Highway 71, International Falls, 218-283-8000, 888-465-4329;
www.holiday-inn.com
127 rooms. Restaurant, bar. Pets accepted. Pool. $61-150

JACKSON
See also Fairmont
A peaceful community on the banks of the Des Moines River, Jackson processes the farm produce of the fertile river valley. Thirteen blocks of Jackson's business district are on the National Register of Historic Places.

WHAT TO SEE
FORT BELMONT
U.S. Highway 71, Jackson, 507-847-3867; www.jacksonmn.com/ft_belmont
This fort includes a blacksmith shop, 19th-century farmhouse, historic church, sodhouse and other buildings, plus American Indian artifacts. Memorial Day-Labor Day, daily 10 a.m.-4 p.m.

KILEN WOODS STATE PARK
Jackson, 507-662-6258
These 219 acres of forested hills in Des Moines Valley offer fishing, hiking, snowmobiling, picnicking, camping and a visitor center.

SPECIAL EVENT
JACKSON COUNTY FAIR
Jackson, 507-847-3867
This county fair has taken place since 1868 and features a 4-H show, carnival, demolition derby, food and music.
Late July-early August.

KABETOGAMA
See also International Falls, Lake Elmo
The tiny town of Kabetogama sits on the shores of deep-blue Kabetogama Lake, which offers more than 500 miles of shoreline and more than 200 small islands. Fishing here is solitary and peaceful, and the waters hold bass, crappies, perch, northern pike, sauger and walleye. In fall, the colors sur-

rounding the lake are spectacular, making it a popular spot for canoeing and kayaking. All year round, the area teems with wildlife, including deer, black bears, moose and wolves. Just a few miles from the town of Kabetogama is the central entrance to Voyageurs National Park.

WHAT TO SEE
ELLSWORTH ROCK GARDENS
Voyageurs National Park, Kabetogama, 218-283-9821; www.ncptt.nps.gov
Located within Voyageurs National Park, the Ellsworth Rock Gardens were created over a span of 20 years by Jack E. Ellsworth, a retired Chicago building contractor. With Kabetogama Lake as a background, large stones and granite mix with flowers, trees and other plantings to create a rich and stunning setting.

KABETOGAMA LAKE
Highway 53, Kabetogama, 800-524-9085; www.kabetogama.com
This lake is 22 miles long and six miles wide with hundreds of miles of rugged shoreline, numerous islands and secluded bays for fishing, sand beaches, woodland trails, snowmobiling and cross-country skiing.

LAKE ELMO
See also International Falls, Kabetogama
For more than 100 years, visitors have sought out Lake Elmo for the excellent fishing opportunities in its five lakes: Horseshoe Lake and Lakes Demontreville, Elmo, Jane and Olson. Anglers catch bluegill, crappie, largemouth bass, northern pike, panfish, sunfish and walleye. In winter, snowmobiling and ice fishing are popular, and summer brings golfing on the four local courses.

WHAT TO SEE
LAKE ELMO PARK RESERVE
1515 Keat Ave. N., Lake Elmo, 651-430-8370; www.co.washington.mn.us
The reserve offers a range of outdoor activities, including archery, canoeing, fishing and swimming. You'll also find trails for cross-country skiing, hiking, horseback riding and mountain biking. The park also offers several orienteering courses, ranging from easy to difficult, plus playground, picnicking and boat launch.
Daily.

WHERE TO EAT
★★★LAKE ELMO INN
3442 Lake Elmo Ave., Lake Elmo, 651-777-8495; www.lakeelmoinn.com
Enjoy the hearty portions of rich, creative cuisine at this state-wide favorite housed in a restored 1881 inn. The charming outdoor seating is a perfect way to enjoy the stellar Sunday brunch.
American menu. Lunch, dinner, Sunday brunch. Bar. Children's menu. Casual attire. $16-35

LE SUEUR

See also Faribault, Mankato, St. Peter

This town on the Minnesota River was named for Pierre Charles le Sueur, who explored the river valley at the end of the 17th century. The Green Giant Company, one of the world's largest packers of peas and corn, was founded here and merged with Pillsbury in 1980.

WHAT TO SEE
W.W. MAYO HOUSE

118 N. Main St., Le Sueur, 507-665-3250; www.mayohouse.org

The home of the founder of the Mayo Clinic, this mansion has been restored to its 1859-1864 period style, when Mayo carried on a typical frontier medical practice from his office on the second floor. The adjacent park is the location of Paul Granlund's bronze sculpture The Mothers Louise.

June-August, Tuesday-Saturday 10 a.m.-4:30 p.m.; May and September-October, Saturday 1-4:30 p.m.

LITCHFIELD

See also Minneapolis, Willmar

Litchfield is best known for its central building, the Grand Army of the Republic Hall, which was built by Union Veterans of the Civil War, a political organization of the late 1800s. As a result, the town is steeped in Civil War history.

WHAT TO SEE
GRAND ARMY OF THE REPUBLIC HALL

308 Marshall Ave. N., Litchfield, 320-693-8911; www.garminnesota.org

Built in 1885, the hall has two rooms in original condition. It commemorates the members of the Grand Army of the Republic.

MEEKER COUNTY HISTORICAL SOCIETY MUSEUM

308 Marshall Ave. N., Litchfield, 320-693-9811; www.litch.com/gar/MCHS.htm

The museum stands behind the Grand Army of the Republic Hall and includes a log cabin, old barn display, blacksmith shop, and Native American display. Original newspapers, furniture and uniforms are also exhibited.

Tuesday-Sunday noon-4 p.m., also by appointment.

LITTLE FALLS

See also Brainerd, Onamia, St. Cloud

This town gets its name from the rapids of the Mississippi River, which flows next to the city and provides opportunities for canoeing and fishing. Little Falls was the hometown of Charles Lindbergh Jr., the first person to fly solo across the Atlantic. The state park in the area bears Lindbergh's name, and his house is open for tours.

WHAT TO SEE
CHARLES A. LINDBERGH HOUSE AND HISTORY CENTER

1620 Lindbergh Drive S., Little Falls, 320-616-5421; www.mnhs.org/places/sites/lh

Home of C.A. Lindbergh, former U.S. congressman, and Charles A. Lind-

bergh, famous aviator, this homestead has been restored to its original appearance with original furniture. The visitor center has exhibits.
Memorial Day-Labor Day, Tuesday-Saturday 10 a.m.-5 p.m., Sunday noon-5 p.m.; September-October, Saturday 10 a.m.-4 p.m., Sunday noon-4 p.m.

CHARLES A. LINDBERGH STATE PARK
1615 Lindbergh Drive S., Little Falls, 320-616-2525; www.dnr.state.mn.us
The 436 acres here provide hiking, cross-country skiing, picnicking and camping.

MINNESOTA MILITARY MUSEUM
15000 Highway 115, Little Falls, 320-632-7374; www.dma.state.mn.us
Located in a former regimental headquarters, this museum documents U.S. military history as it was experienced by Minnesotans, from frontier garrisons to the Persian Gulf. Look for exhibits, military decorations, tanks and aircraft.
September-May, Thursday-Friday 9 a.m.-4 p.m.; June-August, daily 10 a.m.-5 p.m.

WHERE TO EAT
★★★KOZLAK'S ROYAL OAK
4785 Hodgson Road, Shoreview, 651-484-8484; www.kozlaks.com
Guests receive the royal treatment here, beginning with personalized note pads or matchbooks left on the table. Take advantage of the scenic garden seating.
American menu. Lunch, dinner, Sunday brunch. Bar. Children's menu. Casual attire. $16-35

★★★OLD LAKE LODGE
3746 Sunset Drive, Spring Park, 952-471-8513; www.lordfletchers.com
This popular nautical respite about 14 miles west of Minnetonka resembles an old lodge, with cozy fireplaces for cooler days. Local ingredients and unusual flavors come together in the kitchen's inventive dishes.
American, International menu. Lunch, dinner, Sunday brunch. Bar. Casual attire. Outdoor seating. $16-35

LUTSEN
See also Grand Marais
Lutsen, situated on Lake Superior and next to Lutsen Mountain, is an outdoors paradise. Visitors can downhill ski, cross-country ski, hike, mountain bike, canoe or kayak, play golf or see fall colors.

WHAT TO SEE
ALPINE SLIDE
467 Ski Hole Road, Lutsen, 218-663-7281; www.lutsen.com
The chairlift here takes riders up the mountain to the slide; riders control the sled on a half-mile track down the mountain.
May-mid-October, days vary.

WHERE TO STAY
★★CARIBOU HIGHLANDS LODGE
371 Ski Hill Road, Lutsen, 218-663-7241, 800-642-6036; www.caribouhighlands.com
110 rooms. Restaurant, bar. Pets accepted. Tennis. Indoor pool. Spa. $61-150

★★CASCADE LODGE
3719 W. Highway 61, Lutsen, 218-387-1112, 800-322-9543;
www.cascadelodgemn.com
23 rooms. Restaurant. Pool, whirlpool. $61-150

LUVERNE
See also Pipestone
Called the Garden of Eden by the man who founded the city, Luverne still evokes such praise for its beautiful natural resources. Craggy cliffs overlook native prairie land where buffalo still roam. Downtown, a walking tour allows visitors to amble among historic buildings.

WHAT TO SEE
BLUE MOUNDS STATE PARK
1410 161st St., Luverne, 507-283-1307; www.dnr.state.mn.us
A 2,028-acre park, this expanse features Blue Mound—a 1½-mile-long quartzite bluff.

MANKATO
See also Faribault, Le Sueur, New Ulm, St. Peter
In a wooded valley where the Minnesota and Blue Earth rivers join, Mankato (Native American for "blue earth") takes its name from the blue clay that lines the riverbanks. Settled by farmers and Scandinavian and German immigrants, Mankato today enjoys an economy based on farming, retailing, manufacturing and distributing.

WHAT TO SEE
HUBBARD HOUSE
415 Cherry St., Mankato, 507-345-4154; www.bechshistory.com
This 1871 historic Victorian home has cherry woodwork, three marble fireplaces, silk wall coverings, a carriage house and Victorian gardens.

MINNEOPA STATE PARK
54497 Gadwall Road, Mankato, 507-389-5464; www.dnr.state.mn.us
This 1,145-acre park has a scenic falls and gorge, a historic mill site, fishing, hiking and camping.

WHERE TO STAY
★DAYS INN
1285 Range St., Mankato, 507-387-3332, 800-329-7466; www.daysinn.com
50 rooms. Complimentary continental breakfast. Wireless Internet access. Pool. Pets accepted. Business center. $61-150

★★HOLIDAY INN

101 E. Main St., Mankato, 507-345-1234, 888-465-4329; www.holiday-inn.com

151 rooms. Restaurant, bar. Pets accepted. Pool, whirlpool. $61-150

MARSHALL

See also Granite Falls, Redwood Falls, Tracy

At the crossroads of five highways, Marshall is a major industrial and retail center for the southwestern part of Minnesota. Thanks to Southwest State University, the town also boasts a fine anthropological museum and a planetarium.

WHAT TO SEE
CAMDEN STATE PARK

1897 County Road 68, Lynd, 507-865-4530; www.dnr.state.mn.us

More than 2,200 acres in the forested Redwood River Valley, this park includes swimming, fishing, hiking, riding, cross-country skiing, snowmobiling, picnicking and camping.

SOUTHWEST MINNESOTA STATE UNIVERSITY

1501 State St., Marshall, 507-537-6255, 800-642-0684; www.southwestmsu.edu

This school specializes in liberal arts and technical programs. The planetarium is well known, and the museum and greenhouse are equally interesting. Daily.

SPECIAL EVENT
SHADES OF THE PAST '50S REVIVAL WEEKEND

Marshall, 507-532-4484; www.marshall-mn.org

This festival features more than 500 classic and collector cars, plus a flea market, swap meet and street dance.

First weekend in June.

WHERE TO STAY
★★BEST WESTERN MARSHALL INN

1500 E. College Drive, Marshall, 507-532-3221, 800-780-7234; www.bestwestern.com

100 rooms. Restaurant, bar. Pets accepted. Pool. Complimentary breakfast. Fitness center. $61-150

MINNEAPOLIS

See also Anoka, Bloomington, Elk River, Hastings, Lakeville, Litchfield, St. Paul

Across the Mississippi River from Minnesota's capital, St. Paul, is this handsome city complete with skyscrapers, lovely parks and thriving businesses. Minneapolis still has a frontier vigor—it's growing and brimming with confidence—and has a clean, modern aesthetic with a vibrant cultural presence.

A surprising array of nightlife, a revitalized downtown, a rich, year-round sports program, a symphony orchestra and a bevy of theaters make the city vibrant. Minneapolis has one of the largest one-campus universities in the country—the University of Minnesota. The Minneapolis parks system, with more than 100 parks, is considered one of the best in the country.

The capital of Upper Midwest agriculture, with one of the largest cash grain markets in the world, Minneapolis is the processing and distribution center for a large sector of America's cattle lands and grain fields. Several of the largest milling companies in the world have their headquarters here. Minneapolis was born when two mills were built to cut lumber and grind flour for the men of a nearby fort. Despite the fact that these were reservation lands and that cabins were torn down by army troops almost as soon as settlers built them, the community of St. Anthony developed at St. Anthony Falls around the twin mills. In 1885, the boundaries of the reservation were changed, and the squatters' claims became valid. The swiftly growing community took the new name of Minneapolis: "minne"—a Sioux word for water—and "polis," a Greek word for city.

WHAT TO SEE
AMERICAN SWEDISH INSTITUTE
2600 Park Ave., Minneapolis, 612-871-4907; www.americanswedishinst.org
This museum is housed in a turn-of-the-century, 33-room mansion and features hand-carved woodwork, porcelain tile stoves and sculpted ceilings.
Tuesday, Thursday-Saturday noon-4 p.m., Wednesday noon-8 p.m., Sunday 1-5 p.m.; closed Monday.

BASILICA OF ST. MARY
88 N. 17th St., Minneapolis, 612-333-1381; www.mary.org
The Renaissance architecture here is patterned after the Basilica of St. John Lateran in Rome.
Daily.

BELL MUSEUM OF NATURAL HISTORY
University and 17th avenues, Minneapolis, 612-624-7083; www.umn.edu
Dioramas show Minnesota birds and mammals in natural settings. Exhibits on art, photography and natural history research change frequently. Special traveling exhibits often visit. The Touch and See Room encourages hands-on exploration and comparison of natural objects.
Tuesday-Friday 9 a.m.-5 p.m., Saturday 10 a.m.-5 p.m., Sunday noon-5 p.m.; closed Monday.

BUCK HILL SKI AREA
15400 Buck Hill Road, Burnsville, 952-435-7174; www.buckhill.com
Quad, three double chairlifts; J-bar; three rope tows; snowmaking; patrol, school, rentals. Late November-March, daily. Also, BMX racing, mountain biking and mountain boarding.
May-August, daily.

ELOISE BUTLER WILDFLOWER GARDEN AND BIRD SANCTUARY
Theodore Wirth Parkway and Glenwood Avenue, Minneapolis, 612-370-4903;
www.minneapolisparks.org
This horseshoe-shape glen contains a natural bog, a swamp and habitat for prairie and woodland flowers and birds. Guided tours.
Early April-mid-October, daily 7:30 a.m.-30 minutes before sunset.

FREDERICK R. WEISMAN ART MUSEUM

333 E. River Road, Minneapolis, 612-625-9494; www.weisman.umn.edu

The striking, stainless steel exterior of this museum was designed by Frank Gehry. Collections of early 20th-century and contemporary American art, Asian ceramics and Native American Mimbres pottery are inside.
Tuesday-Wednesday, Friday 10 a.m.-5 p.m., Thursday 10 a.m.-8 p.m., Saturday-Sunday 11 a.m.-5 p.m.; closed Monday.

GUTHRIE THEATER

818 S. Second St., Minneapolis, 612-225-6000; www.guthrietheater.org

This world-renowned theater produces classic plays in repertory, as well as new works.
Nightly Tuesday-Sunday; matinees Wednesday, Saturday-Sunday.

HENNEPIN HISTORY MUSEUM

2303 Third Ave. S., Minneapolis, 612-870-1329; www.hhmuseum.org

This museum features permanent and temporary exhibits on the history of Minneapolis and Hennepin County, including collection of textiles, costumes, toys and material unique to central Minnesota.
Sunday, Wednesday, Friday-Saturday 10 a.m.-5 p.m., Tuesday 10 a.m.-2 p.m., Thursday 1-8 p.m.; closed Monday.

HUBERT H. HUMPHREY METRODOME

900 S. Fifth St., Minneapolis, 612-332-0386; www.msfc.com

Home of the Minnesota Twins (baseball), the Minnesota Vikings (football) and University of Minnesota football, this stadium seats up to 63,000.
Monday-Friday.

IDS TOWER

80 S. Eighth St., Minneapolis

At 775 feet and 57 stories, this is one of the tallest buildings between Chicago and the West Coast.

JAMES SEWELL BALLET

528 Hennepin Ave., Minneapolis, 612-672-0480; www.jsballet.org

The James Sewell Ballet performs beautiful and uniquely choreographed ballets with a small ensemble of eight dancers. Two ballets are created each year by critically acclaimed choreographer James Sewell, and many of the company's performances have a contemporary, creative and bold bent.
Mid-August-mid-May.

LAKEWOOD CEMETERY MEMORIAL CHAPEL

3600 Hennepin Ave., Minneapolis, 612-822-2171; www.lakewoodcemetery.com

A cemetery is rarely the first stop on a vacation, but the chapel at Lakewood Cemetery is an architectural wonder worth visiting. Stained-glass windows reflect brilliant light off the more than 10 million half-inch tiles that line the walls. (If the door is locked, stop by the cemetery administration building.) The cemetery grounds are also lovely.
Daily.

LYNDALE PARK GARDENS

1500 E. Lake Harriet Parkway, Minneapolis, 612-230-6400; www.minneapolisparks.org

These four distinctive gardens—one for roses, two for perennials and the Peace Garden—are a treasure. Look for displays of roses, bulbs and other annuals and perennials, exotic and native trees, rock gardens, two decorative fountains, and the adjacent bird sanctuary. April to September is the best time to visit.

Daily 7:30 a.m.-10 p.m.

METROCONNECTIONS

1219 Marquette Ave., Minneapolis, 612-333-8687, 800-747-8687; www.metroconnections.com

Motor coach tours include Twin Cities Highlights (January-November); Stillwater, a historic river town (June-October); and Lake Minnetonka (June-August).

MINNEAPOLIS CITY HALL

350 S. Fifth St., Minneapolis, 612-673-2491; www.municipalbuildingcommission.org

Built in 1891, City Hall's Father of Waters statue in the rotunda is carved out of the largest single block of marble produced from quarries of Carrara, Italy. Take a self-guided tour or join a guided tour on the first Wednesday of the month.

Monday-Friday.

MINNEAPOLIS COLLEGE OF ART AND DESIGN (MCAD)

2501 Stevens Ave. S., Minneapolis, 612-874-3700; www.mcad.edu

Established in 1886, 560-student, four-year college of fine arts, media arts and design. Also includes the MCAD Gallery, which features a rotating collection of student works.

Daily.

MINNEAPOLIS GRAIN EXCHANGE

400 S. Fourth St., Minneapolis, 612-321-7101; www.mgex.com

Tour cash grain market and futures market (Tuesday-Thursday) or the visitors' balcony. Reservations required: mornings.

MINNEAPOLIS INSTITUTE OF ARTS

2400 Third Ave. S., Minneapolis, 612-870-3131, 888-642-2787; www.artsmia.org

Spotlighting masterpieces from every age and culture, the collection of more than 80,000 objects at this museum covers American and European painting, sculpture and decorative arts; period rooms, prints and drawings, textiles, photography; and American, African, Oceanic, Asian and ancient Asian objects.

Tuesday-Wednesday, Friday-Saturday 10 a.m.-5 p.m., Thursday 10 a.m.-9 p.m., Sunday 11 a.m.-5 p.m.

MINNEAPOLIS SCULPTURE GARDEN

Vineland Place and Lyndale Avenue South, Minneapolis, 612-375-7577

This 10-acre urban garden features more than 40 sculptures by leading American and international artists. Daily 6 a.m.-midnight.

MINNESOTA LYNX (WNBA)

Target Center, 600 First Ave. N., Minneapolis, 612-673-1600; www.wnba.com/lynx
Professional women's basketball team.

MINNESOTA TIMBERWOLVES (NBA)

Target Center, 600 First Ave. N., Minneapolis, 612-673-1600;
www.nba.com/timberwolves
Professional men's basketball team.

MINNESOTA TWINS (MLB)

Metrodome, 900 S. Fifth Ave., Minneapolis, 612-375-1366; www.twins.mlb.com
Professional baseball team.

MINNESOTA VIKINGS (NFL)

Metrodome, 900 S. Fifth Ave., Minneapolis, 612-338-4537; www.vikings.com
Professional football team.

RIVER CITY TROLLEY

Minneapolis Convention Center, 1301 Second Ave. S., Minneapolis, 612-378-7833;
www.rivercitytrolley.com
See the city aboard one of these trolleys. The trolleys make a 40-minute loop that traverses the core of the downtown area, passing through the Mississippi Mile, St. Anthony Falls, the Warehouse District and other points of interest. A Chain of Lakes tour is also available. With on-board narration the tours run approximately every 20 minutes.
May-October, daily, also Friday-Saturday evenings.

ST. ANTHONY FALLS

Main Street Southeast and Central Avenue, Minneapolis
At the head of the navigable Mississippi River, the falls is the site of the village of St. Anthony. A public vantage point at the upper locks and dam provides a view of the falls and of the operation of the locks. Also includes a renovated warehouse with shops, a movie theater and restaurants.

UNIVERSITY OF MINNESOTA

77 Pleasant St. S.E., Minneapolis, 612-624-6888; www.umn.edu
Founded in 1851, the University of Minnesota hosts more than 46,000 students on one of the largest single campuses in the United States.

WALKER ART CENTER

1750 Hennepin Ave., Minneapolis, 612-375-7622; www.walkerart.org
The permanent collection of 20th-century paintings, sculpture, prints and photographs here is impressive. Also keep an eye out for changing exhibits, performances, concerts, films and lectures. Free admission on the first Thursday and Saturday of each month.
Gallery open Tuesday-Wednesday, Friday-Saturday 10 a.m.-5 p.m., Thursday 10 a.m.-9 p.m., Sunday 11 a.m.-5 p.m.; closed Monday.

SPECIAL EVENTS
MINNESOTA ORCHESTRA
Orchestra Hall, 1111 Nicollet Mall, Minneapolis, 612-371-5656;
www.minnesotaorchestra.org
A highly regarded orchestra, the Minnesota Orchestra invariably presents a varied repertoire of top-notch classical music, as well as special guests of other genres.
Mid-September-June.

SHOWBOAT
University Theatre, 330 21st Ave S., Minneapolis, 612-625-4001; www.theatre.umn.edu
On the University of Minnesota campus on the Mississippi River, the Showboat harkens back to a day when melodramas, comedies and light opera were presented on riverboats. Here, University Theatre productions preserve the tradition aboard an authentic sternwheeler moored on the river.
July-August.

SOMMERFEST
Orchestra Hall, 1111 Nicollet Mall, Minneapolis, 612-371-5656;
www.minnesotaorchestra.org
This summer concert series, hosted by the Minnesota Orchestra, has a Viennese flavor and food booths.
Mid-July-late August.

UNIVERSITY THEATRE
330 21st Ave. S., Minneapolis, 612-625-4001; www.theatre.umn.edu
Student-professional productions of musicals, comedies and dramas in this four-theater complex draw large crowds.
Early October-late May.

WHERE TO STAY

163

★★★CHAMBERS MINNEAPOLIS
901 Hennepin Ave. S., Minneapolis, 612-767-6900; www.chambersminneapolis.com
This sister property to New York's chic and trendy Chambers hotel has 60 guest rooms loaded with luxuries such as flatscreen TVs, iPod docking stations, rain showers and fluffy pillow-top beds. Chambers owner Ralph Burnett uses the hotel's public spaces to display pieces from his contemporary art collection, which includes works by Damien Hirst, Gary Hume and others. An outdoor courtyard, with tables for dining arranged around a streamlined fire pit, features artist Angus Fairhurst's life-sized gorilla sculpture, a favorite of Burnett.
60 rooms. Restaurant, bar. Wireless Internet access. $251-350

★★★CROWNE PLAZA NORTHSTAR DOWNTOWN
618 Second Ave. S., Minneapolis, 612-338-2288, 800-556-7827;
www.cpminneapolis.com
Located in downtown Minneapolis, this budget-friendly hotel is connected to the city's skywalk system, which makes for easy access to shopping, dining, sports and entertainment. Guest rooms are comfortable and offer sleep kits (relaxation CD and book, lavender spray, an eye mask, ear plugs), marble

bathrooms and work desks with ergonomic chairs.

222 rooms. Restaurant, bar. Fitness center. Business center. $61-150

★★★DEPOT HOTEL, A RENAISSANCE HOTEL
225 S. Third Ave., Minneapolis, 612-375-1700, 800-321-2211;
www.thedepotminneapolis.com

A portion of this downtown Minneapolis hotel was formerly a historic old train depot for the city. The actual depot portion is now a meeting space, and in the winter, an indoor skating rink. The attractive guest rooms feature flatscreen televisions, overstuffed leather chairs and ottomans, decorative mirrors and many historic framed photos. Guests can soothe sore muscles in the indoor pool and whirlpool or work out their muscles in the well-appointed fitness room. The Metrodome, the University of Minnesota, the Guthrie Theater, Target Center and the Minneapolis Convention Center are all nearby, making this property convenient for business or leisure travelers.

225 rooms. High-speed Internet access. Restaurant, bar. Pool. Business center. $251-350

★★DOUBLETREE HOTEL
1101 LaSalle Ave., Minneapolis, 612-332-6800, 800-228-7337;
www.minneapolisdoubletree.com

230 rooms, all suites. High-speed Internet access. Restaurant, bar. Fitness room. Business center. Spa. $151-250

★★EMBASSY SUITES
425 S. Seventh St., Minneapolis, 612-333-3111, 800-362-2779;
www.embassysuites.com

216 rooms, all suites. Complimentary full breakfast. Wireless Internet access. Restaurant, bar. Business center. Pool. $61-150

164   ### ★★★GRAND HOTEL MINNEAPOLIS
615 Second Ave. S., Minneapolis, 612-288-8888, 866-843-4726;
www.grandhotelminneapolis.com

This elegant boutique hotel is a favorite of vacationers to the Twin Cities. The guest rooms and suites are tastefully appointed with Tuscan-style furnishings and stylish artwork, Egyptian cotton linens, plush towels and Aveda bath products. The Grand's Martini BLU restaurant attracts a scene, while the sushi bar and spa deli are convenient stops for quick meals. Guests receive complimentary access to the 58,000-square-foot LifeTime Fitness facility, which has an indoor pool, racquetball and squash courts, and an aerobics studio in addition to the cardiovascular and weight-training equipment.

140 rooms. Wireless Internet access. Restaurant, bar. Airport transportation available. Pool. Business center. Spa. Fitness center. $151-250

★★★GRAVES 601
601 First Ave. N., Minneapolis, 612-677-1100, 866-523-1100;
www.graves601hotel.com

Housed in a 22-story theater district building, this contemporary hotel has a sleek, minimalist lobby, stylish restaurant and rooms filled with luxury amenities. Bathrooms feature rain showers, limestone and Hermés bath products,

while bedrooms have plush beds, plasma TVs and high-speed Internet access. The onsite restaurant, Cosmos, serves sophisticated food like vanilla butter lobster with sweet onion risotto.
255 rooms. Restaurant, bar. $151-250

★★★HILTON MINNEAPOLIS
1001 Marquette Ave. S., Minneapolis, 612-376-1000, 800-445-8667;
www.hiltonminneapolis.com
Located downtown, this expansive hotel is connected by skyway to the Minneapolis Convention Center. The attractive guest rooms are nicely furnished and feature wireless Internet access, plasma televisions and upscale granite bathrooms. Take advantage of the indoor pool and whirlpool or the well-appointed fitness center. Skywater restaurant, which specializes in regional fare, keeps guests well fed. Feel free to bring Fido along for the trip since pets are welcome.
821 rooms. Wireless Internet access. Restaurant, bar. Pool, whirlpool. Fitness center. Business center. Pets accepted. $61-150

★★★★HOTEL IVY
201 S. 11th St., Minneapolis, 612-746-4600; www.thehotelivy.com
Some modern design can be as cold as a Midwestern blizzard, but Hotel Ivy's contemporary style is warm and inviting. This hotel, located in downtown Minneapolis, looks like a boutique hotel, but functions with the amenities of the luxury Starwood chain of which it is a member. The hotel is connected by skyway to Orchestra Hall and other local attractions, but with a 17,000-square-foot spa and one of the city's top restaurants, Porter & Frye, you might just want to hole up right here.
115 rooms, 21 suites. Wireless Internet access. Restaurant, bar. Fitness center. Spa. Business center. $151-250

★★★HYATT REGENCY MINNEAPOLIS
1300 Nicollet Mall, Minneapolis, 612-370-1234, 800-233-1234;
www.minneapolis.hyatt.com
This hotel has an expansive lobby with fountains and plenty of greenery, as well as attractive guest rooms with luxury bedding. Guests can relax in the indoor pool or get a workout at the expansive fitness center, which includes a full-size basketball court, group classes and state-of-the-art machines.
533 rooms. Wireless Internet access. Two restaurants, bar. Airport transportation available. Business center. Pool. Fitness center. Pets accepted; some restrictions. $151-250

★★★THE MARQUETTE HOTEL
Seventh Street and Marquette Avenue, Minneapolis, 612-333-4545;
www.marquettehotel.com
Located downtown, this hotel is connected to shops, restaurants and entertainment by the city's skyway system. The contemporary guest rooms are spacious and feature attractive furnishings, large work desk areas, over-stuffed leather chairs and attractive bathrooms. For a lovely dinner, head to Basil's, the in-house restaurant, which overlooks the IDS Building's Crystal Court and offers dishes such as creamy wild rice chowder with almonds or

Nori seaweed-seared sushi-grade tuna.

281 rooms. Wireless Internet access. Restaurant, bar. Airport transportation available. Pets accepted. $151-250

★★★MARRIOTT MINNEAPOLIS CITY CENTER

30 S. Seventh St., Minneapolis, 612-349-4000, 800-228-9290;
www.minneapolismarriott.com

This hotel has spacious guest rooms decorated with thick gold carpet and crisp white bed linens. Business travelers will appreciate the large work desks and the upscale granite and marble bathrooms. There is a business center and a well-equipped fitness center onsite, and golf courses and tennis facilities are nearby.

583 rooms. High-speed Internet access. Restaurant, bar. Fitness center. Business center. Pets accepted. $151-250

★★NICOLLET ISLAND INN

95 Merriam St., Minneapolis, 612-331-1800; www.nicolletislandinn.com

24 rooms. Wireless Internet access. Restaurant, bar. $151-250

★★RADISSON PLAZA HOTEL MINNEAPOLIS

35 S. Seventh St., Minneapolis, 612-339-4900, 800-333-3333; www.radisson.com

360 rooms. Restaurant, bar. Pets accepted. Fitness center. $151-250

★★RADISSON UNIVERSITY HOTEL

615 Washington Ave. S.E., Minneapolis, 612-379-8888, 800-822-6757;
www.radisson.com

304 rooms. Wireless Internet access. Restaurant, bar. Fitness room. Business center. $61-150

WHERE TO EAT

★★★112 EATERY

112 N. Third St., Minneapolis, 612-343-7696; www.112eatery.com

Located in the historic Amsterdam building in Minneapolis' warehouse district, this restaurant beckons funky foodies with its eclectic menu and convivial spirit. The menu is a veritable melting pot of Italian, Asian and down-home American flavors. Hard-to-resist items include lamb scottadito with goat's milk yogurt and tagliatelle with foie gras meatballs. Side dishes like cauliflower fritters and creamed corn will leave you sated, and the wine list is well-priced and well-rounded.

Contemporary American menu. Dinner. $16-35

★★★B.A.N.K.

The Westin, 88 S. Sixth St., Minneapolis, 612-656-3255; www.bankmpls.com

Past and present come together beautifully at B.A.N.K. This restaurant, located in the former Farmers and Mechanics Bank, is right on the money with its seductive retro styling and fine food. From mac-and-cheese to salmon tartare, there's a mix of highbrow and comfy classics. It's all about tasting and sharing here, where you can even shake and stir your own signature cocktail. Grab a seat at the former teller counter and watch the chefs in action.

American. Breakfast, lunch, dinner, Saturday-Sunday brunch. Bar. $36-85

*BLACK FOREST INN

1 E. 26th St., Minneapolis, 612-872-0812; www.blackforestinnmpls.com

German menu. Breakfast, lunch, dinner. Bar. Children's menu. Casual attire. Outdoor seating. $16-35

★★★BLACKBIRD

815 W. 50th St., Minneapolis, 612-823-4790; www.blackbirdmpls.com

You'll find a little bit of everything on this slightly schizophrenic, internationally influenced menu at this casual neighborhood spot. There's Vietnamese pork sandwiches, cornmeal-crusted walleye po'boys, chicken marsala and fried-liver salad. Weekends were made for breakfast at Blackbird. Chinese-spiced French toast, oxtail hash and huevos rancheros prove that breakfast is indeed the most important meal of the day.
American menu. Lunch, dinner, Saturday-Sunday breakfast. Closed for dinner on Sundays. $16-35

★★CAFE BRENDA

300 First Ave. N., Minneapolis, 612-342-9230; www.cafebrenda.com

American menu. Lunch, dinner. Closed Sunday. Bar. Children's menu. Casual attire. Reservations recommended. $16-35

★★★CAMPIELLO

1320 W. Lake St., Minneapolis, 612-825-2222; www.campiello.damico.com

Located in Uptown, this romantic Italian restaurant is a great choice for a special-occasion meal. Tables are set with white tablecloths and wine glasses. The open kitchen allows diners to watch their meals being prepared, and the service is always top notch. There are many delicious entrées to choose from, but one of the most popular is the balsamic-glazed short ribs. The limoncello syrup cake is the perfect ending to a meal.
Italian menu. Dinner, Sunday brunch. Bar. Business casual attire. Reservations recommended. Valet parking. Outdoor seating. $16-35

★★★CHIANG MAI THAI

3001 Hennepin Ave. S., Minneapolis, 612-827-1606; www.chiangmaithai.com

For those in search of authentic Thai cuisine in Minneapolis, Chiang Mai Thai is a good choice. Go for one of the many curry dishes and the extensive wine list. The restaurant, which is part of the Calhoun Square Mall, also does a large carryout business.
Thai menu. Lunch, dinner. Bar. Reservations recommended. Outdoor seating. $16-35

★★CHRISTOS

2632 Nicollet Ave. S., Minneapolis, 612-871-2111; www.christos.com

Greek menu. Lunch, dinner. Casual attire. $16-35

★★★COSMOS

Graves 601 Hotel, 601 First Ave. N., Minneapolis, 612-312-1168;
www.cosmosrestaurant.com

There's a groovy feel to this signature restaurant inside the Graves 601. Cosmos has an out-of-this-world all-day menu with unusual offerings like foie gras Benedict and bacon-brown sugar waffles at breakfast, grilled cheese sandwiches with seven-year cheddar and green-tea poached chicken at lunch, and chicken sausage-stuffed chicken breast at dinner. Three-course pre-theater menus are featured nightly, while seven and nine-course chef's tasting menus can be arranged with prior notice.

American menu. Breakfast, lunch, dinner. $36-85

★EMILY'S LEBANESE DELI
641 University Ave. N.E., Minneapolis, 612-379-4069
Lebanese menu. Lunch, dinner. Closed Tuesday. Casual attire. Outdoor seating. $16-35

★★FIGLIO
3001 Hennepin Ave. S., Minneapolis, 612-822-1688; www.figlio.com
Italian menu. Lunch, dinner, late-night. Bar. Casual attire. Outdoor seating. $16-35

★★GARDENS OF SALONICA
19 Fifth St. N.E., Minneapolis, 612-378-0611; www.gardensofsalonica.com
Greek menu. Lunch, dinner. Closed Sunday-Monday. Bar. Casual attire. $16-35

★★GIORGIO
2451 Hennepin Ave., Minneapolis, 612-374-5131; www.giorgiociao.com
Italian menu. Dinner. Casual attire. Outdoor seating. $16-35

★ICHIBAN JAPANESE STEAK HOUSE
1333 Nicollet Mall, Minneapolis, 612-339-0540; www.ichiban.ca
Japanese menu. Dinner. Bar. Children's menu. $16-35

★★IT'S GREEK TO ME
626 W. Lake St., Minneapolis, 612-825-9922; www.itsgreektomemn.com
Greek menu. Lunch, dinner. Closed Monday. Bar. Casual attire. Reservations recommended. $16-35

★★J.D. HOYT'S
301 Washington Ave. N., Minneapolis, 612-338-1560; www.jdhoyts.com
American, Cajun/Creole menu. Dinner, Sunday brunch. Bar. Casual attire. Reservations recommended. Valet parking. Outdoor seating. $16-35

★★★JAX CAFÉ
1928 University Ave. N.E., Minneapolis, 612-789-7297; www.jaxcafe.com
Upscale and elegant, Jax Café is an institution famous for its extravagant brunches and perfectly prepared steaks. The main dining room overlooks an outdoor patio and a small trout stream, where diners can catch their own trout. Another more private dining area features a gas fireplace. A bar, which is adorned with stained-glass windows of the Seven Dwarfs, is located in the large lounge area.

American menu. Lunch, dinner, Sunday brunch. Bar. Children's menu. Business casual attire. Reservations recommended. Outdoor seating. $36-85

★★KIKUGAWA
43 S.E. Main St., Minneapolis, 612-378-3006; www.kikugawa-restaurant.com
Japanese menu. Lunch, dinner. Bar. Business casual attire. Reservations recommended. $16-35

★THE KING AND I THAI
1346 LaSalle Ave., Minneapolis, 612-332-6928; www.kingandithai.com
Thai menu. Dinner. Closed Sunday. Bar. Casual attire. Outdoor seating. $16-35

★★★★LA BELLE VIE
510 Groveland Ave., Minneapolis, 612-874-6440; www.labellevie.us
Located in downtown Minneapolis near the Walker Arts Center, La Belle Vie brings new meaning to pre-theater dining. This restaurant is not just the first act, it's the entire show. Its talented team of chefs deliver applause-worthy performances. The staff is equally well trained, and the atmosphere is sophisticated and refined—appropriate for its location within the elegant 510 Groveland residence building. There's a five-course prix-fixe menu, and flights of wine can be selected to round out the experience. Or order from the à la carte menu, with selections such as succulent pork tenderloin and flavorful sea bass with a saffron-orange emulsion.
Continental menu. Dinner. $16-35

★★★LUCIA'S
1432 W. 31st St., Minneapolis, 612-825-1572; www.lucias.com
This quaint 11-table restaurant is a charming Uptown spot. Chef Lucia Watson, who was recognized by the James Beard Award as one of the top five chefs in the Midwest, offers a well-edited menu. She uses fresh, seasonal food along with local products, and everything is made onsite. The adjacent wine bar allows diners to choose from an ever-evolving wine list, with many options by the glass. The brunch is a weekend favorite.
American menu. Lunch, dinner, Saturday-Sunday brunch. Closed Monday. Bar. Casual attire. Valet parking. Outdoor seating. $36-85

★★★MANNY'S
821 Marquette Ave. S., Minneapolis, 612-339-9900; www.mannyssteakhouse.com
A large framed picture of a raging black bull greets guests at this New York-style steakhouse, which offers traditional meat entrées and à la carte sides served family style. The "beef cart"—wheeled tableside and accompanied by an unscripted description of each cut by the server—is what makes Manny's famous, along with dishes like the 40-ounce rib-eye, the 48-ounce double porterhouse and live lobsters. The lounge side of the restaurant also seats guests for dinner.
Steak menu. Breakfast, lunch, dinner. Bar. Business casual attire. Reservations recommended. $36-85

★★★MORTON'S, THE STEAKHOUSE
555 Nicollet Mall, Minneapolis, 612-673-9700; www.mortons.com
Consistent with expectations, this warm, club-like restaurant serves steaks and seafood. The décor is masculine, yet it has romantic touches. Tables

are topped with white cloths and candles, wine is displayed throughout and black-and-white framed photos of celebrities hang upon the walls. A knowledgeable staff explains the menu in a fun tableside presentation.

Steak menu. Lunch, dinner. Bar. Reservations recommended. $36-85

★★NYE'S POLONAISE
112 E. Hennepin Ave., Minneapolis, 612-379-2021; www.nyespolonaise.com

American, Polish menu. Lunch, dinner. Bar. Valet parking. Outdoor seating. $16-35

★★★THE OCEANAIRE SEAFOOD ROOM
1300 Nicollet Mall, Minneapolis, 612-333-2277; www.theoceanaire.com

Fresh fish is served at this sophisticated yet comfortable restaurant located in downtown Minneapolis on the second story of the Hyatt Regency Hotel. Reminiscent of a 1930s ocean liner, Oceanaire serves both simple preparations and more involved specialties. An oyster bar displaying eight different varieties glistens with shaved ice. All-American childhood dessert favorites, including root beer floats and Dixie cups, are a fun touch.

American, seafood menu. Dinner. Bar. Reservations recommended. $36-85

★★ORIGAMI
30 N. First St., Minneapolis, 612-333-8430; www.origamirestaurant.com

Japanese menu. Lunch, dinner. Bar. Casual attire. $16-35

★★★PALOMINO
825 Hennepin Ave., Minneapolis, 612-339-3800; www.r-u-i.com

This European bistro-style restaurant offers an unusual combination of rustic, hardwood-fired Mediterranean cooking and a chic ambience. The oft-changing menu offers the season's best, prepared in a distinctive style. Mediterranean menu. Lunch, dinner. Bar. Children's menu. Casual attire. $36-85

★PHO 79 RESTAURANT
2529 Nicollet Ave. S., Minneapolis, 612-871-4602

Vietnamese menu. Lunch, dinner. Casual attire. $16-35

★★PING'S SZECHUAN BAR AND GRILL
1401 Nicollet Ave. S., Minneapolis, 612-874-9404; www.pingsmpls.com

Chinese menu. Lunch, dinner. Bar. Casual attire. Valet parking. $16-35

★★★PORTER & FRYE
Hotel Ivy, 1115 Second Ave. S., Minneapolis, 612-353-3500; www.porterandfrye.com

It may be located inside the historic Hotel Ivy, but Porter & Frye isn't your typical hotel restaurant. This all-day dining spot's fashionable setting, downtown location and "haute Heartland" cooking make it a favorite of visitors and city dwellers alike. The names may sound familiar, but the gourmet takes on standards like Reuben and grilled cheese sandwiches are like nothing you've ever tasted. Dinner selections, such as tenderloin with dolce Gorgonzola, cater to an epicurean crowd.

American menu. Breakfast, lunch, dinner. $16-35

★PRACNA ON MAIN
117 Main St. S.E., Minneapolis, 612-379-3200; www.saintanthonymain.com
American menu. Lunch, dinner. Bar. Children's menu. Outdoor seating.
$16-35

★★★RUTH'S CHRIS STEAK HOUSE
920 Second Ave. S., Minneapolis, 612-672-9000, 888-722-4398; www.ruthschris.com
This classic steakhouse serves the fast-paced business crowd at its central
downtown location. Only prime steak is offered, each broiled at 1,800° F
and served sizzling hot. A large selection of wine is offered in addition to the
steaks and seafood.
Steak menu. Dinner. Bar. Business casual attire. Reservations recommended.
$36-85

★SAWATDEE
607 Washington Ave. S., Minneapolis, 612-338-6451; www.sawatdee.com
Thai menu. Lunch, dinner. Bar. Casual attire. $16-35

★★★SOLERA
900 Hennepin Ave., Minneapolis, 612-338-0062; www.solera-restaurant.com
Sample the sunny cuisine of Spain at the upbeat Solera. This place knows
how to entertain, especially on its rooftop, where live DJs spin tunes on the
weekends and movies are played on Sundays and Mondays. There's even a
late-night happy hour and menu offered until 2 a.m. (weekends only). Traditional tapas let diners taste a variety of items and many selections change
with the seasons, and the paella is fantastic.
Spanish menu. Dinner, late-night on weekends. $16-35

MINNETONKA
See also Crookston, Thief River Falls
Minnetonka, the Ojibwe name for "big water," sits on the shores of Lake
Minnetonka, a prime tourist attraction only 10 miles from Minneapolis. Ton-
ka Trucks were first manufactured near here in 1947, and Tonka Toy Group, a
division of Hasbro, has its world headquarters in the nearby city of Mound.

WHERE TO EAT
★THE MARSH
15000 Minnetonka Blvd., Minnetonka, 952-935-2202; www.themarsh.com
American menu. Breakfast, lunch, dinner, Sunday brunch. Bar. Children's
menu. Casual attire. Outdoor seating. $16-35

MOORHEAD
See also Detroit Lakes, Fergus Falls
Along with its neighboring city to the west, Fargo, N.D., Moorhead is considered an agricultural capital. Millions of pounds of sugar are produced
annually from beets raised in and near Clay County. Moorhead is the home
of Moorhead State University, Concordia College and Northwest Technical
College at Moorhead.

WHAT TO SEE
COMSTOCK HISTORIC HOUSE
506 Eighth St. S., Moorhead, 218-291-4211; www.mnhs.org/places/sites/ch
This 11-room house built in 1882 was the home of Solomon Comstock, the founder of Moorhead State University, and his daughter Ada Louise Comstock, who was the first full-time president of Radcliffe College from 1923 to 1943. The house has period furniture and historical artifacts. Guided tours. June-September, Saturday-Sunday.

HJEMKOMST CENTER
202 First Ave. N., Moorhead, 218-299-5511; www.hjemkomstcenter.com
Home of the Hjemkomst, a Viking ship replica that sailed to Norway in 1982, the Stave Church and the Red River Valley Heritage exhibit. Look for major traveling exhibits. Monday-Saturday, also Sunday afternoons.

REGIONAL SCIENCE CENTER-PLANETARIUM
1104 Seventh Ave. S., Moorhead, 218-236-3982; www.mnstate.edu/regsci
This planetarium offers a variety of astronomy programs on the Minnesota State University Moorhead campus.
September-May, Sunday-Monday; summer, Thursday.

SPECIAL EVENT
SCANDINAVIAN HJEMKOMST FESTIVAL
Moorhead, 218-299-5452; www.scandinavianhjemkomstfestival.org
The Scandinavian Hjemkomst Festival (meaning "homecoming" in Norwegian) features ethnic foods, folk dancing, storytellers, art exhibits and more. Late June.

MORA

See also Hinckley, Onamia
Rich in Swedish heritage, Mora's name led to its sister-city affiliation with Mora, Sweden. Mora is the place for outdoor enthusiasts, whether you play golf, fish, canoe, kayak, cross-country ski, snowmobile or bird-watch. The downtown area also offers opportunities to stroll past—and perhaps into—charming boutiques.

WHAT TO SEE
KANABEC HISTORY CENTER
805 Forest Ave. W., Mora, 320-679-1665
Exhibits, picnic area and hiking and ski trails; plus research information. Daily.

SPECIAL EVENTS
MORA BIKE TOUR
Mora, 320-679-9195; www.morabiketour.org
This bike tour, which starts and finishes on Ninth Street, offers tours of 30, 60 and 100 miles.
Third Saturday in September.

MORA HALF MARATHON

Mora, 320-679-5091; www.morahalfmarathon.org
Starting on Union Street in downtown Mora, this 13.1-mile race goes through the Kanabec County countryside.
Third Saturday in August.

SNAKE RIVER CANOE RACE

Mora, 320-679-4748; www.snakerivercanoerace.org
This 25-kilometer course runs down the Snake River from the Hinckley Road Bridge to the landing in Mora below the Kanabec History Center. First Saturday in May.

VASALOPPET CROSS-COUNTRY SKI RACE

Mora, 800-368-6672; www.vasaloppet.org
This race has separate 58- and 35-kilometer courses, wooded trails and an exciting finish line in downtown Mora.
Second Sunday in February.

MORRIS

See also Fergus Falls, Glenwood, Willmar
Morris is the county seat of Stevens County and provides a regional shopping center for West Central Minnesota. The surrounding area offers good fishing and hunting and is known for wildfowl, especially pheasants.

WHAT TO SEE
POMME DE TERRE CITY PARK

County Road 10, Morris, 320-589-3141
A 363-acre public recreational area along the Pomme de Terre River offers picnicking, canoeing and fishing; camping, nature and bicycle trail; swimming beach; sand volleyball court; concession. April-October, daily.

UNIVERSITY OF MINNESOTA, MORRIS

600 E. Fourth St., Morris, 320-589-6050, 888-866-3382; www.morris.umn.edu
The Humanities Fine Arts Center Gallery at this school, which was established in 1960, presents changing contemporary exhibits (October-mid-June, Monday-Friday) and performing arts series (October-April). Tours.

SPECIAL EVENT
PRAIRIE PIONEER DAYS

Morris, 320-589-1242; www.morrismnchamber.org
Arts and crafts, a parade, games and activities.
Second weekend in July.

WHERE TO STAY
★★BEST WESTERN PRAIRIE INN

200 Highway 28 E., Morris, 320-589-3030, 800-565-3035; www.bestwestern.com
92 rooms. Complimentary continental breakfast. Restaurant, bar. Pool. $61-150

NEW ULM

See also Mankato, Redwood Falls, St. Peter

Settled by German immigrants who borrowed the name of their home city, New Ulm is one of the few planned communities in the state. After more than a century, it still retains the order and cleanliness of the original settlement.

WHAT TO SEE
BROWN COUNTY HISTORICAL MUSEUM

2 N. Broadway St., New Ulm, 507-354-2016

This former post office houses historical exhibits on Native Americans and pioneers, and artwork, plus a research library with 5,000 family files.
Monday-Friday, also Saturday-Sunday afternoons.

FLANDRAU

1300 Summit Ave., New Ulm, 507-233-9800; www.dnr.state.mn.us

Comprised of 801 acres on the Cottonwood River, there's swimming, cross-country skiing (rentals), camping and hiking at this park.

FORT RIDGELY

New Ulm, 507-426-7840; www.dnr.state.mn.us

This 584-acre park is home to the partially restored fort and interpretive center (May-Labor Day, daily). Also look for the nine-hole golf course, cross-country skiing, camping, hiking and an annual historical festival.

GLOCKENSPIEL

Fourth N. and Minnesota streets, New Ulm, 507-354-4217

A 45-foot-high musical clock tower with performing animated figures and carillon with 37 bells.
Performances three times daily; noon, 3 p.m. and 5 p.m.

HARKIN STORE

2 N. Broadway St., New Ulm, 507-354-8666; www.mnhs.org

This general store built by Alexander Harkin in 1870 was in the small town of West Newton, which died when it was bypassed by the railroad. The store stayed open as a convenience until 1901, when rural free delivery closed the post office. The store has been restored to its original appearance and still has many original items on the shelves.
Special programs. Summer, Tuesday-Sunday; May-September, weekends.

HERMANN'S MONUMENT

Hermann Heights Park, Center and Monument streets, New Ulm, 507-354-4217; www.hermannmonument.com

Erected by a fraternal order, this monument recalls Hermann the Cheruscan, a German hero of A.D. 9. Towering more than 100 feet tall, the monument has a winding stairway that leads to a platform with views of the city and the Minnesota Valley.
June-Labor Day, daily.

SCHELL GARDEN AND DEER PARK
Schells Park, New Ulm, 507-354-5528
This garden hosts deer and peacocks year-round. Brewery tours, a museum and a gift shop round out the offerings.
Memorial Day-Labor Day, daily; rest of the year, Saturday.

SPECIAL EVENTS
BROWN COUNTY FAIR
Fairgrounds, 1200 N. State St., New Ulm, 507-354-2223;
www.browncountyfreefair.com
This county fair, which has been held for more than 130 years, features 4-H Club exhibits, carnival rides, pony rides, music and more.
Mid-August.

FASCHING
118 N. Minnesota St., New Ulm, 507-354-8850
This traditional German winter festival includes German food, music and a costume ball. Late February.

HERITAGEFEST
118 N. Minnesota St., New Ulm, 507-354-8850
This old world style celebration highlights German traditions and culture through music, food, arts and crafts. Look for entertainers from around the area and from Europe. Two weekends in mid-July.

WHERE TO STAY
★★HOLIDAY INN
2101 S. Broadway St., New Ulm, 507-359-2941, 888-465-4329; www.holiday-inn.com
120 rooms. Restaurant, bar. Pets accepted. Pool. $61-150

WHERE TO EAT
★VEIGEL'S KAISERHOF
221 N. Minnesota St., New Ulm, 507-359-2071
German menu. Lunch, dinner. Bar. Casual attire. $16-35

NORTHFIELD
See also Faribault, Hastings, Lakeville, Minneapolis, Owatonna, Red Wing, St. Paul
This historic river town located 30 miles south of the Twin Cities offers a captivating blend of old and new. Its history is one of the most dramatic of any Midwestern community. Each year on the weekend after Labor Day, thousands come here to share in the retelling of the defeat of Jesse James and his gang who, on September 7, 1876, were foiled in their attempt to raid the Northfield Bank in what proved to be one of the last chapters in the saga of the Old West. This history has been preserved in the Northfield Bank Museum (408 Division St.). The storefronts house boutiques, antique stores and other interesting shops.

WHAT TO SEE
CARLETON COLLEGE
1 N. College St., Northfield, 507-222-4000; www.carleton.edu
This small (1,800 students) liberal arts school was established in 1866 and features a lovely arboretum with hiking and running trails along the Cannon River. A 35-acre prairie maintained by the college is a nice place to visit. Tours of the arboretum and the prairie are available with advance notice. Summer theater programs are also available. Check the Web site for details.

NERSTRAND-BIG WOODS STATE PARK
9700 170th St. E., Nerstrand, 507-333-4840; www.dnr.state.mn.us
At more than 1,280 acres, this heavily wooded park has hiking, cross-country skiing, snowmobiling, picnicking and camping.

NORTHFIELD ARTS GUILD
304 Division St. S., Northfield, 507-645-8877; www.northfieldartsguild.org
Exhibits of local and regional fine arts housed in a historic 1885 YMCA Building, as well as juried handcrafted items.
Monday-Saturday.

ST. OLAF COLLEGE
1520 St. Olaf Ave., Northfield, 507-786-2222; www.stolaf.edu
Established 1874; 3,000 students. Famous for its choir, band and orchestra, which tour nationally and abroad, St. Olaf also offers its Steensland Art Gallery (daily). The school is home of the national offices and archives of the Norwegian American Historical Association.

SPECIAL EVENT
DEFEAT OF JESSE JAMES DAYS
Northfield, 507-645-5604; www.djjd.org
Raid reenactment, parade, outdoor arts fair and rodeo. Four days, beginning the weekend after Labor Day.

WHERE TO STAY
★COUNTRY INN BY CARLSON NORTHFIELD
300 S. Highway 3, Northfield, 507-645-2286, 800-456-4000;
www.countryinns.com/northfieldmn
54 rooms. Complimentary continental breakfast. Pool. $61-150

SPECIALTY LODGING
ARCHER HOUSE HOTEL
212 Division St., Northfield, 507-645-5661, 800-247-2235; www.archerhouse.com
36 rooms. High-speed Internet access. Restaurant. $

ONAMIA
See also Aitkin, Brainerd, Little Falls
Tourists tend to visit Onamia because of Mille Lacs Lake, situated just north of town. The largest city in the Mille Lacs area, Onamia is a good place to browse a few boutiques and gift shops.

WHAT TO SEE
MILLE LACS KATHIO STATE PARK
15066 Kathio Park Road, Onamia, 320-532-3523; www.dnr.state.mn.us
Comprises 10,577 acres surrounding the main outlet of Mille Lacs Lake. There's evidence of Native American habitation and culture dating back more than 4,000 years. In 1679, Daniel Greysolon, Sieur du Lhut, claimed the upper Mississippi region for France.
Swimming, fishing, boating, hiking, riding trails, cross-country skiing (rentals), snowmobiling.

MILLE LACS LAKE
Highway 169, Onamia, 888-350-2692; www.millelacs.com
This lake has 150 miles of beaches and shoreline—some of the largest and loveliest in the state. Nearly 9,000 Native American mounds are near the lakeshore.
Fishing, boating, camping as well.

WHERE TO STAY
★★IZATY'S GOLF AND YACHT CLUB
40005 85th Ave., Onamia, 320-532-3101, 800-533-1728; www.izatys.com
28 rooms. Restaurant, bar. Children's activity center. Pool. Golf. $61-150

OWATONNA
See also Albert Lea, Austin, Faribault, Northfield, Rochester
Legend has it that the city was named after a beautiful but frail Native American princess named Owatonna. It is said that her father, Chief Wabena, had heard about the healing water called "Minnewaucan." When the waters' curing powers restored his daughter's health, he moved his entire village to the site now known as Mineral Springs Park. A statue of Princess Owatonna stands in the park and watches over the springs that still provide cold, fresh mineral water.

WHAT TO SEE
MINNESOTA STATE PUBLIC SCHOOL ORPHANAGE MUSEUM
540 West Hills Circle, Owatonna, 507-451-7970, 800-423-6466;
www.orphanagemuseum.com
This museum is on the site of a former orphanage that housed nearly 13,000 children from 1886 to 1945. The main building is on the National Register of Historic Places. Daily.

NORWEST BANK OWATONNA, NA BUILDING
101 N. Cedar Ave., Owatonna, 507-451-7970
Completed in 1908 as the National Farmers Bank, this nationally acclaimed architectural treasure was designed by one of America's outstanding architects, Louis H. Sullivan. The cubelike exterior with huge arched stained-glass windows by Louis Millet quickly earned widespread recognition.

OWATONNA ARTS CENTER

West Hills Complex, 435 Garden View Lane, Owatonna, 507-451-0533;
www.oacarts.org

Housed in a historic Romanesque structure, this permanent collection includes a 100-piece collection of garments from around the world, and 14-foot stained-glass panels featured in the Performing Arts Hall. An outdoor sculpture garden includes works by Minnesota artists such as John Rood, Richard and Donald Hammel, Paul Grandlund and Charles Gagnon. There are changing gallery shows every month.
Tuesday-Sunday.

VILLAGE OF YESTERYEAR

1448 Austin Road, Owatonna, 507-451-1420; www.steelecohistoricalsociety.org

The 11 restored pioneer buildings here (from the mid-1800s) include a church, two log cabins, a schoolhouse, a large family home, an old fire department and a country store, plus a depot, a farm machinery building, a blacksmith shop; and a museum. Period furnishings, memorabilia and a 1905 C-52 locomotive caboose.
May-September, afternoons except Monday.

WHERE TO STAY
★★HOLIDAY INN HOTEL & SUITES

2365 43rd St. N.W., Owatonna, 507-446-8900, 888-465-4329; www.holiday-inn.com
130 rooms. Restaurant, bar. Airport transportation available. Pool. $61-150

PARK RAPIDS

See also Detroit Lakes, Walker

This resort center is surrounded by 400 lakes, nearly as many streams, and beautiful woods. There are more than 200 resorts within 20 miles, and fishing is excellent for bass, walleye, northern pike, muskie and trout.

WHAT TO SEE
HUBBARD COUNTY HISTORICAL MUSEUM/NORTH COUNTRY MUSEUM OF ARTS

Court Avenue and Third Street, Park Rapids, 218-732-5237

This historical museum has displays on pioneer life, including pioneer farm implements, a one-room schoolhouse and foreign wars. The museum of arts has five galleries of contemporary art and also features a section on 15th- to 18th-century European art.
May-September, Tuesday-Saturday; February-April, Tuesday-Sunday.

RAPID RIVER LOGGING CAMP

15073 County Road, Park Rapids, 218-732-3444

This authentic logging camp has a nature trail, antiques, lumberjack meals and logging demonstrations (Tuesday and Friday).
Memorial Day weekend-Labor Day weekend, daily.

PINE RIVER

See also Brainerd, Walker

The city and the river for which it is named are inseparable. Tourists visit Pine River to fish for bass, northern pike and walleye and to canoe down the river, a 19-mile paddle to the mighty Mississippi. Snowmobiling, hiking and cycling are also popular activities in the area.

WHERE TO STAY

★★PINEY RIDGE LODGE

34700 Piney Ridge Lane, Pine River, 218-587-2296, 800-450-3333;
www.pineyridge.com

26 rooms. Closed late September-April. Restaurant. Children's activity center. $61-150

PIPESTONE

See also Luverne

Pipestone often hosts visitors en route to Pipestone National Monument. Some of the red Sioux quartzite from the quarries shows up in Pipestone's public buildings. George Catlin, a famous painter of Native Americans, was the first white man to report on the area.

WHAT TO SEE

PIPESTONE COUNTY MUSEUM

113 S. Hiawatha Ave., Pipestone, 507-825-2563; www.pipestoneminnesota.com
Prehistory, information on early settlements, and Native American and pioneer exhibits.
Tours. Daily.

PIPESTONE NATIONAL MONUMENT

36 N. Reservation Ave., Pipestone, 507-825-5464
The ancient pipestone in the quarries of this 283-acre area is found in few other places. The Native Americans quarried this reddish stone and carved it into ceremonial pipes. The Pipestone deposits, named catlinite for George Catlin, who first described the stone, run about a foot thick (most usable sections are about two inches thick). Principal features of the monument are Winnewissa Falls, which flow over quartzite outcroppings; Three Maidens, a group of glacial boulders near quarries; Leaping Rock, used by Native Americans as a test of strength of young men; and Nicollet Marker, an inscription on a boulder which recalls the 1838 visit of Joseph Nicollet's exploring party. He carved his name and the initials of members of his party, including Lieutenant John C. Fremont. Established as a national monument in 1937, Pipestone protects the remaining red stone and preserves it for use by Native Americans of all tribes.
Daily.

SPLIT ROCK CREEK STATE PARK

Pipestone, 507-348-7908, 800-766-6000; www.pipestoneminnesota.com
Covering more than 1,300 acres, this park offers swimming, fishing, boating, hiking, cross-country skiing, picnicking and camping.

SPECIAL EVENTS
HIAWATHA PAGEANT
117 Eighth Ave. S.E., Pipestone, 507-825-3316, 800-336-6125
This outdoor performance is a tradition for many. All seats are reserved; ticket office opens 1 p.m. on show dates.
Last two weekends in July; first weekend in August.

WATERTOWER FESTIVAL
Pipestone, 507-825-3316; www.pipestoneminnesota.com
Large arts and crafts show and parade.
Last Friday and Saturday in June.

WHERE TO STAY
★★★HISTORIC CALUMET INN
104 W. Main St., Pipestone, 507-825-5871, 800-535-7610; www.calumetinn.com
This historic inn, which features rooms full of antiques, was built from Sioux Quartzite in 1888. The two-story lobby with its lofty tin ceiling is a sight, and the large antique oak bar in Cally's Lounge (which was once a bank) is a perfect spot for a nightcap.
38 rooms. Complimentary full breakfast. Restaurant, bar. Pets accepted. $61-150

WHERE TO EAT
★LANGE'S CAFÉ
110 Eighth Ave. S.E., Pipestone, 507-825-4488
American menu. Breakfast, lunch, dinner, late-night, brunch. Children's menu. $15 and under

RED WING
See also Hastings, Lakeville, Northfield, St. Paul
Established as a missionary society outpost, this community bears the name of one of the great Dakota chiefs, Koo-Poo-Hoo-Sha ("wing of the wild swan dyed scarlet").

WHAT TO SEE
CANNON VALLEY TRAIL
Highway 19, 825 Cannon River Ave., Cannon Falls, 507-263-0508;
www.cannonvalleytrail.com
Twenty-mile cross-country skiing trail connects Cannon Falls, Welch and Red Wing.

GOODHUE COUNTY HISTORICAL MUSEUM
1166 Oak St., Red Wing, 651-388-6024; www.goodhuehistory.mus.mn.us
This is one of the state's most comprehensive museums. Permanent exhibits explore local and regional history from the glacial age to present, and an extensive collection of Red Wing pottery and artifacts from the Prairie Island Native American community is also on display. Tuesday-Sunday.

HIKING
Red Wing
A 1½-mile hiking trail to the top of Mount LaGrange (Barn Bluff) offers a scenic overlook of the Mississippi River. The Cannon Valley Trail provides 25 miles of improved trail following Cannon Bottom River to Cannon Falls.

MOUNT FRONTENAC
31099 Ski Road, 651-388-5826; www.mountfrontenac.com
18-hole golf course. Mid-April-October.

RED WING STONEWARE
4909 Moundview Drive, Red Wing, 651-388-4610; www.redwingstoneware.com
This popular stoneware facility allows visitors to watch artisans create various types of pottery.

SHELDON THEATRE
443 W. Third St., Red Wing, 651-388-8700; www.sheldontheatre.org
This is the first municipal theater in the United States, and opened in 1904. Performances available regularly.
Group tours available. June-October, Friday-Saturday; November-May, Saturday.

SOLDIERS' MEMORIAL PARK/EAST END RECREATION AREA
Skyline Drive, Red Wing
On a plateau overlooking the city and the river, these 476 acres include five miles of hiking trails.

WELCH VILLAGE
26685 County Seven Blvd., Welch, 651-258-4567; www.welchvillage.com
Three quad, five double, triple chairlifts and Mitey-mite, plus patrol, rentals, snowmaking and cafeteria. Longest run is 4,000 feet with a vertical drop of 350 feet. November-March, daily.

SPECIAL EVENTS
FALL FESTIVAL OF THE ARTS
Red Wing, 651-388-7569
This fine arts show features more than 80 artists, live music, food and children's activities.
First weekend in October.

RIVER CITY DAYS
Red Wing, 651-385-5934; www.rivercitydays.org
A lumberjack show, carnival, parade, concession stands and an arts and crafts fair are among the activities at this annual celebration.
First weekend in August.

WHERE TO STAY
★BEST WESTERN QUIET HOUSE & SUITES
752 Withers Harbor Drive, Red Wing, 651-388-1577, 800-780-7234;
www.bestwesternminnesota.com
51 rooms. Pets accepted. Pool. $61-150

★★ST. JAMES HOTEL
406 Main St., Red Wing, 651-388-2846, 800-252-1875; www.st-james-hotel.com
61 rooms. Restaurant, bar. Airport transportation available. $61-150

REDWOOD FALLS
See also Granite Falls, Marshall, New Ulm
The main attraction in the town of Redwood Falls is Ramsey Park, which highlights both the falls for which the city is named and Ramsey Falls.

WHAT TO SEE
LOWER SIOUX AGENCY AND HISTORIC SITE
32469 Redwood County Highway 2, Morton, 507-697-6321;
www.mnhs.org/places/sites/lsa
Exhibits, a trail system and a restored 1861 warehouse trace the history of the Dakota tribe in Minnesota from the mid-17th century through the present. May-September, daily; rest of year, by appointment.

RAMSEY PARK
Redwood Falls; www.redwoodfalls.org
A 200-acre park of rugged woodland carved by the Redwood River and Ramsey Creek. Includes picnicking, trail riding, cross-country ski trail, hiking, golf and camping. There is also a small zoo, a playground shelter and a 30-foot waterfall.

SPECIAL EVENT
MINNESOTA INVENTORS CONGRESS
Redwood Valley School, 805 E. Bridge St., Redwood Falls, 507-637-2344
Exhibit of inventions by adult and student inventors, plus seminars, food, arts and crafts, a parade and a resource center.
Three days of the second full weekend in June.

ROCHESTER
See also Owatonna, Spring Valley
The world-famous Mayo Clinic has transformed what was once a crossroads campground for immigrant wagon trains into city of doctors, hospitals and lodging places. Each year thousands of people come here for medical treatment. One of the first dairy farms in the state began here, and Rochester still remains a central point for this industry.

WHAT TO SEE
MAYO CLINIC
200 First St. S.W., Rochester, 507-284-2511; www.mayo.edu
More than 30 buildings now accommodate the famous group practice of medicine that grew from the work of Dr. William Worrall Mayo and his sons,

Dr. William James Mayo and Dr. Charles Horace Mayo. There are now 1,041 doctors at the clinic as well as 935 residents in training in virtually every medical and surgical specialty. The 14-story Plummer Building includes a medical library and historical exhibit. The Conrad N. Hilton and Guggenheim buildings house clinical and research laboratories. The 19-story Mayo Building covers an entire block. It houses facilities for diagnosis and treatment. Clinic tours Monday-Friday.

MAYOWOOD

1195 W. Circle Drive S.W., Rochester, 507-282-9447
Home of Doctors C.H. and C.W. Mayo, this historic 38-room country mansion is on 15 acres and is full of period antiques and works of art.

OLMSTED COUNTY HISTORY CENTER AND MUSEUM

1195 W. Circle Drive S.W., Rochester, 507-282-9447; www.olmstedhistory.com
Changing historical exhibits. Daily.

PLUMMER HOUSE OF THE ARTS

1091 Plummer Lane S.W., Rochester, 507-328-2525; www.rochestercvb.org
This is the former estate of Dr. Henry S. Plummer, a 35-year member of the Mayo Clinic. Today, 11 acres remain, with formal gardens, a quarry and a water tower. The five-story, circa 1920 house is an English Tudor mansion with 49 rooms, original furnishings and a slate roof.
Tours June-August, Wednesday afternoons, also first and third Sunday afternoons.

WHITEWATER STATE PARK

19041 Highway 74, Altura, 507-932-3007; www.dnr.state.mn.us
A 1,822-acre park contains limestone formations in a hardwood forest and offers swimming, fishing, hiking, cross-country skiing, picnicking and primitive camping.

WHERE TO STAY
★★BEST WESTERN SOLDIERS FIELD TOWER & SUITES

401 Sixth St. S.W., Rochester, 507-288-2677, 800-366-2067; www.bestwestern.com
218 rooms. Complimentary continental breakfast. Restaurant, bar. Airport transportation available. Pool. Fitness center. High-speed Internet access. $61-150

★HAMPTON INN

1755 S. Broadway, Rochester, 507-287-9050, 800-426-7866;
www.hamptoninnrochester.com
105 rooms. Complimentary breakfast. Pool. Business center. $61-150

★★HOLIDAY INN

1630 S. Broadway, Rochester, 507-288-1844, 888-465-4329; www.holiday-inn.com
195 rooms. Restaurant, bar. Pets accepted. Indoor pool, whirlpool. $61-150

★★★KAHLER GRAND

20 Second Ave. S.W., Rochester, 507-280-6200, 800-533-1655;
www.thekahlerhotel.com

This original English Tudor structure has vaulted ceilings and paneling. It is located across from the Mayo Clinic in the downtown area.
688 rooms. Restaurant, bar. Airport transportation available. Pets accepted. Pool. Fitness center. Complementary parking, shuttle. High-speed Internet access. $61-150

★★★MARRIOTT ROCHESTER MAYO CLINIC

101 First Ave. S.W., Rochester, 507-280-6000, 877-623-7775;
www.rochestermarriott.com

Located near the Galleria Mall and Miracle Mile Shopping Complex, with tennis facilities and many golf courses, this hotel is a convenient choice.
203 rooms. High-speed Internet access. Restaurant, bar. Pets accepted. Pool. $151-250

★★RADISSON PLAZA HOTEL ROCHESTER

150 S. Broadway, Rochester, 507-281-8000, 800-333-3333;
www.radisson.com/rochestermn

212 rooms. High-speed Internet access. Restaurant, bar. Pets accepted. $61-150

★★RAMADA HOTEL & CONFERENCE CENTER

1517 16th St. S.W., Rochester, 507-289-8866, 800-272-6232; www.ramada.com

149 rooms. Complimentary continental breakfast. Restaurant, bar. Airport transportation available. Pool. Business center. Fitness center. High-speed Internet access. $61-150

WHERE TO EAT

★★BROADSTREET CAFÉ AND BAR

300 First Ave. N.E., Rochester, 507-281-2451; www.broadstreet-cafe.com.

Mediterranean menu. Lunch, dinner. Bar. Children's menu. Casual attire. Reservations recommended. $16-35

★★CHARDONNAY

723 Second St. S.W., Rochester, 507-252-1310

International menu. Dinner. Closed Sunday. Casual attire. Reservations recommended. Four dining rooms in a remodeled house. $36-85

★★MICHAEL'S FINE DINING

15 S. Broadway, Rochester, 507-288-2020; www.michaelsfinedining.com

Seafood, steak menu. Lunch, dinner. Closed Sunday. Bar. Children's menu. Casual attire. Reservations recommended. $16-35

ROSEAU

See also Baudette, Thief River Falls

More than 150 years ago, Roseau was the site of a busy Hudson Bay Company fur-trading post. Today, the city is a snowmobiler's dream, with a number of snowmobile trails. Polaris Industries, the first mass producer of snowmobiles and today a leading snowmobile manufacturer, is located here and offers tours at its facility.

WHAT TO SEE
HAYES LAKE STATE PARK
48990 County Road 4, Roseau, 218-425-7504; www.dnr.state.mn.us
A 2,950-acre park with swimming, fishing, hiking, cross-country skiing, snowmobiling, picnicking and camping.

PIONEER FARM AND VILLAGE
Highway 11, Roseau, 218-463-3052; www.roseaupioneerfarm.com
Restored buildings include a log barn, a museum, a church, a parish hall, equipped printery, log house, school, store, blacksmith shop and post office. Picnicking.
Mid-May-mid-September, schedule varies.

POLARIS EXPERIENCE CENTER
205 Fifth Ave. S.W., Roseau, 218-463-4999; www.polarisindustries.com
In essence a snowmobile museum, the center mixes exhibits of snowmobile designs throughout history with photographs and videos, all of which are featured on the self-guided tour.
Monday-Saturday noon-8 p.m., Sunday noon-6 p.m. The main Polaris manufacturing plant is also open for tours daily 4 p.m.

ROSEAU COUNTY HISTORICAL MUSEUM AND INTERPRETIVE CENTER
110 Second Ave. N.E., Roseau, 218-463-1918
This museum focuses on natural history and features a collection of mounted birds and eggs, plus Native American artifacts and pioneer history.
Tuesday-Saturday.

ROSEAU RIVER WILDLIFE MANAGEMENT AREA
27952 400th St., Roseau, 218-463-1557
More than 2,000 ducks are raised here annually on 65,000 acres. There's also a bird-watching area, canoeing on the river and hunting during season.

SAUK CENTRE
See also Alexandria, Glenwood, Little Falls
Sauk Centre is "Gopher Prairie," the boyhood home of Nobel Prize-winning novelist Sinclair Lewis. Sauk Centre was the setting for his best-known novel, Main Street, as well as many of his other works. The town is at the southern tip of Big Sauk Lake.

WHAT TO SEE
SINCLAIR LEWIS BOYHOOD HOME
812 Sinclair Lewis Ave., Sauk Centre, 320-352-5201; www.saukcentrechamber.com
This restored home of America's first Nobel Prize-winning novelist features original furnishings and family memorabilia.
Memorial Day-Labor Day, Tuesday-Sunday; rest of year, by appointment.

SINCLAIR LEWIS INTERPRETIVE CENTER

1220 Main St. S., Sauk Centre, 320-352-5201

Exhibits include original manuscripts, photographs and letters, plus a 15-minute video on the author's life and a research library.

Labor Day-Memorial Day, Monday-Friday; Memorial Day-Labor Day, daily.

SPECIAL EVENT
SINCLAIR LEWIS DAYS

Sauk Centre, 320-352-5201; www.saukcentrechamber.com

Activities at this event include a battle of the bands, a concert in the park, a parade, craft show and fireworks.

Mid-July.

SPRING VALLEY

See also Austin, Rochester

As the name suggests, there are many large springs in this area, and the underground rivers, caves and limestone outcroppings here are of particular interest. This was the hometown of Almanzo Wilder. He and wife Laura Ingalls Wilder briefly attended church here.

WHAT TO SEE
FORESTVILLE/MYSTERY CAVE STATE PARK

21071 County 118, Preston, 507-352-5111; www.dnr.state.mn.us

This 3,075-acre park in the Root River Valley includes a historic town site. Fishing, hiking, bridle trails, cross-country skiing, snowmobiling, picnicking and camping also available.

METHODIST CHURCH

221 W. Courtland St., Spring Valley, 507-346-7659

This circa-1876 church features Victorian Gothic architecture and 23 stained-glass windows and is a Laura Ingalls Wilder site. The lower-level displays include a country store, a history room, and military and business displays.

June-August, daily; September-October, weekends, also by appointment.

WASHBURN-ZITTLEMAN HOUSE

220 W. Courtland St., Spring Valley, 507-346-7659; www.springvalley.govoffice.com

This two-story frame house from 1886 has period furnishings, quilts, farm equipment, a one-room school and toys.

Memorial Day-Labor Day, daily; September-October, weekends, also by appointment.

ST. CLOUD

See also Elk River, Litchfield, Little Falls, Minneapolis

Its central location makes St. Cloud a convention hub and retail center for the area. The granite quarried here is prized throughout the United States. This Mississippi River community's architecture reflects the German and New England roots of its early settlers.

WHAT TO SEE
CLEMENS GARDENS & MUNSINGER GARDENS
13th Street and Kilian Boulevard, St. Cloud, 320-258-0389, 800-264-2940;
www.munsingerclemens.com
Clemens Gardens features the White Garden, based on the White Garden at Sissinghurst Garden in Kent, England. Munsinger Gardens is surrounded by pine and hemlock trees.
Memorial Day-Labor Day.

COLLEGE OF ST. BENEDICT
37 S. College Ave., St. Joseph, 320-363-5777; www.csbsju.edu
On campus is the $6 million Ardolf Science Center. Guided tours. Art exhibits, concerts, plays, lectures and films in Benedicta Arts Center.

MINNESOTA BASEBALL HALL OF FAME
St. Cloud Civic Center, St. Cloud, 320-255-7272
Features great moments from amateur and professional baseball. Monday-Friday.

POWDER RIDGE SKI AREA
15015 93rd Ave., Kimball, 320-398-7200, 800-348-7734; www.powderridge.com
Quad, two double chairlifts, J-bar, rope tow; patrol, school, rentals; snowmaking; bar, cafeteria.
Mid-November-March, daily. Fifteen runs.

ST. BENEDICT'S CONVENT
104 Chapel Lane, St. Joseph, 320-363-7100; www.sbm.osb.org
Community of more than 400 Benedictine women. Tours of historic Sacred Heart Chapel, built in 1913, and archives.

ST. CLOUD STATE UNIVERSITY
Fourth Avenue South, St. Cloud, 320-308-3223
Established 1869; 15,600 students. Marked historical sites; anthropology museum, planetarium, art gallery.

ST. JOHN'S UNIVERSITY AND ABBEY, PREPARATORY SCHOOL
1857 Watertower Road, Collegeville, 320-363-3321, 800-525-7737; www.sjprep.net
Established 1857; 1,900 students. Impressive modern abbey, university, church and Hill Monastic manuscript library, other buildings designed by the late Marcel Breuer; 2,450 acres of woodlands and lakes.

STEARNS HISTORY MUSEUM
235 S. 33rd Ave., St. Cloud, 320-253-8424; www.stearns-museum.org
Located in a 100-acre park, the center showcases cultural and historical aspects of past and present life in central Minnesota. It contains a replica of a working granite quarry, agricultural and automobile displays and a research center and archives.
Daily.

WHERE TO STAY

★FAIRFIELD INN

4120 Second St. S., St. Cloud, 320-654-1881, 800-828-2800; www.marriott.com

57 rooms. Complimentary continental breakfast. High-speed Internet access. Pool. $61-150

★★HOLIDAY INN

75 37th Ave. S., St. Cloud, 320-253-9000, 888-465-4329; www.holiday-inn.com

257 rooms. High-speed Internet access. Restaurant, bar. Children's activity center. Pets accepted. Pool. $61-150

WHERE TO EAT

★DB SEARLE'S

18 Fifth Ave. S., St. Cloud, 320-253-0655; www.dbsearles.com

American menu. Dinner. Closed Sunday. Bar. Children's menu. Casual attire. Reservations recommended. $$

ST. PAUL

See also Anoka, Elk River, Hastings, Lakeville, Minneapolis, Northfield, Red Wing, Stillwater

The distribution center for the great Northwest and the dignified capital of Minnesota, stately St. Paul had its humble beginnings as a settlement known as "Pig's Eye." At the bend of the Mississippi and tangential to the point where the waters of the Mississippi and Minnesota rivers meet, St. Paul and its twin city, Minneapolis, form a northern metropolis. Together, they are a center for computers, electronics, medical technology, printing and publishing. In many ways they complement each other, yet they are also friendly rivals. Fiercely proud of their professional sports teams (baseball's Minnesota Twins, football's Minnesota Vikings and basketball's Minnesota Timberwolves), the partisans of both cities troop to the Hubert H. Humphrey Metrodome in Minneapolis, as well as other arenas in the area—the Minnesota Wild hockey team plays at Xcel Energy Center—to watch their heroes in action.

A terraced city of diversified industry and lovely homes, St. Paul boasts 30 lakes within a 30-minute drive, as well as more than 90 parks. It's also home to 3M and other major corporations. The junction of the Mississippi and Minnesota rivers was chosen in 1807 as the site for a fort that later became known as Fort Snelling. Squatters soon settled on the reservation lands nearby, only to be expelled in 1840 with one group moving a few miles east and a French-Canadian trader, Pierre Parrant, settling at the landing near Fort Snelling. Parrant was nicknamed "Pig's Eye," and the settlement that developed at the landing took this name.

When Father Lucien Galtier built a log cabin chapel there in 1841, he prevailed on the settlers to rename their community for St. Paul. A Mississippi steamboat terminus since 1823, St. Paul prospered on river trade, furs, pioneer traffic and agricultural commerce. Incorporated as a town in 1849, it was host to the first legislature of the Minnesota Territory and has been the capital ever since.

A number of institutions of higher education are located in St. Paul, including the University of Minnesota Twin Cities Campus, University of St.

Thomas, College of St. Catherine, Macalester College, Hamline University, Concordia University, Bethel College and William Mitchell College of Law.

WHAT TO SEE
ALEXANDER RAMSEY HOUSE

265 S. Exchange St., St. Paul, 651-296-8760; www.mnhs.org/places/sites/arh

This was the home of Minnesota's first territorial governor and his wife, Anne. The house, built in 1872, is full of original Victorian furnishings and features carved walnut woodwork, marble fireplaces and crystal chandeliers. Guided tours show visitors what life was like in the 1870s; reservations are suggested. Friday-Saturday 10 a.m.-3 p.m., expanded holiday hours.

CAPITAL CITY TROLLEY

525 Farwell Ave., St. Paul, 651-223-5600; www.capitalcitytrolleys.com

This hour-long narrated tour takes visitors through the downtown area and along the Mississippi riverfront, stopping at historical sites such as the mansion of railroad magnate James J. Hill on Summit Avenue.
Reservations are required. May-October, Thursday.

CATHEDRAL OF ST. PAUL

239 Selby Ave., St. Paul, 651-228-1766; www.cathedralsaintpaul.org

The dome of this Classical Renaissance-style Roman Catholic cathedral, in which services began in 1915, is 175 feet high. The central rose window is a dominant feature. Daily.

CITY HALL AND COURTHOUSE

15 W. Kellogg Blvd., St. Paul

This 1932 building, listed on the National Register of Historic Places, is a prominent example of Art Deco. Carl Milles's 60-ton, 36-foot-tall onyx Vision of Peace statue graces the lobby.

COMO PARK

Midway and Lexington parkways, St. Paul, 651-266-6400;
www.comozooconservatory.org

A 448-acre park with a 70-acre lake. The glass-domed conservatory features an authentic Japanese garden (May-September) and the Enchanted Garden and Frog Pond. The Como Zoo includes bison, lions and other big cats and Galapagos tortoises. There is also an amusement area (Memorial Day-Labor Day) with a carousel and other children's rides and a miniature golf course.
Daily 10 a.m.-4 p.m.; April-September until 6 p.m.

FORT SNELLING STATE PARK

1 Post Road, St. Paul, 612-725-2389; www.dnr.state.mn.us

This 4,000-acre park is at the confluence of the Minnesota and Mississippi rivers. Swimming, fishing, boating; hiking, biking, cross-country skiing; picnicking; visitor center. Includes historic Fort Snelling, a stone frontier fortress restored to its appearance in the 1820s. Daily drills and cannon firings; craft demonstrations.
Daily 8 a.m.-4 p.m.

GREAT AMERICAN HISTORY THEATRE

30 10th St. E., St. Paul, 651-292-4323; www.historytheatre.com
Original plays and musicals with American and Midwestern themes.
Thursday-Sunday.

INDIAN MOUNDS PARK

Earl Street and Mounds Boulevard, St. Paul, 651-266-6400;
www.nps.gov/miss/planyourvisit/indimoun.htm
This park, one of the oldest in the region, is made up of more than 25 acres
and contains prehistoric Native American burial mounds built 1,500 to 2,000
years ago. Eighteen mounds existed on this site in 1856, but only six remain.
The park also has picnic facilities, paved trails and outstanding views of the
Mississippi River and the city skyline. Daily, half an hour before sunrise to
half an hour after sunset.

JAMES J. HILL HOUSE

240 Summit Ave., St. Paul, 651-297-2555
This 1891 house, made of red sandstone, was the showplace of the city when
it was built for the famous railroad magnate. Reservations are recommended
for the guided tours, which depart every 30 minutes.
Wednesday-Saturday 10 a.m.-3:30 p.m., Sunday 1-3:30 p.m.

LANDMARK CENTER

75 W. Fifth St., St. Paul, 651-292-3233; www.landmarkcenter.org
This restored Federal Courts Building was constructed in 1902. It is currently the center for cultural programs and gangster history tours. It houses
four courtrooms, a four-story indoor courtyard (the Musser Cortile), and the
Minnesota Museum of American Art.
Visitors can take 45-minute guided tours Thursday and Sunday; also by appointment. Daily; closed holidays.

LUTHER SEMINARY

2481 Como Ave., St. Paul, 651-641-3456; www.luthersem.edu
Established 1869; 780 students. On campus is the Old Muskego Church, the
first church built by Norse immigrants in America, which was constructed in
1844. It was moved to its present site in 1904. Tours.

MINNESOTA CHILDREN'S MUSEUM

10 W. Seventh St., St. Paul, 651-225-6000; www.mcm.org
This museum features hands-on learning exhibits for children and their adult
companions. The museum store is stocked with unique puzzles, maps, toys,
games and books.
Memorial Day-Labor Day, daily; rest of year, Tuesday-Sunday.

MINNESOTA HISTORICAL SOCIETY CENTER

345 Kellogg Blvd. W., St. Paul, 651-296-6126, 800-657-3773; www.mnhs.org
Home to the Historical Society, the center houses a museum with interactive
exhibits and an extensive genealogical and research library, as well as special
events, two museum shops and a café.

Museum: Memorial Day-Labor Day, daily; rest of the year, Tuesday-Sunday.
Library: Tuesday-Saturday.

MINNESOTA MUSEUM OF AMERICAN ART—LANDMARK CENTER

Kellogg Boulevard at Market Street, St. Paul, 651-266-1030; www.mmaa.org

This museum includes changing exhibits and a permanent collection of American art from the 19th century to the present. Artists such as Thomas Hart Benton are featured, as are new art forms. There's also a Museum School and store. Tuesday-Sunday.

MINNESOTA TRANSPORTATION MUSEUM

193 Pennsylvania Ave. E., St. Paul, 651-228-0263; www.mtmuseum.org

Display museum and restoration shop; two-mile rides in early 1900s electric streetcars along reconstructed Como-Harriet line.
Memorial Day weekend-Labor Day, daily; after Labor Day-October, weekends.

MINNESOTA WILD (NHL)

Xcel Energy Center, 175 W. Kellogg Blvd., St. Paul, 651-222-9453; www.wild.com

Professional hockey team.

SCIENCE MUSEUM OF MINNESOTA

120 W. Kellogg Blvd., St. Paul, 651-221-9444; www.smm.org

This eight-acre museum showcases technology, anthropology, paleontology, geography and biology exhibits and a 3-D cinema. The William L. McKnight 3M Omnitheater shows IMAX films, and there's a new Mississippi River Visitor Center. Daily.

SIBLEY HISTORIC SITE

1357 Sibley Memorial Highway, Mendota, 651-452-1596; www.mnhs.org

On this site sits the 1838 home of General Henry Sibley, Minnesota's first governor, now preserved as a museum. Also on the grounds are three other restored limestone buildings, including the Faribault House Museum and the home of pioneer fur trader Jean-Baptiste Faribault, now a museum.
May-October, Tuesday-Sunday.

SIXTH STREET CENTER SKYWAY

56 E. Sixth St., St. Paul

Built from sections of the second level of Sixth Street Center's five-story parking garage, the center includes shops and restaurants.
Daily.

STATE CAPITOL

75 Constitution Ave., St. Paul, 651-296-2881; www.mnhs.org/places/sites/msc

Designed in the Italian Renaissance style by Cass Gilbert and decorated with murals, sculptures, stencils and marble, the capitol opened in 1905. Guided 45-minute tours leave on the hour; the last tour leaves one hour before closing. Daily.

UNIVERSITY OF MINNESOTA, TWIN CITIES CAMPUS

56 Delaware S.E., St. Paul, 612-625-5000; www.umn.edu

Established 1851; 39,315 students. Campus tours; animal barn tours for small children. Near campus is the Gibbs Museum of Pioneer & Dakota Life. This restored and furnished farmhouse dating to 1854 depicts the lives of pioneers and the Dakotahs at the turn of the 20th century. The site includes two barns, two Dakotah-style teepees and a one-room schoolhouse.

Mid-April-mid-November, Tuesday-Friday 10 a.m.-4 p.m., Saturday-Sunday noon-4 p.m.

SPECIAL EVENTS
MINNESOTA STATE FAIR

Fairgrounds, 1265 Snelling Ave. N., St. Paul, 651-288-4400; www.mnstatefair.org

Midway, thrill show, horse show, kids' days, all-star revue; more than a million visitors each year; 300 acres of attractions.

Late August-early September.

WINTER CARNIVAL

75 Fifth St. W., St. Paul, 651-223-4700; www.winter-carnival.com

One of the leading winter festivals in America, this event features ice and snow carving, parades, sports events, parties and pageants. The highlight of the festival is a remarkable ice palace that rivals traditionally built mansions and castles in terms of scale and grandeur. Visitors can walk through the palace's rooms and hallways.

Last weekend in January-first weekend in February.

WHERE TO STAY
★★CROWNE PLAZA RIVERFRONT

11 E. Kellogg Blvd., St. Paul, 651-292-1900, 800-227-6963; www.crowneplaza.com

470 rooms. Wireless Internet access. Restaurant, bar. Pool. $151-250

★★EMBASSY SUITES HOTEL ST. PAUL-DOWNTOWN

175 E. 10th St., St. Paul, 651-224-5400, 800-362-2779; www.embassystpaul.com

210 rooms, all suites. Complimentary full breakfast. Wireless Internet access. Restaurant, bar. Airport transportation available. Pool. $60-150

★★★THE SAINT PAUL HOTEL

350 Market St., St. Paul, 651-292-9292, 800-292-9292; www.stpaulhotel.com

A historic hotel of America, this beautifully restored property was founded in 1910 by wealthy businessman Lucius P. Ordway (the hotel is within walking distance of the Ordway Center for the Performing Arts) and still maintains an old, European charm. Connected to the downtown skyway system, the hotel has hosted presidents Herbert Hoover, Woodrow Wilson and George W. Bush. The elegant guest rooms (all renovated in 2005) have splendid views of downtown, Rice Park or the St. Paul Cathedral, and feature dark wood furniture and upscale linens. The St. Paul Grill is known for steaks.

254 rooms. Restaurant, Bar. $151-250

WHERE TO EAT

★★DAKOTA BAR AND GRILL
1021 E. Bandana Blvd., St. Paul, 651-642-1442
American menu. Dinner. Closed Sunday. Bar. Casual attire. Outdoor seating. $16-35

★DIXIE'S
695 Grand Ave., St. Paul, 651-222-7345; www.dixiesongrand.com
American, Cajun menu. Lunch, dinner, Sunday brunch. Bar. Children's menu. Casual attire. Outdoor seating. $15 and under

★★★FOREPAUGH'S
276 S. Exchange St., St. Paul, 651-224-5606; www.forepaughs.com
Some say the ghost of the former owner, St. Paul pioneer Joseph Lybrandt Forepaugh, haunts this romantic Victorian three-story 1879 house. That doesn't stop diners from visiting for the restaurant's French-inspired dishes. Try shrimp scampi Marseillaise, entrecôte au poivre vert (New York sirloin with a peppercorn sauce) or grilled brochette of lamb. The restaurant offers shuttle service to nearby theaters.
French menu. Lunch, dinner, Sunday brunch. Bar. Children's menu. Casual attire. Valet parking. Outdoor seating. $16-35

★★THE LEXINGTON
1096 Grand Ave., St. Paul, 651-222-5878; www.the-lexington.com
American menu. Lunch, dinner, Sunday brunch. Bar. Children's menu. $36-85

★MANCINI'S CHAR HOUSE
531 W. Seventh St., St. Paul, 651-224-7345
Steak menu. Dinner. Bar. Children's menu. Casual attire. $36-85

★★MUFFULETTA IN THE PARK
2260 Como Ave., St. Paul, 651-644-9116; www.muffuletta.com
International menu. Lunch, dinner, Sunday brunch. Casual attire. Outdoor seating. $16-35

★★RISTORANTE LUCI
470 Cleveland Ave. S., St. Paul, 651-699-8258; www.ristoranteluci.com
Italian menu. Dinner. Closed Sunday-Monday. Children's menu. Casual attire. $16-35

★★SAKURA
350 St. Peter St., St. Paul, 651-224-0185; www.sakurastpaul.com
Japanese menu. Lunch, dinner. Bar. Casual attire. $16-35

★★THE ST. PAUL GRILL
350 Market St., St. Paul, 651-224-7455; www.stpaulhotel.com
American menu. Lunch, dinner, late-night, Sunday brunch. Bar. $15 and under

★★★ W. A. FROST AND COMPANY
374 Selby Ave., St. Paul, 651-224-5715; www.wafrost.com
Located in the historic Dakotah Building, the four dining rooms of this restaurant are decorated with Victorian-style wallpaper, furnishings and oil paintings.
American menu. Lunch, dinner, late-night, Sunday brunch. Bar. Children's menu. Casual attire. Valet parking Friday-Saturday. Outdoor seating. $36-85

ST. PETER
See also Faribault, Le Sueur, Mankato, Minneapolis, New Ulm, St. Paul
Located in Nicollet County, St. Peter was named in honor of the St. Pierre River, which was an early moniker of the Minnesota River. The city is a college town and its historic sites include the Nicollet Country Historical Museum and the Soderlund Pharmacy Museum.

WHAT TO SEE
EUGENE SAINT JULIEN COX HOUSE
500 N. Washington Ave., St. Peter, 507-934-4309; www.nchsmn.org/sites.html
This fully restored house from 1871 is the best example of Gothic Italianate architecture in the state. Built by the town's first mayor, it's filled with late Victorian furnishings. Guided tours. June-August, Wednesday-Sunday; May and September, Saturday-Sunday afternoons.

GUSTAVUS ADOLPHUS COLLEGE
800 W. College Ave., St. Peter, 507-933-8000; www.gustavus.edu
Established 1862; 2,300 students. On campus are Old Main; Alfred Nobel Hall of Science and Gallery; Lund Center for Physical Education; Folke Bernadotte Memorial Library; Linnaeus Arboretum; Schaefer Fine Arts Gallery; Christ Chapel, featuring door and narthex art by noted sculptor Paul Granlund. At various other locations on campus are sculptures by Granlund, sculptor-in-residence, including one depicting Joseph Nicollet, mid-19th-century French explorer and cartographer of the Minnesota River Valley.
Campus tours. In October, the college hosts the nationally known Nobel Conference, which has been held annually since 1965.

TREATY SITE HISTORY CENTER
1851 N. Minnesota Ave., St. Peter, 507-931-2160; www.nchsmn.org/sites.html
This interesting center features county historical items relating to the Dakota people, explorers, settlers, traders and cartographers and their impact on the 1851 Treaty of Traverse des Sioux.
Archives. Museum shop. Daily.

STILLWATER
See also St. Paul, Taylors Falls
A center of the logging industry in pioneer days, Stillwater became a busy river town. An 1848 convention in Stillwater led to the creation of the Minnesota Territory, leading to the town's nickname: "the birthplace of Minnesota." The charming downtown area is filled with antique shops, clothing boutiques and crafts stores.

WHAT TO SEE
ST. CROIX SCENIC HIGHWAY
Highway 95, Stillwater

Highway 95 runs 50 miles from Afton to Taylors Falls along the "Rhine of America," the St. Croix River.

WASHINGTON COUNTY HISTORICAL MUSEUM
602 Main St. N., Stillwater, 651-439-5956

A former warden's house at an old prison site contains mementos of lumbering days, including a pioneer kitchen and furniture.
May-October, Thursday-Sunday; also by appointment.

WILLIAM O'BRIEN STATE PARK
16 miles north on Highway 95, Stillwater, 651-433-0500; www.dnr.state.mn.us

A 1,273-acre park. Swimming, fishing, boating (ramp); hiking, cross-country skiing, picnicking, camping.

SPECIAL EVENTS
LUMBERJACK DAYS
423 Main St. S., Stillwater, 651-430-2306; www.lumberjackdays.com

Lumberjack shows, a parade and musically choreographed fireworks are at this annual summer celebration. Festivities are held in Lowell Park. Late July.

RIVERTOWN ART FAIR
201 Main St., Stillwater, Lowell Park, 651-430-2306

Hundreds of area artisans and craftspeople participate in this annual two-day event along the banks of the St. Croix River. Third weekend in May.

WHERE TO STAY
★★★AFTON HOUSE INN
3291 S. St. Croix Trail, Afton, 651-436-8883, 877-436-8883; www.aftonhouseinn.com

Whether curling up with a book in the pine loft or taking a cruise on the St. Croix River in one of the inn's charter vessels, guests will find uninterrupted peace here. The various rooms have their own personalities, including a corner room with a quad of tall windows and an original exposed beam ceiling and another with an antique piano desk.
25 rooms. Restaurant, bar. $60-150

★COUNTRY INN & SUITES BY CARLSON STILLWATER
2200 W. Frontage Road, Stillwater, 651-430-2699, 800-456-4000;
www.countryinns.com/stillwatermn

66 rooms. Complimentary continental breakfast. Pool. $60-150

★★★LOWELL INN
102 Second St. N., Stillwater, 651-439-1100, 888-569-3554; www.lowellinn.com

Located in the historic area of Stillwater, on the banks of the beautiful St. Croix River, this hotel was built in 1927. It features newly renovated guest rooms and three dining rooms—the George Washington Room (Colonial

finery), the Garden Room (stained glass and a spring-fed fountain) and the Matterhorn Room (Swiss themed, complete with fondue).
23 rooms. Complimentary full breakfast. Restaurant, bar. $151-250

★★★WATER STREET INN
101 S. Water St., Stillwater, 651-439-6000; www.waterstreetinn.us
This intimate Victorian-style hotel offers guest rooms that overlook the scenic St. Croix River. Located in the old Lumber Exchange Building, the inn has rooms that run the gamut from St. Croix suites (queen-size canopied bed, sitting room) to Water Street rooms (balconies, some gas fireplaces). The inn serves a popular Sunday brunch, and dinner offers dishes such as sautéed duck breast with mixed mushrooms, figs and a garlic port sauce or honey-and sage-roasted chicken.
41 rooms. Complimentary full breakfast. Restaurant, bar. $61-150

WHERE TO EAT
★GASTHAUS BAVARIAN HUNTER
8390 Lofton Ave. N., Stillwater, 651-439-7128; www.gasthausbavarianhunter.com
German menu. Lunch, dinner, Sunday brunch. Bar. Children's menu. Casual attire. Outdoor seating. Accordianist Friday evening, Sunday afternoon. $15 and under

★★LOWELL INN RESTAURANT
102 N. Second St., Stillwater, 651-439-1100, 888-569-3554; www.lowellinn.com
American, Continental menu. Breakfast, lunch, dinner, Sunday brunch. Bar. Children's menu. Casual attire. $36-85

SUPERIOR NATIONAL FOREST
See also Ely, Grand Marais, Grand Portage, Virginia
With more than 2,000 beautiful clear lakes, rugged shorelines, picturesque islands and deep woods, this park covers a magnificent portion of Minnesota's famous northern area. Scenic water routes through the Boundary Waters Canoe Area Wilderness and near the international border offer opportunities for adventure.

TAYLORS FALLS
See also St. Paul, Stillwater
Located on the Wisconsin border and just 40 miles from the Twin Cities, Taylors Falls is named for a series of rapids on the St. Croix River. The falls have now been dammed, but the name remains. The downtown area, which reminds tourists of a quaint New England town, has preserved its historic buildings, including the oldest schoolhouse in the state, a number of churches and several houses from the mid-1800s.

WHAT TO SEE
ST. CROIX AND LOWER ST. CROIX NATIONAL SCENIC RIVERWAY
Taylors Falls, 715-483-3284; www.nps.gov/sacn
From its origins in northern Wisconsin, the St. Croix flows southward to form part of the Minnesota-Wisconsin border before joining the Mississippi

near Point Douglas. Two segments of the river totaling more than 250 miles have been designated National Scenic Riverways and are administered by the National Park Service.

TAYLORS FALLS SCENIC BOAT TOUR
37350 Wild Mountain Road, Taylors Falls, 612-465-6315, 800-447-4958; www.taylorsfallsboat.com
Trips through St. Croix Dalles; also 1-hour, seven-mile trip on Taylors Falls Queen or Princess. Scenic, brunch, luncheon and dinner cruises; fall color cruises. Also Taylors Falls one-way canoe rentals to Osceola or Williams O'Brien State Park.
May-mid-October, daily.

W.H.C. FOLSOM HOUSE
120 Government Road, Taylors Falls, 612-465-3125; www.mnhs.org/places/sites/fh
This Federal/Greek Revival mansion, built in 1855, reflects the New England heritage of early settlers and includes many original furnishings.
Memorial Day weekend-mid-October, daily.

WILD MOUNTAIN SKI AREA
County Road 16, Taylors Falls, 651-257-3550, 800-447-4958; www.wildmountain.com
Four quad chairlifts, two rope tows; patrol, school, rentals; snowmaking; cafeteria. Twenty-three runs, longest run 5,000 feet; vertical drop 300 feet.
November-March, daily.

THIEF RIVER FALLS
See also Crookston, Minnetonka, Roseau
The town of Thief River Falls, sitting at the confluence of the Thief and Red Lake rivers, claims more residents of Norwegian descent than any other city in the United States. Both Dakotas (Sioux) and Ojibwes lived in small villages here before the Norwegian settlers arrived. Today, the area's biggest attraction is the Agassiz National Wildlife Refuge, which teems with migratory birds and other wildlife.

WHAT TO SEE
AGASSIZ NATIONAL WILDLIFE REFUGE
Marshall County Road 7 E., Middle River Falls, 218-449-4115; www.fws.gov
This wildlife refuge is made up of approximately 61,500 acres of forest, water and marshland. It is a haven for 280 species of migratory and upland game birds and includes 41 species of resident mammals.
Refuge headquarters Monday-Friday; auto tour route daily, except winter.

PEDER ENGELSTAD PIONEER VILLAGE
Highway 32 S. and Oakland Park Boulevard, Thief River Falls, 218-681-5767; www.exploreminnesota.com
A reconstructed village features 19 turn-of-the-century buildings, including a one-room schoolhouse, a general store, a candy shop, a blacksmith shop, a barber shop and a church, along with two railroad depots and several homes and cabins. Museum houses historic vehicles and farm equipment and Nor-

wegian and Native American artifacts, reflecting the town's history. Memorial Day-Labor Day, 1-5 p.m.

WHERE TO STAY
★★BEST WESTERN INN OF THIEF RIVER FALLS
1060 Highway 32 S., Thief River Falls, 218-681-7555, 800-780-7234;
www.bestwestern.com
39 rooms. Restaurant, bar. Airport transportation available. Pool. $60-150

TOWER
See also Ely, Eveleth, Superior National Forest
A tiny town that offers spectacular natural resources, Tower was once a flourishing mining and lumber town. You can tour the state's first underground mine at the nearby state park. Tower sits just off Lake Vermillion, the state's fifth-largest lake, which harbors bald eagles and loons.

WHAT TO SEE
ARROWHEAD SNOWMOBILE/BIKE TRAIL
Tower, two miles west of Highway 169 on Highway 1; www.dnr.state.mn.us
This 135-mile footpath, which extends approximately from Tower to International Falls, is used by hikers, mountain bikers, horseback riders and snowmobilers. Fall colors are spectacular. Adjoining seven other state trails along its route, the Arrowhead Trail passes near the Boundary Waters Canoe Area Wilderness, Superior National Forest and Voyageurs National Park. The trail ranges from flat and easy sections to hilly and strenuous areas.

LAKE VERMILION
515 Main St., Tower, 218-753-2301
This lake is 40 miles long, with 1,250 miles of wooded shoreline and 365 islands varying in size from speck-like rocks to Pine Island, which is nine miles long and contains its own lake. Fishing for walleye, northern pike, bass and panfish. Swimming, boating, water sports; hunting for duck, deer and small game in fall; snowmobiling and cross-country skiing; camping and lodging. Primarily located in Superior National Forest.

SOUDAN UNDERGROUND MINE STATE PARK
1379 Stuntz Bay Road, Soudan, 218-753-2245; www.dnr.state.mn.us/state
This 1,300 acre park included the site of the Soudan Mine, the state's first underground iron mine ($52°$ F; 2,400 feet) in operation from 1882 to 1962. Self-guided tour of open pits, engine house, crusher building, drill shop, interpretive center; one-hour guided underground mine tour includes train ride. Memorial Day-Labor Day daily.

STEAM LOCOMOTIVE AND COACH
515 Main St., Tower, 218-753-2301
Locomotive from 1910 served Duluth & Iron Range Railroad. Coach is now a museum housing early logging, mining and Native American displays. Memorial Day-Labor Day, daily; early spring and late fall, by appointment.

TRACY

See also Marshall, Pipestone, Redwood Falls

The town of Tracy could well be called Laura Ingalls Wilder Town, because it is forever linked to the author of numerous children's books. Laura's first train ride was from her home in Walnut Grove to the train depot in Tracy, eight miles away. A passage in By the Shores of Silver Lake describes the adventure. The town celebrates the Laura Ingalls Wilder Pageant each year, and the museum and tourist center named for the novelist is just seven miles away.

WHAT TO SEE
LAKE SHETEK STATE PARK

163 State Park Road, Currie, 507-763-3256; www.dnr.state.mn.us

Comprises 1,011 acres on one of largest lakes in Southwest Minnesota. Monument to settlers who were victims of the Dakota Conflict in 1862; restored pioneer cabin. Swimming, fishing, boating (ramp, rentals); hiking, snowmobiling, picnicking, camping.

LAURA INGALLS WILDER MUSEUM AND TOURIST CENTER

330 Eighth St., Walnut Grove, 507-859-2358

This tribute to Laura Ingalls Wilder contains five buildings of museums. The depression in the ground where the dugout used to be, and the rock and spring mentioned in On the Banks of Plum Creek are all 1½ miles north of Walnut Grove.

May-October, daily; rest of year by appointment.

SPECIAL EVENT
LAURA INGALLS WILDER PAGEANT

770 Main St., Walnut Grove, Tracy, 507-859-2174; www.walnutgrove.org

Story of the Ingalls family of Walnut Grove in the 1870s.
July.

TWO HARBORS

See also Duluth

Two Harbors was given its start when the Duluth & Iron Range Railroad reached Lake Superior at Agate Bay. Ore docks were constructed immediately and the city became an important ore shipping terminal. Today, it is a harbor community nestled between the twin harbors of Agate Bay and Burlington Bay.

WHAT TO SEE
DEPOT MUSEUM

520 South Ave., Two Harbors, 218-834-4898

Historic depot highlights the geological history and the discovery and mining of iron ore. Mallet locomotive, world's most powerful steam engine, on display.

May, weekends; Memorial Day-October, daily.

GOOSEBERRY FALLS STATE PARK

3206 Highway 61, Two Harbors, 218-834-3855

Visitors to this 1,662-acre park can enjoy fishing, hiking, cross-country skiing, snowmobiling, picnicking and camping. State park vehicle permit required.

LIGHTHOUSE POINT AND HARBOR MUSEUM

520 South Ave., Two Harbors, 218-834-4898;
www.twoharborschamber.com/lighthouse.htm

Displays tell the story of iron ore shipping and the development of the first iron ore port in the state. A renovated pilot house from an ore boat is located on the site. Shipwreck display.

Tours of operating lighthouse. May-early November, daily.

SPLIT ROCK LIGHTHOUSE STATE PARK

3755 Split Rock Lighthouse, Two Harbors, 218-226-6377; www.dnr.state.mn.us

The lighthouse served as the guiding sentinel for the north shore of Lake Superior from 1910 to 1969. Also in the park is a historic complex that includes a fog signal building, keeper's dwellings, several outbuildings and the ruins of a tramway. The Gitchi-Gami State Trail, a 10-foot-wide paved walking trail, stretches seven miles from Beaver Bay to the Split Rock River and will eventually run 86 miles from Two Harbors to Grand Marais. Waterfalls. Picnicking.

Cart-in camping on Lake Superior, access to Superior Hiking Trail. State park vehicle permit required. Daily.

SUPERIOR HIKING TRAIL

Two Harbors, 218-834-2700; www.shta.org

This 205-mile footpath extends from Two Harbors to the Canadian border, following the rocky hills and ridgeline along Lake Superior. Thirty trailheads and parking areas make the trail ideal for day hiking; 75 rustic campsites are available for thru-hikes. New sections of the trail open periodically.

THE EDNA G

Waterfront Drive, Two Harbors, 218-834-4898

The Edna G served Two Harbors from 1896 to 1981. It was designated a National Historic Site in 1974 as the only steam-powered tug still operating on the Great Lakes. Now retired, the Edna G features seasonal tours where visitors can see its beautiful interior décor of wood paneling and brass fittings.

WHERE TO STAY

★★SUPERIOR SHORES RESORT

1521 Superior Shores Drive, Two Harbors, 218-834-5671, 800-242-1988;
www.superiorshores.com

104 rooms. Restaurant, bar. Pets accepted. $

VIRGINIA
See also Eveleth, Hibbing, Tower
Born of lumbering, Virginia is nurtured by mining and vacationing. Great open iron ore pits mark the surrounding green countryside—man-made canyons are right at the city limits. Vacationers come to Virginia en route to the Boundary Waters Canoe Area Wilderness, Superior National Forest and Voyageurs National Park.

WHAT TO SEE
MINE VIEW IN THE SKY
403 First St. N., Virginia, 218-741-2717
Observation building (and visitors information center) gives view of a Mesabi Range open-pit mine 650 feet below.
May-September, daily.

WORLD'S LARGEST FLOATING LOON
1409 N. Broadway, Virginia, 218-748-7500
Listed in the Guinness Book of World Records, this 20-foot-long, 10-foot-high, 7½-foot-wide fiberglass loon swims on Silver Lake, which is located in the heart of the city, during the summer months.

WHERE TO STAY
★AMERICINN VIRGINIA
5480 Mountain Iron Drive, Virginia, 218-741-7839
45 rooms. High-speed Internet access. Complimentary breakfast. Pets accepted. $61-150

VOYAGEURS NATIONAL PARK
Voyageurs National Park is on Minnesota's northern border and lies in the southern part of the Canadian Shield, which contains some of the oldest rock formations in the world. More than one-third water, the park is rugged but varied, with most trails and campsites accessible by boat. Rolling hills, bogs, beaver ponds, swamps, islands and large and small lakes make up the vast scenery. Voyageurs has a cool climate with short, warm summers and long winters. Common summer activities include boating, swimming, hiking, camping and fishing, since some of the best bass and walleye in the United States are here. In winter, there is skiing, snowmobiling and snowshoeing. A rich location for wildlife viewing, Voyageurs is located in black bear country, and designated campsites are equipped with bear lockers for food storage. If a locker is not available, be prepared to hang your food, as bear-proofing food storage is required. In the summer, park-sponsored programs include interpretive walks, children's -activities and canoe trips. In the winter, activities include candlelight skiing and snowshoe hikes. Also in the park, Kettle Falls Dam, built by the Minnesota and Ontario Paper Company, converted 20-foot falls to a 12-foot dam. Lodging is available in the park during the summer months at Kettle Falls Hotel (listed on the National Register of Historic Places), and houseboats are available for rent.

WALKER

See also Bemidji, Park Rapids, Pine River

At the foot of Chippewa National Forest and Leech Lake, Walker serves tourists heading for adventures among woods and waters. Snowmobiling and cross-country skiing are popular sports here. The town is named for a pioneer lumberman and landowner.

WHAT TO SEE
LEECH LAKE
Walker

Third-largest lake in the state; fishing and swimming.

WHERE TO STAY
★AMERICINN

905 Minnesota Ave, Walker, 218-547-2200, 800-634-3444; www.americinn.com

37 rooms. Complimentary breakfast. Business center. Pool. $61-150

WILLMAR

See also Granite Falls, Litchfield

Founded as a railroad town, Willmar is still linked to the train industry today. This area's rich farmland and peaceful scenery make it one of the fastest growing cities in Minnesota.

WHAT TO SEE
KANDIYOHI COUNTY HISTORICAL SOCIETY MUSEUM

610 Highway 71 N.E., Willmar, 320-235-1881; www.kandiyohi.com

Steam locomotive, country schoolhouse, restored house; historical exhibits, agriculture building, research library. Memorial Day-Labor Day, daily; rest of year, Monday-Friday; also by appointment.

SIBLEY STATE PARK

800 Sibley Park Road, New London, 320-354-2055; www.dnr.state.mn.us

A 2,600-acre park, this was a favorite hunting ground of Minnesota's first governor, for whom the park is named. Swimming, fishing, boating (ramps, rentals); horseback riding, hiking; cross-country skiing, snowmobiling; camping; nature center.

WHERE TO STAY
★DAYS INN

225 28th St. S.e., Willmar, 320-231-1275, 877-241-5235; www.daysinnwillmar.com

59 rooms. Complimentary continental breakfast. Pets accepted. $60-150

★★HOLIDAY INN

2100 E. Highway 12, Willmar, 320-235-6060, 888-465-4329; www.holiday-inn.com

98 rooms. High-speed Internet access. Restaurant, bar. Pets accepted. $60-150

WINONA
See also Rochester

New Englanders and Germans came to this site on the west bank of the Mississippi and built an industrial city graced with three colleges. An early lumbering town, Winona today is one of the state's leading business and industrial centers and home of Winona State University.

WHAT TO SEE
BUNNELL HOUSE
710 Johnson St., Homer, 507-452-7575; www.winona.edu
Unusual mid-19th-century Steamboat Gothic architecture; period furnishings. Also here is Carriage House Museum Shop.
Memorial Day-Labor Day, Wednesday-Saturday 10 a.m.-5 p.m., Sunday 1-5 p.m.; Labor Day-mid-October, weekends only; rest of year by appointment.

GARVIN HEIGHTS
Huff Street and Garvin Heights Road, Winona
Park with 575-foot bluff, offering majestic views of the Mississippi River Valley. Picnic area.
Dawn-dusk.

PRAIRIE ISLAND PARK
Prairie Island Road, Winona
Camping (April-October), picnicking, water, restrooms, fireplaces. Fishing (all year).

UPPER MISSISSIPPI RIVER NATIONAL WILDLIFE AND FISH REFUGE
51 E. Fourth St., Winona, 507-452-4232
From Wabasha, Minnesota, extending 261 miles to Rock Island, Illinois, the refuge encompasses 200,000 acres of wooded islands, marshes, sloughs and backwaters. Twenty percent of the refuge is closed for hunting and trapping until after duck hunting season. Boat required for access to most parts of refuge.
Daily.

WINONA COUNTY HISTORICAL SOCIETY MUSEUM
160 Johnson St., Winona, 507-454-2723; www.winonahistory.org
Country store; blacksmith, barber shops; Native American artifacts; logging and lumbering exhibits; early vehicles and fire fighting equipment, award-winning children's exhibit, gift shop, library.
Daily

SPECIAL EVENTS
VICTORIAN FAIR
160 Johnson St., Winona, 507-452-0735
Living history; costumed guides; boat rides. Late September.

WINONA STEAMBOAT DAYS

Winona, 507-452-2272; www.winonasteamboatdays.com

Activities at this annual celebration include a lumberjack show, craft fair, water-ski show, food court and arcade and boat rides.
Mid-June.

WHERE TO STAY

★★BEST WESTERN RIVERPORT INN & SUITES

900 Bruski Drive, Winona, 507-452-0606, 800-595-0606; www.bestwestern.com

106 rooms. Complimentary continental breakfast. High-speed Internet access. Restaurant, bar. Pets accepted. Pool. $60-150

WISCONSIN

FORESTS BLOTTED OUT THE SKY OVER WISCONSIN WHEN THE FIRST FRENCH VOYAGEURS arrived more than three centuries ago. Rich in natural resources, modern conservation concepts took strong root here—Wisconsin's 15,000 lakes and 2,200 streams are teeming with fish, and millions of acres of its publicly owned forests are abundant with game.

Wisconsin is famous for breweries, universities, forests, paper mills, dairy products and diverse vacation attractions. Wisconsin is also the birthplace of the statewide primary election law, workers' compensation law, unemployment compensation and many other reforms that have since been widely adopted.

The Badger State acquired its nickname during the lead rush of 1827, when miners built their homes by digging into the hillsides like badgers. The state is America's dairyland, producing much of the nation's milk and more than 30 percent of all cheese consumed in the United States. It is a leader in the production of hay, cranberries and ginseng, and harvests huge crops of peas, beans, carrots, corn and oats. It is the leading canner of fresh vegetables and an important source of cherries, apples, maple syrup and wood pulp. A great part of the nation's paper products, agricultural implements and nonferrous metal products and alloys are manufactured here as well.

Wisconsin summers are balmy, and winter offers plenty of cold-weather activities, making the state a year-round vacationland that lures millions of visitors annually. This is a land of many contrasts: rounded hills and narrow valleys to the southwest, a huge central plain, rolling prairie in the southeast and the north filled with majestic forests, marshes and lakes.

Native Americans called this land Ouisconsin ("where the waters gather"). French explorer Jean Nicolet, seeking the Northwest Passage to the Orient, landed near Green Bay in 1634 and greeted whom he thought were Asians. The people were actually part of the Winnebago tribe, which made a treaty of alliance with the French that resulted in a brisk fur trade for the next 125 years. The British won Wisconsin from the French in 1760 and lost it to the United States after the American Revolution.

Shortly before Wisconsin became a state, it was a battleground in the Black Hawk War. After the campaign, word spread of the state's beauty and fertile land in the East, and a flood of settlers arrived. Diversified industry and the bounty of the many farms promise continuing prosperity for Wisconsin.

ALGOMA
See also Green Bay. Sturgeon Bay
This lakeshore town is home to Wisconsin's oldest winery, Von Steihl Winery.

WHAT TO SEE
VON STIEHL WINERY
115 Navarino St., Algoma, 920-487-5208, 800-955-5208; www.vonstiehl.com

Housed in a 140-year-old brewery, this winery offers wine, cheese and jelly tastings at the end of each tour. May-October, daily; rest of year, Friday-Sunday.

WHERE TO STAY
★RIVER HILLS MOTEL
820 N. Water St., Algoma, 920-487-3451, 800-236-3451; www.wi-lodges-review.com
30 rooms. Pets accepted. $61-150

ANTIGO
See also Wausau
Antigo calls itself the "Gateway to Wisconsin's Northwoods"—an appropriate moniker for this town about 90 miles northwest of Green Bay.

WHAT TO SEE
F.A. DELEGLISE CABIN
404 Superior St., Antigo, 715-627-4464; www.wisconsinhistory.org
This is the first home of the city's founder.
May-October, daily.

APPLETON
See also Green Bay, Neenah-Menasha, Oshkosh
Located astride the Fox River, Appleton's economy thrives on the manufacture of paper and paper products, insurance and service industries.

WHAT TO SEE
CHARLES A. GRIGNON MANSION
1313 Augustine St., Kaukauna, 920-766-3122; www.foxvalleyhistory.org
This is the first deeded property in Wisconsin and the restored Greek Revival house of one of the area's early French-Canadian settlers. Expect period furnishings, displays and summer events.
June-August, Friday-Saturday; September-May, by appointment.

FOX CITIES CHILDREN'S MUSEUM
100 W. College Ave., Appleton, 920-734-3226; www.kidmuseum.org
The hands-on exhibits here include climbing through a human heart, playing in the New Happy Baby Garden or visiting Grandma's Attic.
Tuesday-Friday 9 a.m.-5 p.m., Saturday 10 a.m.-5 p.m., Sunday noon-5 p.m.; closed Monday.

MUSIC-DRAMA CENTER
420 E. College Ave., Appleton, 920-832-6611; www.lawrence.edu
The center houses the Cloak Theater, an experimental arena playhouse and Stansbury Theater, and offers concerts and plays during the academic year.

OUTAGAMIE MUSEUM
330 E. College Ave., Appleton, 920-735-9370; www.myhistorymuseum.org
Major exhibit themes include electricity, papermaking, agriculture, transpor-

tation and communications. There is also an extensive exhibit devoted to Appleton native Harry Houdini.
Tuesday-Sunday.

WHERE TO STAY
★★BEST WESTERN MIDWAY HOTEL
3033 W. College Ave., Appleton, 920-731-4141, 800-482-3879; www.bestwestern.com
105 rooms. Complimentary continental breakfast. Wireless Internet access. Restaurant, bar. Airport transportation available. Pets accepted. Fitness center. $61-150

★★HOLIDAY INN
150 S. Nicolet Road, Appleton, 920-735-9955, 800-465-4329; www.holidayinn.com
228 rooms. Wireless Internet access. Restaurant, bar. Airport transportation available. Pool. Pets accepted. Complimentary continental breakfast. Fitness center. Business center. $61-150

★★RADISSON PAPER VALLEY HOTEL
333 W. College Ave., Appleton, 920-733-8000, 800-333-3333; www.radisson.com
390 rooms. Restaurant, bar. Pool. Pets accepted. Complimentary breakfast. $60-150

★WOODFIELD SUITES
3730 W. College Ave., Appleton, 800-531-5900
98 rooms, all suites. Complimentary continental breakfast. $61-150

WHERE TO EAT
★★GEORGE'S STEAK HOUSE
2208 S. Memorial Drive, Appleton, 920-733-4939; www.foodspot.com
Steak menu. Lunch, dinner. Closed Sunday. Bar. Children's menu. Casual attire. Reservations recommended. $16-35

ASHLAND
See also Bayfield
Located on Chequamegon Bay, which legend says is the "shining big sea water" of Longfellow's Hiawatha, Ashland is a port for Great Lakes ships delivering coal for the Midwest. It is also a gateway to the Apostle Islands. Papermaking machinery, fabricated steel and other industrial products provide a diversified economy.

WHAT TO SEE
COPPER FALLS STATE PARK
Highway 169 and Copper Falls Road, Mellen, 715-274-5123; www.dnr.wi.gov
This 2,500-acre park has more than eight miles of river, plus nature and hiking trails that provide spectacular views of the river gorge and the falls. Attractions include swimming, fishing, canoeing, backpacking, cross-country skiing, picnicking and a playground.
Daily.

NORTHLAND COLLEGE

1411 Ellis Ave., Ashland, 715-682-1699; www.northland.edu

Northland was founded to bring higher education to the people of the isolated logging camps and farm communities of northern Wisconsin. Students here learn through a lens of environmentalism. On campus find the Sigurd Olson Environmental Institute in an earth-sheltered, solar-heated building and historic Wheeler Hall, which is constructed of brownstone from the nearby Apostle Islands.

WHERE TO STAY
★★BEST WESTERN LAKE SUPERIOR INN

30600 Highway 2, Ashland, 715-682-5235, 800-452-7749; www.bestwestern.com

64 rooms. Restaurant, bar. Fitness center. Pets accepted. High-speed Internet access. Business center. Indoor pool. $61-150

★★HOTEL CHEQUAMEGON

101 W. Lakeshore Drive, Ashland, 715-682-9095, 800-946-5555; www.hotelc.com

65 rooms. Restaurant, bar. Pool. Complimentary breakfast. $61-150

BAILEYS HARBOR

See also Marinette, Menominee, Peshtigo, Sturgeon Bay

Baileys Harbor is the oldest village in Door County, with one of the best harbors on the east shore. Range lights, built in 1870 to guide ships into the harbor, still operate. Its waters feature charter fishing for trout and salmon.

WHAT TO SEE
BJORKLUNDEN

7603 Chapel Lane, Baileys Harbor, 920-839-2216; www.lawrence.edu/dept/bjork

This 425-acre estate, owned by Lawrence University in Appleton, has a replica of a Norwegian wooden chapel. The chapel was handcrafted by the original owners, the Boynton family, during the summers of 1939 to 1947. Seminars in the humanities are held on the estate each summer.

Tours of chapel: Mid-June-August, daily.

WHERE TO STAY
★★GORDON LODGE

1420 Pine Drive, Baileys Harbor, 920-839-2331, 800-830-6235; www.gordonlodge.com

40 rooms. Closed mid-October-mid-May. Complimentary full breakfast. Restaurant, bar. Beach. Tennis. Outdoor pool. $151-250

WHERE TO EAT
★★COMMON HOUSE

8041 Highway 57, Baileys Harbor, 920-839-2708; www.commonhouserestaurant.com

American menu. Dinner. Bar. Children's menu. $36-85

★SANDPIPER

8177 Highway 57, Baileys Harbor, 920-839-2528; www.sandpiperfishboil.com

American menu. Breakfast, lunch. Closed November-April. Children's menu. Casual attire. Outdoor seating. $16-35

BARABOO

See also Portage, Prairie du Sac, Wisconsin Dells

A center for the distribution of dairy products, Baraboo is a neatly ordered town of lawns, gardens, parks, homes and factories. The city was home to Ringling Brothers and Gollmar circuses, and still holds memories. Jean Baribeau founded it as a trading post for the Hudson Bay Company. Beautiful, spring-fed Devil's Lake is three miles south of town.

WHAT TO SEE
CIRCUS WORLD MUSEUM

550 Water St., Baraboo, 608-356-8341; www.circusworldmuseum.com

This museum has 50 acres and eight buildings of circus lore and is the original summer quarters of Ringling Brothers Circus. Live circus acts perform under the Big Top, plus there is a daily circus parade, a display of circus parade wagons, steam calliope concerts, a P.T. Barnum sideshow, a wild animal menagerie, a carousel and a band organ.

Early May-mid-September, daily.

HO-CHUNK CASINO & BINGO

S3214A Highway 12, Baraboo, 800-746-2486; www.ho-chunk.com

This gaming casino features 48 blackjack tables, 1,200 slot machines, video poker and keno.

Daily, 24 hours.

INTERNATIONAL CRANE FOUNDATION

E11376 Shady Lane Road, Baraboo, 608-356-9462; www.savingcranes.org

This nonprofit organization promotes the study and preservation of cranes, featuring the birds and their chicks from all over the world.

Guided tours: Memorial Day-Labor Day, Daily; September-October, weekends.

MID-CONTINENT RAILWAY MUSEUM

E8948 Diamond Hill Road, North Freedom, 608-522-4261; www.midcontinent.org

This restored 1894 depot is a complete 1900 rail environment with steam locomotives, coaches, a steam wrecker and snowplows, plus artifacts and historical exhibits.

MIRROR LAKE STATE PARK

E10320 Fern Dell Road, Baraboo, 608-254-2333; www.mirrorlakewisconsin.com

This 2,050-acre park features swimming, fishing, boating and canoeing, plus hiking, cross-country skiing, picnicking, a playground and camping.

Daily.

SAUK COUNTY HISTORICAL MUSEUM

531 Fourth Ave., Baraboo, 608-356-1001; www.saukcounty.com

This museum houses 19th-century household goods, textiles, toys, china, military items, a pioneer collection, Native American artifacts, circus memorabilia, a natural history display and photos.

Tuesday-Saturday noon-5 p.m.

WHERE TO STAY

★BEST WESTERN

725 W. Pine st., West Baraboo, 608-356-1100, 800-831-3881; www.bestwestern.com
82 rooms. Complimentary continental breakfast. Fitness center. Pool.
$61-150

★★HO-CHUNK HOTEL & CASINO

S3214 Highway 12, Baraboo, 608-356-6210, 800-746-2486; www.ho-chunk.com
315 rooms. Restaurant, bar. Casino. Pool. Fitness center. $151-250

BAYFIELD

See also Ashland
Considered a gateway to the Apostle Islands, Bayfield is a charming community filled with orchards, inns, berry farms and a host of seasonal activities.

WHAT TO SEE

APOSTLE ISLANDS NATIONAL LAKESHORE

415 Washington Ave., Bayfield, 715-779-3397; www.nps.gov
These 11 miles of mainland shoreline and 21 islands of varying size feature
hiking, boating, fishing, plus primitive campsites on 18 islands. Visit one of
the two visitor centers, in Bayfield (daily) and at Little Sand Bay (Memorial
Day-September).

LAKE SUPERIOR BIG TOP CHAUTAUQUA

Ski Hill Road, Bayfield, 715-373-5552, 888-244-8368; www.bigtop.org
Outdoor venue featuring folk and bluegrass, musicals and theater.
June-Labor Day, Wednesday-Sunday evenings; some Tuesday and matinee
performances.

MADELINE ISLAND FERRY LINE

1 Washington Ave., Bayfield, 715-747-2051; www.madferry.com
The Island Queen, Nichevo II and the Madeline Bayfield make frequent
trips.
April-January, daily.

MADELINE ISLAND HISTORICAL MUSEUM

Colonel Wood Avenue and Main Street, Bayfield, 715-747-2415;
www.madelineislandmuseum.wisconsinhistory.org
This museum is located near the site of an American Fur Company post and
housed in a single building combining four pioneer log structures.
Late May-early October, daily.

SPECIAL EVENTS

APPLE FESTIVAL

42 S. Broad St., Bayfield, 800-447-4094; www.bayfield.org
For three days orchard owners, artists, musicians, street entertainers, crafters and festival food vendors line the historic streets of this quaint fishing
village.
First weekend in October.

BAYFIELD FESTIVAL OF ARTS

Memorial Park, 2 E. Front St., Bayfield, 800-447-4094; www.bayfield.org

The Bayfield Festival of Arts has been held for more than 40 years on Lake Superior. Artists and crafters from across the Midwest gather in Bayfield's picturesque waterfront park to display their work.

Last weekend in July.

RUN ON WATER

Bayfield Lakeside Pavilion, 2 E. Front St., Bayfield, 800-447-4094; www.bayfield.org

When Lake Superior freezes, there is no better way to celebrate the winter or the road between Bayfield and Madeline Island than to run across it.

First Saturday in February.

SAILBOAT RACE WEEK

Bayfield Lakeside Pavilion, 2 E. Front St., Bayfield, 800-447-4094;
www.bayfieldraceweek.org

As Lake Superior's premier sailboat regatta, this is the high point of sailboat racing on the lake. About 40 boats and more than 400 sailors from throughout the upper Midwest and Canada participate in this event.

First week in July.

WHERE TO STAY
★★BAYFIELD INN

20 Rittenhouse Ave., Bayfield, 715-779-3363, 800-382-0995; www.bayfieldinn.com

21 rooms. Complimentary continental breakfast. Restaurant. $61-150

★★★OLD RITTENHOUSE INN

301 Rittenhouse Ave., Bayfield, 1-888-611-4667, 800-779-2129;
www.rittenhouseinn.com

Travelers looking for something a bit different can find it in this whimsical and charming inn. Considered by many as the preferred lodging for romance and weekend getaways, the inn consists of the lovely Victorian Old Rittenhouse Inn itself, which also houses a restaurant. Guests can enjoy the comfortably appointed guest rooms, all of which feature lovely antiques, and enjoy fine dining that covers everything from hearty breakfasts to elegant dinners.

19 rooms. Complimentary continental breakfast. Restaurant. $60-150

WHERE TO EAT
★★OLD RITTENHOUSE

301 Rittenhouse Ave., Bayfield, 715-779-5111, 800-779-2129; www.rittenhouseinn.com

American menu. Breakfast, lunch, dinner. Children's menu. Casual attire. $251-350

BEAVER DAM

See also Watertown, Waupun

Located in south-central Wisconsin, Beaver Dam is a small town close to Milwaukee (90-minute drive) and Madison (40-minute drive).

WHAT TO SEE
DODGE COUNTY HISTORICAL MUSEUM

105 Park Ave., Beaver Dam, 920-887-1266; www.dodgecountyhistory.org
Housed in an 1890 Romanesque building, this museum spotlights Chinese and Native American artifacts, spinning wheels and dolls.
Tuesday-Saturday, afternoons.

SPECIAL EVENT
DODGE COUNTY FAIR

Fairgrounds, N6885 High Point Road, Beaver Dam, 920-885-3586;
www.dodgecountyfairgrounds.com
Includes country artists, a demolition derby and pig races.
Five days in mid-August.

WHERE TO STAY
★★BEST WESTERN CAMPUS INN MOTOR LODGE

815 Park Ave., Beaver Dam, 920-887-7171, 800-572-4891; www.bestwestern.com
94 rooms. Restaurant, bar. Pool. Complimentary breakfast. Fitness center.
$60-150

BELOIT
See also Delavan, Janesville
In 1837, the town of Colebrook, N.H., moved almost en masse to this point at the confluence of Turtle Creek and the Rock River. The community, successively known as Turtle, Blodgett's Settlement and New Albany, was finally named Beloit in 1857. The New Englanders, determined to sustain standards of Eastern culture and education, founded Beloit Seminary soon after settling. This small coeducational school became Beloit College. Today, the city's economy centers on the college, food processing and the production of heavy machinery.

WHAT TO SEE
ANGEL MUSEUM

656 Pleasant St., Beloit, 608-362-9099; www.angelmuseum.com
This museum features a collection of 11,000 angels made from everything from leather to china. Oprah Winfrey has donated more than 500 angels from her private collection.
Tuesday-Saturday 10 a.m.-4 p.m.; June-August, Sunday 1-4 p.m.

BELOIT COLLEGE

700 College St., Beloit, 608-363-2000; www.beloit.edu
Noted for the Theodore Lyman Wright Museum of Art, Beloit College also houses the Logan Museum of Anthropology, which has changing displays of Native American and Stone Age artifacts. The campus also contains prehistoric mounds.
Campus tours by appointment.

HANCHETT-BARTLETT HOMESTEAD

2149 St. Lawrence Ave., Beloit, 608-365-7835; www.beloithistoricalsociety.com

This restored historic limestone homestead on 15 acres was built in 1857 in the transitional Greek Revival style with Italianate details and has been restored in period colors. The house contains furnishings from the mid-19th century; the limestone barn houses collection of farm implements. June-September, Wednesday-Sunday afternoons; also by appointment.

SPECIAL EVENT
RIVERFEST

Riverside Park, Beloit, 53511, 608-365-4838; www.beloitriverfest.com

This music festival of top-name performers pulls in more than 50 bands. There is also food, carnival rides and children's entertainment. Mid-July.

WHERE TO STAY
★HOLIDAY INN EXPRESS

2790 Milwaukee Road, Beloit, 608-365-6000, 800-465-4329; www.holidayinn.com

73 rooms. Complimentary continental breakfast. Pets accepted. Pool. $61-150

BLACK RIVER FALLS

See also Sparta, Tomah

In 1819, when the Black River countryside was a wilderness of pine, one of the first sawmills in Wisconsin was built here. Among the early settlers were a group of Mormons from Nauvoo, Ill. Conflict developed with local landowners, and the Mormons soon returned to Nauvoo. The seat of Jackson County, Black River Falls is situated on the Black River, which offers boating and canoeing. The area is also noted for deer hunting and winter sports.

WHAT TO SEE
BLACK RIVER FALLS STATE FOREST

910 Highway 54 E., Black River Falls, 715-284-1406; www.dnr.wi.gov

A 66,000-acre area, this state forest offers swimming, fishing, boating, canoeing, hiking, cross-country skiing, snowmobiling, a bridle trail, picnicking, a playground and camping. There is also a lookout tower and wildlife. Daily.

WHERE TO STAY
★★BEST WESTERN ARROWHEAD LODGE & SUITES

600 Oasis Road, Black River Falls, 715-284-9471, 800-284-9471;
www.bestwestern.com

143 rooms. Complimentary breakfast. Restaurant, bar. Pets accepted. Fitness center. Business center. Indoor pool. $61-150

★DAYS INN

919 Highway 54 E., Black River Falls, 715-284-4333, 800-356-8018; www.daysinn.com

86 rooms. Complimentary breakfast. Pets accepted. Pool. Business center. $61-150

BOULDER JUNCTION

See also Eagle River, Manitowish Waters, Minocqua

This secluded little village within the Northern Highland-American Legion State Forest is the gateway to a vast recreational area with woodlands, scenic drives, streams and several hundred lakes where fishing for muskellunge is excellent. The town also offers various winter activities, including snowmobiling, cross-country skiing and ice fishing. In nearby state nurseries, millions of young pine trees are raised and shipped all over the state for forest planting.

WHAT TO SEE
NORTHERN HIGHLAND-AMERICAN LEGION STATE FOREST
4125 County Highway M, Boulder Junction, 715-385-3521

This 225,000-acre forest has swimming beaches, water skiing, fishing, boating, canoeing, hiking, cross-country skiing, snowmobiling, picnicking and improved and primitive camping.
Daily.

BURLINGTON

See also Delavan, Elkhorn, Fontana, Lake Geneva

Originally called Foxville, Burlington was renamed for the city in Vermont by a group of settlers arriving in 1835. It is the home of the Liar's Club, an organization dedicated to the preservation of the art of telling tall tales. A prize is awarded each year to the contributor who submits the most incredible "stretcher."

WHAT TO SEE
GREEN MEADOWS FARM
33603 High Drive, Burlington, 262-534-2891

This operating farm offers daily guided tours, pony rides, tractor-drawn hayrides, more than 20 hands-on animal areas and picnic areas.
May-June, Tuesday-Saturday; October, daily; closed September.

SPINNING TOP EXPLORATORY MUSEUM
533 Milwaukee Ave., Burlington, 262-763-3946; www.wisconline.com

Find exhibits and displays dealing with tops, yo-yos and gyroscopes, plus top games, demonstrations, hands-on experiments and video presentations.

SPECIAL EVENTS
AQUADUCKS WATER SKI SHOW
Fischer County Park, Highway 11, Burlington, 262-763-6044; www.aquaducks.org

Water skiers perform each Saturday evening.
June-Labor Day.

CHOCOLATE CITY FESTIVAL
Maryland Avenue, Burlington, 262-763-3300; www.chocolatefest.com

The two-day, citywide celebration includes an arts and crafts fair, a parade and entertainment.
Weekend after Mother's Day.

WHERE TO STAY
★AMERICINN
2709 Brown's Lake Drive, Burlington, 262-534-2125, 800-634-3444;
www.americinn.com
50 rooms. Complimentary breakfast. Pool. Business center. $60-150

CABLE
See also Hayward
Outdoor enthusiasts will enjoy Cable, which is located in the heart of Chequamegon-Nicolet National Forest in northwest Wisconsin. Spend a day on the golf course or hiking though the forest, fish for your dinner or opt for one of the area's delicious restaurants.

WHERE TO EAT
★★RIVER'S BEND
792 Riverview Drive, Howard, 920-434-1383; www.epictrip.com
American menu. Lunch, dinner. Bar. Children's menu. Casual attire. $16-35

CEDAR GROVE
See also Port Washington, Sheboygan
Dutch settlers founded this village on the edge of Lake Michigan. Many of those settlers' descendants still live in the area, and they celebrate their Dutch heritage each year during the Holland Fest.

SPECIAL EVENT
HOLLAND FEST
118 Main St., Cedar Grove, 920-457-9491; www.hollandfest.com
This fest includes Dutch traditions such as wooden-shoe dancing, street scrubbing, a folk fair, food, music, an art fair and a parade.
Last Friday-Saturday in July.

CEDARBURG
See also Milwaukee, Port Washington
Cedarburg, surrounded by rich farmlands and protected forests and wetlands, has many beautiful old homes that were built in the 1800s. Many buildings in the historic downtown area have been restored.

WHAT TO SEE
CEDAR CREEK SETTLEMENT AND WINERY
N70W6340 Bridge Road, Cedarburg, 262-377-8020, 800-827-8020;
www.cedarcreeksettlement.com
This stone woolen mill was converted into a winery and houses shops, art studios and restaurants. The winery makes strawberry, cranberry and grape wines and there is a museum of antique wine-making tools.
Daily.

SPECIAL EVENT
WINTER FESTIVAL
W63N641 Washington Ave., Cedarburg, 262-377-9620, 800-827-8020;
www.cedarburgfestivals.org

This festival features ice carving and snow sculpture contests, bed and barrel races across the ice, winter softball and volleyball, an Alaskan malamute weight pull, a snow goose egg hunt, a torchlight parade and horse-drawn sleigh rides.

First full weekend in February.

WHERE TO STAY
★BEST WESTERN QUIET HOUSE & SUITES
10330 N. Port Washington Road, Mequon, 262-241-3677, 800-780-7234;
www.bestwestern.com

54 rooms. Complimentary continental breakfast. High-speed Internet access. Airport transportation available. Pets accepted. Fitness center. Business center. Indoor pool. $61-150

CHIPPEWA FALLS
See also Eau Claire, Menomonie

Water has replaced lumber as the prime natural resource of this city on the Chippewa River. Jean Brunet, a pioneer settler, built a sawmill and then a dam here. Soon the area was populated by lumberjacks. Today, hydroelectric power is channeled to the industries of Chippewa Falls, whose water is noted for its purity.

WHAT TO SEE
BRUNET ISLAND STATE PARK
23125 255th St., Cornell, 715-239-6888; www.dnr.wi.gov

This 1,032-acre river island park features swimming, fishing, boating, canoeing, nature and hiking trails, cross-country skiing, picnicking, a playground and camping.

CHIPPEWA FALLS ZOO
Irvine Park, Bridgewater Ave., Chippewa Falls, 715-723-3090, 715-723-0051;
www.chippewachamber.org

This zoo concentrates on native animals.
May-October, daily.

COOK-RUTLEDGE MANSION
505 W. Grand Ave., Chippewa Falls, 715-723-7181; www.cookrutledgemansion.com

This restored Victorian mansion offers guided tours.
June-August, Thursday-Sunday; September-May, by appointment.

LAKE WISSOTA STATE PARK
18127 County Highway O, Chippewa Falls, 715-382-4574; www.dnr.wi.gov

This 1,062-acre park offers swimming, water-skiing, fishing, boating, canoeing, hiking, cross-country skiing, picnicking, a playground and camping.
Daily.

WHERE TO STAY
★COUNTRY INN & SUITES BY CARLSON CHIPPEWA FALLS
1021 W. Park Ave., Chippewa Falls, 715-720-1414, 888-201-1746;
www.countryinns.com
62 rooms. Complimentary breakfast. Indoor pool. $61-150

WHERE TO EAT
★LINDSAY'S ON GRAND
24 W. Grand Ave., Chippewa Falls, 715-723-4025
American menu. Breakfast, lunch, dinner. Children's menu. Casual attire.
$15 and under

CRANDON
See also Rhinelander, Three Lakes
This town is the perfect destination for travelers searching for a rustic adventure. There are four lakes in Crandon, which offer opportunities for fishing, swimming and boating in summer. In winter, enjoy cross-country skiing and snowmobiling across the scenic terrain.

WHAT TO SEE
CAMP FIVE MUSEUM AND "LUMBERJACK SPECIAL" STEAM TRAIN TOUR
Highway 8 and Highway 32, Laona, 715-674-3414, 800-774-3414;
www.camp5museum.org
Take this old steam train ride to the Camp Five Museum complex, where you will find an active blacksmith shop, a 1900s country store, a logging museum with audiovisual presentation, a nature center with a diorama featuring area wildlife and a 30-minute guided forest tour.
Mid-June-late August, four departures Monday-Saturday.

DELAVAN
See also Beloit, Burlington, Elkhorn, Fontana, Lake Geneva
Between 1847 and 1894, Delavan was the headquarters of 28 different circuses. The original P. T. Barnum circus was organized here during the winter of 1870-1871 by William C. Coup. Spring Grove and St. Andrew's cemeteries are "last lot" resting places for more than 100 members of the 19th-century circus colony. Today, many flowering crabapple trees grace the town, usually blooming in mid-May.

WHERE TO EAT
★★MILLIE'S
N2484 County Road O, Delavan, 262-728-2434; www.millieswi.com
American menu. Breakfast, lunch. Closed Monday (except July-August); closed Tuesday-Friday January-February. Bar. $16-35

DEVIL'S LAKE STATE PARK
See also Baraboo
These 11,050 acres, with spring-fed Devil's Lake as the greatest single attraction, form one of Wisconsin's most beautiful state parks. Remnants of

an ancient mountain range surround the lake, providing unique scenery. The lake, 1.25 miles long, is in the midst of sheer cliffs of quartzite that rise as high as 500 feet above the water. Unusual rock formations may be found at the top of the bluffs. The park has a naturalist in residence who may be contacted for information concerning year-round nature hikes and programs. Sandy swimming beaches with bathhouses, concessions and boat landings are at either end. No motorboats are permitted. The park provides hiking and cross-country skiing trails, picnic grounds, improved tent and trailer facilities and a nature center. The lake is restocked yearly. Native American mounds include the Eagle, Bear and Lynx mounds. General tourist supplies are available at the north and south shores.

DODGEVILLE
See also Mount Horeb, New Glarus, Platteville
This town in southwestern Wisconsin offers plenty of opportunities to play outdoors year-round. Do not miss the American Players Theatre in nearby Spring Green if you visit in the summer.

WHAT TO SEE
GOVERNOR DODGE STATE PARK
4175 Highway 23, Dodgeville, 608-935-2315; www.dnr.state.wi.us
A 5,029-acre park with 95-acre and 150-acre lakes, Governor Dodge includes rock formations and white pine and offers swimming, fishing, boating and canoeing; bicycle, hiking and bridle trails; cross-country skiing, snowmobiling, picnicking, playgrounds, concessions, camping, backpack campsites and a horse campground.
Nature programs: June-August, daily.

WHERE TO STAY
★THE HOUSE ON THE ROCK INN
3591 Highway 23, Dodgeville, 608-935-3711, 888-935-3960;
www.thehouseontherock.com
114 rooms. Pool. Bar. $151-250

DOOR COUNTY
See also Baileys Harbor, Egg Harbor, Ellison Bay, Ephraim, Sister Bay
Famous for its foliage and 250 miles of shoreline, Door County is a peninsula with Green Bay on the west and Lake Michigan on the east. Its picturesque villages, rolling woodlands, limestone bluffs and beautiful vistas are the reason the area is often referred to as the Cape Cod of the Midwest.

Door County offers year-round attractions. Spring and summer bring fishing, sailing, beachcombing, camping, hiking, biking and horseback riding. Thousands of acres of apple and cherry blossoms color the landscape in late May. There is excellent scuba diving in the Portes des Mortes (Death's Door) Straits at the tip of the peninsula, where hundreds of shipwrecks lie in the shifting freshwater sands. Fall colors can be viewed from the endless miles of trails and country roads, which become cross-country ski routes in winter.

Many artists reside here, as evidenced by the towns' shops, galleries and boutiques. Summertime theater and concerts also attract tourists.

The taste of the peninsula is unquestionably the legendary fish boil. Trout or whitefish and potatoes and onions are cooked in a cauldron over an open fire. When the fish has almost finished cooking, kerosene is thrown onto the fire, creating a huge flame and causing the unwanted oils to boil out and over the pot.

WHERE TO STAY
★CEDAR COURT

9429 Cedar St., Fish Creek, 920-868-3361; www.cedarcourt.com
16 rooms. Outdoor pool, whirlpool. $61-150

★★FINDLAY'S HOLIDAY INN

1 Main Road, Washington Island, 920-847-2526, 800-522-5469; www.holidayinn.net
16 rooms. Closed November-April. Restaurant. $61-150

★★GORDON LODGE

1420 Pine Drive, Baileys Harbor, 920-839-2331, 800-830-6235; www.gordonlodge.com
40 rooms. Closed mid-October-mid-May. Complimentary full breakfast. Restaurant, bar. Tennis. $151-250

★★LEATHEM SMITH LODGE AND MARINA

1640 Memorial Drive, Sturgeon Bay, 920-743-5555, 800-366-7947; www.lslodge.com
63 rooms. Complimentary continental breakfast. Restaurant, bar. Golf. Tennis. $60-150

★★WAGON TRAIL

1041 County Road ZZ, Ellison Bay, 920-854-2385, 800-999-2466; www.wagontrail.com
72 rooms. Restaurant. Pool. Tennis. Wireless Internet access. $151-250

EAGLE RIVER

219

See also Boulder Junction, Rhinelander, Three Lakes
The bald eagles that gave this town its name are still occasionally seen, and the Eagle River chain of 28 lakes, the largest inland chain of freshwater lakes in the world, is an outstanding tourist attraction. Eagle River has developed as a center of winter sports. The result is lake vacationers in summer and ski fans, both cross-country and downhill, and snowmobilers in winter. There are more than 11 miles of cross-country ski trails on Anvil Lake trail, and 600 miles of snowmobile trails and several hiking areas are in the Nicolet National Forest.

WHAT TO SEE
TREES FOR TOMORROW NATURAL RESOURCES EDUCATION CENTER

519 Sheridan St., Eagle River, 715-479-6456, 800-838-9472;
www.treesfortomorrow.com
You'll find demonstration forests, nature trail and a "talking tree" here. There are also outdoor skills and natural resource programs with an emphasis on forest ecology and conservation.
Guided tours: Tuesday, Thursday in summer.

WHERE TO STAY
★DAYS INN
844 Highway 45 N., Eagle River, 715-479-5151, 800-356-8018; www.daysinn.com
93 rooms. Complimentary continental breakfast. Pets accepted. Pool. Airport shuttle. Business center. High-speed Internet access. Fitness center. Restaurant. $61-150

EAU CLAIRE
See also Chippewa Falls, Menomonie
Once a wild and robust lumber camp and sawmill on the shores of the Eau Claire and Chippewa rivers, the city has turned to diversified industry. The name is French for "clear water."

WHAT TO SEE
DELLS MILLS MUSEUM
E. 18855 County Road V, Augusta, 715-286-2714; www.dellsmill.com
This historic five-story water-powered flour and grist mill was built in 1864 out of hand-hewn timbers.
May-October, Daily.

PAUL BUNYAN LOGGING CAMP
Carson Park, 1110 Carson Park Drive, Eau Claire, 715-835-6200;
www.paulbunyancamp.org
This restored 1890s logging camp has a bunkhouse, cook shack, blacksmith shop, dingle, filers shack, barn and heavy equipment display.
First Monday in April-first Monday in October.

UNIVERSITY OF WISCONSIN-EAU CLAIRE
105 Garfield Ave., Eau Claire, 715-836-4411; www.uwec.edu
The university houses a planetarium, bird museum, greenhouses, musical events and an art gallery. Putnam Park arboretum, a 230-acre tract of forest land kept in its natural state, has self-guided nature trails.

WHERE TO STAY
★★★FANNY HILL VICTORIAN INN & DINNER THEATER
3919 Crescent Ave., Eau Claire, 715-836-8184, 800-292-8026; www.fannyhill.com
A beautiful river view is the claim to fame at this elegant inn, which has a classic flair. Each room is appointed with Victorian touches, which cap off the romantic surroundings. A Victorian garden overlooking the Chippewa River and a dinner theater (productions have included Neil Simon's Last of the Red Hot Lovers and Noises Off) on the premises are nice touches.
11 rooms. Complimentary full breakfast. High-speed Internet access. Bar. $151-250

★HAMPTON INN
2622 Craig Road, Eau Claire, 715-833-0003, 800-426-7866; www.hamptoninn.com
106 rooms. Complimentary continental breakfast. Wireless Internet access. Business center. Fitness center. Pool. Restaurant $60-150

★★PLAZA HOTEL AND SUITES EAU CLAIRE

1202 W. Clairemont Ave., Eau Claire, 715-834-3181; www.plazaeauclaire.com
233 rooms. Restaurant, bar. Airport transportation available. Indoor pool, whirlpool, children's pool. Fitness center. $60-150

EGG HARBOR
See also Baileys Harbor, Ephraim, Sister Bay, Sturgeon Bay
This Door County town is located on the shore of Green Bay.

SPECIAL EVENT
BIRCH CREEK MUSIC CENTER
3821 County East, Egg Harbor, 920-868-3763; www.birchcreek.org
This concert series takes place in a unique barn concert hall. Early-mid-July: percussion series; mid-July mid-August: big band series. Other concerts and events through Labor Day.

ELKHART LAKE
See also Fond du Lac, Sheboygan
This lake resort, famous for its good beaches, is one of the state's oldest vacation spots.

WHAT TO SEE
BROUGHTON-SHEBOYGAN COUNTY MARSH
W7039 County Road SR, Elkhart Lake, 920-876-2535; www.elkhartlake.com/attractions
This 14,000-acre wildlife area offers fishing, boating, canoeing, duck hunting, camping and a lodge and restaurant.

LITTLE ELKHART LAKE
Elkhart Lake, www.co.sheboygan.wi.us
This 131-acre lake has heavy concentrations of pike, walleye, bass and panfish.

OLD WADE HOUSE HISTORIC SITE
W7824 Center Road, Greenbush, 920-526-3271; www.wisconsinhistory.org
The restored Old Wade House is an early stagecoach inn with a nearby smokehouse, blacksmith shop and mill dam site, plus the Jung Carriage Museum housing more than 100 restored horse- and hand-drawn vehicles. May-October.

SPECIAL EVENT
ROAD AMERICA
N7390 Highway 67, Elkhart Lake, 800-365-7223; www.roadamerica.com
Located on 525 rolling, wooded acres, this racecourse is a closed-circuit four-mile sports car track with 14 turns. One of the most popular events of the season is the CART Indy race, which draws top-name race teams. June-September.

WHERE TO STAY
★★VICTORIAN VILLAGE ON ELKHART LAKE
279 Lake St., Elkhart Lake, 920-876-3323, 877-860-9988; www.vicvill.com
120 rooms. Restaurant, bar. $61-150

★★★52 STAFFORD
52 S. Stafford St., Plymouth, 920-893-0552, 800-421-4667
Remodeled to be reminiscent of a fine Irish manor home, the luxurious furnishings and atmosphere of this restored 1892 home make guests feel more like they are on the Emerald Isle than in Wisconsin.
23 rooms. Complimentary continental breakfast. Restaurant. $60-150

ELKHORN
See also Burlington, Delavan, Fort Atkinson, Janesville, Waukesha
In southeast Wisconsin, Elkhorn is a picturesque town, which has inspired generations of painters to capture the essence of small-town America.

WHERE TO EAT
★★JERRY'S OLD TOWN INN
N116 W15841 Main St., Germantown, 262-251-4455; www.jerrysworldfamousribs.com
American menu. Dinner. Bar. Children's menu. Casual attire. $15 and under

ELLISON BAY
See also Baileys Harbor, Door County, Egg Harbor, Ephraim, Sister Bay
This resort area is near the northern end of Door County. Fishing and boating are popular here; public launching ramps and charter boats are available. This is also considered a good area for scuba diving.

WHAT TO SEE
FERRY TO WASHINGTON ISLAND
Northport Pier, Detroit Harbor Road, Gills Rock, 920-847-2546; www.wisfery.com
This ferry has an enclosed cabin and open deck seating. Trips are 30 minutes and accommodate cars and bicycles.
Daily.

NEWPORT STATE PARK
475 County Road NP, Ellison Bay, 920-854-2500; www.dnr.state.wi.us/Org
The 2,370-acre wilderness park includes 11 miles of Lake Michigan shoreline, a beach, hiking, cross-country ski trails, picnicking, backpacking and winter camping.

WHERE TO EAT
★VIKING GRILL
12029 Highway 42, Ellison Bay, 920-854-2998; www.thevikinggrill.com
American menu. Breakfast, lunch, dinner. Closed early February-late March. Bar. Children's menu. Casual attire. Outdoor seating. $16-35

EPHRAIM

See also Baileys Harbor, Egg Harbor, Ellison Bay, Sister Bay
Moravian colonists founded the second Ephraim here after leaving the first town of that name, now a part of Green Bay; a monument at the harbor commemorates the landing of Moravians in 1853. The village is now a quaint resort community and a center for exploration of the north and west shores of Door County.

SPECIAL EVENT
FYR BAL FESTIVAL
Ephraim Village Hall, Highway 42, Ephraim, 920-854-4989;
www.ephraim-doorcounty.com/fyr_bal.html
This Scandinavian welcome to summer includes a fish boil, a Blessing of the Fleet, an art fair, a lighting of the bonfires on the beach at dusk and a coronation of Viking Chieftain.
Three days in mid-June.

WHERE TO STAY
★★EDGEWATER RESORT MOTEL
10040 Water St., Ephraim, 920-854-2734; www.edge-waterresort.com
38 rooms. Closed November-April. Restaurant. Pool. $61-150

★EVERGREEN BEACH
9944 Water St., Ephraim, 920-854-2831, 800-420-8130; www.evergreenbeach.com
30 rooms. Closed late October-late May. Complimentary continental breakfast. $60-150

ALSO RECOMMENDED
EAGLE HARBOR INN
9914 Water St., Ephraim, 920-854-2121, 800-324-5427; www.eagleharbor.com
41 rooms. Complimentary full breakfast. Pool. $60-150

EPHRAIM INN
9994 Pioneer Lane, Ephraim, 920-854-4515; www.theephraiminn.com
16 rooms. Closed November-April (Monday-Thursday). No children allowed. $61-150

WHERE TO EAT
★OLD POST OFFICE RESTAURANT
10040 Water St., Ephraim, 920-854-4034; www.oldpostoffice-doorcounty.com
American menu. Breakfast, dinner. Closed November-April. Casual attire. Outdoor seating. $16-35

FISH CREEK

See also Baileys Harbor, Egg Harbor, Ellison Bay, Ephraim, Sister Bay
This picturesque Green Bay resort village, with its many interesting shops, is in Door County.

WHAT TO SEE
PENINSULA STATE PARK
9462 Shore Road, Fish Creek, 920-868-3258; www.dnr.state.wi.us
This 3,763-acre park has nine miles of waterfront including sandy and cobblestone beaches, caves and cliffs and an observation tower. Swimming, fishing, boating, water skiing, hiking, bicycle trails, cross-country skiing, snowmobiling, picnic grounds, a playground, concessions and camping are all available.

SPECIAL EVENT
AMERICAN FOLKLORE THEATRE
Peninsula State Park Amphitheater, 9462 Shore Road, Fish Creek, 920-854-6117;
www.folkloretheatre.com
See original folk musical productions based on American lore and literature at this theatre.
July-August.

WHERE TO STAY
★CEDAR COURT
9429 Cedar St., Fish Creek, 920-868-3361; www.cedarcourt.com
16 rooms. Pool. $61-150

★HOMESTEAD SUITES
4006 Highway, 42, Fish Creek, 920-868-3748, 800-686-6621;
www.homesteadsuites.com
48 rooms, all suites. Complimentary continental breakfast. Pool. $151-250

★★★WHITE GULL INN
4225 Main St., Fish Creek, 920-868-3517, 888-364-9542; www.whitegullinn.com
Built in 1896, this longstanding charmer features antiques in the lovely suites, rooms and cottages. Accommodations have been fully restored (fireplaces and whirlpool baths are common) and the seven houses and cottages offer distinctly period details whirlpool baths like a maple canopied bed or French doors leading to a private deck. Have a candlelight dinner at the onsite restaurant, which serves dishes such as herbed lamb shank and Parmesan-dusted halibut fillet. Don't miss the traditional fish boil.
17 rooms. Complimentary full breakfast. Restaurant, bar. $151-250

WHERE TO EAT
★★C AND C SUPPER CLUB
4170 Main St., Fish Creek, 920-868-3412; www.ccsupperclub.com
American menu. Lunch, dinner. Closed three weeks in March. Bar. Children's menu. Business casual attire. Reservations recommended. $16-35

★THE COOKERY
Highway 42, Fish Creek, 920-868-3634; www.cookeryfishcreek.com
American menu. Breakfast, lunch, dinner. Closed Monday-Thursday, November-March. Children's menu. Casual attire. $16-35

★PELLETIER'S

4199 Main St., Fish Creek, 920-868-3313; www.doorcountyfishboil.com

American menu. Breakfast, lunch, dinner. Closed late Oct-mid-May. Children's menu. Casual attire. Reservations recommended. Outdoor seating. $16-35

★★SUMMERTIME

1 N. Spruce St., Fish Creek, 920-868-3738; www.thesummertime.com

American menu. Breakfast, lunch, dinner. Closed November-April. Children's menu. Casual attire. Outdoor seating. $16-35

FOND DU LAC

See also Elkhart Lake, Green Lake, Oshkosh, Waupun

Located at the foot of Lake Winnebago and named by French explorers in the 1600s, Fond du Lac—"foot of the lake"—was an early outpost for fur trading, later achieving prominence as a lumbering center and railroad city.

WHAT TO SEE
GALLOWAY HOUSE AND VILLAGE

336 Old Pioneer Road, Fond du Lac, 920-922-6390, 920-922-0991; www.fdl.com

This restored 30-room Victorian mansion has four fireplaces, carved woodwork and stenciled ceilings. The village features 24 buildings including a one-room schoolhouse, a print shop, a general store, an operating gristmill, a museum with a collection of Native American artifacts, war displays and other area artifacts.

Memorial Day-Labor Day, Daily; rest of September, Saturday-Sunday.

ICE AGE VISITOR CENTER

N2875 Highway 67, Campbellsport, 920-533-8322; www.dnr.state.wi.us

Films, slides and panoramas show visitors how glaciers molded Wisconsin's terrain; naturalists answer questions.

Daily.

NORTHERN UNIT

N1765 Highway G, Campbellsport, 262-626-2116; www.dnr.state.wi.us

The forest is being developed as part of an Ice Age National Scientific Reserve. Its 30,000 acres include Long and Mauthe Lake Recreation Areas and scenic Kettle Moraine Drive.

OCTAGON HOUSE

276 Linden St., Fond du Lac, 920-922-1608; www.marlenesheirlooms.com

This 12-room octagonal house was built in 1856 by Isaac Brown and designed by Orson Fowler. It has a hidden room, secret passageways and an underground tunnel, plus period antiques, dolls, and spinning wheel demonstrations.

Monday, Wednesday, Friday afternoons.

ST. PAUL'S CATHEDRAL

51 W. Division, Fond du Lac, 920-921-3363; www.saintpaulsepiscopalcathedral.org

The English Gothic limestone structure has wood carvings from Oberammergau, Germany, rare ecclesiastical artifacts and a variety of stained-glass windows, plus a cloister garden. Self-guided tours by appointment.

WHERE TO STAY
★DAYS INN
107 N. Pioneer Road, Fond du Lac, 920-923-6790, 800-329-7466; www.daysinn.com
59 rooms. Complimentary continental breakfast. Pets accepted. $61-150

★HOLIDAY INN
625 W. Rolling Meadows Drive, Fond du Lac, 920-923-1440, 800-465-4329;
www.holidayinn.com
139 rooms. Restaurant, bar. Airport transportation available. Pets accepted. Pool. $61-150

WHERE TO EAT
★SALTY'S SEAFOOD AND SPIRITS
503 N. Park Ave., Fond du Lac, 920-922-9940; www.fdlfeatures.com
Seafood menu. Lunch, dinner. Bar. Children's menu. Casual attire. $16-35

★★SCHREINER'S
168 N. Pioneer Road, Fond du Lac, 920-922-0590; www.fdlchowder.com
American menu. Breakfast, lunch, dinner. Bar. Children's menu. $15 and under

★★SEVEN SEAS
1807 Nagawicka Road, Hartland, 262-367-3903; www.weissgerbers.com
Seafood menu. Dinner, Sunday brunch. Bar. Children's menu. Business casual attire. Reservations recommended. Outdoor seating. $36-85

FONTANA
See also Beloit, Burlington, Delavan, Elkhorn, Lake Geneva
Located on the western shore of Lake Geneva in territory once occupied by the Potawatomi, this town was named for its many springs.

WHERE TO STAY
★★★THE ABBEY RESORT
269 Fontana Blvd., Fontana, 262-275-6811, 800-558-2405, 800-709-1323;
www.theabbeyresort.com
Situated on 90 lush acres and set on the water's edge, this elegant resort and spa delights with its restaurants (Porto serves Mediterranean dishes). The atmosphere of quiet elegance makes for an enjoyable stay.
334 rooms. Restaurant, bar. Pool. Tennis. Business Center. $60-150

FORT ATKINSON
See also Elkhorn, Janesville, Madison, Watertown
In 1872, William Dempster Hoard, later governor of Wisconsin, organized the Wisconsin State Dairyman's Association here. He toured the area, drumming up support by preaching the virtues of the cow, "the foster mother of the human race." More than any other man, Hoard was responsible for Wis-

consin's development as a leading dairy state. Nearby are Lake Koshkonong, a popular recreation area, and Lake Ripley, where Ole Evinrude invented the outboard motor in 1908.

WHAT TO SEE
DWIGHT FOSTER HOUSE
407 Merchants Ave., Fort Atkinson, 920-563-7769; www.hoardmuseum.org
The historic home of the city's founder, this five-room, two-story Greek Revival frame house has period furnishings and many original pieces.
Tuesday-Saturday.

HOARD HISTORICAL MUSEUM
401 Whitewater Ave., Fort Atkinson, 920-563-7769; www.hoardmuseum.org
Housed in a historic home, this museum features pioneer history and archaeology of the area, period rooms, an antique quilt, a bird room, old costumes and clothing, antique firearms, a reference library and permanent and changing displays.
Tuesday-Sunday.

NATIONAL DAIRY SHRINE MUSEUM
407 Merchants Ave., Fort Atkinson, 920-563-7769; www.roadsideamerica.com
This museum traces the development of the dairy industry for the past 100 years. A collection of memorabilia, the exhibits include an old creamery, a replica of an early dairy farm kitchen, an old barn and milk-hauling equipment, and more.
Tuesday-Saturday.

GALESVILLE
See also La Crosse, Sparta, Tomah
Twenty miles north of La Crosse, Galesville is in the Coulee Region of the Mississippi River Valley.

WHAT TO SEE
MERRICK STATE PARK
S2965 Highway, 101 S. Webster St., 608-687-4936; www.dnr.state.wi.us
A 324-acre park along the Mississippi River, Merrick features canoeing and camping.
Daily.

PERROT STATE PARK
W26247 Sullivan Road, Trempealeau, 608-534-6409; www.dnr.state.wi.us
Trempealeau Mountain, a beacon for voyageurs for more than 300 years, is in this 1,425-acre park. Nicolas Perrot set up winter quarters here in 1686. A French fort was built on the site in 1731.
Daily.

GREEN BAY
See also Algoma, Appleton, Door County

The strategic location that made Green Bay a trading center as far back as 1669, today enables this port city to handle nearly 1.8 million tons of cargo a year. The region was claimed for the King of France in 1634, and was named La Baye in 1669 when it became the site of the mission of St. Francis. It then saw the rise of fur trading, a series of Native American wars and French, British and U.S. conflicts. Although it became part of the United States in 1783, Green Bay did not yield to American influence until after the War of 1812, when agents of John Jacob Astor gained control of the fur trade. The oldest settlement in the state, Green Bay is a paper and cheese producing center as well as a hub for health care and insurance. It is also famous for its professional football team, the Green Bay Packers.

WHAT TO SEE
GREEN BAY BOTANICAL GARDENS
2600 Larsen Road, Green Bay, 920-490-9457; www.gbbg.org
An educational and recreational facility, these botanical gardens have a formal rose, children's and four-season garden.
May-October, Daily; November-April, Monday-Friday.

GREEN BAY PACKERS (NFL)
Lambeau Field, 1265 Lombardi Ave., Green Bay, 920-469-7500; www.packers.com
Probably the most storied football venue in the NFL, Curly Lambeau Field is home to the Green Bay Packers. Site of the famous Ice Bowl, the stadium is known for its harsh weather (it's commonly referred to as the "frozen tundra of Lambeau Field"), as well as for the "Lambeau Leaps" that Packer players take into the waiting arms of fans in the front row of the end zone.

GREEN BAY PACKERS HALL OF FAME
Lambeau Field Atrium, 1265 Lombardi Ave., Green Bay, 920-499-4281, 888-442-7225; www.packers.com
This museum chronicles the history of the Green Bay Packers from 1919 to present and also houses a unique collection of multimedia presentations, memorabilia, hands-on activities and NFL films.
Daily.

HAZELWOOD HISTORIC HOME MUSEUM
1008 S. Monroe Ave., Green Bay, 920-437-1840; www.browncohistoricalsoc.org
This Greek Revival house is where the state constitution was drafted.
Memorial Day-Labor Day, Wednesday-Monday; rest of year, by appointment.

HERITAGE HILL STATE PARK
2640 S. Webster, Green Bay, 920-448-5150; www.heritagehillgb.org
The park includes a 40-acre living history museum and a complex of 26 historical buildings that illustrate the development of northeast Wisconsin.
Memorial Day-late-October, Daily; December, Friday-Saturday. Christmas festival, Friday-Sunday in December.

ONEIDA NATION MUSEUM

W892 County Road EE, De Pere, 920-869-2768;museum.oneidanation.org
Permanent and hands-on exhibits tell the story of the Oneida Nation.
September-May, Tuesday-Friday; June-August, Tuesday-Saturday.

UNIVERSITY OF WISCONSIN-GREEN BAY

2420 Nicolet Drive, Green Bay, 920-465-2000; www.uwgb.edu
The campus, built on 700 acres, houses the Weidner Center for the Performing Arts and the Cofrin Memorial Arboretum, as well as a nine-hole golf course and Bayshore picnic area. Tours of campus by appointment.

SPECIAL EVENT
WATERBOARD WARRIORS

Brown County Park, Green Bay, 920-448-4466; www.waterboardwarriors.org
Water ski shows performed by skiers from the area. Tuesday and Thursday evenings, June-August.

WHERE TO STAY
★BAYMONT INN

2840 S. Oneida St., Green Bay, 920-494-7887, 877-229-6668; www.baymontinns.com
77 rooms. Complimentary breakfast. Pets accepted. $61-150

★★BEST WESTERN MIDWAY HOTEL

780 Packer Drive, Green Bay, 920-499-3161, 800-780-7234; www.bestwestern.com
145 rooms. Restaurant, bar. Airport transportation available. Pool. $61-150

★FAIRFIELD INN

2850 S. Oneida St., Green Bay, 920-497-1010, 800-228-2800; www.fairfieldinn.com
63 rooms. Complimentary continental breakfast. Pool. $60-150

★★HOLIDAY INN

200 Main St., Green Bay, 920-437-5900, 800-457-2929; www.holidayinn.com
149 rooms. Restaurant, bar. Pets accepted. $61-150

★★RADISSON HOTEL & CONFERENCE CENTER GREEN BAY

2040 Airport Drive, Green Bay, 920-494-7300, 800-333-3333; www.radisson.com
408 rooms. Restaurants, bar. Airport transportation available. $61-150

WHERE TO EAT
★★EVE'S SUPPER CLUB

2020 Riverside Drive, Green Bay, 920-435-1571; www.evessupperclub.com
American menu. Lunch, dinner. Closed Sunday. Bar. Casual attire. Reservations recommended. $36-85

★★WELLINGTON

1060 Hansen Road, Green Bay, 920-499-2000; www.thewellingtongb.com
American menu. Lunch, dinner. Closed Sunday. Children's menu. Outdoor seating. $16-35

GREEN LAKE

See also Fond du Lac, Waupun

This county seat, known as the oldest resort community west of Niagara Falls, is a popular four-season recreational area. Green Lake, at 7,325 acres, is the deepest natural lake in the state and affords good fishing (including lake trout), swimming, sailing, power boating and iceboating.

WHAT TO SEE
GREEN LAKE CONFERENCE CENTER

West 2511 Highway 23, Green Lake, 920-294-3323; www.glcc.org

A 1,000-acre, year-round vacation conference center, Green Lake offers indoor swimming, fishing, cross-country skiing, tobogganing, ice skating, camping, hiking, biking, tennis and a 36-hole golf Course. Daily.

WHERE TO STAY
★AMERICINN

1219 W. Fond du Lac St., Ripon, 920-748-7578; www.americinnripon.net

42 rooms. Complimentary continental breakfast. Pets accepted. Pool. $61-150

★★★HEIDEL HOUSE RESORT & CONFERENCE CENTER

643 Illinois Ave., Green Lake, 920-294-3344; www.heidelhouse.com

Set on 20 acres on Green Lake, Heidel House offers something for everyone no matter the season including hiking trails, an ice rink in winter, fishing charters, yacht cruises and plenty of activities for children. From the Main Lodge to the lofty Estate Rooms, accommodations are comfortable and well-appointed. And four restaurants—Grey Rock, the Sunroom, Boathouse and the Pump House Parlor—offer an array of dining options for every taste. 205 rooms. Restaurant. Fitness center. Pool. Spa. Business center. $151-250

HUDSON

See also Menomonie

On the St. Croix River, Hudson's keepers have worked hard to preserve the town's historic buildings—and its charm—despite the fact that this area is one of the fastest growing in Wisconsin.

WHAT TO SEE
WILLOW RIVER STATE PARK

1034 County Trunk A, Hudson, 715-386-5931; www.dnr.state.wi.us

This 2,800-acre park offers swimming, fishing, boating, canoeing, cross-country skiing, picnicking and camping.
Daily.

WHERE TO STAY
★★BEST WESTERN HUDSON HOUSE INN

1616 Crest View Drive, Hudson, 715-386-2394, 800-780-7234; www.bestwestern.com

100 rooms. Restaurant, bar. Pool. $60-150

HURLEY
See also Ironwood, Manitowish Waters
Originally a lumber and mining town, Hurley is now a winter sports center.

WHAT TO SEE
IRON COUNTY HISTORICAL MUSEUM
303 Iron St., Hurley, 715-561-2244; www.hurleywi.com
This museum includes exhibits of the county's iron mining past, plus local artifacts and a photo gallery. Monday, Wednesday, Friday-Saturday.

SPECIAL EVENT
PAAVO NURMI MARATHON
316 Silver St., Hurley, 715-561-3290, 866-340-4334; www.hurleywi.com
The oldest marathon in the state, Paavo also has related activities Friday-Saturday.
Second weekend in August.

JANESVILLE
See also Beloit, Elkhorn, Fort Atkinson, Madison
In 1836, pioneer Henry F. Janes carved his initials into a tree on the bank of the Rock River. The site is now the intersection of the two main streets of industrial Janesville. Janes went on to found other Janesvilles in Iowa and Minnesota. Wisconsin's Janesville has a truck and bus assembly plant that offers tours.

WHAT TO SEE
LINCOLN-TALLMAN RESTORATIONS
440 N. Jackson St., Janesville, 608-752-4519; www.rchs.us
The Tallman House is a 26-room antebellum mansion of Italianate design considered among the top 10 mid-19th-century structures built at the time of the Civil War. Restorations include the Greek Revival Stone House and the horse barn that serves as a visitor center and museum shop. Tours: Daily.

MILTON HOUSE MUSEUM
18 S. Janesville St., Milton, 608-868-7772; www.miltonhouse.org
This hexagonal building was constructed of grout. An underground railroad tunnel connects it with the original log cabin.
Memorial Day-Labor Day, Daily; May and September-mid-October, weekends, also Monday-Friday by appointment.

SPECIAL EVENT
ROCK COUNTY 4-H FAIR
Rock County 4-H Fairgrounds, 1301 Craig Ave., Janesville, 608-755-1470;
www.rockcounty4hfair.com
One of the largest 4-H fairs in the country, this one includes exhibits, competitions, a carnival, grandstand shows and concerts.
Last week in July.

WHERE TO STAY
★★BEST WESTERN JANESVILLE
3900 Milton Ave., Janesville, 608-756-4511, 800-334-4271; www.bestwestern.com
105 rooms. Complimentary breakfast. Restaurant, bar. Pets accepted. $61-150

KENOSHA
See also Lake Geneva, Milwaukee, Racine
A major industrial city, port and transportation center near Chicago, Kenosha was settled by New Englanders. The city owns 84 percent of its Lake Michigan frontage, most of it developed as parks.

WHAT TO SEE
BONG STATE RECREATION AREA
26313 Burlington Road, Kansasville, 262-878-5600; www.dnr.state.wi.us
This 4,515-acre area offers swimming, fishing, boating, hiking, bridle and off-road motorcycle trails, cross-country skiing, snowmobiling, picnicking, guided nature hikes, a nature center, a special events area and camping.

CARTHAGE COLLEGE
2001 Alford Park Drive, Kenosha, 262-551-8500; www.carthage.edu
The Civil War Museum is located in the Johnson Art Center.
Monday-Friday.

KEMPER CENTER
6501 Third Ave., Kenosha, 262-657-6005; www.kempercenter.com
Composed of approximately 11 acres, this area houses several buildings including an Italianate Victorian mansion. The complex has more than 100 different trees, a rose collection, a mosaic mural, outdoor tennis courts, a picnic area and the Anderson Art Gallery (Thursday-Sunday afternoons).

RAMBLER LEGACY GALLERY
220 51st Place, Kenosha, 262-654-5770; www.kenoshahistorycenter.org
This gallery features Lorado Taft dioramas of famous art studios; Native American, Oceanic and African arts; Asian ivory and porcelain, Wisconsin folk pottery; a mammals exhibit and a dinosaur exhibit.
Tuesday-Sunday.

UNIVERSITY OF WISCONSIN-PARKSIDE
900 Wood Road, Kenosha, 262-595-2345; www.uwp.edu
This 700-acre campus has buildings connected by glass-walled interior corridors that radiate from the $8-million, tri-level Wyllie Library Learning Center.

SPECIAL EVENT
BRISTOL RENAISSANCE FAIRE
12550 120th Ave., Kenosha, 847-395-7773, 800-523-2473; www.renfair.com/bristol
Step back into a 16th-century European marketplace. Stop in at a comedy

show, a sword fight or a jousting competition.

Open nine weekends beginning July 9, plus Labor Day, Saturday-Sunday 10 a.m.-7 p.m.

WHERE TO STAY
★BAYMONT INN
7601 118th Ave., Pleasant Prairie, 262-857-7963, 877-229-6668;
www.baymontinns.com
93 rooms. Complimentary continental breakfast. Pets accepted. $61-150

WHERE TO EAT
★★HOUSE OF GERHARD
3927 75th St., Kenosha, 262-694-5212; www.foodspot.com
German menu. Lunch, dinner. Closed Sunday; also one week in early July. Bar. Children's menu. Casual attire. Reservations recommended. $16-35

★★MANGIA TRATTORIA
5717 Sheridan Road, Kenosha, 262-652-4285; www.kenoshamangia.com
Italian menu. Lunch, dinner. Bar. Children's menu. Casual attire. Reservations recommended. Outdoor seating. $36-85

KOHLER
See also Sheboygan
Kohler, a small town near Sheboygan, has gained a reputation as one of the region's top resort destinations. One of the nation's first planned communities, designed with the help of the Olmsted Brothers firm of Boston, Kohler began as a garden at the factory gate and headquarters for the country's largest plumbing manufacturer. Today, the resort and spa offer unparalleled relaxation in a charming, quiet setting. Running through Kohler is seven miles of the Sheboygan River and a 500-acre wildlife sanctuary.

WHAT TO SEE
JOHN MICHAEL KOHLER ARTS CENTER
608 New York Ave., Kohler, 920-458-6144; www.jmkac.org
Visit here for changing contemporary art exhibitions, galleries, a shop, an historic house, theater and dance and concert series. The exhibitions emphasize craft-related forms, installation works, photography, new genres, ongoing cultural traditions and the work of self-taught artists.
Daily.

OLD PLANK ROAD RECREATIONAL TRAIL
101 Upper Rd., Kohler, 920-457-3699; www.us.kohler.com/designcenter/designcenter.jsp
Bike along Lake Michigan all the way to the Kettle Moraine State Forest on this 17-mile trail. The concierge at the American Club can hook you up with a bike, helmet, map and even a boxed lunch to take with you on your scenic hoof.

RIVER WILDLIFE

411 Highland Dr., Kohler, 920-457-0134, 800-344-2838

This "country club in the woods" is a private recreational center and dining club located on a 500-acre wildlife preserve. If you're staying at the American Club, you can buy a pass that allows you to get away from it all and enjoy a secluded morning in mother nature, or get in a day of hiking, horseback riding, canoeing, kayaking, fishing, and more. Afterward, you can relax in the rustic log cabin, which is just as you may picture it, replete with a requisite massive fieldstone fireplace, pine floors and antique wood furnishings. You'll definitely want to stick around for dinner too. The menu features a regionally-inspired menu that includes such hearty bites as wild mushroom bruschetta, and pan seared medallions of elk. Members also have access to four hike-in camp sites and the Tomczyk, a secluded one-room lodging cabin with a wood burning sauna. The cabin sleeps up to eight people and can only be reached by a half-mile hike. Advanced reservations are required for most activities and dining.

SHOPS AT WOODLAKE

Kohler, 920-459-1713; www.destinationkohler.com

Pick up clothing, fly-fishing supplies, furniture, home accessories and other specialty goods at this small shopping center in Kohler village.
Monday-Friday 10 a.m.-6 p.m., Saturday 10 a.m.-5 p.m., Sunday noon-5 p.m.

SPECIAL EVENTS
KOHLER FOOD & WINE EXPERIENCE

110 Upper Road, Kohler, 800-344-2838; www.destinationkohler.com

This annual event features cooking demonstrations, food and wine tastings and seminars.
Three days in late October.

TRADITIONAL HOLIDAY ILLUMINATION

419 Highland Drive, Kohler, 920-457-8000; www.destinationkohler.com

More than 200,000 lights on trees surrounding Kohler hospitality facilities create a winter fantasy land in the Kohler Village.
Thanksgiving-February.

WHERE TO STAY
★★★★THE AMERICAN CLUB

419 Highland Drive, Kohler, 920-457-8000, 800-344-2838; www.americanclub.com

Located in the charming village of Kohler, the American Club is a cozy country getaway. In addition to access to world-class golf, you get friendly, warm service, and a relaxing spot in which to lounge around. The rooms are simple but comfortable with wood-beamed ceilings, white duvets and Kohler bathrooms. The Kohler spa is the centerpiece of the resort and sets the relaxing, happy atmosphere. You'll find guests walking around in spa robes throughout the day and into the evening, when everyone mingles in the lobby over wine, cheese and other nibbles. Afterward, you can easily pop around to the different restaurants; many are in walking distance or you can hop on a shuttle. It's almost like you're trapped in this pretty little

Kohler factory, and that's the appeal. For two or three days, life is sweet. 240 rooms. Wireless Internet access. Three restaurants, three bars. Children's activity center. Airport transportation available. Beach. Golf. Tennis. $251-350

★★INN ON WOODLAKE
705 Woodlake Road, Kohler, 920-452-7800, 800-919-3600; www.innonwoodlake.com
121 rooms. Complimentary breakfast. Restaurant, bar. Golf. Tennis. $151-250

WHERE TO EAT
CUCINA
725 E. Woodlake Rd., Kohler, 920-457-8888
Fill up on hearty plates of pasta at this casual Italian restaurant with a domed ceiling and Roman columns overlooking Wood Lake. There's nothing fancy about the tortelloni or the seafood linguini, which is what makes this restaurant the perfect choice for that evening you simply don't want to make a fuss. Italian menu. Lunch, dinner, Sunday brunch. Casual attire. Reservations recommended. $16-35

★★RICHARD'S
501 Monroe St., Sheboygan Falls, 920-467-6401; www.richardsoffalls.com
American menu. Dinner. Closed Monday. Bar. Business casual attire. Reservations recommended. $16-35

★★★★THE IMMIGRANT RESTAURANT
419 Highland Dr., Kohler, 920-457-8888, 800-344-2838;
www.destinationkohler.com
The remnants of Walter J. Kohler Sr.'s boarding house are the basis for the opulent yet inviting Immigrant Restaurant and Winery Bar. No expense was spared when it came to the creation of the building. The Immigrant Restaurant is divided into six rooms, each of which represents the nationalities that populated Wisconsin in its early days—Dutch, German, Norman, Danish, French and English. The wonderful dishes include pan-seared scallops with heirloom carrot purée and vodka caviar butter, or slow-cooked Wagyu beef cheeks with celery root. For those who want to try a little bit of everything, the restaurant offers a sampling menu, with such delectable items as deep fried quail eggs with sweet chili sauce and sirloin carpaccio with garlic chips. Paired with one of the excellent wines, this may be just the ticket. Afterward, head to the bar, a popular gathering spot, and order yet another exquisite wine and enjoy a dessert such as vanilla-and-Armagnac-roasted bananas, lemon-raspberry cake or the chocolate trilogy. While you're here, ask about wine and cheese tastings. American menu. Dinner. Closed Sunday. Bar. Jacket required. Reservations recommended. Valet parking. $36-85

THE WISCONSIN ROOM
119 Highland Dr., Kohler, 920-457-8888
The original dining hall of immigrant workers for Kohler, the Wisconsin Room features regional Midwestern fare, including pepper-crusted venison steak with wild mushroom risotto, braised red cabbage and blackberry preserves; grilled tenderloin with a delicious foyot sauce; and cinnamon laven-

der duck breast. The professional service and the nostalgic setting, with antique chandeliers and leaded glass windows, will draw you in. Friday nights feature a seafood buffet. America menu. Breakfast, dinner, Sunday brunch. Reservations recommended. $36-85

SPA
★★★★KOHLER WATERS SPA
419 Highland Drive, 920-457-8000; www.destinationkohler.com/spa
Kohler Waters Spa, located adjacent to the American Club, takes full advantage of its namesake's long history in the fixture and bath business. Water plays a part in just about everything at this spa, from the design (waterfalls abound from the relaxation pool to some treatment rooms) to the services (water therapies such as aromatherapy baths are the highlight). A new rooftop deck includes both an outdoor sunning space and an indoor lounge. The spa offers a complete menu for couples and specialty treatments for men, including scrubs, baths and a golfer's massage.

LA CROSSE
See also Galesville, Sparta
An agricultural, commercial, and industrial city, La Crosse is washed by the waters of the Mississippi, Black and La Crosse rivers. Once a trading post, it was named by the French for the native game the French called lacrosse.

WHAT TO SEE
HIXON HOUSE
429 N. Seventh St., La Crosse, 608-782-1980; www.lchsweb.org
This 15-room home features Victorian and Asian furnishings. A visitor information center and gift shop is located in the building that once served as a wash house.
Memorial Day-Labor Day, Tuesday-Sunday.

LA CROSSE QUEEN CRUISES
La Crosse, 608-784-2893; www.lacrossequeen.com
This sightseeing cruise on the Mississippi River is aboard a 150 passenger, double-deck paddle wheeler.
Early May-mid-October, daily. Dinner cruise: Friday night, Saturday-Sunday.

PUMP HOUSE REGIONAL ARTS CENTER
119 King St., La Crosse, 608-785-1434; www.thepumphouse.org
Find regional art exhibits and performing arts here.
Tuesday-Saturday, afternoons.

SPECIAL EVENT
RIVERFEST
Riverside Park, 410 Veteran's Memorial Drive, La Crosse, 608-782-6000; www.riverfest.org
Five-day festival features river events, music, food, entertainment, fireworks and -children's events.
Late June-early July.

WHERE TO STAY
★★BEST WESTERN MIDWAY HOTEL
1835 Rose St., La Crosse, 608-781-7000, 877-688-9260; www.midwayhotels.com
121 rooms. Restaurant, bar. Pets accepted. $60-150

★★RADISSON HOTEL LA CROSSE
200 Harborview Plaza, La Crosse, 608-784-6680, 800-333-3333; www.radisson.com
169 rooms. High-speed Internet access. Restaurant, bar. Pets accepted. Pool.
$60-150

WHERE TO EAT
★★FREIGHTHOUSE
107 Vine St., La Crosse, 608-784-6211; www.freighthouserestaurant.com
Steak menu. Dinner. Bar. Casual attire. $36-85

★★PIGGY'S
501 S. Front St., La Crosse, 608-784-4877, 888-865-9632; www.piggys.com
American menu. Dinner. Bar. Children's menu. Reservations recommended.
$16-35

LADYSMITH
See also Chippewa Falls, Rice Lake
Ladysmith, the seat of Rusk County, is located along the Flambeau River.
The economy is based on processing lumber and marketing dairy and farm
produce. There are fishing and canoeing facilities in the area.

WHAT TO SEE
FLAMBEAU RIVER STATE FOREST
W1613 County Road W., Winter, 715-332-5271; www.dnr.wi.gov
This 91,000-acre forest offers a canoeing, swimming, fishing, boating, back-
packing, nature and hiking trails, mountain biking, cross-country skiing,
snowmobiling, picnicking and camping.
Daily.

LAKE DELTON
See also Baraboo, Portage, Wisconsin Dells
This town is in the Wisconsin Dells, the tourist destination that calls itself
"the Waterpark Capital of the World."

WHERE TO EAT
★★DEL-BAR
800 Wisconsin Dells Parkway, Lake Delton, 608-253-1861, 866-888-1861;
www.del-bar.com
American menu. Dinner. Bar. Children's menu. Casual attire. Reservations
recommended. Outdoor seating. $36-85

★★WALLY'S HOUSE OF EMBERS
935 Wisconsin Dells Parkway, Lake Delton, 608-253-6411; www.houseofembers.com
American. Dinner. Bar. Children's menu. Outdoor seating. $16-35

LAKE GENEVA

See also Burlington, Delavan, Elkhorn, Fontana, Kenosha

This is a popular and attractive four-season resort area. Recreational activities include boating, fishing, swimming, horseback riding, camping, hiking, biking, golf, tennis, skiing, cross-country skiing, ice fishing, snowmobiling and ice boating.

WHAT TO SEE
BIG FOOT BEACH STATE PARK

1452 Highway H, Lake Geneva, 262-248-2528; www.dnr.state.wi.us

This 272-acre beach park on Geneva Lake offers swimming (lifeguard on duty mid-June-Labor Day, weekends only), fishing, picnicking, a playground, winter sports and camping.
Daily.

WHERE TO STAY
★★BEST WESTERN HARBOR SHORES

300 Wrigley Drive, Lake Geneva, 262-248-9181, 888-746-7371; www.bestwestern.com

108 rooms. Complimentary continental breakfast. Restaurant, bar. Pool. $61-150

★★★GRAND GENEVA RESORT & SPA

7036 Grand Geneva Way, Lake Geneva, 262-248-8811, 262-248-2556, 800-558-3417; www.grandgeneva.com

This resort and spa is situated on 1,300 acres of wooded meadowland with a private lake. A 36-hole golf course, the luxurious Well Spa and a host of dining options makes this spot a treat. Guest rooms are equipped with everything you'd expect from an upscale resort (Aveda amenities, balconies). Well Spa offers a full range of treatments, from various massage modalities to hydrotherapy. Hitting upon delicious food is easy at one of the resort's three main restaurants: Ristorante Brissago, Geneva ChopHouse and Grand Café. 355 rooms. Restaurant, bar. Airport transportation available. Golf. Tennis. Spa. Fitness center. $151-250

★★★THE LODGE AT GENEVA RIDGE

W4240 Highway 50, Lake Geneva, 262-248-9121, 800-225-5558; www.generaridge.com

The Lodge has 146 guest rooms, golf, various water sports, horseback riding, hayrides, hot air balloon rides and a petting zoo. The full-service spa offers a full menu of treatments and services. The country style fare in the dining room (find something lighter at the Lake View Lounge) offers hearty meals. 144 rooms. Restaurant, Bar. Spa. Tennis. $61-150

★★★TIMBER RIDGE LODGE & WATERPARK

7020 Grand Geneva Way, Lake Geneva, 262-249-8811, 866-636-4502; www.timberridgeresort.com

Moose Mountain Falls Waterpark resides here, but there's plenty more to take advantage of at this all-season, all-suite resort. The 1,300-acre spread is known for its spacious suites and its close proximity to nearby cities—it's just an hour's drive from Milwaukee. The Spa & Sport Center, along with the championship golf course, keeps guests moving. A diverse set of dining options such as Smokey's Bar-B-Que House and the Hungry Moose Food Court. And a full lineup of children's activities makes this place perfect for families.

225 rooms, all suites. High-speed Internet access. Restaurant, bar. $151-250

SPECIALTY LODGING
FRENCH COUNTRY INN
W4190 West End Road, Lake Geneva, 262-245-5220; www.frenchcountryinn.com

Portions of the guest house were built in Denmark and shipped to the United States for the Danish exhibit at the 1893 Columbian Exposition in Chicago.

124 rooms. Restaurant. Pool. $251-350

WHERE TO EAT
★CACTUS CLUB
430 Broad St., Lake Geneva, 262-248-1999; www.foodspot.com

American, Mexican menu. Lunch, dinner. Bar. Children's menu. Casual attire. $16-35

★POPEYE'S GALLEY AND GROG
811 Wrigley Drive, Lake Geneva, 262-248-4381; www.popeyesonlakegeneva.com

American menu. Lunch, dinner. Bar. Children's menu. $16-35

★★★RISTORANTE BRISSAGO
7036 Grand Geneva Way, Lake Geneva, 262-248-8811; www.grandgeneva.com

Named after a town on Lake Maggiore in the Italian-Swiss countryside, this restaurant enjoys a Midwestern, countryside home all its own. Executive Chef Robert Fedorko turns fresh ingredients imported from Italy into delicious dishes such as pasta marinara with garlic shrimp, filet mignon in a gorgonzola crust and Parmesan mashed potatoes or pizza with four cheeses. The dining room is just one of the options at the Grand Geneva Resort & Spa.

Italian menu. Dinner. Closed Monday. Bar. Valet parking. $36-85

MADISON
See also Fort Atkinson, Janesville, Mount Horeb, New Glarus, Prairie du Sac

Madison was a virgin wilderness in 1836 when the territorial legislature selected the spot for the capital and the state university. Today, this "City of Four Lakes," located on an isthmus between Lake Mendota and Lake Monona, is a recreational, cultural and manufacturing center. Both the university and state government play important roles in the community. Madison has a rich architectural heritage left by Frank Lloyd Wright who led the Prairie School movement here. There are a number of Wright buildings; many are private homes and not open to the public.

WHAT TO SEE
EDGEWOOD COLLEGE
1000 Edgewood College Drive, Madison, 608-257-4861,800-444-4861; www.edgewood.edu

A 55-acre campus on Lake Wingra, Edgewood includes Native American burial mounds.

GEOLOGY MUSEUM

1215 W. Dayton St., Madison, 608-262-2399; www.geology.wisc.edu

Exhibits include a six-foot rotating globe, rocks, minerals, a black light display, a walk-through cave, meteorites and fossils including the skeletons of a giant mastodon and dinosaurs.

Monday-Friday, Saturday mornings.

HENRY VILAS PARK ZOO

702 S. Randall Ave., Madison, 608-258-9490; www.vilaszoo.org

World famous for successful orangutan, Siberian tiger, spectacle bear, penguin and camel breeding programs, this zoo's exhibits include 600 specimens consisting of 140 species.

Daily.

LAKE KEGONSA STATE PARK

2405 Door Creek Road, Stoughton, 608-873-9695; www.dnr.wi.gov

This 343-acre park offers swimming, water-skiing, fishing, boating, hiking and nature trails, picnicking, a playground and camping.

Daily.

MADISON CHILDREN'S MUSEUM

100 State St., Madison, 608-256-6445; www.madisonchildrensmuseum.com

This hands-on museum offers special craft and activity programs every weekend. Tuesday-Sunday; closed holidays.

STATE CAPITAL

Capital Square, 2 E. Main St., Madison, 608-266-0382; www.wisconsin.gov

A focal point of the city, the white granite capitol building has a classic dome topped by Daniel Chester French's gilded bronze statue "Wisconsin." Tours: daily.

STATE HISTORICAL MUSEUM

30 N. Carroll St., Madison, 608-264-6555; www.wisconsinhistory.org/museum

Permanent exhibits explore the history of Native American life in Wisconsin and a gallery features changing Wisconsin and U.S. history exhibits.

Tuesday-Saturday.

UNIVERSITY OF WISCONSIN-MADISON

716 Langdon St., Madison, 608-263-2400; www.wisc.edu

The 929-acre campus extends for more than two miles along the south shore of Lake Mendota.

SPECIAL EVENT
ART FAIR ON THE SQUARE

227 State St., Madison, 608-257-0158; www.mmoca.org

The art fair features exhibits by 500 artists, plus food and entertainment.

Mid-July.

WHERE TO STAY

★★BEST WESTERN INN ON THE PARK
22 S. Carroll St., Madison, 608-257-8811, 608-285-8800, 800-279-8811;
www.innonthepark.net
212 rooms. Restaurant, bar. Airport transportation available. $61-150

★★★EDGEWATER HOTEL
666 Wisconsin Ave., Madison, 608-256-9071, 800-922-5512; www.theedgewater.com
Lakeview rooms loaded with the latest in modern features await guests at this getaway on Lake Mendota. The Admiralty Dining Room offers an upscale menu in a setting that provides some of the best views available. Enjoy a cocktail in the Cove Lounge or outdoor dining at Café on the Pier.
108 rooms. Restaurant, bar. Airport transportation available. Pets accepted. $61-150

★HAMPTON INN
4820 Hayes Road, Madison, 608-244-9400, 800-426-7866; www.hamptoninn.com
115 rooms. Complimentary continental breakfast. Pool. $61-150

★★★MADISON CONCOURSE HOTEL & GOVERNOR'S CLUB
1 W. Dayton St., Madison, 608-257-6000, 800-356-8293; www.concoursehotel.com
The Madison Concourse is situated in the heart of downtown Madison. The Dayton Street Café and Ovations provide reliable dining, and guest rooms are all well-appointed. The Governor's Club Executive Level, which encompasses the top three floors of the hotel, provides views of the State Capital and the city skyline, plus complimentary top-shelf cocktails, hors d'ouevres and other special amenities.
356 rooms. Restaurant, bar. Airport transportation available. Pool. $61-150

★★★SHERATON MADISON HOTEL
706 John Nolen Drive, Madison, 608-251-2300, 800-325-3535; www.sheraton.com
The stately exterior of this Sheraton is a welcome sight for business and pleasure travelers alike. Rooms are comforable (especially because of the Sheraton's new beds) and the hotel is centrally located. Lobby Wi-Fi stations are convenient and there's a pool if you have some free time.
239 rooms. Restaurant, bar. Pets accepted. Pool. $61-150

WHERE TO EAT

★★★ADMIRALTY
666 Wisconsin Ave., Madison, 608-256-9071; www.theedgewater.com
This dining room boasts spectacular sunset views over Lake Mendota and a classic, international menu. The space carries old-world charm with its leather chairs, framed photographs and tableside preparations of dishes.
International menu. Breakfast, lunch, dinner, Sunday brunch. Bar. Outdoor seating. $16-35

★AMY'S CAFÉ
414 W. Gilman St., Madison, 608-255-8172; www.amyscafe.com
American menu. Lunch, dinner. Bar. Outdoor seating. $15 and under

★ELLA'S DELI

2902 E. Washington Ave., Madison, 608-241-5291; www.ellas-deli.com

American menu. Lunch, dinner. Children's menu. $15 and under

★ESSENHAUS

514 E. Wilson St., Madison, 608-255-4674; www.essenhaus.com

German menu. Dinner. Closed Monday. Bar. Children's menu. Outdoor seating. $16-35

★★★L'ETOILE

25 N. Pinckney, Madison, 608-251-0500; www.letoile-restaurant.com

Chef Tory Miller and his wife, Traci, are now at the helm of this landmark Madison restaurant, where the focus on local, sustainable products continues. Menus change seasonally and ingredients are sourced from a variety of local, small-scale farmers. Although it may be hard to find (it's on the second floor), it's worth the search to experience some of this university town's best dining. Don't miss the outstanding cheese course, offering a choice of artisan Wisconsin cheeses. Try the ground floor Café Soleil, which serves an array of sandwiches, soups, salads and sweet or savory pastries.

French menu. Dinner. Closed Sunday-Monday. Bar. $36-85

★★NAU-TI-GAL

5360 Westport Road, Madison, 608-246-3130; www.nautigal.com

American menu. Lunch, dinner, Sunday brunch. Bar. Children's menu. Outdoor seating. $16-35

★★NORTH SHORE BISTRO

8649 N. Port Washington Road, Fox Point, 414-351-6100; www.northshorebistro.com

American menu. Lunch, dinner. Bar. Casual attire. Outdoor seating. $16-35

★★QUIVEY'S GROVE

6261 Nesbitt Road, Madison, 608-273-4900; www.quiveysgrove.com

American menu. Lunch, dinner. Bar. Children's menu. Outdoor seating. $16-35

★SA-BAI THONG

2840 University Ave., Madison, 608-238-3100; www.sabaithong.com

Thai menu. Lunch, dinner. $16-35

MANITOWISH WATERS

See also Boulder Junction, Hurley, Minocqua

Manitowish Waters is in Northern Highland-American Legion State Forest, which abounds in small- and medium-size lakes linked by streams. Ten of the 14 lakes are navigable without portaging, making them ideal for canoeing. There are 16 campgrounds on lakes in the forest and 135 overnight campsites on water trails. Canoe trips, fishing, swimming, boating, water-skiing and snowmobiling are popular here.

WHAT TO SEE
CRANBERRY BOG TOURS

Community Center, Highway 51 Airport Road, Manitowish Waters, 715-543-8488;
www.manitowishwaters.org
Begin your tour with a video and samples and then follow guides in your own vehicle. Late July-early October, Friday.

WHERE TO EAT
★★LITTLE BOHEMIA

142 Highway 51 S, Manitowish Waters, 715-543-8800; www.littlebohemia.net
Steak menu. Dinner. Closed Wednesday; February-March. Bar. Children's menu. $16-35

MANITOWOC

See also Green Bay, Sheboygan, Two Rivers
A shipping, shopping and industrial center, Manitowoc has an excellent harbor and a geographical position improved by the completion of the St. Lawrence Seaway. Shipbuilding has been an important industry since its earliest days. During World War II, Manitowoc shipyards produced nearly 100 vessels for the United States Navy including landing craft, wooden minesweepers, sub chasers and 28 submarines.

WHAT TO SEE
RAHR-WEST ART MUSEUM

610 N. Eighth St., Manitowoc, 920-683-4501; www.rahrwestartmuseum.org
This Victorian house has period rooms, American art and a collection of Chinese ivory carvings. A modern art wing features changing exhibits.
Monday-Tuesday, Thursday-Friday 10 a.m.-4 p.m., Wednesday 10 a.m.-8 p.m., Saturday-sunday 11 a.m.-4 p.m.

WISCONSIN MARITIME MUSEUM

75 Maritime Drive, Manitowoc, 920-758-2210; www.wisconsinmaritime.org
The exhibits here depict 150 years of maritime history including a model ship gallery and narrated tours through the USS Cobia, a 312-foot World War II submarine.
Hours vary slightly by season. Memorial Day-Labor Day 9 a.m.-6 p.m., Labor day-Memorial day 9 a.m.-5 p.m.

MARINETTE

See also Peshtigo
Located along the south bank of the Menominee River, Marinette is named for Queen Marinette, daughter of a Menominee chief. An industrial and port city, it is also the retail trade center for the surrounding recreational area.

WHERE TO STAY
★★BEST WESTERN RIVERFRONT INN

1821 Riverside Ave., Marinette, 715-732-1000, 800-338-3305; www.bestwestern.com
120 rooms. Restaurant, bar. Pool. Fitness center. Complimentary breakfast. $60-150

MARSHFIELD

See also Stevens Point, Wisconsin Rapids

Marshfield, a city that once boasted one sawmill and 19 taverns, was almost destroyed by fire in 1887. It was rebuilt on a more substantial structural and industrial basis. This is a busy northern dairy center, noted for its large medical clinic, manufactured housing wood products and steel fabrication industries.

WHAT TO SEE
WILDWOOD PARK AND ZOO
1800 S. Central Ave., Marshfield, 715-384-4642, 800-422-4541;
www.ci.marshfield.wi.us
This zoo houses a variety of animals and birds, mostly native to Wisconsin. Mid-May-late September, Daily; October-April, Monday-Friday.

MAUSTON

See also Wisconsin Dells

This town, in central Wisconsin, is midway between Chicago and the Twin Cities in Minnesota. The area offers extensive bike trails, several golf courses and, of course, delicious cheese.

WHAT TO SEE
BUCKHORN STATE PARK
W8450 Buckhorn Park Ave., Necedah, 608-565-2789; www.dnr.wi.gov
A 2,504-acre park, Buckhorn has facilities for swimming, water-skiing, fishing, boating, canoeing, hunting, hiking, nature trails, picnicking and a playground.
Daily.

WHERE TO STAY
★★WOODSIDE RANCH RESORT & CONFERENCE CENTER
W. 4015 State Highway 82, Mauston, 608-847-4275, 800-626-4275;
www.woodsideranch.com
37 rooms. Wireless Internet access. Restaurant, bar. Pets accepted. Tennis. $151-250

MENOMONEE FALLS

See also Milwaukee, Wauwatosa

The town's keepers call Menomonee Falls "the world's largest village." Northwest of Milwaukee, the town offers a downtown historic district with buildings nearly 100 years old. Here you'll find shops, restaurants and special events such as farmers markets or holiday parades.

WHERE TO EAT
★★★FOX AND HOUNDS
1298 Friess Lake Road, Hubertus, 262-628-1111; www.foodspot.com/foxandhounds
This renowned spot, located a few miles west of Milwaukee, is set in an 1845 log cabin that was built by the first clerk of Washington County. It's worth planning ahead for a reservation at the Friday fish fry.

American menu. Dinner. Closed Sunday-Monday. Bar. Children's menu. $36-85

MENOMONIE
See also Chippewa Falls, Eau Claire
Located on the banks of the Red Cedar River, Menomonie is the home of the University of Wisconsin-Stout and was once headquarters for one of the largest lumber corporations in the country. The decline of the lumber industry diverted the economy to dairy products.

WHAT TO SEE
MABEL TAINTER MEMORIAL BUILDING
205 Main St. East, Menomonie, 715-235-0001, 715-235-9726; www.mabeltainter.com
This hand-stenciled and ornately carved cultural center was constructed in 1889 by lumber baron Andrew Tainter in memory of his daughter Mabel. Guided tours: Daily.

WILSON PLACE MUSEUM
101 Wilson Circle, Menomonie, 715-235-2283; www.discover-net.net
This Victorian mansion is the former residence of Senator James H. Stout, founder of the University of Wisconsin. Nearly all furnishings are original. Guided tours Memorial Day-Labor Day, Friday-Sunday afternoons.

WHERE TO STAY
★BEST WESTERN INN OF MENOMONIE
1815 N. Broadway, Menomonie, 715-235-9651, 800-622-0504; www.bestwestern.com
102 rooms. Complimentary breakfast. Pets accepted. Pool. $61-150

MILWAUKEE
See also Cedarburg, Kenosha, Menomonee Falls

Thriving and progressive, Milwaukee has retained its Gemutlichkeit (German for "coziness"), though today's conviviality is as likely to be expressed at a soccer game or at a symphony concert as at the beer garden. While Milwaukee is still the beer capital of the nation, its leading single industry is not brewing but the manufacture of X-ray apparatus and tubes.
Long a French trading post and an early campsite between Chicago and Green Bay, the city was founded by Solomon Juneau, who settled on the east side of the Milwaukee River. English settlement began in significant numbers in 1833 and was followed by an influx of Germans, Scandinavians, Dutch, Bohemians, Irish, Austrians and large numbers of Poles. By 1846, Milwaukee was big and prosperous enough to be incorporated as a city. In its recent history, perhaps the most colorful period was from 1916 to 1940 when socialist mayor Daniel Webster Hoan held the reins of government.
   The city's Teutonic personality has dimmed, becoming only a part of the local color of a city long famous for good government, a low crime rate and high standards of civic performance. With a history going back to the days when Native Americans called this area Millioki, "gathering place by the waters," Milwaukee is a city of 96.5 square miles on the west shore of Lake Michigan, where the Milwaukee, Menomonee and Kinnickinnic rivers meet.

As a result of the St. Lawrence Seaway, Milwaukee has become a major seaport on America's new fourth seacoast. Docks and piers handle traffic of 10 lines of oceangoing ships.

The city provides abundant tourist attractions including professional and college basketball, hockey, football and baseball, top-rated polo, soccer and auto racing. Milwaukee has art exhibits, museums, music programs, ballet and theater including the Marcus Center for Performing Arts. Its many beautiful churches include the Basilica of St. Josaphat, St. John Cathedral and the Gesu Church.

WHAT TO SEE
ARTS MARCUS CENTER FOR THE PERFORMING

929 N. Water St., Milwaukee, 414-273-7206; www.marcuscenter.org
This strikingly beautiful structure, overlooking the Milwaukee River, has four theaters, reception areas and a parking facility connected by a skywalk.

BETTY BRINN CHILDREN'S MUSEUM

O'Donnell Park, 929 E. Wisconsin Ave., Milwaukee, 414-390-5437; www.bbcmkids.org
Kids 10 and under will have a blast at this interactive museum, where they can enter a digestion tunnel and hear what their body sounds like as it's digesting food, or create their own racetrack and test drive golf ball-shaped push carts on different road surfaces.
Tuesday-Saturday 9 a.m.-5 p.m., Sunday noon-5 p.m., June-August, Monday 9 a.m.-5 p.m.

CAPTAIN FREDERICK PABST MANSION

2000 W. Wisconsin Ave., Milwaukee, 414-931-0808; www.pabstmansion.com
This magnificent 1893 house once owned by a beer baron features exquisite woodwork, wrought iron and stained glass, plus a restored interior.
Guided tours: Daily.

CITY HALL

200 E. Wells St., Milwaukee, 414-286-3285; www.ci.mil.wi.us
This Milwaukee landmark is of Flemish Renaissance design. The Common Council Chamber and Anteroom retain their turn-of-the-century character featuring ornately carved woodwork, leaded glass, stenciled ceilings, two large stained-glass windows and ironwork balconies surrounding the eight-story atrium.
Monday-Friday.

DISCOVERY WORLD: THE JAMES LOVELL MUSEUM OF SCIENCE, ECONOMICS AND TECHNOLOGY

815 N. James Lovell St., Milwaukee, 414-765-9966; www.discoveryworld.org
Discovery World, aimed at kids 14 and under, is filled with 150 interactive exhibits. At the 4Cast Center, try your hand at weather forecasting with live Doppler Radar, the Lightning Track and a seismograph.
Daily 9 a.m.-5 p.m.

HAGGERTY MUSEUM OF ART

530 N. 13th St., Milwaukee, 414-288-7290; www.marquette.edu/haggerty

On the Marquette campus, this museum includes paintings, prints, drawings, sculpture and decorative arts.

Daily.

IROQUOIS BOAT LINE TOURS

445 W. Oklahoma Ave., Milwaukee, 414-294-9450

View the lakefront, harbor, lighthouse, breakwater and foreign ships in port.

Early June-August, daily.

MILLER BREWERY TOUR

4251 W. State St., Milwaukee, 414-931-2337, 800-944-5483; www.millerbrewing.com

Milwaukee is synonymous with beer, so take the one hour guided tour of Miller Brewing Company, Milwaukee's sole remaining large-scale brewery and the nation's second largest. At the end of the tour, adults receive free beer samples while kids get root beer.

Labor Day-Memorial Day, Monday-Saturday 10 a.m.-5 p.m., October-April, 10 a.m.-5:30 p.m., last tour at 3:30 p.m.

MILWAUKEE COUNTY ZOO

10001 W. Blue Mound Road, Milwaukee, 414-771-3040; www.milwaukeezoo.org

See 2,500 mammals, birds, reptiles and fish at the Milwaukee County Zoo, which is renowned for displaying predators next to their prey. The zoo features an animal health center with a public viewing area; make sure to catch a treatment procedure or surgery (mornings are best). Sea lion show, miniature zoo train, zoomobile with guided tours and carousel are available for a fee.

May-September, Monday-Saturday 9 a.m.-5 p.m., Sunday and holidays 9 a.m.-6 p.m.; October-April, Daily 9 a.m.-4:30 p.m.

MILWAUKEE PUBLIC MUSEUM

800 W. Wells St., Milwaukee, 414-278-2700; www.mpm.edu

This natural and human history museum features unique "walk-through" dioramas and exhibits and life-size replicas of dinosaurs.

Daily 9 a.m.-5 p.m.

MITCHELL PARK HORTICULTURAL CONSERVATORY

524 S. Layton Blvd., Milwaukee, 414-649-9800; www.county.milwaukee.gov

The superb modern design here features three self-supporting domes (tropical, arid and show dome) and outstanding seasonal shows and beautiful exhibits all year. Each dome is almost half the length of a football field in diameter and nearly as tall as a seven-story building.

Daily.

PABST THEATER

144 E. Wells St., Milwaukee, 414-286-3663; www.pabsttheater.org

The center of Milwaukee's earlier cultural life, this restored theater has excellent acoustics and hosts musical and drama events.

Tours: Saturday.

PARK SYSTEM

9480 W. Watertown Plank Road, Milwaukee, 414-257-6100; www.county.milwaukee.gov
One of the largest in the nation at 14,681 acres, this system includes 137 parks and parkways, community centers, five beaches, 19 pools, 16 golf courses, 134 tennis courts and winter activities such as cross-country skiing, skating and sledding.

SCHLITZ AUDUBON CENTER

1111 E. Brown Deer Road, Milwaukee, 414-352-2880
The center has 225 acres of shoreline, grassland, bluff, ravine and woodland habitats with a variety of plants and wildlife including fox, deer, skunk and opossum.
Daily.

ST. JOAN OF ARC CHAPEL

14th Street and Wisconsin Avenue, Milwaukee, 414-288-6873; www.marquette.edu/ul
Brought from France and reconstructed on Long Island, New York, in 1927, this 15th-century chapel was brought here in 1964.
Tours daily.

UNIVERSITY OF WISCONSIN-MILWAUKEE

2200 E. Kenwood Blvd., Milwaukee, 414-229-1122; www4.uwm.edu
The Manfred Olson Planetarium offers programs Friday and Saturday evenings during the academic year. There is also an art museum and three art galleries that are open to the public at 3203 N. Downer Ave.

VILLA TERRACE DECORATIVE ARTS MUSEUM

2220 N. Terrace Ave., Milwaukee, 414-271-3656;
www.cavtmuseums.org, www.villaterracemuseum.org
This Italian Renaissance-style house serves as a museum for decorative arts.
Guided tours: Wednesday-Sunday afternoons.

SPECIAL EVENTS
GREAT CIRCUS PARADE

550 Water St., Milwaukee, 608-356-8341; www.circusworldmuseum.com
This re-creation of an old-time circus parade includes bands, animals and an unusual collection of horse-drawn wagons from the Circus World Museum.
Late June.

SUMMERFEST

Henry Maier Festival Grounds, 200 N. Harbor Drive, Milwaukee, 800-273-3378;
www.summerfest.com
Milwaukee's premier event, this popular festival (many people take the train in from Chicago) goes on for days and includes 11 different music stages and scores of food stands.
Late June-early July.

WHERE TO STAY

★★COURTYARD BY MARRIOTT

300 W. Michigan St., Milwaukee, 414-291-4122, 800-321-2211

169 rooms. Restaurant. Airport transportation available. $61-150

★★EMBASSY SUITES

1200 South Moorland Road, Brookfield, 262-782-2900, 800-362-2779;
www.brookfieldsuiteshotel.com

203 rooms, all suites. Complimentary breakfast. Restaurant, bar. $61-150

★★★HILTON MILWAUKEE CITY CENTER

509 W. Wisconsin Ave., Milwaukee, 414-271-7250, 800-774-1500;
www.hiltonmilwaukee.com

Those looking to stay in the downtown area will enjoy all this comfortable hotel has to offer, with its location near local theaters, museums and major businesses. This hotel recently underwent an extensive renovation, which helped bring the space back to its 1920s splendor. The traditionally-designed rooms are pleasant and spacious. The Milwaukee Chophouse features steaks and seafood. There's even a 20,000-square-foot indoor waterpark (in true Wisconsin style).

730 rooms. Restaurant, bar. Pool. $61-150

★★★HILTON MILWAUKEE RIVER

4700 N. Port Washington Road, Milwaukee, 414-962-6040, 800-445-8667;
www.milwaukeeriver.hilton.com

Overlooking the banks of the Milwaukee River, this Hilton is within striking distance of nearly everything Milwaukee has to offer. Rooms are spacious and well-appointed, and a few face the river. The Anchorage offers a stately spot for a seafood dinner.

161 rooms. Wireless Internet access. Restaurant, bar. Pool. $151-250

★★HOLIDAY INN

611 W. Wisconsin Ave., Milwaukee, 414-273-2950, 800-465-4329;
www.ichotelsgroup.com

247 rooms. Restaurant, bar. Business Center. $61-150

★★★HOTEL METRO

411 Mason Ave., Milwaukee, 414-272-1937

This European-style boutique hotel is within walking distance of several of Milwaukee's main attractions, including the Milwaukee Art Museum and the Milwaukee Public Market. The various suites (all equipped with refreshment bars and Aveda bath products) range from master suites with separate sitting areas and whirlpool baths to the even more spacious (600-square-feet) deluxe suites. The rooftop spa has everything from a saltwater hot tub and fitness equipment to a sun garden. Metro Bar & Café offers upscale bistro fare using seasonal, fresh ingredients and a selection of more than 60 wines.

65 rooms, all suites. Restaurant, bar. Pets accepted. $151-250

★★★HYATT REGENCY MILWAUKEE

411 E. Mason St., Milwaukee, 414-276-1234, 800-233-1234; www.milwaukee.hyatt.com

This hotel delights with spacious and elegantly appointed guest rooms and offers Milwaukee's only revolving rooftop restaurant, which affords panoramic views of the city's skyline. Oversized work stations and wireless Internet also make this a good choice for business travelers.

484 rooms. Wireless Internet access. Restaurant, bar. $151-250

★★★THE PFISTER HOTEL

424 E. Wisconsin Ave., Milwaukee, 414-273-8222, 800-558-8222;
www.thepfisterhotel.com

The Pfister has been a perennial favorite of Milwaukee natives since 1893. The hotel embraces its past with a museum-quality collection of Victorian artwork. The views of the city and Lake Michigan are particularly alluring, and the restaurants and lounges are the places to see and be seen in the city. Sunday brunch at Café Rouge is popular with guests and locals, while Blu spices up the scene with special martinis and flights of wine.

307 rooms. Wireless Internet access. Restaurant, bar. Spa. $151-250

★★★SHERATON MILWAUKEE BROOKFIELD HOTEL

375 S. Moorland Road, Brookfield, 262-786-1100, 800-325-3535; www.sheraton.com

Guest rooms are updated with flat-screen TVs, high-speed Internet access, and the signature Sweet Sleeper bed guarantees a restful night's sleep. Downtown area shopping and nightlife are close at hand here, as well as Brookfield Hills Golf Club.

389 rooms. Restaurant. Pets accepted. Pool. $151-250

★★★WYNDHAM MILWAUKEE CENTER

139 E. Kilbourn Ave., Milwaukee, 414-276-8686, 800-996-3426;
www.intercontinentalmilwaukee.com

Located in Milwaukee's charming theater district, this elegant hotel is actually within the same building complex as the Milwaukee Repertory and Pabst Theaters. Well-appointed rooms overlook the Milwaukee River and guests are within walking distance of the Marcus Center, City Hall and plenty of shopping and dining.

220 rooms. Wireless Internet access. Restaurant, bar. Fitness center. Whirlpool. $61-150

WHERE TO EAT

★AU BON APPETIT

219 N. Milwaukee St., Second floor, 414-223-3222; www.aubonappetit.com

Mediterranean menu. Dinner. Closed Sunday-Monday. Casual attire. Reservations recommended. $16-35

★BALISTRERI'S BLUE MOUND INN

6501 W. Bluemound Road, Milwaukee, 414-258-9881; www.balistreris.com

Italian, American menu. Lunch Monday-Friday, dinner. Bar. $16-35

★★★BARTOLOTTA'S LAKE PARK BISTRO

3133 E. Newberry Blvd., Milwaukee, 414-962-6300; www.lakeparkbistro.com

This restaurant serves authentic French dishes and many wood-fired oven specialties in this Parisian-style dining room. Chef Adam Siegel was a James Beard Award nominee in 2007. Such dishes as steamed mussels in a creamy white wine broth with garlic and shallots, filet mignon au poivre and roasted halibut with caramelized fennel, sautéed spinach and a Provencal-style olive tapenade show off the chef's talent. The sizeable wine list is worth perusing French menu. Lunch, dinner, Sunday brunch. Bar. Children's menu. $16-35

★COUNTY CLARE IRISH INN & PUB
1234 N. Astor St., Milwaukee, 414-272-5273; www.countyclareinn.com
Irish menu. Lunch, dinner. Bar. Children's menu. Casual attire. Outdoor seating. $16-35

★★EAGAN'S
1030 N. Water St., Milwaukee, 414-271-6900; www.eagansonwater.com
Seafood menu. Lunch, dinner, Sunday brunch. Bar. Business casual attire. Outdoor seating. $16-35

★IZUMI'S
2150 N. Prospect Ave., Milwaukee, 414-271-5278; www.izumisrestaurant.com
Japanese menu. Lunch, dinner. $16-35

★★KARL RATZSCH'S
320 E. Mason St., Milwaukee, 414-276-2720; www.karlratzsch.com
German menu. Lunch (Wednesday-Saturday), dinner. Closed Sunday. Bar. Children's menu. Casual attire. Valet parking. $36-85

★★THE KING AND I
823 N. Second St., Milwaukee, 414-276-4181; www.kingandirestaurant.com
Thai menu. Lunch (Monday-Friday), dinner. Bar. Casual attire. Reservations recommended. $16-35

★THE KNICK
1030 E. Juneau Ave., Milwaukee, 414-272-0011; www.theknickrestaurant.com
American menu. Breakfast, lunch, dinner, brunch. Bar. Casual attire. Valet parking. Outdoor seating. $16-35

★★MADER'S
1037 N. Old World Third St., Milwaukee, 414-271-3377; www.maders.com
German menu. Lunch, dinner, Sunday brunch. Bar. Children's menu. Valet parking. $16-35

★★★MIMMA'S CAFÉ
1307 E. Brady St., Milwaukee, 414-271-7337; www.mimmas.com
This family-run restaurant has grown from an eight-seat eatery to a 150-seat, fine Italian restaurant with impressive faux-marble walls, paintings, chandeliers and polished-tile flooring. Try inventive dishes such as lemon pepper fettuccini with mussels, tomatoes, basil and garlic, or black pasta with scallops, shrimp, crab and sun-dried tomatoes in a porcini cream sauce.
Italian menu. Dinner. Bar. Business casual attire. Outdoor seating. $16-35

★OLD TOWN SERBIAN GOURMET HOUSE
522 W. Lincoln Ave., Milwaukee, 414-672-0206
American, Serbian menu. Lunch, dinner. Closed Monday. Bar. Children's menu. $16-35

★★★OSTERIA DEL MONDO
1028 E. Juneau Ave., Milwaukee, 414-291-3770; www.osteria.com
Chef/owner Marc Bianchini enhances the German landscape of Wisconsin with this authentic Italian café, located in the Knickerbocker Hotel. The wine, food—for example, bucatini with onions and Italian bacon—and desserts are transporting. The wine bar adds a lively touch to this casual yet intimate restaurant.
Italian menu. Dinner. Bar. Business casual attire. Reservations recommended. Valet parking. Outdoor seating. $16-35

★★★PANDL'S BAYSIDE
8825 N. Lake Drive, Milwaukee, 414-352-7300; www.pandls.com
This restaurant serves up a wonderfully cozy atmosphere in an attractive setting with an elaborate salad bar, family-friendly brunches and good value. Enjoy fresh fish, steaks and the ever-popular duckling with raspberry sauce.
American menu. Lunch, dinner. Bar. Children's menu. $36-85

★PLEASANT VALLEY INN
9801 W. Dakota St., Milwaukee, 414-321-4321; www.foodspot.com/pleasantvalleyinn
American menu. Dinner. Closed Monday. Bar. Children's menu. $16-35

★★POLARIS
333 W. Kilbourn Ave., Milwaukee, 414-270-6130; www.foodspot.com/polaris
American menu. Dinner, brunch. Bar. Children's menu. Casual attire. Reservations recommended. $16-35

★★SAFE HOUSE
779 N. Front St., Milwaukee, 414-271-2007; www.safe-house.com
American menu. Lunch (Monday-Saturday), dinner. Bar. Children's menu. $16-35

★★★SANFORD
1547 N. Jackson St., Milwaukee, 414-276-9608; www.sanfordrestaurant.com
The site, once a grocery store owned by the Sanford family, houses a modern, sophisticated dining room offering New American cuisine from an à la carte menu. There is also a four-course seasonal menu and an additional, five-course ethnic tasting menu offered on weeknights.
American menu. Dinner. Closed Sunday. Business casual attire. Reservations recommended. Valet parking. $36-85

★SARAPHINO'S ITALIAN RESTAURANT
3074 E. Layton Ave., St. Francis, 414-744-0303; www.foodspot.com/saraphinos
American, Italian menu. Breakfast, lunch, dinner. Children's menu. Casual attire. $16-35

★SAZ'S STATE HOUSE
5539 W. State St., Milwaukee, 414-453-2410; www.sazs.com
American menu. Lunch, dinner, Sunday brunch. Bar. Outdoor seating.
$16-35

★★THIRD STREET PIER
1110 N. Old World Third St., Milwaukee, 414-272-0330; www.weissgerbers.com
American menu. Dinner, brunch. Bar. Children's menu. Outdoor seating.
$16-35

★THREE BROTHERS
2414 S. St. Clair St., Milwaukee, 414-481-7530; www.3brothersrestaurant.com
Serbian menu. Dinner. Closed Monday. $16-35

★YEN CHING
7630 W. Good Hope Road, Milwaukee, 414-353-6677; www.yenchingchinese.com
Chinese menu. Lunch, dinner. $16-35

MINERAL POINT
See also Dodgeville, New Glarus, Platteville
The first settlers were New Englanders and Southerners attracted by the lead
deposits. In the 1830s, miners from Cornwall, England settled here. These
"Cousin Jacks," as they were called, introduced superior mining methods
and also built the first permanent homes, duplicating the rock houses they
had left in Cornwall. Since the mines were in sight of their homes their wives
called them to meals by stepping to the door and shaking a rag—the town
was first called "Shake Rag." The city offers a wide variety of shopping opportunities, including artisan galleries and working studios.

WHERE TO EAT
★★★RAY RADIGAN'S
11712 S. Sheridan Road, Pleasant Prairie, 262-694-0455;
www.foodspot.com/rayradigans
Just three miles from town, this popular stop has been a beloved local institution since 1933, dishing out superb steaks. The lobster thermidor and the
LeBlanc special, a prime blue ribbon T-bone steak, are both standouts.
American menu. Lunch, dinner. Closed Monday. Bar. Children's menu. Casual attire. Reservations recommended. $16-35

MINOCQUA
See also Boulder Junction, Eagle River, Manitowish Waters, Rhinelander
Minocqua is a four-season resort area known for its thousands of acres of
lakes. The area contains one of the largest concentrations of freshwater bod-
ies in America. Minocqua, the "Island City," was once completely surrounded
by Lake Minocqua. Now youth camps and resorts are along the lakeshore.

WHAT TO SEE
JIM PECK'S WILDWOOD
10094 State Highway 70, Minocqua, 715-356-5588; www.wildwoodwildlifepark.com
A wildlife park featuring hundreds of tame animals and birds native to the

area, many can be pet at the baby animal nursery.
May-mid-October, daily.

MINOCQUA WINTER PARK NORDIC CENTER
12375 Scotchman Lake Road, Minocqua, 715-356-3309; www.skimwp.org
This center has more than 35 miles of groomed and tracked cross-country trails, two groomed telemarking slopes and more than one mile of lighted trails for night skiing (Thursday-Friday only).
December-March, Thursday-Tuesday.

SPECIAL EVENT
NORTHERN LIGHTS PLAYHOUSE
5611 Highway 51, Hazelhurst, 715-356-7173; www.nl-playhouse.com
This professional repertory theater presents Broadway plays, musicals and comedies and also offers a children's theatre.
Memorial Day-early October.

WHERE TO STAY
★BEST WESTERN CONCORD INN
320 Front St., Minocqua, 715-356-1800, 800-356-8888; www.newconcordinn.com
53 rooms. Complimentary continental breakfast. Pets accepted. Pool.
$61-150

WHERE TO EAT
★★NORWOOD PINES
10171 Highway 70 W., Minocqua, 715-356-3666; www.norwoodpines.com
Steak menu. Dinner. Closed Sunday. Children's menu. $36-85

★PAUL BUNYAN'S
8653 Highway 51 North, Minocqua, 715-356-6270; www.paulbunyans.com
American menu. Breakfast, lunch, dinner. Closed October-April. Bar. Children's menu. $16-35

★RED STEER
Highway 51 S., Minocqua, 715-356-6332; www.chysredsteer.com
Seafood, steak menu. Dinner. Bar. Children's menu. $16-35

MONROE
See also Janesville, New Glarus
A well-known community of Swiss heritage in an area of abundant dairy production, Monroe is the site of a unique courthouse with a 120-foot tall clock tower.

WHAT TO SEE
YELLOWSTONE LAKE STATE PARK
8495 Lake Road, Blanchardville, 608-523-4427, 800-947-8757; www.dnr.wi.gov
This 968-acre park on Yellowstone Lake offers swimming, fishing, boating, hiking, cross-country skiing, snowmobiling, picnicking, concessions and camping.
Daily.

WHERE TO STAY
★AMERICINN MONROE
424 Fourth Ave., Monroe, 608-328-3444
54 rooms. Business Center. Fitness center. Complimentary breakfast. Pool.
$61-151

NEENAH-MENASHA
See also Appleton, Green Bay, Oshkosh
Wisconsin's great paper industry started in Neenah and its twin city, Menasha.

WHAT TO SEE
BARLOW PLANETARIUM
1478 Midway Road, Menasha, 920-832-2848; www.uwfox.uwc.edu/Barlow
3-D projections explain the stars.
Thursday-Friday evening, Saturday-Sunday.

BERGSTROM-MAHLER MUSEUM
165 N. Park Ave., Neenah, 920-751-4658; www.bergstrom-mahlermuseum.com
The museum showcases more than 1,800 glass paperweights, antique German glass, American regional paintings and changing exhibits.
Tuesday-Sunday.

HIGH CLIFF GENERAL STORE MUSEUM
N7630 State Park Road, Sherwood, 920-989-1106; www.dnr.state.wi.us
The museum depicts life in the area from 1850 to the early 1900s.
Mid-May-September, Friday-Sunday.

NEW GLARUS
See also Dodgeville, Madison, Mineral Point, Mount Horeb
When bad times struck the Swiss canton of Glarus in 1845, a group of 108 settlers set out for the New World and settled New Glarus. Their knowledge of dairying brought prosperity. The town is still predominantly Swiss in character and ancestry.

WHERE TO STAY
★★★CHALET LANDHAUS INN
801 Highway 69, New Glarus, 608-527-5234, 800-944-1716; www.chaletlandhaus.com
An all-encompassing inn with a distinctly Swiss influence, this place is a quaint, homey escape. Enjoy the Swiss barbecue buffet.
67 rooms. Restaurant. Fitness center. Business Center. Pets accepted. $151-250

WHERE TO EAT
★★NEW GLARUS HOTEL
100 Sixth Ave., New Glarus, 608-527-5244; www.newglarushotel.com
American, Continental menu. Lunch, dinner, Sunday brunch. Closed Tuesday in November-April. Bar. Children's menu. $16-35

OCONOMOWOC

See also Milwaukee, Watertown

Native Americans called this place "the gathering of waters" because of its location between Fowler Lake and Lake Lac La Belle.

WHAT TO SEE
HONEY OF A MUSEUM

Honey Acres, N1557 Highway 67, Ashippun, 920-474-4411, 800-558-7745;
www.honeyacres.com

This museum is dedicated to beekeeping and honey making. An onsite shop sells many products made with honey and other honey products.

Monday-Friday 9 a.m.-3:30 p.m., Saturday-Sunday noon-4 p.m.

WHERE TO EAT
★★★GOLDEN MAST INN

W349 N5253 Lacy's Lane, Okauchee, 262-567-7047; www.weissgerbers.com

This local restaurant offers a wide array of entrées with a German flair. Try sauerbraten, red cabbage and spaetzle or authentic Wiener schnitzel.

American, German menu. Dinner, brunch. Closed Monday. Bar. Children's menu. Reservations recommended. Outdoor seating. $36-85

OSHKOSH

See also Appleton, Fond du Lac, Neenah-Menasha

Named for the chief of the Menominee, Oshkosh is located on the west shore of Lake Winnebago, the largest freshwater lake within the state. The city is known for the many recreational activities offered by its lakes and rivers. This is the original home of the company that produces the famous overalls that helped make Oshkosh a household word.

WHAT TO SEE
EAA AIR ADVENTURE MUSEUM

3000 Poberezny Road, Oshkosh, 920-426-4818; www.airventuremuseum.org

More than 90 aircraft are on display at this museum including home-built aircraft, antiques, classics, ultralights, aerobatic and rotary-winged planes. It also features a special World War II collection and extensive collections of aviation art and photography. Antique airplanes fly on weekends.

May-October. Daily.

GRAND OPERA HOUSE

100 High Ave., Oshkosh, 920-424-2350; www.grandoperahouse.org

This restored 1883 Victorian theater offers a variety of performing arts.

OSHKOSH PUBLIC MUSEUM

1331 Algoma Blvd., Oshkosh, 920-424-4731; www.oshkoshmuseum.org

Housed in a turn-of-the-century, Tudor-style mansion with Tiffany stained-glass windows and interior, this museum also occupies an adjacent addition. Exhibits include a china and glassware collection and life-sized dioramas depicting French exploration, British occupation, pioneer settlement and native wildlife.

Tuesday-Sunday.

UNIVERSITY OF WISCONSIN-OSHKOSH

800 Algoma Blvd., Oshkosh, 920-424-0202, 800-624-1466; www.uwosh.edu
This university includes the Priebe Art Gallery, Reeve Memorial Union and Kolf Sports and Recreation Center.
Campus tours: Monday-Friday; Saturday by appointment.

SPECIAL EVENTS
EXPERIMENTAL AIRCRAFT ASSOCIATION AIR VENTURE

3000 Poberezny Road, Oshkosh, 920-426-4800; www.airventure.org
Held at Wittman Regional Airport, this is one of the nation's largest aviation events with more than 500 educational forums, workshops and seminars; daily air shows; exhibits and more than 12,000 aircraft.
Late July-early August.

OSHKOSH PUBLIC MUSEUM ART FAIR

1331 Algoma Blvd., Oshkosh, 920-424-4731; www.oshkoshmuseum.org
On the Oshkosh Public Museum grounds, this fair features original fine art by more than 200 high-quality artists from around the country.
Early July.

WHERE TO STAY
★HOLIDAY INN EXPRESS

2251 Westowne Ave., Oshkosh, 920-303-1300; www.hiexpress.com
68 rooms. Pets accepted. Fitness center. Indoor pool. Business center. Complimentary breakfast. $61-150

WHERE TO EAT
★★ROBBINS

1810 Omro Road, Oshkosh, 920-235-2840; www.robbinsrestaurant.com
American menu. Lunch, dinner, brunch. Bar. Children's menu. Casual attire. Reservations recommended. Outdoor seating. $16-35

PLATTEVILLE

See also Dodgeville, Mineral Point
Sport fishing is very popular in the many streams in the area. The world's largest letter "M" was built on Platteville Mound in 1936 by mining engineering students—it is lit twice each year for the University of Wisconsin-Platteville's homecoming and Miner's Ball.

WHAT TO SEE
ROLLO JAMISON MUSEUM

405 Main St., Platteville, 608-348-3301; www.mining.jamison.museum
This museum contains a large collection of everyday items amassed by Rollo Jamison during his lifetime, including horse-drawn vehicles, tools and musical instruments.
May-October, daily.

STONE COTTAGE

2785 W., Highway 151, Platteville, 608-348-8888; www.platteville.com

Much of the interior of this 1837 cottage is the original furnishing of the home. It was built with two-foot-thick walls of dolomite Galena limestone and was a private residence until the 1960s.

Saturday-Sunday afternoons.

WHERE TO STAY
★★GOVERNOR DODGE HOTEL

300 W. Highway 151, Platteville, 608-348-2301; www.governordodge.com

72 rooms. Restaurant. Pets accepted. $60-150

PORT WASHINGTON

See also Cedarburg, Milwaukee, Sheboygan

Located along the shore of Lake Michigan, Port Washington has many pre-Civil War homes. The Port Washington Marina, one of the finest on Lake Michigan, provides exceptional facilities for boating and fishing.

WHAT TO SEE
EGHART HOUSE

302 W. Grand Ave., Port Washington; www.egharthouse.org

Built in 1872, this house has Victorian furnishings from 1850 to 1900 in the hall, parlor, dining-living room, bedroom, kitchen and pantry.

Tours: Late May-Labor Day, Sunday afternoons; weekdays by appointment.

WHERE TO STAY
★★HOLIDAY INN PORT WASHINGTON

135 E. Grand Ave., Port Washington, 262-284-9461

96 rooms. Restaurant, bar. Pets accepted. Pool. Fitness center. $61-150

PORTAGE

See also Baraboo, Prairie du Sac, Wisconsin Dells

Portage is built on a narrow strip of land separating the Fox and Wisconsin rivers. In the early flow of traffic, goods were hauled from one river to another, providing the name for the city. Before permanent settlement, Fort Winnebago occupied this site. Several historic buildings remain. Modern Portage is the business center of Columbia County.

WHAT TO SEE
OLD INDIAN AGENCY HOUSE

RR 1, Portage, 608-742-6362; www.nscda.org

This restored house was the home of John Kinzie, U.S. Indian Agent to the Winnebago and an important pioneer; his wife Juliette wrote Wau-bun, an early history of their voyages to Fort Winnebago.

May-October, Daily; November-April, by appointment.

PRAIRIE DU CHIEN

See also Dodgeville, Platteville

Dating to 1673, Prairie du Chien is the second-oldest European settlement in Wisconsin. Marquette and Jolliet discovered the Mississippi River just south of the prairie that the French adventurers then named Prairie du Chien ("prairie of the dog") for Chief Alim, whose name meant "dog." The site became a popular gathering place and trading post. The War of 1812 led to the construction of Fort Shelby and Fort Crawford on an ancient American Indian burial ground in the village. Jefferson Davis, later president of the Confederacy, and Zachary Taylor, later president of the United States were both stationed here. In 1826, Hercules Dousman, an agent for John Jacob Astor's American Fur Company, came and built a personal fortune, becoming Wisconsin's first millionaire. When Fort Crawford was moved, Dousman bought the site and erected Villa Louis, the "House of the Mound," a palatial mansion.

WHAT TO SEE
FORT CRAWFORD MUSEUM

717 S. Beaumont Road, Prairie du Chien, 608-326-6960;

www.fortcrawfordmuseum.com

This museum features relics of 19th-century medicine, Native American herbal remedies, drugstores and dentist and physicians' offices.

May-October, daily.

KICKAPOO INDIAN CAVERNS AND AMERICAN INDIAN MUSEUM

54850 Rhein Hollow Road, Wauzeka, 608-875-7723; www.kickapooindiancaverns.com

These are the largest caverns in Wisconsin, used by Native Americans for centuries as a shelter. Sights include a subterranean lake, cathedral room, turquoise room, stalactite chamber and chamber of the lost waters.

Mid-May-October, daily.

NELSON DEWEY STATE PARK

12190 County Road W., Cassville, 608-725-5374; www.dnr.wi.gov

This 756-acre park offers nature and hiking trails and camping.

Daily

STONEFIELD

12195 County Road W., Cassville, 608-725-5210; www.stonefield.wisconsinhistory.org

Named for a rock-studded, 2,000-acre farm that Dewey (the first elected governor of Wisconsin) established on the bluffs of the Mississippi River, the State Agricultural Museum contains displays of farm machinery and the site also features a recreation of an 1890 Stonefield Village comprising a blacksmith, general store, print shop, school, church and 26 other buildings.

Memorial Day-early September, daly; Early September-mid-October, Saturday-Sunday.

VILLA LOUIS

521 N. Villa Louis Road, Prairie du Chien, 608-326-2721;

www.villalouis.wisconsinhistory.org

Built on site of Fort Crawford, this restored 1870 home contains original furnishings and a collection of Victorian decorative arts.

May-October, daily 10 a.m.-4 p.m.

WYALUSING STATE PARK

13081 State Park Lane, Bagley, 608-996-2261; www.dnr.state.wi.us

A 2,654-acre park at the confluence of the Mississippi and Wisconsin rivers, Wyalusing features the Sentinel Ridge, which provides a commanding view of the area. Other features include fishing, boating, canoeing and 18 miles of nature, hiking and cross-country ski trails.

Daily.

WHERE TO STAY

★BEST WESTERN QUIET HOUSE & SUITES

Highways 18 and 35 S., Prairie du Chien, 608-326-4777, 800-780-7234;

www.bestwestern.com

42 rooms. Wireless Internet access. Indoor pool. Complimentary full breakfast. $61-150

PRAIRIE DU SAC

See also Baraboo, Madison, Portage, Spring Green

This spot is a favorite launching area for canoeists on the Wisconsin River. It is possible to see bald eagles south of the village at Ferry Bluff.

SPECIAL EVENT

HARVEST FESTIVAL

Wollersheim Winery, 7876 Highway 188, Prairie du Sac, 608-643-6515, 800-847-9463;

www.wollersheim.com

Fest includes a grape stomping competition, music, a cork toss, a grape spitting contest and food.

First full weekend in October.

RACINE

See also Burlington, Kenosha, Milwaukee

Racine is situated on a thumb of land jutting into Lake Michigan. The largest concentration of people of Danish descent in the United States can be found here. West Racine is known as "Kringleville" because of its Danish pastry.

WHAT TO SEE

RACINE HERITAGE MUSEUM

701 S. Main St., Racine, 262-636-3926; www.racineheritagemuseum.org

This museum features the cultural history of Racine and includes permanent and temporary exhibits, archives and a photographic collection.

Tuesday-Saturday

WHERE TO STAY
★★DAYS INN
3700 Northwestern Ave., Racine, 262-637-9311, 888-242-6494; www.daysinn.com
110 rooms. Complimentary breakfast. Restaurant, bar. Pets accepted. Pool. $61-150

WHERE TO EAT
★★HOB NOB
277 S. Sheridan Road, Racine, 262-552-8008; www.thehobnob.com
American menu. Dinner. Bar. Children's menu. Business casual attire. Reservations recommended. $16-35

RHINELANDER
See also Crandon, Eagle River, Minocqua, Three Lakes
Located at the junction of the Wisconsin and Pelican rivers, Rhinelander is close to 232 lakes, 11 trout streams and two rivers within a 12-mile radius. The logging industry, which built this area, still thrives and the many miles of old logging roads are excellent for hiking and mountain biking. Paved bicycle trails, cross-country skiing and snowmobiling are also popular in this northwoods area.

WHAT TO SEE
RHINELANDER LOGGING MUSEUM
810 Keenan St., Rhinelander, 715-369-5004; www.rhinelanders-morningside.com
The most complete displays of old-time lumbering in the Midwest are found here. On the grounds are the Five Spot, which is the last narrow-gauge railroad locomotive to work Wisconsin's northwoods, and a restored depot dating from late 1800s. The museum also displays the "hodag"—called "the strangest animal known to man" because, well, it's a hoax. It has become the symbol of the city.
Memorial Day-Labor Day, daily.

SPECIAL EVENT
HODAG COUNTRY FESTIVAL
4270 River Road, Rhinelander, 715-369-1300, 800-762-3803; www.hodag.com
This three-day country music festival features top-name entertainment. Mid-July.

WHERE TO STAY
★★BEST WESTERN CLARIDGE MOTOR INN
70 N. Stevens St., Rhinelander, 715-362-7100, 800-427-1377; www.bestwestern.com
85 rooms. Restaurant, bar. Airport transportation available. Pets accepted. Indoor pool. Fitness center. Business Center. High-speed Internet access. $61-150

★★HOLIDAY INN EXPRESS
668 W. Kemp St., Rhinelander, 715-369-3600, 800-465-4329; www.holidayinn.com
101 rooms. Restaurant, bar. Airport transportation available. Pets accepted. $61-150

RICE LAKE

See also Chippewa Falls, Ladysmith

Formerly headquarters for the world's largest hardwood mills, Rice Lake has an economy based on industry and retail trade. The city and lake were named for nearby wild rice sloughs, which were an important Sioux and Chippewa food source. Surrounded by 84 lakes, the city is in a major recreation area.

WHERE TO STAY

★AMERICINN

2906 Pioneer Ave., Rice Lake, 715-234-9060

43 rooms. Complimentary continental breakfast. Pool. Wireless Internet access. $61-150

★★★★CANOE BAY

Off Hogback Road, Rice Lake, 715-924-4594; www.canoebay.com

Canoe Bay is rather like a luxurious camp for adults, with gourmet dining, an award-winning wine cellar and extensive amenities. Situated on 280 acres in northwestern Wisconsin, the resort's three private, spring-fed lakes are perfect for a multitude of recreational opportunities. The wilderness trails are ideal for hiking in summer months, while snowshoeing and cross-country skiing are popular during the winter. The resort has no telephones or televisions to distract from the peaceful setting. Choose from either well-appointed rooms at the lodge or the inn or cozy private cottages. Linger over dinner in the candlelit Dining Room, where dishes are prepared with organic produce and locally produced ingredients.

19 rooms. No children allowed. Complimentary full breakfast. Restaurant. $251-350

WHERE TO EAT

★★NORSKE NOOK

2900 Pioneer Ave., Rice Lake, 715-234-1733; www.norskenook.com

American menu. Breakfast, lunch, dinner. Children's menu. Casual attire. $15 and under

RICHLAND CENTER

See also Spring Green

Famed architect Frank Lloyd Wright was born in this small town in 1867.

WHAT TO SEE

EAGLE CAVE

16320 Cavern Lane, Blue River, 608-537-2988; www.eaglecave.net

This large onyx cavern contains stalactites, stalagmites and fossils. Guided tours: Memorial Day-Labor Day, Daily.

SHAWANO

See also Appleton, Green Bay, Wausau

A city born during the lumber boom, Shawano is now a retail trade center for the small surrounding farms and produces dairy and wood products.

WHAT TO SEE
SHAWANO LAKE

Highway 22 and Lake Drive, Shawano, 800-235-8528; www.shawanolakeresort.com
This lake is four miles wide and seven miles long and offers fishing, boating, ice fishing, hunting and camping.

WHERE TO STAY
★AMERICINN

1330 E. Green Bay St., Shawano, 715-524-5111
45 rooms. Complimentary continental breakfast. Business center. High-speed Internet access. Fitness center. Pool. $61-150

★★BEST WESTERN VILLAGE HAUS MOTOR LODGE

201 N. Airport Drive, Shawano, 715-526-9595, 800-553-4479; www.bestwestern.com
89 rooms. Restaurant, bar. Pool. $61-150

SHEBOYGAN

See also Elkhart Lake, Kohler, Manitowoc, Port Washington
A harbor city on the west shore of Lake Michigan, Sheboygan is a major industrial city and a popular fishing port.

WHAT TO SEE
KOHLER ANDRAE STATE PARK

1020 Beach Park Lane, Sheboygan, 920-451-4080; www.dnr.wi.gov/org
This park includes 1,000 acres of woods and sand dunes and offers swimming, nature and cross-country ski trails, picnicking, playgrounds, concessions and camping. Daily.

SPECIAL EVENTS
BRAT DAYS

Kiwanis Park, 17th and New Jersey streets, Sheboygan, 920-457-9491;
www.sheboyganjaycees.com
This celebration of the area's German heritage and its famous bratwurst began in 1953, and is the biggest festival in the city each year.
Early August.

HOLLAND FEST

118 Main St., Cedar Grove, 920-457-9491; www.hollandfest.com
A celebration of Dutch traditions, Holland Fest includes wooden-shoe dancing, street scrubbing, a folk fair, food, music, an art fair and a parade.
Last Friday-Saturday in July.

POLAR BEAR SWIM

712 Riverfront Drive, Suite 101, Sheboygan, 920-457-9491; www.sheboygan.org
More than 350 swimmers brave Lake Michigan's icy winter waters.
January 1.

WHERE TO STAY
★BAYMONT INN
2932 Kohler Memorial Drive, Sheboygan, 920-457-2321, 800-301-0200;
www.baymontinn.com
98 rooms. Complimentary continental breakfast. Pets accepted. $61-150

★★★BLUE HARBOR RESORT & CONFERENCE CENTER
725 Blue Harbor Drive, Sheboygan, 920-452-2900, 866-701-2583;
www.blueharborresort.com
This massive resort also houses a 54,000-square-foot indoor entertainment area and waterpark and the Northern Lights Arcade. Elements Spa is a lovely retreat and restaurants include On the Rocks Bar & Grille and the Rusty Anchor Buffet.
183 rooms, all suites. Restaurants, bar. $151-250

SISTER BAY
See also Door County
Near the northern tip of Door County, Sister Bay was settled in 1857 by Norwegian immigrants. Today it's known for its shopping, dining and boating, but still retains a distinct Scandinavian flavor.

WHERE TO STAY
★OPEN HEARTH LODGE
2669 S. Bay Shore Drive, Sister Bay, 920-854-4890; www.openhearthlodge.com
32 rooms. Complimentary continental breakfast. Pool. $61-150

WHERE TO EAT
★AL JOHNSON'S SWEDISH RESTAURANT
710 Bay Shore Drive, Sister Bay, 920-854-2626, 920-854-9650; www.aljohnsons.com
Continental menu. Breakfast, lunch, dinner. Children's menu. Casual attire. $16-35

SPARTA
See also Black River Falls, La Crosse, Tomah
Sparta is home to several small manufacturing industries including dairy products, brushes and automobile parts. The area is well known for its biking trails. Fort McCoy, a U.S. Army base, is five miles northeast on Highway 21.

WHAT TO SEE
ELROY-SPARTA STATE TRAIL
113 White St., Kendall, 608-337-4775; www.wiparks.net
Built on an old railroad bed, this 32-mile hard-surfaced trail passes through three tunnels and over 23 trestles.
April-October, daily.

WHERE TO STAY
★COUNTRY INN & SUITES BY CARLSON SPARTA
737 Avon Road, Sparta, 608-269-3110, 888-201-1746; www.countryinns.com
61 rooms. Complimentary continental breakfast. Bar. Pets accepted. Pool. $61-150

WHERE TO EAT
★BACK DOOR CAFÉ
1223 Front St., Cashton, 888-322-5494; www.agespast.net
American menu. Lunch, dinner. Closed Sunday. $15 and under

SPRING GREEN
See also Dodgeville, Mineral Point, Prairie du Sac, Richland Center
Spring Green's claim to fame is that architect Frank Lloyd Wright grew up in this community, built his home, Taliesin East, here and established the Taliesin Fellowship for the training of apprentice architects.

WHAT TO SEE
HOUSE ON THE ROCK
5754 Highway 23, Spring Green, 608-935-3639; www.thehouseontherock.com
Designed and built by Alexander J. Jordan atop a chimney-like rock, 450 feet above a valley, waterfalls and trees are located throughout house along with collections of antiques.
Mid-March-late October, daily.

TOWER HILL STATE PARK
5808 County Highway C, Spring Green, 608-588-2116; www.dnr.state.wi.us
T state park includes 77 acres of wooded hills and bluffs overlooking the Wisconsin River. The site has a pre-Civil War shot tower and lead-mining village of Helena.
Daily.

WHERE TO STAY
★★HOUSE ON THE ROCK RESORT
5754 Highway 23, Spring Green, 608-935-3639; www.houseontherock.com
80 rooms, all suites. Restaurant, bar. Pool. Tennis. $151-250

ST. CROIX FALLS
See also Hudson, Rice Lake
Headquarters of the Interstate State Park, St. Croix Falls has become a summer and winter resort area. Lions Park, north of town, has picnicking and boat launching, and there are many miles of groomed snowmobile trails in Polk County.

WHAT TO SEE
CREX MEADOWS WILDLIFE AREA
102 E. Crex Ave., St. Croix Falls, 715-463-2896; www.crexmeadows.org
This 30,000-acre state-owned wildlife area is a prairie-wetlands habitat,

breeding wildlife species including giant Canada geese, 11 species of ducks, sharp-tailed grouse, sandhill cranes, bald eagles, ospreys, trumpeter swans and loons.
Daily.

GOVERNOR KNOWLES STATE FOREST
325 Highway 70, Grantsburg, 715-463-2898; www.dnr.state.wi.us
A 33,000-acre expanse extending north and south along the St. Croix River, this forest offers fishing, boating, canoeing, hiking, bridle, snowmobile and cross-country ski trails, picnicking and group camping.
Daily.

INTERSTATE STATE PARK
Highway 35, St. Croix Falls, 715-483-3747; www.dnr.wi.gov
At 1,325-acres, this is Wisconsin's oldest state park. It offers swimming, fishing, boating, canoeing, picnicking, camping and nature, hiking and cross-country ski trails. The Ice Age National Scientific Reserve operates a visitor center here. Daily.

STEVENS POINT
See also Marshfield, Wisconsin Rapids
A diversified community on the Wisconsin River, near the middle of the state, Stevens Point was established as a trading post by George Stevens, who bartered with the Potawatomi. Incorporated as a city in 1858, today it has a number of industries and markets the dairy produce and vegetable crops of Portage County.

WHAT TO SEE
STEVENS POINT BREWERY

2617 Water St., Stevens Point, 715-344-9310; www.pointbeer.com
The 1857 brewery offers tours. Monday-Saturday, reservations suggested.

UNIVERSITY OF WISCONSIN-STEVENS POINT
2100 Main St., Stevens Point, 715-346-0123; www.uwsp.edu
Across the entire front of the four-story Natural Resources Building is the world's largest computer-assisted mosaic mural. The Museum of Natural History has one of the most complete collections of preserved birds and bird eggs in the country.

WHERE TO STAY
★COMFORT SUITES
300 N. Division St., Stevens Point, 715-341-6000
105 rooms. Complimentary continental breakfast. Pool. Fitness center.
$61-150

STURGEON BAY
See also Door County
Door County's Sturgeon Bay sits at the farthest inland point of a bay where

swarms of sturgeon were once caught and piled like cordwood along the shore. The historic portage from the bay to Lake Michigan, used for centuries by Native Americans and early explorers, began here. The Sturgeon Bay ship canal now makes the route a waterway used by lake freighters and pleasure craft. The city is the county seat and trading center. Two shipyards and a number of other industries are located here. Ten million pounds of cherries are processed every year in Door County.

WHAT TO SEE
ROBERT LA SALLE COUNTY PARK
1015 Green Bay Road, Sturgeon Bay, 800-527-3529; www.doorcounty.com
This site is where La Salle and his band of explorers were rescued from starvation by friendly Native Americans. A monument marks the location of La Salle's fortified camp.

THE FARM
4285 State Highway 57, Sturgeon Bay, 920-743-6666; www.thefarmindoorcounty.com
The Farm features animals and fowl in natural surroundings, plus a pioneer farmstead and wildlife display.
Memorial Day-Mid-October, daily.

WHERE TO STAY
★BAY SHORE INN
4205 N. Bay Shore Drive, Sturgeon Bay, 920-743-4551, 800-556-4551; www.bayshoreinn.net
30 rooms. Pool. Tennis. $61-150

★BEST WESTERN MARITIME INN
1001 N. 14th Ave., Sturgeon Bay, 920-743-7231, 800-780-7234; www.bestwestern.com
91 rooms. Complimentary breakfast. Pets accepted. Pool. Fitness center. $61-150

★★LEATHEM SMITH LODGE AND MARINA
1640 Memorial Drive, Sturgeon Bay, 920-743-5555, 800-366-7947; www.lslodge.com
63 rooms. Complimentary continental breakfast. Restaurant, bar. Golf. Tennis. $61-150

WHERE TO EAT
★★INN AT CEDAR CROSSING
336 Louisiana St., Sturgeon Bay, 920-743-4249; www.innatcedarcrossing.com
American menu. Breakfast, lunch, dinner. Bar. Children's menu. Casual attire. Reservations recommended. $16-35

SUPERIOR
See also Ashland, Duluth
At the head of Lake Superior, with the finest natural harbor on the Great Lakes, Superior-Duluth has been one of the leading ports in the country in volume of tonnage for many years. The Burlington Northern Docks and taconite pellet handling complex are the largest in the United States. More than

200 million bushels of grain are shipped in and out of the area's elevators each year. Superior is also the largest coal-loading terminal in the United States with 12 coal docks in the Superior-Duluth area. Long before its founding date, the city was the site of a series of trading posts. The University of Wisconsin-Superior is located here.

WHAT TO SEE
BRULE RIVER STATE FOREST
6250 S. Ranger Road, Brule, 715-372-5678; www.dnr.wi.gov
On 40,218 acres, this forest offers fishing, boating, canoeing and nature, hiking, snowmobile and cross-country ski trails.

PATTISON STATE PARK
6294 Highway 35 S., Superior, 715-399-3111; www.dnr.state.wi.us
This state park has 1,476 acres of sand beach and woodlands and offers swimming, fishing, canoeing, a nature center, playgrounds and nature, hiking and cross-country ski trails. The outstanding park attraction is Big Manitou Falls, which at 165 feet is the highest waterfall in the state. Little Manitou Falls, a 31-foot drop, is located upstream of the main falls.
Daily.

WHERE TO STAY
★BEST WESTERN BAY WALK INN
1405 Susquehanna Ave., Superior, 715-392-7600, 800-780-7234;
www.bestwestern.com
50 rooms. Complimentary breakfast. Pets accepted. Pool. $61-150

★BEST WESTERN BRIDGEVIEW MOTOR INN
415 Hammond Ave., Superior, 715-392-8174, 800-777-5572; www.bestwestern.com
96 rooms. Complimentary breakfast. Pets accepted. $61-150

★★DAYS INN
110 Harbor View Parkway, Superior, 715-392-4783, 888-515-5040;
www.daysinnsuperior.com
111 rooms. Complimentary breakfast. Restaurant, bar. Pets accepted.
$61-150

WHERE TO EAT
★★SHACK SMOKEHOUSE AND GRILLE
3301 Belknap St., Superior, 715-392-9836; www.shackonline.com
American menu. Lunch, dinner. Bar. Children's menu. Casual attire. Reservations recommended. $16-36

THREE LAKES
See also Crandon, Eagle River, Rhinelander
Between Thunder Lake and the interlocking series of 28 lakes on the west boundary of Nicolet National Forest, Three Lakes is a provisioning point for parties exploring the forest and lake country.

WHAT TO SEE
CHEQUAMEGON-NICOLET NATIONAL FOREST

4364 Wall St., Eagle River, 715-479-2827; www.fs.fed.us/r9/cnnf

This forest has 661,000 acres and is 62 miles long and 36 miles wide; elevation ranges from 860 feet to 1,880 feet. It is noted for scenic drives through pine, spruce, fir, sugar maple, oak and birch trees.
Daily.

TOMAH

See also Black River Falls, Sparta

Tomah is Wisconsin's gateway to Cranberry Country. It was also the home of Frank King, the creator of the comic strip Gasoline Alley; the main street was named after him. Lake Tomah, on the west edge of town, has boating, waterskiing, fishing, ice-fishing and snowmobiling.

WHAT TO SEE
MILL BLUFF STATE PARK

15819 Funnel Road, Camp Douglas, 608-427-6692; www.dnr.wi.gov

This park has 1,258 acres with rock bluffs, swimming, picnicking and camping.
Daily.

NECEDAH NATIONAL WILDLIFE REFUGE

W7996 20th St. West, Necedah, 608-565-2551; www.fws.gov/refuges

Water birds may be seen during seasonal migrations with lesser numbers present during the summer. Resident wildlife include deer, wild turkeys, ruffed grouse, wolves and bears.
Daily.

WILDCAT MOUNTAIN STATE PARK

E13660 State Highway 33, Ontario; www.dnr.wi.gov., Ontario, 608-337-4775

This park has 3,470 acres of hills and valleys and offers trout fishing in Kickapoo River, Billings and Cheyenne creeks, canoeing and nature, hiking, bridle and cross-country ski trails. Observation points provide panoramic view of the countryside. Daily.

WHERE TO STAY
★COMFORT INN

305 Wittig Road, Tomah, 608-372-6600, 800-228-5150; www.comfortinn.com

52 rooms. Complimentary continental breakfast. Pets accepted. Pool.
$61-150

★★HOLIDAY INN

1017 E. McCoy Blvd., Tomah, 608-372-3211, 866-372-3211; www.holidayinn.com

100 rooms. High-speed Internet access. Restaurant, bar. Pets accepted.
$61-150

WHERE TO EAT
★★BURNSTAD'S EUROPEAN CAFÉ
701 E. Clifton, Tomah, 608-372-4040, 888-378-5985; www.burnstads.com
American menu. Breakfast, lunch, dinner. Bar. Casual attire. Outdoor seating. $16-36

TWO RIVERS
See also Green Bay, Manitowoc, Sheboygan
A fishing fleet in Lake Michigan and light industry support Two Rivers.

WHAT TO SEE
POINT BEACH STATE FOREST
9400 County Trunk O, Two Rivers, 920-794-7480; www.dnr.wi.gov
A 2,900-acre park with heavily wooded areas, sand dunes and a beach along Lake Michigan, Point Beach offers nature, hiking, snowmobile and cross-country ski trails, and ice skating. Daily.

ROGERS STREET FISHING VILLAGE MUSEUM
2102 Jackson St., Two Rivers, 920-793-5905
The museum features artifacts of the commercial fishing industry, a 60-year-old diesel engine, artifacts from sunken vessels, life-size woodcarvings and arts and crafts galleries featuring local area artists. June-August, daily.

WASHINGTON ISLAND
See also Door County
Washington Island, six miles off the coast of Door County, is one of the oldest Icelandic settlements in the United States. Many Scandinavian festivals are still celebrated. The island may be reached by ferry.

WHAT TO SEE
ROCK ISLAND STATE PARK
Little Lake Road, Washington Island, 920-847-2235; www.dnr.state.wi.us
This 912-acre park was the summer home of electric tycoon C.H. Thordarson. It features buildings in Icelandic architectural style, and it provides plenty of recreational activities, including swimming, fishing, boating, nature trails and more than nine miles of hiking and snowmobile trails. Daily

WHERE TO STAY
★★FINDLAY'S HOLIDAY INN AND VIKING VILLAGE
1 Main Road, Washington Island, 920-847-2526, 800-522-5469; www.holidayinn.net
16 rooms. Closed November-April. Restaurant. $61-150

WHERE TO EAT
★★FINDLAY'S HOLIDAY INN
1 Main Road, Washington Island, 920-847-2526, 800-522-5469; www.holidayinn.net
American menu. Breakfast, lunch. Closed November-April. Casual attire. $16-35

WATERTOWN

See also Beaver Dam, Fort Atkinson, Oconomowoc

Waterpower, created where the Rock River falls 20 feet in two miles, attracted the first New England settlers. A vast number of German immigrants followed, including Carl Schurz, who became Lincoln's minister to Spain and secretary of the interior under President Hayes. His wife, Margarethe Meyer Schurz, established the first kindergarten in the United States. Watertown, with diversified industries, is in the center of an important farming and dairy community.

WHAT TO SEE

OCTAGON HOUSE AND FIRST KINDERGARTEN IN USA

919 Charles St., Watertown, 920-261-2796; www.watertownhistory.org

Completed in 1854, the 57-room mansion has a 40-foot spiral cantilever-hanging staircase, Victorian-style furnishings throughout and many original pieces. The grounds include a restored kindergarten founded in 1856 and a 100-year-old barn with early farm implements.

May-October, daily.

WAUKESHA

See also Elkhorn, Milwaukee

Mineral springs found here by pioneer settlers made Waukesha famous as a health resort. In the latter half of the 19th century, it was one of the nation's most fashionable vacation spots. Before that it was an important point on the Underground Railroad. The American Freeman was published here. Today the city is enjoying industrial growth. Carroll College lends the city an academic atmosphere. The name Waukesha ("by the little fox") comes from the river that runs through it. The river, along with the city's many parks and wooded areas, adds to a beautiful atmosphere for leisure activities.

WHAT TO SEE

OLD WORLD WISCONSIN

S103W 37890 Highway 67, Eagle, 262-594-6300;

www.oldworldwisconsin.wisconsinhistory.org

This museum fills 576 acres with more than 65 historic structures reflecting various ethnic backgrounds of Wisconsin history. Restored buildings include church, town hall, schoolhouse, stagecoach inn, blacksmith shop and 10 complete 19th-century farmsteads. All buildings are furnished with period artifacts and staffed by costumed interpreters.

May-October, daily.

WHERE TO STAY

★★★MILWAUKEE MARRIOTT WEST

W231N 1600 Corporate Court, Waukesha, 262-574-0888, 800-228-9290;

www.marriott.com

This modern, comfortable hotel overlooks a small pond and features an upscale lobby. The hotel offers convenient access to highways and area activities and an indoor pool and whirlpool. Guest rooms have pillow-top beds and large picture windows.

281 rooms. Restaurant, bar. Pool. $61-150

WAUPACA

See also Stevens Point, Wautoma

This community, near a chain of 22 lakes to the southwest, is a boating, fishing and tourist recreation area.

WHAT TO SEE
HARTMAN CREEK STATE PARK

N2480 Hartman Creek Road, Waupaca, 715-258-2372; www.dnr.state.wi.us

A 1,400-acre park with 300-foot sand beach on Hartman Lake, attractions include swimming, fishing, boating, canoeing and nature, hiking, snowmobile and cross-country ski trails.

WHERE TO STAY
★★BEST WESTERN GRAND SEASONS HOTEL

110 Grand Seasons Drive, Waupaca, 715-258-9212

90 rooms. Complimentary breakfast. Restaurant, bar. Pets accepted. $61-150

WAUPUN

See also Beaver Dam, Fond du Lac, Green Lake

The city's American Indian name means "early dawn of day." Diversified crops, light industry and three state institutions contribute to this city's economy.

WHAT TO SEE
HORICON NATIONAL WILDLIFE REFUGE

W4279 Headquarters Road, Mayville, 920-387-2658; www.fws.gov/midwest/horicon

Large flocks of Canada geese and various species of ducks can be seen October, November, March and April. Monday-Friday.

WAUSAU

See also Antigo, Stevens Point

Known as Big Bull Falls when it was settled as a lumber camp, the town was renamed Wausau, Native American for "faraway place." When the big timber was gone, the lumber barons started paper mills. Paper products are still one of the city's many industries.

WHAT TO SEE
MARATHON COUNTY HISTORICAL MUSEUM

403 McIndoe St., Wausau, 715-848-6143; www.marathoncountyhistory.com

This former home of early lumberman Cyrus C. Yawkey has Victorian period rooms, a model railroad display and changing theme exhibits.
Tuesday-Thursday, Saturday-Sunday.

RIB MOUNTAIN STATE PARK

4200 Park Road, Rib Mountain Drive, Wausau, 715-842-2522; www.dnr.wi.gov

Part of an 860-acre park, the summit of Rib Mountain is one of the highest points in the state. Hiking trails wind past rocky ridges and natural oddities in quartzite rocks.
Daily.

WHERE TO STAY
★★BEST WESTERN MIDWAY HOTEL
2901 Martin Ave., Wausau, 715-842-1616, 800-780-7234; www.bestwestern.com
98 rooms. Restaurant, bar. Pets accepted. Pool. Fitness center. $61-150

WHERE TO EAT
★★GULLIVER'S LANDING
1701 Mallard Lane, Wausau, 715-849-8409; www.gulliverslanding.com
American menu. Dinner. Bar. Children's menu. Outdoor seating. $36-85

★WAUSAU MINE CO.
3904 W. Stewart Ave., Wausau, 715-845-7304; www.wausaumine.com
American menu. Lunch, dinner. Bar. Children's menu. $16-35

WAUTOMA
See also Green Lake, Waupaca
In the central part of the state, Wautoma and surrounding areas have cross-country skiing and snowmobiling trails, miles of bike routes and plenty of areas to camp.

WHAT TO SEE
NORDIC MOUNTAIN SKI AREA
W5806 County Road West, Wautoma, 920-787-3324, 800-253-7266;
www.nordicmountain.com
The longest run here is one mile with a vertical drop of 265 feet. The ski area also features 13 miles of cross country trails, rentals and a ski school.
Night skiing: December-mid-March, Thursday-Tuesday.

WAUWATOSA
See also Menomonee Falls, Milwaukee
About eight miles northwest of Milwaukee, Wauwatosa has a historic village area well worth an afternoon stroll.

WHAT TO SEE
HARLEY-DAVIDSON TOUR
11700 W. Capitol Drive, Wauwatosa, 414-343-7850, 877-883-1450;
www.harley-davidson.com
Milwaukee is Hog Heaven, so it's only fitting to tour the propeller-factory-turned-Harley-facility and see transmission and engine assembly from start to finish. Tickets for tours are handed out at 9 a.m. on a first-come, first-served basis; arrive early.
Monday-Friday 9:30 a.m.-1 p.m.

LOWELL DAMON HOUSE
2107 Wauwatosa Ave., Wauwatosa, 414-273-8288; www.milwaukeecountyhistsoc.org
The community's oldest home is a classic example of colonial architecture and period furnishings.
Tours: Sunday, Wednesday.

WHERE TO STAY
★HOLIDAY INN EXPRESS
11111 W. North Ave., Wauwatosa, 414-778-0333, 800-465-4329; www.holidayinn.com
122 rooms. Complimentary breakfast. Pets accepted. $61-150

WHERE TO EAT
★★BALISTRERI'S ITALIAN RESTAURANT
812 N. 68th St., Wauwatosa, 414-475-1414; www.balistreris.com
Italian menu. Lunch, dinner. Casual attire. $16-35

★★★RISTORANTE BARTOLOTTA
7616 W. State St., Wauwatosa, 414-771-7910; www.bartolottas.com
A classic representation of trattoria-style dining, this restaurant features a menu that highlights fresh and authentic ingredients. The eatery has a loyal following and delivers a casual dining experience.
Italian menu. Dinner. Bar. Children's menu. Casual attire. Reservations recommended. Outdoor seating. $16-35

WEST ALLIS
See also Menomonee Falls, Milwaukee, Waukesha
This town near Milwaukee offers plenty of places to play outdoors: golf, hike, shop at the summer farmers market or take a bike ride.

SPECIAL EVENT
WISCONSIN STATE FAIR
State Fair Park, 640 S. 84th St., West Allis, 414-266-7000, 800-884-3247;
www.wistatefair.com
The fair features entertainment on 12 stages, auto races, exhibits, contests, demonstrations and fireworks. August.

WISCONSIN DELLS
See also Baraboo, Mauston, Portage, Prairie du Sac
Until 1931, this city was called Kilbourn, but it changed its name in the hope of attracting tourists to the nearby Dells. It seems to have worked—the Wisconsin Dells has become the state's prime tourist attraction. Although some aspects of the Dells lean toward the tacky side, the overall feel is good clean fun.

The region offers a wide selection of campgrounds, bed and breakfasts, hotels, motels, resorts, condos and cottages. Of these, more than 40 welcome guests with pets and 17 house indoor water parks. Man-made and natural attractions keep visitors from lingering too long at area accommodations.

Families can explore the Upper and Lower Dells on a Dells Boat Tour or the water- and land-based environs on an original World War II Duck. Take to the water in the largest indoor water park in the United States at Kalahari Resort & Convention Center, or at Noah's Ark, America's largest water park, housing five million gallons of water and three miles of water slides. Uncover the enchantment under the Big Top at Circus World Museum in nearby Baraboo, take a wagon tour through a working elk ranch (Nanchas Elk Ranch Tours), or ride the rails through the Baraboo Hills at the Mid-Continent Railway Museum.

Spectators flock to the Tommy Bartlett show, where entertainers amaze through daring feats, on stage and in the sky. Fast-paced action circles the track at the Dells Motor Speedway—the place to head for stock car racing. Those in search of quieter pursuits can stroll along the new RiverWalk in the downtown Dells River District. The 1,100-foot walkway is equipped with a bicycle path, benches and game tables. Mirror Lake State Park and Rocky Arbor State Park are two other places to commune with nature, or tour the vineyards at Prairie du Sac's Wollersheim Winery, the largest producer of wine in Wisconsin.

WHAT TO SEE

BEAVER SPRINGS FISHING PARK AND RIDING STABLES

600 Trout Road, Wisconsin Dells, 608-254-2735; www.beaverspringsfun.com
Guided one-hour rides tour spring-fed ponds stocked with trout, catfish, bass and other fish. April-October, daily.

DELLS DUCKS

1550 Wisconsin Dells Parkway, Wisconsin Dells, 608-254-6080; www.dellsducks.com
The one-hour land/water tour offers views of scenic rock formations along the Wisconsin River.
Late May-late October, daily.

H.H. BENNETT STUDIO AND HISTORY CENTER

215 Broadway, Wisconsin Dells, 608-253-3523; www.hhbennett.com
The oldest photographic studio in the United States features the landscape and nature photography of H. H. Bennett that helped make the Dells area famous. The studio is still in operation and it is possible to purchase enlargements made from Bennett's original glass negatives.
Memorial Day-late October, daily; November-April, by appointment.

RIVERVIEW PARK & WATERWORLD

Highway 12, Wisconsin Dells, 608-254-2608; www.riverviewpark.com
Waterworld features a wave pool, speed slides, tube rides and kids' pools with the park offers go-carts.
Park: late May-early September, Waterworld: late May-early September, daily.

TOMMY BARTLETT'S ROBOT WORLD & EXPLORATORY

560 Wisconsin Dells Parkway, Wisconsin Dells, 608-254-2525; www.tommybartlett.com
More than 150 hands-on exhibits include the world's only Russian Mir Space Station core module and explore principles of light, sound and motion.
Features robot-guided tours are offered daily.

WHERE TO STAY

★BEST WESTERN AMBASSADOR INN & SUITES

610 Frontage Road South, Wisconsin Dells, 608-254-4477, 800-828-6888;
www.bestwestern-dells.com
181 rooms. High-speed Internet access. Pool. $61-150

★COMFORT INN
703 Frontage Road North, Wisconsin Dells, 608-253-3711, 800-424-6423;
www.comfortinn.com
75 rooms. Complimentary full breakfast. Wireless Internet access. Pool.
$61-150

★★RIVERWALK HOTEL
1015 River Road, Wisconsin Dells, 608-253-1231, 800-659-5395;
www.dellsriverwalkhotel.com
54 rooms. Restaurant, bar. Pool. $61-150

★★WILDERNESS HOTEL & GOLF RESORT
511 E. Adams St., Wisconsin Dells, 608-253-9729, 800-867-9453;
www.wildernessresort.com
483 rooms. High-speed Internet access. Restaurant, bar. Airport transportation available. Golf. $151-250

★★WINTERGREEN RESORT AND CONFERENCE CENTER
60 Gasser Road, Wisconsin Dells, 608-254-2285, 800-648-4765;
www.wintergreen-resort.com
111 rooms. Restaurant, bar. Pool. $60-150

WHERE TO EAT
★MESA GRILLE CHULA VISTA RESORT
N 4021 River Road, Wisconsin Dells, 608-254-8366; www.chulavistaresort.com
Mexican menu. Breakfast, lunch, dinner. Bar. Children's menu. Reservations recommended. $16-35

WISCONSIN RAPIDS
See also Marshfield, Stevens Point

A paper manufacturing and cranberry center, Wisconsin Rapids was formed in 1900 by consolidating the two towns of Grand Rapids and Centralia after the Wisconsin River had devastated large sections of both communities. At first the combined town was called Grand Rapids, but the name was changed when confusion with the Michigan city developed. Cranberry marshes here produce the largest inland cranberry crop in the world.

WHERE TO STAY
★BEST WESTERN RAPIDS MOTOR INN
911 Huntington Ave., Wisconsin Rapids, 715-423-3211, 800-780-7234;
www.bestwestern.com
43 rooms. Pets accepted. $60-150

★QUALITY INN
3120 Eighth St., Wisconsin Rapids, 715-423-5506, 800-755-1336; www.qualityinn.com
36 rooms. Complimentary continental breakfast. Pets accepted. $60-150

★★★HOTEL MEAD

451 E. Grand Ave., Wisconsin Rapids, 715-423-1500,800-843-6323;
www.hotelmead.com
Centrally located and considered by many as the hospitality center of central
Wisconsin, this hotel caters to business, leisure and adventure travelers.
157 rooms. Restaurant, bar. Pets accepted. Pool. $60-150

INDEX

NUMBERS

279

★★★★★ INDEX

291

M

★
★★
★★
★★
★

INDEX

303

Villa Louis (Prairie Du Chien), *260*

Villa Terrace Decorative Arts Museum (Milwaukee), *248*

Village of Yesteryear (Owatonna), *178*

The Vineyard (Anoka), *132*

Von Stiehl Winery (Algoma), *205*

Voyageur Winter Festival (Ely), *145*

W

W. A. Frost and Company (St. Paul), *194*

W.H.C. Folsom House (Taylors Falls), *197*

W.J. Hayes State Park (Brooklyn), *22*

W.K. Kellogg Bird Sanctuary of Michigan State University (Battle Creek), *15-16*

W.W. Mayo House (Le Sueur), *155*

Wagon Trail (Door County), *219*

Walker Art Center (Minneapolis), *162*

Wally's House of Embers (Lake Delton), *237*

Warner Vineyards (Paw Paw), *103*

Warren Dunes State Park (New Buffalo), *98*

Warren Dunes State Park (St. Joseph), *120*

Washburn-Zittleman House (Spring Valley), *186*

Washington County Historical Museum (Stillwater), *195*

Water Lily (Mount Pleasant), *95*

Water Street Inn (Stillwater), *196*

Waterboard Warriors (Green Bay), *229*

Waterfront Art Fair (Charlevoix), *25*

Waterloo Farm Museum (Jackson), *71*

Watertower Festival (Pipestone), *180*

Wausau Mine Co. (Wausau), *273*

Wayne State University (Detroit), *36*

Weathervane Terrace Inn & Suites (Charlevoix), *25*

Weber's Inn (Ann Arbor), *12*

Webster's (Kalamazoo), *74*

Welch Village (Red Wing), *181*

Welcome To My Garden Tour (Marshall), *89*

Wellington (Green Bay), *229*

Western Avenue Grill (Glen Arbor), *49*

Western Michigan University (Kalamazoo), *73*

Wharton Center for the Performing Arts (East Lansing), *41*

Whitcomb Conservatory (Detroit), *36*

White Gull Inn (Fish Creek), *224*

White Lake Arts & Crafts Festival (Whitehall), *127*

White Pine Village (Ludington), *78*

White River Light Station Museum (Whitehall), *127*

Whitewater State Park (Rochester), *183*

The Whitney (Detroit), *40*

Wild Mountain Ski Area (Taylors Falls), *197*

Wildcat Mountain State Park (Tomah), *269*

Wilderness Hotel & Golf Resort (Wisconsin Dells), *276*

Wilderness State Park (Mackinaw City), *83*

Wildwood Park and Zoo (Marshfield), *244*

Willard Beach (Battle Creek), *15*

William Mitchell State Park (Cadillac), *23*

William O'Brien State Park (Stillwater), *195*

Willow River State Park (Hudson), *230*

Wilson Place Museum (Menomonie), *245*

Windmill Island (Holland), *59*

DETROIT

MICHIGAN

MINNESOTA

WISCONSIN

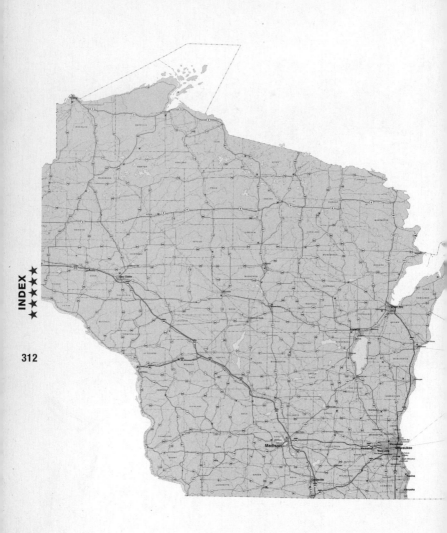